Economic Effects
of Antidumping

World Scientific Studies in International Economics
(ISSN: 1793-3641)

World Scientific Studies in International Economics includes works dealing with the theory, empirical analysis, and evaluation of international economic policies and institutions, with topics covering international macroeconomics and finance, international trade theory and policy, as well as international legal and political economy. Monographs and edited volumes will comprise the core of the publications.

Vol. 77   *Economic Effects of Antidumping*
edited by Thomas J. Prusa (Rutgers University, USA)

Vol. 76   *Policy Analysis and Modeling of the Global Economy: A Festschrift Celebrating Thomas Hertel*
edited by Peter Dixon (Victoria University, Australia),
Joseph Francois (University of Bern, Switzerland) &
Dominique van der Mensbrugghe (Purdue University, USA)

Vol. 75   *Competition, Innovation and Trade*
edited by Larry D. Qiu (Lingnan University, Hong Kong)

Vol. 74   *Understanding the Implications of Trade and Financial Market Integration for Business Cycles*
edited by Mario J. Crucini (Vanderbilt University, USA)

Vol. 73   *The International Economics of Wine*
edited by Kym Anderson (University of Adelaide, Australia &
Australian National University, Australia)

Vol. 72   *Foreign Direct Investment*
by Bruce A. Blonigen (University of Oregon, USA & National Bureau of Economic Research, USA)

Vol. 71   *Offshoring: Causes and Consequences at the Firm and Worker Level*
edited by Holger Görg (Kiel Institute for the World Economy, Germany) &
Aoife Hanley (Kiel Institute for the World Economy, Germany)

Vol. 70   *Policy Externalities and International Trade Agreements*
by Nuno Limão (University of Maryland, USA)

Vol. 69   *Economic Analysis of the Rules and Regulations of the World Trade Organization*

The complete list of the published volumes in the series can be found at
https://www.worldscientific.com/series/wssie

77 World Scientific Studies in International Economics

Economic Effects
of Antidumping

editor

Thomas J Prusa
Rutgers University, USA

World Scientific

NEW JERSEY · LONDON · SINGAPORE · BEIJING · SHANGHAI · HONG KONG · TAIPEI · CHENNAI · TOKYO

Published by

World Scientific Publishing Co. Pte. Ltd.
5 Toh Tuck Link, Singapore 596224
USA office: 27 Warren Street, Suite 401-402, Hackensack, NJ 07601
UK office: 57 Shelton Street, Covent Garden, London WC2H 9HE

Library of Congress Cataloging-in-Publication Data
Names: Prusa, Thomas John, editor.
Title: Economic effects of antidumping / editor, Thomas J. Prusa, Rutgers University, USA.
Description: USA : World Scientific, 2021. | Series: World scientific studies in
    international economics, 1793-3641 ; Vol. 77 | Includes bibliographical references.
Identifiers: LCCN 2020043893 | ISBN 9789811225246 (hardcover) |
    ISBN 9789811225253 (ebook) | ISBN 9789811225260 (ebook other)
Subjects: LCSH: Antidumping duties--Law and legislation--History. | Antidumping duties--
    Economic aspects. | Dumping (International trade)--Law and legislation.
Classification: LCC K4635 .E29 2021 | DDC 343.08/7--dc23
LC record available at https://lccn.loc.gov/2020043893

British Library Cataloguing-in-Publication Data
A catalogue record for this book is available from the British Library.

For any available supplementary material, please visit
https://www.worldscientific.com/worldscibooks/10.1142/11964#t=suppl

Desk Editors: Priyanka Murugan/Karimah Samsudin

Typeset by Stallion Press
Email: enquiries@stallionpress.com

Printed in Singapore

About the Editor

 **Thomas J. Prusa** is a Professor of Economics at Rutgers University, New Brunswick, New Jersey. For almost 30 years, Professor Prusa's research has focused on trade policy decision-making by the U.S. International Trade Commission. His research has addressed all of the main statutes administered by the USITC, including countervailing duty, global safeguards, Section 337, and especially antidumping.

Professor Prusa has lectured in conferences and seminars to the World Trade Organization (WTO), European Union, the World Bank, the Federal Reserve, the World Trade Institute, the CATO Institute, the American Enterprise Institute, the United Nations (UN), Stanford University, Princeton University, New York University, and many others. Professor Prusa has also provided expert testimony before the U.S. International Trade Commission on many occasions.

Acknowledgments

I would like to thank the following publishers and journals for granting their permissions to reproduce the articles:

Publishers
Canadian Economics Association Publishers
Elsevier Science
John Wiley & Sons
Sejong University Publishers
Springer Nature
The World Bank Group Publishers
University of Chicago Press Publishers

Journals
Economic Inquiry
International Economic Review
Journal of International Economics
Journal of Economic Integration
Japan and the World Economy
Policy Research Working Paper Series
Review of World Economics
Review of International Economics
The Canadian Journal of Economics
The Great Recession and Import Protection
National Bureau of Economic Research

Contents

About the Editor   v

Acknowledgments   vii

Introduction   xi

Chapter 1   Why are so Many Antidumping Petitions
             Withdrawn?   1

Chapter 2   The Trade Effects of U.S. Antidumping Actions   21

Chapter 3   On the Spread and Impact of Anti-Dumping   45

Chapter 4   USA: Evolving Trends in Temporary
             Trade Barriers   67

Chapter 5   Pricing Behavior in the Presence
             of Antidumping Law   99

Chapter 6   Dumping and Double Crossing: The
             (In)Effectiveness of Cost-Based Trade
             Policy Under Incomplete Information   129

Chapter 7   Macroeconomic Factors and Antidumping
             Filings: Evidence from Four Countries   153

Chapter 8   Cumulation and ITC Decision-Making:
             The Sum of the Parts is Greater
             than the Whole   171

Chapter 9   U.S. Anti-dumping: Much Ado About Zeroing   195

Chapter 10   The Economic and Strategic Motives
             for Antidumping Filings   233

Chapter 11   WTO Exceptions as Insurance   259

Chapter 12   Using Safeguard Protection to Raise
             Domestic Rivals' Costs   273

Introduction

Thomas J. Prusa*

1. Introduction and Background

Antidumping (AD) is the oldest and most widely used of the administrative protection statutes. AD's origins date back to 1904 when Canada became the first country to adopt a law that allowed for special duties on "under-valued goods", where the duty would be calculated as the difference between the price in Canada and the price at which goods were sold in the exporter's own market. New Zealand (1905) and Australia (1906) quickly followed Canada's lead in implementing their own AD statutes. The broader context to the origin of these laws was the public response to the large monopolies and cartels that had arisen in the late 19th and early 20th centuries in a number of Western developed countries, particularly in the U.S.

Beginning with the Sherman Antitrust Act of 1890 and followed by other refinements, including the Clayton Act of 1914 and the Robinson–Patman Act of 1936, the U.S. made illegal many business practices that harmed or limited market competition. One of the business practices made illegal with the Clayton Act of 1914 and the Robinson–Patman Act of 1936 was price discrimination that is

*Department of Economics, New Jersey Hall, 75 Hamilton St, Rutgers University, New Brunswick, NJ, 08901-1248; Ph: 848-932-8646; Email: prusa@rutgers.edu.

predatory in its intent, i.e., pricing low with the intent of driving competitors out of the marketplace. The first AD legislation in the U.S., the Antidumping Act of 1916, largely applied this principle to imports, making it illegal to sell imports at low prices with the intent of destroying or injuring an industry in the U.S.

Showing (predatory) intent on the part of a firm to injure competitors is legally difficult and a U.S. Tariff Commission report in 1919 concluded that the 1916 law did not cover a broad enough range of dumping activities that could be harmful to U.S. producers, whether there was predatory intent or not. As a result, the U.S. enacted the Antidumping Act of 1921, which provides a considerably different standard, morphing AD from a criminal statute with criminal punishments for predatory pricing practices to an administered import policy that levies duties on a foreign firm for simply charging lower prices in the U.S. than the firm's own home market. In effect, the 1921 law brought U.S. practice into conformity with the other AD users of the era.

In the decades that followed, administrative forms of protection like AD were rarely used as countries began to implement substantial increases in tariffs and quotas after the crash of 1929 and the onset of the Great Depression. Nevertheless, AD was not forgotten in the initial negotiations and adoption of the GATT. Article VI of the original GATT in 1947 enshrines general language allowing signatories to employ AD and closely follows the provisions of the 1921 U.S. Antidumping Act.

The early rounds of GATT were focused on reducing traditional forms of trade protection and did not make any substantive changes or additions to the AD provisions in Article VI. The Tokyo Round (1973–1979) included the first significant changes to GATT AD rules, broadening the rules for determining dumping to include "sales below costs" and clarifying what constitutes material injury (essentially codifying evolving European Community and U.S. practices).

The Uruguay Round (1986–1994) made the most substantive changes to AD provisions in the GATT by rewriting Article VI from a set of general guiding principles to a very detailed description of how AD actions are to be implemented by WTO member countries.[1] While there were some refinements and innovations to AD rules in this rewriting, the fundamental concepts of applying AD measures were unaltered and continued to be quite consistent with the existing national laws of the "traditional users" of AD laws (Australia, Canada, EU, and U.S.).

2. Economics and Antidumping

One of the first things that an economist discovers when studying AD is that at least since GATT 1947, the legal basis for imposing AD has had nothing to do with an economic understanding of dumping. For instance, economists often argue that dumping is only economically meaningful if imperfect competition exists, products are not homogeneous, and markets are segmented (e.g., limited price arbitrage). None of these economically meaningful concepts appear in the GATT (and later WTO) AD rules. The lack of economic principles makes AD very different from most other GATT provisions and is perhaps the greatest frustration of economists with respect to AD.

That the implementation and justification for AD lack economic foundation hardly means that AD is not a powerful laboratory for understanding economic incentives and effects of protection. To the contrary, there are unique features of AD actions and policies that allow one to gain richer insights into application and consequences of trade policies than is typically true for other forms of trade policies.

First, AD actions are frequent and disperse, occurring across scores of countries, products, and firms every year. This leads to rich data with substantial heterogeneity for analysis. In contrast, many trade actions, such as country-level tariff reforms or other forms of administrative protection (e.g., safeguards) are much rarer and, thus, provide fewer observations.

---

[1]The changes to the rules were substantial enough to warrant moving the AD text to a new agreement, often called the Antidumping Agreement. Article I of the Antidumping Agreement refers back to Article VI of GATT.

Second, unlike many trade actions that require legislation, AD trade policies are administered on a rolling basis by country-level government agencies. In a number of the major countries, including the U.S. and the European Union, these agencies provide substantial public information about the investigations. This along with the targeted nature of AD actions (investigations must name each country-product source where unfair trade practices are occurring) allows better and more refined evaluation of the effects of trade policies. As one example, foreign firms who are investigated for unfair trade practices are named and even given their own AD duty if they are found to be conducting unfair trade. Such targeted trade actions then allow one to very explicitly and cleanly measure firm- and even plant-level responses by these foreign firms in response to trade actions specifically targeted at them, which is not true of most other forms of trade policy.

Finally, political economy issues are important and likely more multi-faceted with AD policies than many other forms of trade policy. As mentioned, each AD investigation involves different combinations of foreign country import sources, as well as related domestic firms producing the targeted product. The political economy around each of these AD cases can be quite different. For example, different local legislators and special interest groups will be involved in each AD action providing, again, a rich and varied set of observations. At the same time, AD actions can also involve national legislation when rule changes are made at the country level. A final interesting political economy aspect of AD policies is their relation to WTO rules and actions. Unlike many other trade protection programs, AD trade actions are WTO-consistent and legal. This opens up a number of interesting theoretical and empirical issues.

3.   Topics Covered in This Volume

In the 1980s, many trade tensions were resolved by the parties agreeing to some form of Voluntary Export Restraint (VER). While the automobile VER is perhaps the most well-known example, there were hundreds of VERs in the 1980s, including many that were the result of AD petitions. The propensity for U.S. firms to file AD actions and then withdraw them once a VER was negotiated is the subject of Chapter 1. This chapter demonstrates that the endogeneity of AD is not only related to the filing decision but also to the outcome of the petition.

Chapters 2, 3, and 4 all discuss various aspects of the growing use of AD protection. Chapter 2 documents the significant impact on imports as a result of AD duties: a large and sharp decrease in imports from targeted suppliers and a subsequent increase in imports from non-targeted suppliers. Chapter 3 discusses the spread of AD over recent decades. Long a trade policy used by just a handful of users – the U.S., EU, Canada, and Australia accounted for over 95% of all AD cases in the 1980s — by the mid-1990s, AD had begun to be used by many countries and by the early 2000s use by developing countries had outstripped that of the traditional users. The hunter was now the hunted! Chapter 4 focuses exclusively on AD use by the U.S. over a three-decade period. While the number of new petitions filed in any year has declined, the long-lived nature of U.S. AD duties means the overall level of U.S. import trade subject to AD duties has not declined.

Chapters 5, 6, and 7 also analyze implications of the endogeneity of the AD process. Chapter 5 discusses how the need to demonstrate material injury influences how the domestic industry will operate prior to the petition filing. The cost of losing sales before the petition is initiated (and allowing imports to fill the void) can be offset by the gain once duties have been applied on the foreign competitors. Chapter 6 focuses on the "less than fair value" criterion. Given that more than two-thirds of cases involve the "sales below cost" methodology, foreign firms have an incentive to make it difficult for the domestic investigative authority to accurately assess their costs. The foreign firm does so by restraining its sales prior to the petition, and by doing so increasing the chance of resolving the dispute via a VER.

In contrast with the theoretical analyses in Chapters 5 and 6. Chapter 7 empirically studies the filing patterns among the major AD users during the 1980s and 1990s: the U.S., the EU, Canada, and

Australia. I find that disputes increase as the exchange rate appreciates (which makes exporting more difficult and increases the competitiveness of foreign competition). A real appreciation of the exchange rate increases filings by about 33%. I also find that a weak domestic economy, as measured by domestic GDP, significantly increases AD activity.

Chapters 8 and 9 analyze implications of specific provisions of the AD statute. In Chapter 8, I study the amendment to allow the trade values from all targeted countries to be treated as if the total trade from all sources were from a single supplier (referred to as the "cumulation" provision). Previously, in a multi-country investigation, the impact on the competing domestic industry of each supplier's sales was evaluated individually. As a result, it was more likely that countries with small import market shares would not be found to have caused material injury. Not surprisingly, I find the cumulation provision increases the probability of an affirmative decision by at least 20 percentage points. The surprising finding is, holding the total value of imports constant, cases involving more countries were increasingly likely to have an affirmative finding. In other words, three suppliers each with a 10% market share were more injurious than a single supplier with a 30% market share.

Chapter 9 examines a long overlooked provision in U.S. AD rules — zeroing. Zeroing refers to the practice of replacing the actual amount of dumping that yields negative dumping margins with a value of zero prior to the final calculation of a weighted-average margin of dumping for the product under investigation with respect to the exporters under investigation. Zeroing drops transactions that have negative margins and, hence, increases the overall dumping margins and the resulting size of the applied AD duty. What makes zeroing important was the U.S.' insistence that the practice was consistent with WTO rules, even after the WTO Appellate Body had issued dozens of rulings against its use and even though no other country in the world used similar methodology. The zeroing fiasco is a key reason for the U.S.'s refusal to allow any new Appellate Body members to be appointed, which has resulted in the collapse of the WTO dispute system.

The final three chapters all examine strategic aspects of AD filings. In Chapter 10, I examine the tendency for a country to file AD petitions against countries who have recently filed AD petitions against it. This tit-for-tat type of AD activity highlights that many AD cases have little to do with actual "unfair trade" but rather reflect other motivations.

Chapter 11 examines the insurance role that AD protection has. That is, when a domestic industry is hit with a "shock" (a downturn), how can the government provide assistance? Given that tariffs are negotiated years in advance and are subject to "bound" maximum rates (which are often zero), there is little ability for developed countries to use the tariff schedule in a contingent manner to offer assistance. I study how contingent, sector-specific tariffs like AD can allow timely but narrow protection that offers superior welfare as compared to other trade policies.

Finally, in Chapter 12, I examine how contingent protection not only affects the competition between domestic and foreign firms but can also alter the competitive conditions among domestic firms. In particular, I examine a situation where the firms are competing across a vertically integrated product line, where at each stage of production products can be sold to end consumers or be further processed into a distinctly different product. In such a scenario, protection on one product (say, hot-rolled steel) will affect competition in the market for hot-rolled steel and also in all the downstream products (such as cold-rolled steel and galvanized steel) that use hot-rolled steel as an input. Moreover, if domestic producers vary in their ability to produce hot-rolled steel and also in their reliance on downstream revenue, protection on hot-rolled steel will have the effect of raising the costs of domestic competitors.

Chapter 1

Why are so many antidumping petitions withdrawn?[†]

Thomas J. Prusa*

Department of Economics, State University of New York at Stony Brook, Stony Brook, NY 11794-4384, USA

Received April 1990, revised version received August 1991

The number of antidumping petitions initiated has increased dramatically in recent years. However, only one-third of antidumping cases actually result in dumping duties being levied. Surprisingly, nearly as many antidumping cases are withdrawn or are voluntarily terminated. We present data that show that these withdrawn cases have at least as great an effect on trade as cases which resulted in duties. We discuss legal reasons why such settlements are possible and present a model of the bargaining process. We find that petitions with low probability of success ('nuisance' suits) actually confer large gains to both domestic and foreign firms.

1. Introduction

The number of antidumping petitions initiated has increased dramatically in recent years. In 1986, for instance, over 70 antidumping petitions were initiated by U.S. firms. This is an extremely large number especially when one realizes that fewer than 20 petitions were initiated in 1981. Many observers interpret this trend as an indication of a greater incidence of dumping than in previous years; however, there is a growing suspicion that countries, limited in their use of tariffs and quotas by GATT agreements, are now using the fair trade laws as a remedy for various economic woes [UNCTAD (1984), Yarrow (1987)]. Moreover, it is becoming increasingly evident that many businessmen view antidumping law as an offensive weapon, even though the law was clearly intended to be a defensive statute. For instance, one author recently wrote

> Every U.S. business should be aware of, and seek protection against, the increasingly pervasive effects of foreign imports with in the U.S. market.

Correspondence to: T.J. Prusa, Department of Economics, State University of New York at Stony Brook, Stony Brook, NY 11794-4384, U.S.A.

*This paper is a revised version of a chapter in my dissertation at Stanford University. I wish to thank Ron McKinnon for suggesting the topic and Tom Campbell, Alan Deardorff, John Litwack, Bob Staiger, and Mike Riordan for their helpful suggestions. Two anonymous referees also made a number of very helpful comments. I gratefully acknowledge the financial support of the Lynde and Harry and Bradley Foundation and the American Council of Learned Societies.

[†]This article originally appeared in *Journal of International Economics*, **33**, pp. 1–20.

> Companies should consider the *offensive* use of the U.S. trade laws as a
> *strategic business tool* in the same sense as more traditional elements of
> business planning such as research and development, capital investment,
> productivity improvements ... [Hartquist (1987, p. 54, emphasis
> added)].

There is, however, very little definitive evidence that firms are in fact
abusing the law. The fact that more cases are being initiated does not imply
that more duties are being levied or that the United States has become more
protectionist. For example, only nine cases resulted in dumping duties in
both 1980 and 1984, even though twice as many cases were initiated in 1984.
One intepretation of the data is that the International Trade Commission
(ITC) is able to maintain its objectivity and eliminate frivolous cases, and
hence that current antidumping law remains an efficient mechanism for
insuring fair trade. Others argue that the large increase in antidumping
petitions reflects that the mere initiation of an investigation against a foreign
rival benefits the domestic industry by harassing the foreign rival, a tactic
referred to in the legal literature as the in terrorem effect.

Since Viner's (1923) seminal exposition on dumping, trade theorists have
been pre-occupied with developing theories that explain why firms might
price discriminate across markets [Brander and Krugman (1933)] or engage
in below-cost sales [Davies and McGuinness (1982), Ethier (1982)], and have
failed to analyze the economic effects of how antidumping law is implemented. Recently, a number of authors have begun to address this issue
[Prusa (1987), Ethier and Fischer (1987), Fischer (1988), Messerlin (1988,
1989)]. There is much to be learned by examining how trade laws are
implemented. For example, a review of antidumping case history reveals that
only a relatively small percentage of cases result in duties, and this is not
because the majority of cases are rejected. Many antidumping cases are
resolved with settlement agreements; moreover, these agreements have significant efficiency and welfare effects. By 'settlement agreement' we mean a
negotiated agreement between the parties (with or without government
intervention) which results in some type of price or quantity undertaking.
Given that many antidumping cases are settled, an accurate understanding of
the welfare affects of antidumping law should account for this outcome.

In the legal literature it is argued that the settlement agreements are
desirable since they save the government investigative expense and also
reduce the international tensions created by dumping actions. This viewpoint,
of course, assumes that the settlements mimic the expected ITC decisions. If,
however, firms use the settlement agreements to achieve collusive outcomes,
the efficacy of such agreements must be severely questioned. This paper will
measure and analyze the effect of the settlement agreements and compare
them with the effect of levying dumping duties. We find that empirically

these settlements entail greater distortions than those associated with the imposition of dumping duties. We interpret this as evidence that an antidumping investigation allows firms to achieve outcomes that are unattainable in a standard noncooperative trade environment.

The paper proceeds as follows. Section 2 presents data on the incidence of antidumping actions and analyzes the economic effect of these cases, and discusses the legal issues behind the settlement option. Section 3 presents a stylized bargaining model that is used to analyze the magnitude of the settlements and the affect of the legal rules governing the agreements. The bargaining over the price undertakings is modelled as a Nash bargaining problem. The use of this solution concept can be justified using the known relationship between the Nash solutions and noncooperative dynamic bargaining. In particular, the outcome of the cooperative bargaining process, as characterized by the Nash bargaining solution, is identical to the subgame perfect equilibrium of a noncooperative bargaining game. Concluding comments are made in section 4.

2. Antidumping investigations and trade

Traditionally, economists have modelled the proceedings of an antidumping investigation as follows [see fig. 1(a)]: (1) a domestic industry bands together, collects data, and files a petition with the ITC against a foreign industry at a cost of C_I;[1] in the absence of governmental intervention, the industries compete noncooperatively; (2) within 45 days the ITC issues a preliminary determination; a negative finding ends the investigation; (3) given the information signalled by the ITC's preliminary finding, the domestic firms have an opportunity to withdraw the petition; if the case is not withdrawn, the industry incurs additional ongoing legal expenses of C_O; (4) if the petition is not withdrawn, the ITC issues its final determination no later than 420 days after the petition was originally initiated.

Referring to fig. 1(a), let $\Pi_N - C_I$ denote the domestic industry's net profit when the petition is withdrawn, where Π_N is the domestic industry's 'no dumping duty' oligopoly profit and C_I reflects the costs of initiating a petition. To keep things as simple as possible we will think of the domestic industry as acting as a single player, and hence we will use the terms industry and firm interchangeably. In section 3 we will specify more carefully how Π_N is determined, but for the time being we will take it as given.

Let ρ denote the probability that the ITC will levy dumping duties and Π_D denote the profit that will be earned by the domestic industry if dumping duties are levied against the foreign industry. Clearly, $\Pi_D > \Pi_N$. The domestic

---

[1]In fact, the petition is filed simultaneously with the ITC and the Commerce Department. For the issues analyzed in this paper, we can assume without loss of generality that the ITC is the lone decision-maker.

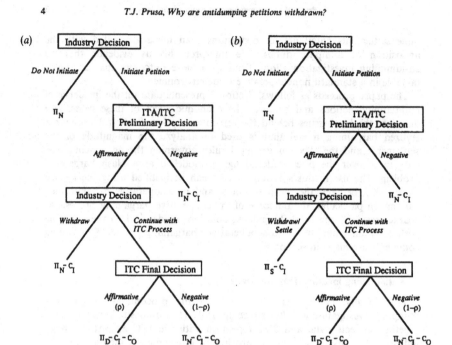

Fig. 1. (a) Extensive form of traditional model of antidumping process. (b) Extensive form of settlement model of antidumping process.

firm's expected profit, given that the investigation proceeds to a final ITC decision, can be written as

$$E\Pi = \rho\Pi_D + (1-\rho)\Pi_N - C_I - C_O,$$

$$= \Pi_N + \rho(\Pi_D - \Pi_N) - C_I - C_O.$$

Under the traditional model of antidumping actions, the case will be withdrawn only if

$$\rho(\Pi_D - \Pi_N) - C_O < 0. \tag{1}$$

However, since the bulk of the legal expenses are sunk and the ongoing legal expenses are relatively small, we would expect most cases to proceed to a

Table 1
Summary of outcomes of U.S. antidumping cases.

Result of case	1980	1981	1982	1983	1984	1985	Total
Dumping duties	10 (27%)	5 (33%)	13 (20%)	19 (41%)	10 (14%)	25 (40%)	82 (27%)
Petition rejected	9 (24%)	6 (40%)	21 (32%)	5 (11%)	43 (58%)	20 (32%)	104 (35%)
Petition withdrawn	18 (49%)	4 (27%)	31 (48%)	22 (48%)	21 (28%)	18 (29%)	114 (38%)
Total no. of cases initiated	37	15	65	46	74	63	300

Note: Numbers in parentheses are the percent of the total cases initiated for that year.
Source: Author's compilation from various issues of U.S. International Trade Commission *Annual Report*.

final ITC decision.[2] In a sense, the null hypothesis of the traditional model is that very few petitions would be withdrawn.

We can use table 1 to help us analyze how well this standard model describes antidumping actions. Table 1 gives a breakdown of the outcomes of antidumping cases initiated between 1980 and 1985. The cases can be broadly classified into one of three ways: petition accepted (duties levied), petition rejected, and petition withdrawn. It is clear that initiating a petition by no means implies that duties will be levied – on average duties were levied only 27 percent of the time. It is somewhat surprising that each of the three possible outcomes accounts for approximately a third of the outcomes. As aforementioned, since the large fraction of legal fees and expenses are sunk we would expect few cases to be withdrawn. The rather large percentage of withdrawn petitions suggests that the characterization depicted in fig. 1(a), and summarized by eq. (1), does not accurately describe the proceedings.

In fact, typically the withdrawal of an antidumping petition is not evidence that the domestic industry's case has failed. Frequently a petition is withdrawn only after the domestic industry has achieved some type of out-of-court settlement with its foreign rival. The settlement may involve either a price undertaking or a quantity restriction. Furthermore, settlements can be made with or without governmental approval. Therefore a more accurate characterization of the proceedings should incorporate the ability of the domestic industry to extract a settlement from its foreign rival. Since settlements are possible, the extensive form representation depicted in fig. 1(b) is more appropriate. This characterization is identical to that in fig. 1(a) except that we allow the domestic and foreign industries to negotiate before

---

[2]The ongoing expenses (for the domestic industry) are relatively small since once the petition is filed, the ITC carries out its own investigation. In a sense, the ITC is an arbitrator, using the data each side presents (along with collecting its own data) to come to a binding decision. See Barshefsky and Cunningham (1981) for a discussion of legal expenses incurred in an antidumping investigation.

the final ITC decision. Referring to fig. 1(b), let $\Pi_S - C_1$ denote the net profit from settling, where Π_S is the profit resulting from a settlement. We would expect $\Pi_S > \Pi_N$. As before, $\Pi_N + \rho(\Pi_D - \Pi_N) - C_1 - C_0$ denotes the expected profit when the investigation proceeds to a final ITC decision. In this framework, if

$$\Pi_N + \rho(\Pi_D - \Pi_N) - C_0 < \Pi_S, \tag{2}$$

the case will be settled. Since the foreign rival can offer to restrict its prices/quantity to insure $\Pi_S > \Pi_N$, this latter model is more consistent with the large number of petition withdrawals.

The ability to achieve a settlement is similar to litigants bargaining over an out-of-court settlement. The domestic industry, or the plaintiff, files a petition against its foreign rival, or the defendant. The award/penalty is the change in profits when the dumping duty is levied. The analogy underlies the legal literature's benign view of settlements. In the standard litigation model [Shavel (1982)] the parties are merely negotiating how to divide the damages and since legal fees are costly, it will be beneficial for risk-neutral parties to settle. In the context of an antidumping case, the parties would negotiate how much prices will be changed.

There are, however, a number of problems with this analogy. Unlike the standard legal examples, the amount of damages is not fixed. In fact, given that the parties are competitors in a market, it is possible that a price restriction could benefit both parties. This issue will be more fully discussed in the following sections. Furthermore, the foreign and domestic firms are competitors in a market, and these price/quantity agreements restrain trade. One would expect that such agreements violate antitrust law. However, there has never been an antitrust action due to an antidumping settlement. There are several reasons why the settlement option is likely to be exempt from antitrust prosecution. First, many cases are settled under the auspices of the U.S. government. That is, the U.S. Trade Representative (USTR) acts on behalf of the domestic industry and negotiates the settlement with the foreign government/industry. Even though these settlements may be anticompetitive, the domestic firms are not directly involved, and therefore they are not directly engaged in anticompetitive behavior. Once the USTR has negotiated the settlement, the domestic industry withdraws its petition. Second, in many other cases the antidumping petition is withdrawn after the foreign industry voluntarily raises its prices or restricts its quantities. Thus, the settlement outcome may involve tacit rather than direct collusion between parties. Third, the settlement process is protected by the legal principle called the *Noerr–Pennington* doctrine. The *Noerr–Pennington* doctrine is a judicially created antitrust exemption for lawful efforts to obtain legislative, judicial, or executive action. The *Noerr–Pennington* doctrine implies that antitrust

Table 2

Trade impact of U.S. antidumping/countervailing duty cases.

(a) Products subject to antidumping/countervailing duty petitions in 1980

Result of case	Ratio of 1981 value of trade to 1980 value of trade
Duties levied	0.44
Petition rejected	1.12
Petition withdrawn	0.57
All cases	0.77
All imports	1.09

(b) Products subject to antidumping/countervailing duty petitions in 1981

Result of case	Ratio of 1982 value of trade to 1981 value of trade
Duties levied	0.84
Petition rejected	1.07
Petition withdrawn	0.80
All cases	0.92
All imports	0.97

Data sources: Antidumping/countervailing trade data, UNCTAD (1984); Value of import data, *Statistical Abstract of the United States – 1986*.

considerations must be subordinated to the firms' constitutional right to participate in the legislative process. Even though the doctrine was formulated with domestic issues in mind,[3] it appears that it applies equally to cases involving international parties.[4] The *Noerr–Pennington* exemption broadens the scope for relief and allows the domestic industry to withdraw its petition after achieving a settlement. All in all, considering that it is the domestic firms who initiate the petition and given the variety of ways a settlement can be achieved, it is plausible that a number of antidumping petitions are filed explicitly with the intent of obtaining a settlement offer.

The data in table 2 quantify the effects of these settlement agreements. The table compares the value of trade in the year after the petition was resolved

[3]The *Noerr* case concerned the right of a group of railroads to mount a campaign encouraging the adoption of certain anti-trucking legislation. The truckers alleged that the lobbying activity was intended to eliminate competition, and hence violated the Sherman Antitrust Act. The Supreme Court ruled in favor of the railroads, writing that 'no violation of antitrust laws can be based on attempts to influence the passage or enforcement of legislation ... (even if) the law restrains trade or creates a monopoly'. The *Pennington* case involved the joint efforts of a union and large coal mine operators to establish a minimum wage. The small mine operators argued that such joint activity was intended to drive them out of business. The Supreme Court ruled against the small mine companies, writing that 'joint efforts to influence public officials do not violate the antitrust laws even though intended to eliminate competition' [Vakerics (1987)].

[4]To date, there have not been any cases challenging the right of domestic firms to initiate (or settle) petitions. Thus, in some respects the legal precedent has not been firmly established. See Barshefsky and Cunningham (1981) and Vakerics (1987).

8   *T.J. Prusa, Why are antidumping petitions withdrawn?*

with the value of trade in the year the petition was filed. A number less than one implies that trade fell the year following the petition. This table is based upon data collected by the United Nations in 1982. The products involved in each antidumping case are identified by a seven-digit TSUSA code. The TSUSA codes were used to calculate trade volume for those products involved in antidumping investigations.[5]

We look first at those products that were subject to investigation during 1980 (the upper panel of table 2). Those products that had antidumping petitions rejected had a 1981 trade value that was 112 percent of their 1980 value – a number nearly the same as the change in the value of all imports (109 percent). This suggests that a petition by itself does not adversely affect competition and hence that the domestic industry does not gain a strategic advantage over its foreign rivals by merely initiating a petition. In other words, this suggests that the in terrorem effect is not evidenced in the data.

In comparison, those products that were granted protection (i.e. had duties levied) had a 1981 trade value that was only 44 percent of its 1980 value. This is exactly what theory suggests should be observed – the imposition of duty on a product will lower the demand for the product. The fall in trade as a result of duties is generally recognized as the main reason why domestic firms initiate antidumping petitions.

Thus, the data clearly show the great advantage to having a petition accepted rather than rejected. Somewhat surprisingly though, we do not observe a great difference between a petition that results in duties being levied and a petition that is withdrawn. For instance in 1980–1981, the value of trade fell to 57 percent of its previous value for those products that had petitions withdrawn. This suggests that, on average, withdrawing a petition has nearly the same effect as having duties levied. The 1981–1982 data confirm these findings. In particular, for the 1981–1982 period, dumping duties lowered the value of trade to 84 percent of its previous value while petition withdrawals were associated with a value of trade that was 80 percent of its previous value. In summary, two key facts emerge from this analysis. First, the imposition of antidumping duties significantly reduces the growth in the value of trade relative to either those products that had petitions rejected or those that were not involved in an antidumping case. Second, petition withdrawals have essentially the same effect on the growth in the value of trade as does levying duties.

While it is possible that these settlements actually increase domestic welfare (since on average they achieve the same outcome as the ITC but save the ITC investigative expense) one must question whether this is a plausible interpretation of the data, especially in light of the fact that not all

[5]Unfortunately, the United Nations does not report trade data for antidumping cases alone. Since the legal procedures involved in countervailing duty investigations are very similar to antidumping investigations, the results are likely to be consistent with antidumping cases alone.

withdrawn cases involve agreements. Unfortunately, given the way the government reports case outcomes, it is difficult to determine precisely which cases are withdrawn with a settlement and which are withdrawn without any type of an agreement. This ambiguity is due in part to the fact that an agreement with governmental assistance is only one way a settlement might be achieved. UNCTAD (1984) estimates that only 50 percent of the withdrawn cases involve agreements.[6] Since many cases do not involve any agreement and those cases withdrawn without an agreement do not restrain trade, the simple averages presented in table 2 underestimate the true restraint of trade that is implied by a settlement. Clearly, UNCTAD's estimate implies that the subset of cases involving agreements must restrain trade by far more than duties. Vermulst (1987) estimates that nearly 80 percent of the petitions withdrawn involved some type of settlement. Although this estimate somewhat attenuates the magnitude of the trade restraint implied by settlements, it still implies that settlement agreements must restrain trade by more than duties do. Regardless which estimate is correct, the general insight – that on average a settlement has a large and significant impact on trade – is nonetheless confirmed. These results make it clear that a normative analysis of antidumping law that only discusses how duties affect consumers ignores an important way in which the law affects welfare.

Using either UNCTAD's or Vermulst's estimate we find that settlement agreements grant significant market power to domestic firms. Even though domestic firms may prefer settling, they cannot unilaterally impose a settlement agreement on their foreign rivals. The foreign firms will only agree to settle with the domestic firms when they too gain from an agreement; however, if the foreign firms prefer settling, the desirability of such agreements must be carefully questioned. For instance, if the settlement implies that the price received by the foreign firm for its products is the same as it would be if the ITC levied duties, the agreement is probably desirable. On the other hand, if the settlement allows the foreign firm to price in such a way that it earns greater profits than it would without an antidumping action, we must question the use of such settlement agreements. This would suggest that the settlements promote collusion rather than fair trade. We analyze this issue in the following section.

3. Price agreements and the nature of competition

The model developed in this section is aimed at explaining the empirical facts discussed in the preceding section and clarifies whether settlements are

---

[6]It should be noted that UNCTAD's method of classifying cases differs slightly from the ITC's method. It seems likely that UNCTAD's calculations underestimate the true percentage of cases involving assurances and thus overestimate the fall in trade involved in a settlement agreement.

welfare-improving. By welfare we are referring to consumer's welfare. In particular, the model shows (1) why initiating a petition creates the opportunity for settlements that are mutually beneficial relative to the expected ITC outcome and also relative to free trade, and (2) why the rules governing the settlement process crucially influence how beneficial such settlements are.

Consider a market with two risk-neutral firms, one foreign and one domestic, which sell slightly differentiated products. For convenience, we will denote foreign variables with an asterisk. Furthermore, we will assume that each firm sets price and can sell all output demanded at that price. Note that in many applications the outcome of the game is extremely sensitive to the choice of strategic variable [Bulow, Geanakoplos and Klemperer (1985)]; however, the results of this model are robust to whether firms choose prices or quantities.[7]

We will assume that there exists a unique, stable Nash equilibrium and that in equilibrium both firms' prices and output are strictly positive.[8] Denote the domestic (foreign) firm's best response function as $\beta(P^*)[\beta^*(P)]$. The Nash equilibrium is defined by the two-tuple (P_N, P_N^*) which satisfies $\beta^*(P_N) = P_N^*$ and $\beta(P_N^*) = P_N$.

Fig. 2 depicts the Bertrand–Nash equilibrium in price space. $\beta(P^*)$ defines the domestic firm's price that allows the highest iso-profit loci to be reached, given P^*. $\beta^*(P)$ can be interpreted in a similar fashion. The Nash equilibrium is at point n. The foreign and domestic firms' Nash profits are $\Pi_N^* \equiv \Pi^*(P_N, P_N^*)$ and $\Pi_N \equiv \Pi(P_N, P_N^*)$, respectively. The point $s^*(s)$ is the Stackelberg leader equilibrium when the foreign (domestic) firm can pre-commit to a price.

Fig. 3 depicts the Nash equilibrium, n, in profit space. The profit possibilities attainable in any period are also depicted in fig. 3. The curve m^*jm is the profit possibilities frontier (PPF). This frontier is the locus of maximum profit attainable by the firms. Any point on or below this frontier is attainable by a suitable pair of prices $\{P, P^*\}$. The point $m^*(m)$ depicts the monopoly level of profit for the foreign (domestic) firm while j depicts the joint profit-maximizing level of profits. As is well known, the Nash profit levels are strictly interior to the efficient locus. It is clear that both firms could be made better off if they could commit to prices that would generate profits on the profit frontier on the segment vy (or, more generally, the region northeast of n).

This simple Nash equilibrium will serve as a benchmark case which we will compare with an alternative situation. Consider the case when an antidumping petition has been initiated, and the ITC has given preliminary

---

[7]The crucial condition is that the joint Nash profits are less than the joint monopoly profits, which is satisfied for both Bertrand and Cournot competition.

[8]Friedman (1983) discusses the sufficient conditions for these conditions to hold.

T.J. Prusa, Why are antidumping petitions withdrawn?   11

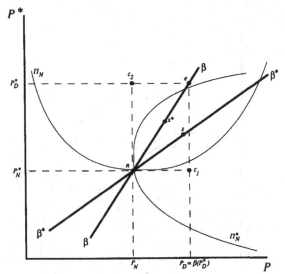

Fig. 2. Bertrand–Nash equilibrium in price space.

approval. This allows us to concentrate on the economic aspects of the bargaining process. From this viewpoint the costs of the petition C_1 are sunk and hence do not affect the bargaining process. Furthermore, for simplicity we assume that $C_0 = 0$. Allowing $C_0 > 0$ does not change the nature of the results and only complicates the notation. If dumping is determined, a specific duty of $(P_D^* - P_N^*)$ will be levied on the foreign product. The price domestic consumers face is $P_D^*, P_D^* > P_N^*$, while P_N^* is collected by the foreign firm. In order to highlight the bargaining process we will assume that if duties are levied, the foreign firm continues to collect only P_N^*; however, it is clear that the foreign firm will have incentives to alter its pricing behavior when faced with the duty.

With the foreign firm burdened with duties, the domestic firm will charge $P_D = \beta(P_D^*), P_D > P_N$. For notational convenience, let $\Pi_D^* \equiv \Pi^*(P_D, P_D^*)$ and $\Pi_D \equiv \Pi(P_D, P_D^*)$. If duties are levied, the foreign firm will earn $\Pi_D - (P_D^* - P_N^*)Q_D^*$, where $(P_D^* - P_N^*)$ is the specific duty and Q_D^* is the quantity demanded of the foreign product at prices $\{P_D, P_D^*\}$. In other words, $(P_D^* - P_N^*)Q_D^*$ is the dumping duty revenue collected by the government. The conditions that guarantee a unique Nash equilibrium [Friedman 1983)] also imply

$$\Pi_D^* - (P_D^* - P_N^*)Q_D^* < \Pi_N^*.$$

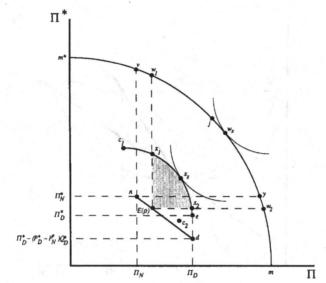

Fig. 3. Bertrand–Nash equilibrium and settlement loci in profit space.

If duties are levied, the domestic firm will earn Π_D. If the petition is rejected, the firms will earn Nash profit levels, $\{\Pi_N, \Pi_N^*\}$. Put another way, the firms' pricing strategies are determined by the ITC's decision. If duties are levied, the foreign firm's price P_D^* is assigned by the ITC; the domestic firm then sets its price knowing that duties have been levied; therefore $P_D = \beta(P_D^*)$. If duties are not levied, the foreign firm's pricing strategy is not hindered by the ITC and thus the firms just charge their Nash equilibrium prices, P_N and P_N^*.

The antidumping duty equilibrium, $\{\Pi_D, \Pi_D^* - (P_D^* - P_N^*)Q_D^*\}$, is depicted by point d in fig. 3. The point e depicts the firms' profits if the foreign firm did not have to pay the dumping duty (i.e. if it collected P_D^* instead of P_N^* per unit). Note that the diagram depicts the case when P_D^* is sufficiently large so that $\Pi_D^* < \Pi_N^*$; this need not be the case. In particular, if P_D^* is in the neighborhood of the Stackelberg leader price, the foreign firm would earn greater profit at the higher price if it did not have to pay the duty.

The ITC has only two options: levying duties or rejecting the petition. However, because the injury and less than fair value determinations involve a tremendous amount of data collection and calculation, it is quite possible the ITC will make mistakes (owing to observation error). Moreover, because many of the calculations involve highly subjective decisions (i.e. which exchange rate is relevant, how much of the import penetration is due to unfair practices, how to adjust for product differences, etc.), even if the foreign firm has not dumped, it may not be able to convince the ITC. Let ρ denote the ex ante probability that the ITC will levy duties. Assuming that the firms are risk-neutral and that ρ is common knowledge, we can write the expected profit of the domestic and foreign firm as

$$E\Pi(\rho) = \rho\Pi_D + (1 - \rho)\Pi_N \tag{3}$$

and

$$E\Pi^*(\rho) = \rho[(\Pi_D^* - (P_D^* - P_N^*)Q_D^*] + (1 - \rho)\Pi_N^*. \tag{4}$$

Let $E(\rho) \equiv (E\Pi(\rho), E\Pi^*(\rho))$. This point is depicted in profit space in fig. 3. The line segment between points n and d depicts the firms' expected profits if the antidumping case is not settled. If it is likely that the ITC will find dumping (e.g. ρ close to one), $E(\rho)$ lies closer to the point d; conversely, if it is extremely unlikely that the ITC will find dumping, $E(\rho)$ lies closer to the point p.

In addition to ITC determined outcomes, the firms always have the option of settling the agreement. We will consider two alternative regulatory environments that govern how the settlement outcome is determined. These two regulatory environments are based on the procedures for expedited relief as defined in the Trade Adjustment Act of 1979. Let $\Pi_S \equiv \Pi(P_S, P_S^*)$ and $\Pi_S^* \equiv \Pi^*(P_S, P_S^*)$ denote profit levels that will be achieved via negotiation for the domestic and foreign industries, respectively. One set of rules governing the settlement process will be referred to as Settlement via ITC Sanctioned Suspension (SANC). The second set of rules governing the settlement process will be referred to as Settlement via Private Negotiation and Withdrawal (PRIV).

Under SANC rules an agreement to suspend the petition must (i) be agreed upon by the parties, and (ii) must be determined (by the ITC) to be in the 'public interest'. We interpret this rule as imposing the following constraints on the settlement offers: (i) $\Pi_S^* \geq \Pi^*(\rho)$ and $\Pi_S \geq \Pi(\rho)$, and (ii) $P_S^* \leq P_D^*$. In other words, SANC rules constrain the potential prices over which the firms can negotiate. This seems to be a plausible interpretation, for according to the antidumping code

> Proceedings may be suspended . . . without the imposition of provisional measures or antidumping duties upon receipt of satisfactory voluntary undertakings. . . . Price increases under such undertakings shall not be higher than necessary to eliminate the margin of dumping [Lorenzen (1979, p. 1429)].

In contrast, under PRIV rules an agreement must only be agreed upon by the parties. There are no explicit restrictions imposed by the antidumping code. Therefore, under this rule a settlement offer only has to satisfy $\Pi_S^* \geqq \Pi^*(\rho)$ and $\Pi_S \geqq \Pi(\rho)$.

If the domestic firm asks for a suspension, the ITC must approve the terms of the settlement offer. On the other hand, the firm may opt to negotiate a settlement unencumbered by the ITC. In this latter case, once an agreement is made the domestic firm will withdraw the petition and petition the ITC to terminate its investigation. While the ITC always has the right to continue the investigation there has never been a case where it has failed to terminate its investigation when requested to do so.

It appears that the main advantage the SANC process offers the domestic firm is that it makes it more difficult for the foreign firm to renege or shirk on its agreement.[9] Within practical limits, the private agreement that instigated the petition withdrawal is also enforceable – the petition can always be refiled.[10] Thus, for the remainder of this paper we will examine settlement offers under each procedure assuming the agreements are enforceable.

We first examine when the firms will opt to settle. The alternative for either firm is to make unacceptable demands, and then wait for the ITC's decision. If the case is not settled, the firms' security level of profits is $E(\rho)$. The bargaining game is solved using the well-known Nash bargaining solution. [See Roth (1979) for an excellent discussion.] The Nash bargaining solution states that if the set of profit opportunities over which the firms bargain is convex, there exists a unique settlement offer, $\{\Pi(P_S, P_S^*), \Pi^*(P_S, P_S^*)\}$, that satisfies

$$\max_{\{P_S^*, P_S\}} [\Pi(P_S, P_S^*) - E\Pi(\rho)][\Pi^*(P_S, P_S^*) - E\Pi^*(\rho)]. \tag{5}$$

The price undertakings, $\{P_S^*, P_S\}$, are implicitly defined by (5). We relegate the proof that the set of prices over which the firms bargain is convex to the appendix.

The negotiation set under SANC rules is defined by the shaded region in fig. 3. The negotiation set is found by maximizing weighted profits subject to the constraints that (i) $\Pi(P_S, P_S^*) \geqq E\Pi(\rho)$ and $\Pi^*(P_S, P_S^*) \geqq E\Pi^*(\rho)$, and (ii) $P_S^* \leqq P_D^*$. Clearly, the restriction on the foreign firm's price also restricts the domestic firm's optimal price. As depicted in fig. 3, the restriction on the

---

[9]The following quote from the U.S. code governing antidumping law suggests that agreements are enforceable. 'Violation of a suspension agreement will lead to ... resumption of the investigation... An intentional violation will result in civil fraud penalties' [Barshefsky and Cunningham (1981)].

[10]There are a number of examples of U.S. firms withdrawing petitions, and then later filing essentially the same complaint with the ITC.

foreign firm's price offers implied by SANC rules causes the boundary of the negotiation set to be strictly interior to the PPF. If P_D^* is sufficiently large, the boundary of the negotiation set could coincide with the PPF.

In contrast, the negotiation set under PRIV rules is defined by the points northeast of $E(\rho)$ in the feasible set. The negotiation set under PRIV rules is found by maximizing weighted profits subject to the constraints that $\Pi(P_S, P_S^*) \geqq E\Pi(\rho)$ and $\Pi^*(P_S, P_S^*) \geqq E\Pi^*(\rho)$. The boundary under PRIV rules is the PPF.

The Nash bargaining solution implies that the firms will choose prices that maximize (5). This in turn implies that the solution must lie on the upper boundary of the negotiation set. We can graphically depict the Nash bargaining solution by finding the tangency of the upper boundary of the negotiation set and a rectangular hyperbola that is asymptotic to the broken lines through $E(\rho)$. Along this rectangular hyperbola $[\Pi(P_S, P_S^*) - E\Pi(\rho)][\Pi^*(P_S, P_S^*) - E\Pi^*(\rho)]$ is constant. In profit space, the point x_S depicts the solution under SANC rules, while w_S depicts the solution under PRIV rules.

We summarize the above discussion with the following proposition.

Proposition 1. Assume common knowledge over ρ. The Nash bargaining solution exists under either set of settlement rules. In other words, under either SANC or PRIV settlement rules, there exist settlement offers that guarantee both firms will earn no less profit than the expected ITC decision.

Proposition 1 states that there exist mutually advantageous settlement possibilities for any ρ and thus that the negotiation set is nonempty under either set of rules. Even in the limit ($\rho = 1$), the firms can always at least bargain over the duty revenue. This suggests that we should not be surprised when we observe so many antidumping cases withdrawn.

The chief advantage of using the Nash bargaining solution is that we do not have to explicitly model the bargaining process. This does not imply that that bargaining game is a black-box. Rather, we can use Binmore's (1987) formulation of the Nash bargaining solution to describe a noncooperative bargaining game whose outcome is defined by (5). Binmore (1987) shows that the solution defined by eq. (5) is equivalent to a subgame perfect equilibrium of a noncooperative bargaining game. The noncooperative bargaining game described by Binmore requires us to assume that (i) a common discount rate summarizes the parties' impatience with respect to the outcome, (ii) the negotiations can be divided into discrete periods, and (iii) the foreign and domestic firms make offers in alternating periods. These are not terribly binding assumptions. For instance, perfect capital mobility will imply a single world interest rate which would justify (i). Furthermore, since the firms have approximately one year to negotiate before the ITC reaches its final decision, it would be natural to divide the bargaining game into a day-by-day negotiation game where we assume the foreign firm makes offers on odd days and the domestic firm makes offers on even days. If an offer is accepted, the petition is settled. A subgame equilibrium of this game is defined by (5).

Since both firms are willing to settle the antidumping case, this implies that both prefer settling to the expected ITC outcome. Even when it is highly unlikely that antidumping duties will be levied (i.e. ρ close to zero) the foreign firm prefers to settle since it allows the firms to revise their prices upwards. The domestic firm will also prefer to settle in this case since continuing with the petition will almost certainly result only in Π_N. Conversely, when it is very likely that antidumping duties will be levied (i.e. ρ close to one) the foreign firm prefers to settle since it avoids paying duties. The domestic firm will settle only if it is assured of at least Π_D; it is always in the best interest of the foreign firm to offer a price undertaking that ensures this.

This does not imply that the foreign firm prefers settling to Nash competition. Certainly, if P_D^* is in the neighborhood of the foreign firm's Stackelberg leader price it will prefer settling to Nash competition, for any value of ρ. However, if P_D^* is sufficiently large, then the foreign firm may benefit from settling ($\Pi_S^* > E\Pi^*(\rho)$) but it will be forced to commit to such large price undertakings that its profits are lower than under Nash competition (i.e. $\Pi_S^* < \Pi_N^*$). For example, under SANC rules and $\rho = 1$ the foreign firm will earn Π_D^* which may be smaller than Π_N^*. In this case, the settlement outcome mimics the expected ITC decision.

Interestingly, a settlement will most clearly fail to mimic the expected ITC decision when ρ is small. From (5) we see that the negotiated outcome will always give both firms no less profit than the expected ITC outcome; if ρ is small, $E\Pi(\rho) \approx (\Pi_N, \Pi_N^*)$. Any small price revision in the neighborhood of n will raise both firms' profits. Thus even under SANC rules we find that a 'nuisance suit' (i.e. a suit with small ρ) will benefit both firms, and hence will promote tacit collusion. This result sharply contrasts with the interpretation of nuisance suits found in the legal literature, where it is argued that they are aimed at harassing the foreign firm and do not directly raise profits. The value of a nuisance suit is most dramatically evidenced when $\rho = 0$; in this case the foreign firm need not make any price revision. One would hope the bargaining outcome would approximate the ITC's own decision. However, the opportunity to cooperate allows the firms to mutually offer to raise their prices and achieve collusive profit levels. In fact, if the firms are symmetric, the Nash bargaining outcome of a nuisance suit will entail the firms sharing the joint profit-maximizing level of profits.

As this discussion suggests, the parameter ρ plays an important role in determining the efficacy of the bargaining game. In this model, the negotiation sets are defined by the legal rules (SANC or PRIV) and prices

$\{P_N, P_N^*, P_D, P_D^*\}$. The parameter ρ shifts the security level of profits. As ρ increases, bargaining power is shifted toward the domestic firm and away from the foreign firm. Changes in ρ will entail changes in the settlement level of profits. As ρ increases, the domestic firm's profits will increase and the foreign firm's profits will decrease. Under SANC rules if $\rho = 1$, the domestic firm is indifferent between settling and letting the case continue through the ITC. In contrast, the foreign firm will strictly prefer to settle and avoid paying the duty. Under SANC rules, the only loss to consumer welfare is the loss of the duty revenue. Under PRIV rules, there will be an additional loss to welfare. For all but the most extreme cases, the point e will be the interior of the PPF. Therefore, from (5) the negotiated outcome under PRIV rules will lead not only to a loss of duties but also to greater profit for both firms relative to $E(\rho)$.

The preceding analysis reveals that under either set of legal rules, the settlement option can lead to collusive outcomes. A few comments are in order. First, the argument that private settlements mimic the expected ITC decision (and therefore are welfare increasing) is fallacious. Note that even if $\rho = 0$ the foreign firm will always benefit from the settlement process. Second, the settlement process in an antidumping investigation is fundamentally different from the typical bargaining games analyzed in the literature. The standard bargaining games analyze how two players should decide to divide a 'pie'. The difference in this problem is that not only are the firms trying to decide their share of the pie, but they also have the ability to increase the size of the pie! By choosing relatively moderate price increases, both firms can earn greater profits, which is far different from the original intent of the law. The ITC could make the settlement process a fixed-size pie problem if it more strictly regulated the settlement process. For instance, the ITC could more tightly restrict price revisions and charge the firms an approval fee equal to the expected duties. Under these circumstances the settlement outcome would more closely parallel the expected ITC decision. This type of scheme is not implemented of course, since settlements are politically desirable. Third, the empirical findings reported in section 2 discussed the effect of settled cases in terms of trade data, while the model in section 3 focuses on the effect of settled cases in terms of profits. In general, the model's predictions are consistent with the empirical results. In particular, the larger profits that emerge from the bargaining game will imply a fall in trade. The model does predict that we should observe significant differences in trade when comparing cases that are settled with those that are rejected. However, the data also suggest that there is a greater restraint of trade when cases are settled than when duties are levied. This may not be implied by the model. For instance, under SANC rules, the settled price P_S^* must be no greater than P_D^*. If the case was not withdrawn and the ITC levied duties, the domestic firm would charge $P_D = \beta(P_D^*)$. By the optimality of the best response function, we know that this is the highest price the domestic firm would offer under SANC rules. This implies that when compared with a settlement under SANC rules, the ITC outcome $\{P_D, P_D^*\}$ would involve the least trade. Therefore, with the bargaining model discussed above, settled outcomes could involve more or less restraints on trade than the ITC decision. Fourth, unless one of the parties fears that the other will cheat on the settlements, the model predicts that firms should prefer settling under PRIV rules rather than SANC rules.

4. Concluding comments

The rise of administered protection during the past twenty years is quite worrisome. Traditional models and analysis of protection do not adequately describe the true effects of the new protectionism. For instance, the data and analysis presented in this paper reveal that antidumping petitions have had a much greater effect on trade than previously thought. Trade data indicate that withdrawn cases restrict trade by at least as much, and probably more than, dumping duties. This behavior is consistent with the argument that U.S. firms are using antidumping laws for reasons other than the original intent of the law. The *Noerr–Pennington* doctrine provides firms with an antitrust exemption and grants them the right to achieve private settlements.

This paper presents a stylized bargaining model of the settlement process. The concept of a Nash bargaining solution is used to solve for a unique equilibrium. The value of the model is that the key incentives driving the settlement process are clarified. Even when the agreement must be in the public interest, the ability to avoid dumping duties and cooperate on pricing decisions makes it strictly preferred to the expected ITC decision. The desirability of achieving a settlement is increased when the firms do not need ITC approval. One interpretation of the model is that antidumping petitions serve as a vehicle to achieve cooperative levels of profits.

Finally, note that economists typically argue that levying dumping duties increases producer surplus at the expense of consumer surplus. If antidumping petitions were resolved only via official ITC decisions, then this is a legitimate argument. However, since many petitions are withdrawn after a settlement agreement one needs to reconsider the traditional analysis of antidumping duties. One possible interpretation of the data and analysis in this paper is that levying duties may actually *increase* consumer surplus since the alternative is not free trade but rather a negotiated outcome.

Appendix

Proof that the bargaining set is convex. We will show the bargaining set is convex under either set of bargaining rules.

Assume SANC rules. In fig. 3 let c_1 depict the profits $(\Pi(P_D, P_N^*), \Pi^*(P_D, P_N^*))$, c_2 depict the profits $(\Pi(P_N, P_D^*), \Pi^*(P_N, P_D^*))$, n depict the profits $(\Pi(P_N, P_N^*), \Pi^*(P_N, P_N^*))$, e depict the profits $(\Pi(P_D, P_D^*), \Pi^*(P_D, P_D^*))$, and finally let d depict the profits $(\Pi(P_D, P_D^*), \Pi^*(P_D, P_D^*) - (P_D^* - P_N^*)Q_D^*)$.

The attainable set is defined by maximizing weighted profits subject to $P_S^* \leqq P_D^*$. In fig. 2 (price space) this set is defined by $\{P, P^*\} \in c_1 n e c_2$. In fig. 3 (profit space) this set is defined by the frontier $c_1 x_1 x_2 e$. Note that this set is concave and compact in both price and profit space. The concavity of this set in profit space follows directly from the concavity of each firm's profit function. The negotiation set is defined as the subset of the attainable set which gives the firms at least $E(\rho)$.

Assume PRIV rules. Without the additional constraint on the foreign prices the attainable set is defined by the PPF. This set is concave and compact in both price and profit space. The concavity of this set in profit space follows directly from the concavity of each firm's profit function. Q.E.D.

References

Barshefsky, C. and R.O. Cunningham, 1981, The prosecution of antidumping actions under the Trade Agreements Act of 1979, North Carolina Journal of International Law and Commercial Regulation 6, 307–362.

Binmore, K., 1987, Perfect equilibrium in bargaining models, in: K. Binmore and P. Dasgupta, eds., Economics of bargaining (Basil Blackwell, Oxford).

Brander, J.A. and P. Krugman, 1983, A 'reciprocal dumping' model if international trade, Journal of International Economics 15, 313–321.

Bulow, J.I., J.D. Geanakoplos and P.D. Klemperer, 1985, Multimarket oligopoly: Strategic substitutes and complements, Journal of Political Economy 93, 488–511.

Bureau of Census, 1987, Statistical abstract of the United States – 1986 (United States Department of Commerce, Washington, DC).

Davies, S. and A. McGuinness, 1982, Dumping at less than marginal cost, Journal of International Economics 12, 169–182.

Ethier, W.J., 1982, Dumping, Journal of Political Economy 90, 481–506.

Ethier, W.J. and R. Fischer, 1987, The new protectionism, Journal of International Economic Integration 2, 1–11.

Fischer, R.D., 1988, Endogenous probability of protection and firm behavior, Mimeo.

Friedman, J., 1983, Oligopoly theory (Cambridge University Press, Cambridge).

Hartquist, D.A., 1987, Trade wars – arming for battle, North Carolina Journal of International Law and Commercial Reglation 12, 37–58.

Hindley, B., 1987, GATT safeguards and voluntary export restraints: What are the interests of developing countries, The World Bank Economic Review 1, 689–705.

Lorenzen, S.A., 1979, Technical analysis of the antidumpting agreement and the trade agreements act, Law and Policy in International Business 11, 1405–1436.

Messerlin, P.A., 1988, The EC antidumping regulations: A first economic appraisal: 1980–85, Mimeo.

Messerlin, P.A., 1989, GATT-inconsistent outcomes of GATT-consistent laws: The long-term evolution of the EC antidumping laws, Mimeo.

Prusa, T.J., 1987, Antidumping law and firm behavior, Mimeo.

Roth, A.E., 1979, Axiomatic models of bargaining (Springer-Verlag, Berlin).

Shavell, S., 1982, Suit, settlement and trial: A theoretical analysis under alternative methods for the allocation of legal costs, Journal of Legal Studies 11, 55–81.

UNCTAD, 1984, Protectionism and structural assistance: Antidumping and countervailing
    practices (UNCTAD, Geneva).
Vakerics, T.V., 1987, Antitrust basics (Law Journal Seminars Press, New York, NY).
Vermulst, E.A., 1987, Antidumping law and practice in the United States and the European
    Communities: A comparative analysis (North-Holland, New York, NY).
Viner, J., 1923, Dumping: A problem in international trade (University of Chicago Press,
    Chicago, IL).
Von Kalinowski, J.O., 1987, Antitrust laws and trade regulation – desk edition (Mathew Bender
    and Company, New York, NY).
Yarrow, G., 1987, Economic aspects of antidumping policies, Oxford Review of Economic Policy
    3, 66–79.

Chapter 2

The Trade Effects of U.S. Antidumping Actions*

Thomas J. Prusa

Even though tariff rates fell throughout the late 1970s and 1980s, there is growing consensus that the overall level of protection in the United States rose during this period. For instance, Bhagwati (1988, 43) states, "The downward trend in trade restrictions resulting from declining tariffs was rudely interrupted in the mid-1970s," and Nivola (1993) points out that between 1975 and 1985 the volume of U.S. import trade affected by some form of trade barriers doubled. In fact, from a historical perspective, what is surprising is not that the long postwar period of trade liberalization was interrupted (at least temporarily) but that the era of trade liberalization lasted so long.[1]

Rather, what is unusual about the recent rise in protectionism is the form that it has taken. In earlier years, increased demand for protection was met with comprehensive tariff bills. By contrast, the recent rise in protection is almost entirely due to administered protection and nontariff barriers such as voluntary export restraints (VERs), which differ in several important ways from traditional tariff protection. First of all, the modern tools of protection are typically more subtle and less transparent than tariffs, falling in the grey area between GATT-consistent and GATT-inconsistent protection. This ambiguity explains why the modern tools are so popular since it allows countries considerable discretion over when and how to implement these policies. Is a health standard that outlaws the sale of beef from cattle injected with growth hormones truly based on concern for public safety, or is it simply an attempt

Thomas J. Prusa is associate professor of economics at Rutgers University and a faculty research fellow of the National Bureau of Economic Research.

The author is indebted to Rob Feenstra for assistance in constructing the data set and to Bob Staiger and the seminar participants at the NBER conference for their helpful comments.

1. For most of U.S. history, periods of trade liberalization were quite short-lived, typically lasting only five or six years (Taussig 1931).

191

---

*This article originally appeared in *National Bureau of Economic Research*, pp. 191–213.

to reduce the amount of imported beef? Are budget cuts that significantly reduce the staff at customs offices a sincere effort to manage the federal deficit or a veiled attempt to raise the cost of exporting into the U.S. market? Is an industry's fall in profits and sales due to increasingly efficient foreign competitors, or is this injury due to dumped imports?

A second key characteristic—and the one that is the focus of this paper—is that the modern instruments are usually not comprehensive. Protection via VERs and the unfair trade statutes is product and country specific. For instance, the 1981 automobile VER with Japan neither restricted automobiles from South Korea nor (initially) restricted light trucks or utility vehicles from Japan. One might expect that the restriction on Japanese automobiles would lead to an increase in the imports of Japanese trucks and utility vehicles and South Korean automobiles.[2] Similarly, an antidumping (AD) duty levied on carbon steel pipes from France is not levied on carbon steel pipes from Germany. One would expect that an antidumping duty levied on a single source would cause exports from the named country (i.e., France) to fall and those from nonnamed countries to increase.

The goal of this paper is to begin to address the issue of how the country-specific nature of AD protection affects its use and effectiveness. I find evidence that AD protection induces substantial trade diversion from named to nonnamed countries. There is also evidence that, the larger the estimated duty, the larger the amount of diversion. Because the magnitude of import diversion is found to be quite large, the results also suggest that AD duties are less restrictive than the domestic industry might expect. Nonetheless, AD duties are valuable since trade is restrained by more in cases resulting in duties than in cases that are rejected. More generally, AD actions are valuable since they induce substantial increases in import prices—by both named and nonnamed countries.

The paper will proceed as follows. In section 7.1, I provide background on the rise of U.S. AD activity and discuss related research. In section 7.2, I present data on the trade effects of AD actions, with particular emphasis on the magnitude of import diversion from named to nonnamed countries. Given that I find import diversion to be substantial, the aggressive U.S. use of AD law has a peculiar side effect—countries that are active in the categories under investigation (but not named) will benefit from the AD sanctions on rivals. In other words, the diversion of imports implies that domestic producers are not the only firms that benefit from an AD action. Countries such as South Korea and Brazil, both of which are frequently named in AD petitions, may nevertheless be net beneficiaries of AD actions since they also gain from sanctions on other countries. This issue of which countries have experienced the most contraction of trade and which have experienced the most expansion as a result

2. For analyses of the VER on Japanese automobiles, see Feenstra (1984, 1987) and Dinopoulos and Kreinin (1988).

of U.S. AD actions is discussed in section 7.3. A few concluding comments are made in section 7.4.

7.1 Background

7.1.1 The Rise of AD Law

During the 1980s, there were more cases filed under AD law (almost five hundred) than under all the other trade statutes combined (Baldwin and Steagall 1994; Hansen and Prusa 1995). AD law, however, is far from an overnight sensation. In fact, AD law is one of the oldest of U.S. trade statutes. The emergence of AD law as the preeminent trade statute is the result of many revisions and amendments over the years; the vast majority of the amendments were geared toward expanding its applicability and increasing the likelihood of an AD case resulting in duties. Prior to 1958, for instance, AD actions were extremely rare. Then, in 1958, Congress amended the rules governing the way in which the dumping margin was calculated, and petition filings increased: about twenty to twenty-five petitions were filed per year between 1958 and 1973; however, the rejection rate was quite high (on average, only two or three cases per year would result in duties). In 1974, AD law was again significantly amended: the definition of dumping was broadened to include sales below cost, and strict time limits on the length of the investigation were imposed. Following the 1974 amendments, AD filings jumped by 50 percent. Despite these changes, the rejection rate remained around 85 percent.

Frustrated by the lack of protection afforded by the law, industries lobbied Congress to make the law more likely to result in duties. These lobbying efforts were manifested in the Trade Agreement Act of 1979, which contained numerous significant changes to AD law. Among them, the power to investigate less than fair value was transferred from the Department of Treasury to the Department of Commerce, use of "best information available" was approved, and time limits on cases were shortened. As a result of these amendments, the use of AD law exploded. During the years following these amendments, AD filings surged, averaging forty-five to fifty cases per year, and the rejection rate dropped to about 50 percent.

The point of this historical background is to emphasize that AD is a malleable, frequently amended statute. AD law is now the most widely used trade statute primarily because congressional amendments have made the statute far more applicable than it was in the 1960s and 1970s. The kinds of pricing behavior that are sanctionable under AD have changed over the years. And, importantly, usually these changes are in response to complaints from U.S. industries who find the current implementation of the law unsatisfactory. One would expect, then, that the country-specific nature of AD protection would be a prime target for change. However, GATT guidelines prevent Congress from amending AD law to apply to imports from all sources.

A more creative solution was needed, and the "cumulation" amendment contained in the Trade and Tariff Act of 1984 is a significant step in the direction of making AD protection more comprehensive. The cumulation provision requires the International Trade Commission (ITC) to cumulate imports when a trade dispute involves imports from multiple sources. Without cumulation, imports are evaluated on a country-by-country basis when determining injury; when cumulation is applied, the ITC aggregates all "like" imports from all countries under investigation and assesses the combined effect on the domestic industry.

When Congress was debating whether to mandate cumulation, the issue of diversion was never mentioned. Rather, the stated reason for the amendment was that the source of the dumped or subsidized imports was irrelevant. What mattered was that the cumulated volume was injurious. This argument in favor of cumulation has been referred to as the "hammering effect" since, according to industries and their representatives, "a domestic industry that suffers material injury by reason of 100,000 tons of unfairly traded imports from a single country is injured to the same degree by 20,000 tons of unfairly traded imports from each of five different countries" (Suder 1983, 470–71). The main goal of mandated cumulation was to reduce the rejection rate at the ITC. Hansen and Prusa (in press) find that this has indeed been the result; they estimate that cumulation increases the probability of an affirmative injury determination by 20-30 percent and has changed the ITC's decision (from negative to affirmative) for about one-third of cumulated cases.

Cumulation may also have important implications for import diversion. For instance, if (i) cumulation increases the number of multiple petition filings and (ii) the greater the number of countries named in the petition, the less significant will be the import diversion, then cumulation will effectively make AD law more comprehensive. The first part of the hypothesis is clearly correct since, during the years following mandated cumulation, there has been a 50 percent increase in multiple petition filings. The second part of the hypothesis is an issue we will want to examine in this paper (i.e., Is diversion less important when more countries are named?).

7.1.2   Related Research

The popularity of AD law has spurred a large body of literature, both theoretical and empirical, but none has focused specifically on the issue of diversion. The theoretical research on AD law has focused on its strategic and incentive effects.[3] Broadly speaking, the empirical literature on AD law can be divided into two groups. One line of research is based on Baldwin's (1985)

---

3. Depending on the precise model specification, AD law can induce a rich variety of strategic effects. For example, in Anderson (1992), the threat of an AD duty induces foreign firms to behave more competitively, while, in Staiger and Wolak (1991), Leidy (1993), and Prusa (1994), AD law can facilitate collusion. Fischer (1992) points out that the nature of the strategic competition influences how AD law affects competition.

seminal work on the determinants of administered protection.[4] Another group of papers empirically estimates the effects of antidumping cases.[5] However, a shortcoming of virtually all the empirical papers is that estimates are based on aggregated data, typically four-digit Standard Industrial Classification (SIC) industry data. For example, Lichtenberg and Tan (1994) estimate the effects of AD cases, but their estimates are for all SIC-level imports (i.e., from all source countries). Given that AD protection is country specific, their aggregated approach will not measure the important trade creation and diversion that are a fundamental characteristic of AD protection.

An important exception is Krupp and Pollard (1992), which examines the effects of AD actions in the chemical industry using monthly Tariff Schedules of the United States Annotated (TSUSA) level import data. Krupp and Pollard's use of disaggregated data allows them to examine the effect of AD actions on the chemical industry. However, since they collect disaggregated data for only a single industry, they cannot address the general issue of diversion.

Staiger and Wolak (1994) also control for the aggregation issue caused by using SIC-level data by normalizing SIC-level imports with the number of TSUSA codes under investigation in each SIC category. Staiger and Wolak estimate trade effects of AD investigation, with particular emphasis on the filing and investigation effects. Even though their estimates are based on SIC data, Staiger and Wolak are still able to find evidence of import diversion and in general find that the restraint on overall imports is about one-third to half as much as on imports from the named country.

7.2 The Trade Effects of AD Actions

7.2.1 The Data

In order to examine the trade effects of AD cases, time-series trade data for each AD case needed to be constructed. To do this, I collected the line-item tariff codes named for each of the 428 AD petitions filed between 1980 and 1988. The product codes and the estimated AD duties are found the *Federal Register* notices accompanying each determination made by the Department of Commerce and the ITC.

Until 1988, products were usually identified by their seven-digit TSUSA code. In a significant number of cases, the products were identified by their five-digit TSUSA code. Because of this difference, and in order to reduce the number of missing values due to the numerous changes in the TSUSA codes, I aggregated all seven-digit codes to their five-digit equivalent. In 1989, the

---

4. Moore (1992), Baldwin and Steagall (1994), and Hansen and Prusa (in press) all focus on the determination of International Trade Commission decisions. A large number of other related papers are cited therein.
5. Work in this area includes Finger, Hall, and Nelson (1982), Harrison (1991), and Hartigan, Kamma, and Perry (1989).

United States adopted the Harmonized Tariff Schedule (HTS). Therefore, in order to extend the time series beyond 1988, the TSUSA codes were concorded with their corresponding HTS codes. Once the TSUSA codes were collected, import trade data for those products under investigation were extracted from the Commerce Department's annual import trade data by source country. Imports were deflated using the GNP price deflator. Time series for the products involved in each case were constructed from 1978 to 1993.

Other work has shown that settled cases can have a significant effect on trade (Prusa 1992; Staiger and Wolak 1994). However, to narrow the analysis, I chose to exclude settled cases in the present analysis and thus compare import diversion in cases that are rejected with diversion in those that result in duties. After dropping cases where only incomplete data series could be constructed, the data set is composed of 109 rejected cases and 126 cases where duties were levied.[6]

The diversity of AD cases complicates matters since trade volume in some cases amounts to only a few million dollars while in others the trade volume is in the hundreds of millions of dollars. To control for these vast differences, I plot all variables as percentage changes relative to their value in the year the petition was filed (year t_0).[7] The year following the petition is denoted t_1, the year after that t_2, etc. Except under unusual circumstances, the case must be decided within one year, so, during year t_1, imports are being investigated.

7.2.2 Filing Behavior: A Look at the Countries Investigated

The set of countries subject to AD investigations between 1980 and 1988 is comprehensive: over fifty countries representing all major U.S. trading partners were subject to investigation. The bulk of cases were against developed countries and the export-oriented growth countries such as South Korea and Taiwan, but countries as small as Trinidad and Tobago, Bangladesh, and Iran were also subject to AD investigations. In table 7.1, the countries most frequently named in AD petitions are listed. As is readily apparent, the countries at the top of the list constitute virtually all important U.S. trading partners.

In addition, I include the percentage of each country's cases resulting in duties. Between 1980 and 1988, about one-third of AD petitions resulted in duties, one-third resulted in settlements, and one-third were rejected. In general, the countries appearing in this table are representative of the general incidence of duties. In the final column, I give information about the number of cases where the listed country was active in an import market that was subject to an AD investigation but where that country was not named. For instance,

---

6. Incomplete data series can arise if a product's TSUSA code changes (with the result that only partial time series could be constructed) or the TSUSA-HTS concordance is unsatisfactory.

7. I also adjusted the trends for macroeconomic trends by measuring relative to changes in overall merchandise trade. The results are qualitatively the same as those presented here and are available on request.

197   The Trade Effects of U.S. Antidumping Actions

Table 7.1   **Countries Most Frequently Named in AD Investigations**

Country	No. of Cases Named	% of Cases Resulting in Duties	No. of Cases Exporting to U.S. but Not Named
Japan	52	33	112
Taiwan	26	46	115
West Germany	25	56	122
Italy	25	40	139
Canada	24	50	142
Brazil	23	30	108
South Korea	23	39	109
France	21	38	136
United Kingdom	17	47	145
Belgium	16	44	131
People's Republic of China	16	31	94
Spain	14	21	115
Venezuela	11	27	61

Japanese industries were named as alleged dumpers in fifty-two cases, of which seventeen (33 percent) resulted in duties. In 112 other AD cases, Japan exported to the U.S. market but was not the country subject to investigation. As I discuss in section 7.3, in these cases, Japanese firms potentially stood to benefit from U.S. AD actions. If AD duties are levied, some other country (a rival) would be subject to duties, thereby giving Japanese firms an opportunity to expand their sales in the U.S. market.

7.2.3   Named Country Imports

The first issue is the effect of AD actions on imports from the named country. In figure 7.1, I present changes in the value of imports. The trends look as one would have expected. On average, when duties are levied, trade from the named country is restricted, especially in comparison to when the case is rejected. In year t_1, import trade from the named country (when duties are levied) was 9 percent less than it was in t_0 and 16 percent less than import trade from named countries in rejected cases. In year t_2, import trade from the named country (when duties are levied) was 25 percent less than trade in rejected cases. While these numbers suggest that AD duties have a substantial effect on trade, at least from the named country, it should be noted that the largest restriction appears to occur in the very short run. By t_2, trade from the named country (when duties are levied) is already rebounding, and by t_3, trade exceeds its prepetition level.

The size of the duty plays a key role in how restrictive an AD case is. In figure 7.1 I also compare those cases that are subject to duties in the top quartile (i.e., duties greater than 36 percent) with those subject to duties in the bottom quartile (i.e., cases with positive duties, but less than 7 percent). For

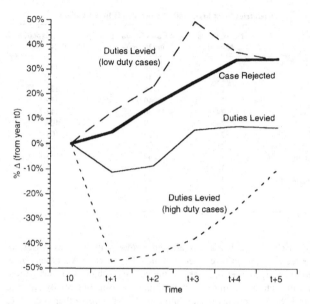

Fig. 7.1   Value of imports (named country)

these two sets of cases, the restrictive effect of AD actions is more marked. For instance, we find that import trade from the named country falls by 47 percent during the first year for countries subject to very high AD duties. By contrast, cases subject to small duties apparently experience no perceptible decline in import trade—and, in fact, imports *grow* by almost 10 percent during the first year following the petition.

While it seems surprising that named imports would grow when duties are levied, this result highlights a unique characteristic of AD protection. If an AD duty is levied and the named country raises its U.S. market price by the full amount of the duty (holding home market prices constant), the assigned duty will never in fact have to be paid. In this case, the AD duty serves to create a price floor for the named country's products. This characteristic likely is part of the explanation for why small duties might be beneficial for the named country. The other key reason is the fact that firms competing noncooperatively typically find that competition forces them to cut their price and that, if they could somehow reduce the incentive to undercut their rivals, they would benefit from higher prices. Since AD duties are essentially government-mandated price floors, and since small duties will raise the named country's AD-distorted price only slightly higher than the original prices, it might easily be the case

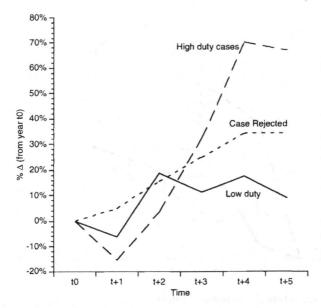

Fig. 7.2   Value of imports (named country), case rejected

that the primary effect of AD duties is the creation of desirable coordination benefits.

It is also instructive to look at imports from named countries in high- and low-duty cases when duties are *not* levied. In figure 7.2, I depict trade patterns for rejected AD cases. What is interesting is that, even when duties are never levied, imports often fall during the investigation. For instance, in cases where high duties are threatened (but ultimately rejected), trade from the named country falls by almost 20 percent during the investigation. This finding is consistent with Staiger and Wolak's (1994) finding that there is a substantial "investigation" effect to an AD petition. It is not surprising that the investigation effect is most apparent for high-duty cases. This effect stems from the fact that, once the Commerce Department makes its preliminary duty calculation, duties are collected (as a bond) pending the final outcome of the investigation. If the case is ultimately rejected, the bond is returned. But, during the investigation, the required bonding creates considerable uncertainty as to the true price of the goods. Once the case is resolved, the uncertainty is resolved, and the investigation effect disappears: imports from named countries (especially those in high-duty cases) rebound sharply.

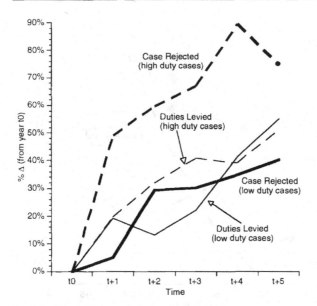

Fig. 7.3   Value of imports (nonnamed countries)

7.2.4   Imports from Nonnamed Countries

Even though successful AD actions restrict imports from the named country, the countries that are not subject to the investigation can offset this restraint by increasing their sales to the United States. This potential diversionary effect of AD actions is, indeed, observed. In figure 7.3, the value of imports from nonnamed countries is depicted. The diversion of trade is large, not only when duties are levied, but also when the case is rejected. In fact, surprisingly, we find that diversion is even more substantial when duties are not levied.

On average, imports from nonnamed countries grow by 22 percent in year t_1. In addition, we find that the diversion is greater for high-duty cases than for low-duty cases. This pattern makes sense given that, in figures 7.1 and 7.2, we saw that the AD actions have a more substantial effect on the named country's imports in high-duty cases than in low-duty cases. For cases where high duties are imposed, nonnamed countries increase their imports 30 percent by year t_2 and 40 percent by year t_3. Diversion is still substantial when low duties are levied, averaging 15-20 percent during each of the first three years following the petition.

In figure 7.4, I again depict imports from nonnamed countries when duties are levied, but here I control for the number of countries named in the petition. As should be expected, diversion is more substantial when only a single coun-

201   The Trade Effects of U.S. Antidumping Actions

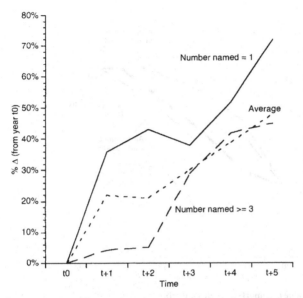

Fig. 7.4   Value of imports (nonnamed countries), duties levied

try is named. In the first year following a petition, nonnamed imports grew by 35 percent when a single country was named, as compared to 4 percent growth when three or more countries are named. This pattern in the amount of diversion persists throughout the years following the case.

7.2.5   Overall Imports

In figure 7.5, the effect on imports (in the investigated product categories) from all source countries is depicted. Two trends emerge. First, the trade effect of AD actions is far less substantial for overall imports than for imports from the named country. For instance, in year t_1, imports from the named country fall by 11 percent when duties are levied. At the same time (year t_1), however, overall imports increase by 15 percent. In year t_2, imports from the named country are still down 9 percent, but overall imports increase by 11 percent. Interestingly, a similar pattern emerges for cases that are rejected. For example, imports from the named country increase by 5 percent in year t_1, but overall imports increase by 19 percent. Clearly, the ability of nonnamed countries to increase imports destined for the United States softens the restrictions imposed by AD duties. Second, diversion does not imply that AD duties have no effect on overall import trade. Overall import growth for cases where duties are levied is about 5–10 percentage points less than for rejected cases during the first

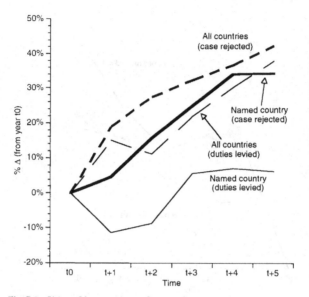

Fig. 7.5   Value of imports (named vs. total)

few years following the AD petition. Taken together, these results indicate that attempts to understand the effect of AD actions will surely fail if one looks only at the effects on import trade from the named country. While AD duties do reduce overall import growth, the effect is more muted than the reduction in imports from the named country.

In figure 7.6, I focus only on cases where duties are levied and again examine imports from all source countries. But the difference here is that I control for the number of countries named in the petition. In figure 7.4, we saw that there is less diversion when three or more countries were named. By contrast, here we see that, overall, imports are not so systematically affected by the number of named countries. During the first two years following the filing, petitions with at least three named countries do appear to have very little import growth, but thereafter overall imports grow more rapidly than in petitions with only a single country. While it is not clear why this is the case, it does reinforce the notion that looking only at the effect of AD on the named country will surely be misleading.

7.2.6   The Effect on Unit Values and Quantities

Underlying the changes in imports are changes in prices (unit values) and quantities. In figure 7.7, the effect of AD actions on unit values (as charged by the named country) is depicted. The results are precisely what one would ex-

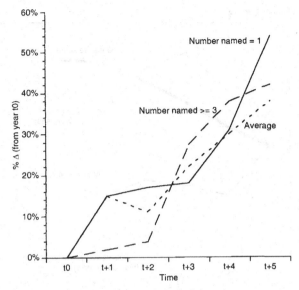

Fig. 7.6   Value of imports (total), duties levied

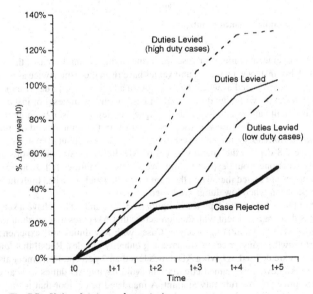

Fig. 7.7   Unit value (named country)

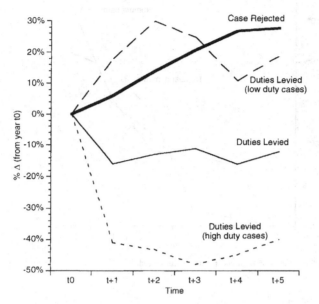

Fig. 7.8   Quantity (named country)

pect. Unit values rise more for cases resulting in duties than for cases that are rejected. For instance, by year t_3, unit values have risen more than twice as much when duties are levied as when they are not. In addition, unit values rise more quickly for cases with high duties than for cases with low duties. For instance, by year t_3, unit values for cases with the highest duties have risen by more than 100 percent since the case was filed; by contrast, in the same period of time, unit values for cases with the lowest duties have risen by about 40 percent.

Figure 7.8 depicts the quantity effect of AD duties. Again, the results are exactly what one would expect to find. We see that quantities fall by more (i) when duties are levied than when the case is rejected and (ii) when high duties are levied than when low duties are levied.

Combining the results depicted in figures 7.3, 7.7, and 7.8, we have a set of patterns that are consistent with the conjecture that AD cases that result in low duties serve as a facilitating practice. Cases with low duties still experience import growth, rising prices, and increasing quantity of sales. Recall that *low-duty cases* are defined as having AD duties less than 7 percent. Remember also that, unlike tariffs, the named country can avoid paying AD duties if it raises its U.S. prices by the full duty amount. A mandated price floor that is only a small amount greater than current prices could easily allow the foreign firm to

205   The Trade Effects of U.S. Antidumping Actions

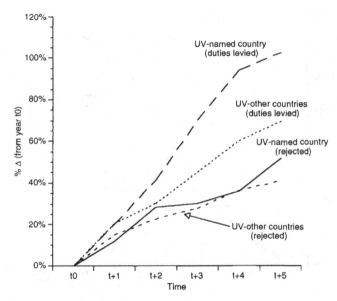

Fig. 7.9   Unit value (named vs. nonnamed)

price more like a Stackelberg leader. It is reasonable to believe that the U.S. industry benefits from higher prices by foreign firms, and, therefore, in this scenario, the AD provides coordination benefits for the rivals.

In a typical model of strategic interaction, other firms in the market respond to price increases by one party. We would expect to observe such strategic interactions in response to AD-induced price changes. In figure 7.9, I depict the unit values for the named country and also for nonnamed countries. (For each case, the nonnamed country's unit value was calculated using a weighted average of the individual countries' imports.)

The results again are clearly consistent with what would be predicted by theory: as the named country's unit values increase, the nonnamed countries' unit values increase, but in general by a somewhat smaller amount (60-70 percent of the named country's change). This trend is found both when cases are rejected and when cases result in duties. This is consistent with the notion that price effects of AD investigation cascade to nonnamed countries. In this respect, AD law is quite effective. The price increases induced by an AD action spur price increases by other foreign rivals.

Finally, in figure 7.10, the effect of duties on unit values is depicted, controlling for the number of countries named in the petition. Certainly, in the short

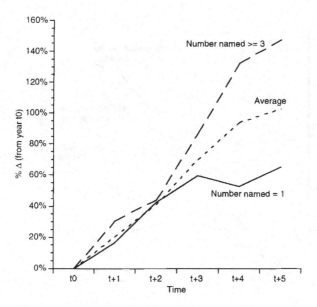

Fig. 7.10   Unit value (named country), duties levied

run, it appears that the number of named countries does not significantly affect the price increases induced by duties. However, in the longer run (greater than three years), it does appear to matter.

7.2.7   Estimation Results

In table 7.2, I present OLS regression results for named imports, nonnamed imports, and overall imports. The basic specification is

$$\ln x_{i,\,t_j} = \alpha + \beta_0 \ln x_{i,t-1} + \beta_1 \ln(x_{i,\,t-1}/x_{i,\,t-2}) + \beta_2 \text{NumNamed}_i$$
$$+ \beta_3 \ln \text{Duty}_i + \beta_4(\text{Dec}_i \ln \text{Duty}_i) + \beta_5 t_j + \beta_6(t_j \text{Dec}_i)$$
$$+ \beta_7 \text{Year}_{t_j}, \quad j = 0, \ldots, 5.$$

The variable x_{i,t_j} denotes imports for case i at time t_j, where t_0 corresponds to the year the petition was filed, t_1 to the period of investigation, and $t_2 \ldots t_5$ are the years following the outcome. The variable Duty_i denotes the size of the duty.[8] Given the discussion above, we might expect the number of countries

---

8. Recall that, even if a case is ultimately rejected, a duty level is estimated by the Commerce Department. Until the final ITC injury determination, duties are collected (as a bond) pending the final outcome of the investigation. If the case is ultimately rejected, the bond is returned.

named (NumNamed$_i$) to have an effect (= 1 when three or more countries are named). The variable Dec$_i$ is a decision dummy (= 1 if duties are levied). Calendar year dummies (Year$_{ij}$) are included in the estimation to control for macroeconomic trends.

A number of the general trends depicted in the figures also emerge from the regressions. Consider first the effect on imports from the named country. The estimated duty effect is negative and significant. The restriction when duties are levied ($-0.158 = -0.055 - 0.103$) is about three times as large as the restriction stemming from the investigation effect alone (-0.055). Results from an alternative specification where a dummy variable is used to capture the duty effect are also reported. In this specification, the restrictions from low and high duties are estimated (relative to moderate duties). Notice that low duties appear to have little effect on import trade, especially if the case does not result in duties. This result is consistent with the notion that the main effect of small AD duties is beneficial coordination. On the other hand, high duties have a large negative effect on imports, especially when duties are levied. Second, note that, in both specifications, the effect of an AD investigation is quite long-lived. The time effects are negative and quite large, although most are insignificantly estimated.

The results for nonnamed imports help characterize the amount of import diversion. Broadly speaking, the results are consistent with the trends depicted in the figures. We find, for instance, that diversion is greater for cases that are rejected (the time-decision cross-effect coefficients are all negative). We also find that, the larger the duties, the more diversion there is, especially for rejected cases. Interestingly, we find that, after controlling for other effects, diversion seems to increase in the number of countries named, a result that bears further study in future work.

The results for overall imports suggest that import diversion mitigates most, if not all, of the effect of AD actions on the value of imports. For instance, note that overall imports increase in cases where no duties are levied. The time-effect dummies are all positive. However, overall imports do fall for cases that result in duties: the estimated decision-duties and decision-time cross-effects are all positive. On net, AD duties do cause overall imports to fall, but the restriction is far less than the restriction to named country imports.

7.3 Net Country Effects of U.S. AD Actions

Interestingly, the import diversion induced by AD actions implies that many foreign countries benefit from aggressive U.S. use of AD law. On average, it seems reasonable to believe that countries that are named will tend to lose from AD actions while those that are not named will in general benefit. Thus, although the countries listed in table 7.1 were all frequently subject to AD investigations, they were also active in many product categories where some other country was subject to AD investigation. Paradoxically, the main bene-

Table 7.2   OLS Estimates

Variable	Named Imports		Nonnamed Imports		Overall Imports	
Constant	1.797	1.448	.521	.605	1.046	1.111
	(.315)***	(.312)***	(.179)**	(.174)***	(.202)***	(.198)***
Ln(value in $t - 1$)	.899	.908	.942	.945	.921	.922
	(.018)***	(.017)***	(.009)***	(.009)***	(.011)***	(.010)***
%Δ value between $t - 1$ and $t - 2$	.155	.166	.264	.267	.107	.110
	(.037)***	(.036)***	(.027)***	(.026)***	(.016)***	(.016)***
Number named ≥ 3 (dummy)	.139	0.01	.120	.132	.097	.103
	(.082)*	(.079)	(.046)**	(.044)**	(.045)**	(.044)**
Size of duty						
Ln(Duty)	−.055		.076		.051	
	(.031)*		(.016)***		(.016)***	
Low duty (dummy)		−.004		−.120		−.146
		(.121)		(.066)*		(.065)**
High duty (dummy)		−.133		.229		.068
		(.129)		(.070)**		(.068)
Cross-effect: Duty × decision						
Ln(Duty), affirmative	−.103		−0.019		−.036	
	(.040)**		(.022)		(.021)*	
Low duty, affirmative (dummy)		.181		.116		.115
		(.157)		(.086)		(.083)
High duty, affirmative (dummy)		−.227		−.098		−.105
		(.162)		(.089)		(.086)

Years following AD petition (dummies)						
t + 1	-.433	-.274	.074	.094	.022	.067
	(.161)**	(.153)*	(.088)	(.083)	(.086)	(.081)
t + 2	-.366	-.212	.166	.191	.111	.159
	(.161)**	(.153)	(.089)*	(.083)**	(.087)	(.081)*
t + 3	-.266	-.104	.207	.232	.099	.150
	(.162)	(.153)	(.090)**	(.084)**	(.087)	(.082)*
t + 4	-.224	-.064	.267	.286	.181	.227
	(.162)	(.153)	(.091)**	(.085)***	(.087)**	(.082)***
t + 5	-.261	-.099	.246	.267	.187	.232
	(.165)	(.156)	(.092)**	(.086)**	(.088)**	(.083)***
Cross-effect: Years × decision						
t + 1 × affirmative	.239	-.051	-.065	-.077	.010	-.050
	(.198)	(.180)	(.109)	(.099)	(.105)	(.095)
t + 2 × affirmative	.002	-.277	-.182	.211	-.142	-.211
	(.198)	(.181)	(.109)*	(.099)**	(.106)	(.096)**
t + 3 × affirmative	-.023	-.316	-.115	-.153	-.032	-.110
	(.199)	(.181)*	(.112)	(.102)	(.108)	(.097)
t + 4 × affirmative	-.096	-.388	-.093	-.126	-.040	-.113
	(.201)	(.183)**	(.113)	(.104)	(.108)	(.099)
t + 5 × affirmative	-.033	-.327	-.017	-.051	-.005	-.077
	(.203)	(.187)*	(.114)	(.105)	(.109)	(.100)
Adjusted R^2	0.758	0.753	0.927	0.931	0.912	0.918
Number of observations	1,164	1,214	1,157	1,207	1,195	1,245

Note: Standard errors are given in parentheses. Calendar year dummies are estimated but not reported. ***, **, and * indicate significance at 1, 5, and 10 percent, respectively.

factors of AD duties may not be the U.S. complainant but rather the other countries competing in the U.S. market. If import diversion were complete and the price effects small, the U.S. industry that spent hundreds of thousands of dollars (if not millions) assembling the forms, mobilizing disparate firms to provide information, lobbying congressmen, and incurring all the other sundry expenses associated with filing a petition might receive little or no gain.

Using the estimates reported in table 7.2, we can measure the effect of AD duties. In particular, when a country is named, we can estimate the value of imports with the duty and also what imports would have been if duties had never been levied. The difference is the effect of AD duties for the named country in that case. If we sum the trade effects over all cases where a country was named, a measure of the AD duties-induced trade contraction can be constructed.

Similarly, using the estimates on nonnamed imports, we can estimate the value of nonnamed imports with the duty and also what nonnamed imports would have been had duties never been levied. The difference is the effect of AD duties for the nonnamed country. Summing over all nonnamed countries would yield the total diversion for that case. If we sum the trade diversion over all cases where a country was not named (but was actively exporting to the United States), a measure of the AD duties-induced trade expansion can be constructed.

In table 7.3, I report the results from performing such calculations using the changes in imports between t_0 and t_1 as the measure of the trade effect. Clearly, this measure does not capture all trade effects of AD actions since it does not control for what trade patterns would have been without any AD activity, but it nonetheless highlights the idea that the distortions caused by AD law can be either a blessing or a curse.[9]

In the upper part of the table, I list the countries that have suffered the greatest trade contraction when named in U.S. AD actions (and subject to duties). Japan, the most frequently named country, easily tops the list as the country whose trade has fallen the most as a result of U.S. AD duties (total estimated losses of $7.6 billion). Note, however, that I estimate that Japan's exports to the United States increase by more than $5 billion, yielding a net trade contraction of about $2 billion. The other countries on the list all suffer sizable import losses (when named), but far less than Japan. It is interesting to note that all the remaining countries, except Iran, are estimated to have a net gain in trade with the United States despite their losses in cases where duties were levied. Of particular interest is the fact that Canada is estimated to be a net gainer from AD duties. Given the highly visible nature of many Canadian-U.S. AD disputes, this is somewhat surprising. However, it does serve as a reminder that politics rather than economics is often more important in explaining the tensions created by a trade suit.

---

9. In addition, the calculation does not include any trade distortions from those cases that were settled.

211 The Trade Effects of U.S. Antidumping Actions

Table 7.3 Effect of U.S. Antidumping Activity

	When Named		When Not Named		Net Effect:
	$\% \Delta$, t_0 and t_1	Δ Imports, t_0 and t_1 ($millions)	$\% \Delta$, t_0 and t_1	Δ Imports, t_0 and t_1 ($millions)	Δ Imports, t_0 and t_1 ($millions)
Countries with the largest trade contraction (when named):					
Japan	−20.37	−7,654	13.46	5,356	−2,298
Brazil	−13.43	−201	17.99	17,962	17,762
Italy	−13.48	−184	18.31	19,514	19,331
South Korea	−8.01	−117	17.62	19,442	19,326
France	−8.07	−109	17.94	20,959	20,850
United Kingdom	−11.56	−69	18.31	21,539	21,470
Taiwan	−5.41	−65	17.29	20,469	20,404
Canada	−6.31	−47	18.98	21,230	21,183
Soviet Union	−25.42	−44	5.42	5,767	5,723
Iran	−62.52	−23	.11	19	−5
People's Republic of China	−14.33	−23	9.46	11,062	11,039
Countries with the largest trade expansion (when not named):					
Belgium	−6.14	−1	18.12	23,110	23,109
Netherlands	−13.99	−4	18.05	23,088	23,084
Austria	...	...	18.25	22,798	22,798
Switzerland	...	...	17.88	22,783	22,783
Australia	−26.00	−2	17.92	22,558	22,556
Spain	−8.56	−14	17.98	22,370	22,356
Denmark	...	...	17.84	22,220	22,220
Mexico	2.74	4	17.91	21,745	21,749
United Kingdom	−11.56	−69	18.31	21,539	21,470
Hong Kong	3.33	3	17.87	21,533	21,536

In the bottom part of the table, I list the ten countries that experience the greatest trade expansion as a result of U.S. AD actions. All the countries on this list are estimated to experience a net gain of over $20 billion as a result of duties being levied on other countries.

7.4 Concluding Comments

Overall, the evidence presented in this paper suggests that the protection offered by AD law is significantly offset by the ability of alternative foreign suppliers to increase their shipments destined for the United States. Even though imports from named countries are restricted, especially for those cases with high duties, most of the protective effect of AD duties is offset by the increased trading activity of nonnamed countries.

The results also suggest that the country-specific nature of AD protection is an important factor both in explaining the surge in AD actions during the 1980s and in evaluating the protective effect of AD actions. In conjunction with previous work on the effect of the cumulation amendment (Hansen and Prusa in press), the results in the paper are consistent with the view that the surge in

AD filings during the 1980s is a strategic attempt to compensate for the limited nature of AD protection and is not evidence of an increase in injurious pricing by foreign competitors.

The fact that almost three hundred AD cases have been filed during the first half of the 1990s leaves little doubt that U.S. firms will continue to use AD law frequently to reduce import competition. The results in this paper suggest that, unless the popularity of multiple petition filings increases the overall share of imports investigated, the other foreign suppliers will mitigate the losses caused by AD protection.

References

Anderson, James E. 1992. Domino dumping, I: Competitive exporters. *American Economic Review* 82 (March): 65–83.

Baldwin, Robert E. 1985. *The political economy of U.S. import policy.* Cambridge, Mass.: MIT Press.

Baldwin, Robert E., and Jeffrey W. Steagall. 1994. An analysis of ITC decisions in antidumping, countervailing duty and safeguard cases. *Weltwirtschaftliches Archiv* 130, no. 2:290–308.

Bhagwati, Jagdish. 1988. *Protectionism.* Cambridge, Mass.: MIT Press.

Dinopoulos, E., and M. Kreinin. 1988. Effects of the U.S.-Japan VER on European prices and on U.S. welfare. *Review of Economics and Statistics* 70, no. 3 (August):484–91.

Feenstra, R. 1984. Voluntary export restraint in U.S. autos, 1980–81: Quality, employment, and welfare effects. In *The structure and evolution of recent U.S. trade policy,* ed. R. E. Baldwin. Chicago: University of Chicago Press.

———. 1987. Gains from trade in differentiated products: Japanese compact trucks. In *Empirical methods for international trade,* ed. R. Feenstra. Cambridge, Mass.: MIT Press.

Finger, J. Michael, H. K. Hall, and D. R. Nelson. 1982. The political economy of administered protection. *American Economic Review* 78, no. 3 (June): 452–66.

Fischer, Ronald D. 1992. Endogenous probability of protection and firm behavior. *Journal of International Economics* 32:149–63.

Hansen, Wendy L., and Thomas J. Prusa. 1995. The road most taken: The rise of Title VII protection. *World Economy* 18, no. 2 (March): 295–313.

———. In press. Cumulation and ITC decision-making: The sum of the parts is greater than the whole. *Economic Inquiry.*

Harrison, Ann. 1991. The new trade protection: Price effects of antidumping and countervailing duty measures in the United States. Working paper. Washington, D.C.: World Bank.

Hartigan, James C., Sreenivas Kamma, and Phillip R. Perry. 1989. The injury determination category and the value of relief from dumping. *Review of Economics and Statistics* 71 (February): 183–86.

Krupp, Corinne M., and Patricia S. Pollard. 1992. Market responses to antidumping laws: Some evidence from the U.S. chemical industry. Michigan State University. Typescript.

Leidy, Michael P. 1993. Quid pro quo restraint and spurious injury: Subsidies and the

213   The Trade Effects of U.S. Antidumping Actions

prospect of CVDs. In *Analytical and negotiating issues in the global trading system,* ed. Alan Deardorff and Robert Stern. Ann Arbor: University of Michigan Press.

Lichtenberg, Frank, and Hong Tan. 1994. An industry level analysis of import relief petitions filed by U.S. manufacturers, 1958–85. In *Troubled industries in the United States and Japan.* New York: St. Martin's.

Moore, Michael. 1992. Rules or politics? An empirical analysis of ITC antidumping decisions. *Economic Inquiry* 30, no. 3 (July): 449–66.

Nivola, Pietro S. 1993. *Regulating unfair trade.* Washington, D.C.: Brookings.

Prusa, Thomas J. 1992. Why are so many antidumping petitions withdrawn? *Journal of International Economics* 33: 1–20.

———. 1994. Pricing behavior in the presence of antidumping law. *Journal of Economic Integration* 9, no. 2:260–89.

Staiger, Robert W., and Frank A. Wolak. 1991. Strategic use of antidumping law to enforce tacit international collusion. Stanford University. Typescript.

———. 1994. Measuring industry-specific protection: Antidumping in the United States. *Brookings Papers on Economic Activity: Microeconomics,* 51–118.

Suder, Jonathan T. 1983. Cumulation of imports in antidumping and countervailing duty investigations. *George Washington Journal of International Law and Economics* 17:463–87.

Taussig, Frank. 1931. *A tariff history of the United States.* 8th ed. New York: A. M. Kelley.

Chapter 3

On the spread and impact of anti-dumping[*]

Thomas J. Prusa   *Department of Economics, Rutgers University*

Abstract. In this paper two key costs of AD protection are documented. First, once AD has been adopted, countries often have a difficult time restraining its use. In recent years 'new' users have accounted for half of the overall world total. Many of the heaviest AD users are countries who did not even have an AD statute a decade ago. Second, I will show that that, on average, AD duties cause the value of imports to fall by 30–50 per cent. I find that trade falls by almost as much for settled cases as for those that result in duties. I also find that, even for those cases that are rejected, imports fall. JEL Classification: F13

A propos de la généralisation et de l'impact des mesures anti-dumping. Ce mémoire souligne deux coûts importants des mesures de protection anti-dumping (AD). D'abord, une fois la mesure en place, les pays ont souvent de grandes difficultés à en restreindre l'usage. Au cours des années récentes, les "nouveaux" utilisateurs de ces mesures comptent pour la moitié de l'activité AD dans le monde. Et plusieurs des pays qui en font un usage intensif n'avaient pas de loi AD il y a une décennie. Ensuite, en moyenne, les droits de douane AD entraînent une chute des importations de l'ordre de 30% à 50%. Et le commerce chute de presque autant pour les cas où il y a résolution du problème que pour ceux où un tarif de rétorsion est imposé. Fait intéressant, il appert que les importations chutent même dans les cas où la plainte est rejetée.

1. Introduction

Of all the issues negotiated under the Uruguay Round, anti-dumping was perhaps the most contentious. Broadly stated, the debate pitted anti-dumping's traditional

Also affiliated with NBER. I would like to thank Jim Anderson, Bob Baldwin, Dick Baldwin, Wolfgang Keller, Arik Levinson, Antonio Spilimbergo, and Ian Wooton for their helpful comments. I would also like to thank Bob and Dick Baldwin for organizing the NBER-sponsored US-EU conference for which the first draft of this paper was prepared. Email: Prusa@econ.rutgers.edu

*This article originally appeared in *The Canadian Journal of Economics/Revue canadienne d'Economique*, **34**(3), pp. 591–611.

592   T.J. Prusa

users, essentially industrialized countries such as the United States and the European Community against traditional non-users, primarily developing countries. Thanks to demands by the United States and the European Community, the Uruguay Round achieved only mixed success at tightening the rules governing antidumping (AD) actions. The strengthening of de minimis rules and the addition of sunset reviews should make AD protection less burdensome for small producers. Unfortunately, the agreement also endorsed the cumulation provision, codified the concept of the AD duty as a cost, and did little to restrain the use of price undertakings. All things considered, there is every reason to believe not only that AD disputes will continue to flourish but also that AD policy will be a key item for the next World Trade Organization (WTO) round.

To many observers, the U.S. and EC embrace of AD is frustrating and perplexing. On the one hand, the United States and the European Community preach that reducing government interference and accepting free markets will maximize growth and welfare. On the other hand, it often seems that just when developing countries begin to efficiently operate and become competitive in particular markets, industrialized countries shut down those precise markets with a trade policy that is universally decried by economists. 'Do as I say, not as I do' seems an apt description of the U.S. and EC view of the efficiency of government involvement in markets – at least with respect to AD.

A growing number of countries however, have not followed that advice. In recent years 'new' AD users (primarily developing countries) have initiated AD complaints at unprecedented rates. Only a decade ago developing countries filed only one or two complaints per year. By contrast, in recent years developing countries account for well over 100 petitions per year, close to half of the overall world total. It appears, then, that developing countries have also been seduced by AD's unique combination of GATT/WTO consistency and ease of use. Now they, too, can levy sector specific tariffs without blatantly violating their tariff bindings.

This surge of AD activity has not gone unnoticed. According to the U.S. Trade Representative, trade negotiations must preserve 'antidumping laws as effective remedies against unfair trade practices' while at the same time 'prevent misuse of other countries' antidumping laws against U.S. exporters.'[1] In other words, traditional AD users are worried that the 'new' users are employing AD to restrict competition and close markets that earlier GATT rounds had opened. The desire to rein in other countries' use of AD may cause industrialized countries to change their tune with respect to AD. Apparently, the United States and the European Community may finally seek to reform AD because other countries have also realized how large a loophole it is, how easy it is to use, and perhaps most important, how easy it is to misuse.

AD has become the trade policy of choice for both developed and developing economies. Unfortunately, it is not clear exactly why so many new countries are

---

1 Letter from U.S. Trade Representative Michael Kantor to Senator Ernest Hollings, 29 June 1993, reprinted inside 'Inside U.S. Trade,' 2 July 1993, page 15.

embracing AD law. Perhaps they believe that if it is good for the United States and the European Community, then it must be good for them too. Perhaps they believe that their use of AD is the only way to defend themselves against other countries' using it against them. Or perhaps AD is simply a policy instrument that their mercantilist instincts can't resist.

Whatever the motivation, it is unlikely that many new AD users are aware of the costs of embracing such a policy. My goal in this paper is to begin the process of educating AD users as to the costs of its use. I will present evidence that shows that countries should be very careful in embracing AD protection. While current proliferation of AD actions might lead to long-run restrictions on anti-dumping, I argue that one should not overlook the short-run costs associated with AD protection.

I will emphasize two main costs of AD protection. First, there is substantial evidence that once AD has been adopted, countries often have a difficult time restraining its use. Many of the reasons why AD is so attractive to policymakers – it is an extremely flexible and timely instrument – are also reasons why it is prone to being misused. AD can be applied in so many circumstances because its rules and procedures can be broadly interpreted. A country may find it advantageous to interpret the GATT/WTO standards in such a way that a particular sector can be protected. Yet this almost always leads other sectors also to seek protection under this newly established precedent. Thus, it is difficult for governments to rein in its use. Industries like AD, since it allows them to seek protection – often with only the skimpiest evidence of injury and little evidence of economically unjustified pricing practices. As a result, countries adopting an AD statute often find it a bit like letting the genie out of the bottle: it is difficult to give one industry protection without encouraging other sectors also to seek protection. So, while it might be conceivable that AD protection raises welfare in certain circumstances, its widespread use suggests that it is often being employed inappropriately.

Second, unlike typical MFN tariffs AD duties are almost always remarkably large. On average, AD duties are 10 to 20 times higher than the MFN level, and it not unheard of to have AD duties more than 100 times higher than the MFN level. Clearly, protection at these levels has dramatic impact on trade. I will provide evidence that that, on average, AD duties cause the value of imports to fall by 30–50 per cent. I will also show that AD actions distort trade patterns even if duties are never levied. Almost one-quarter of all AD cases are settled, often via some form of VER or marketing arrangement. I find that trade falls by almost as much for these cases as those that result in duties. As a matter of interest, I also find that even for those cases that are rejected imports fall, evidence that the mere investigation distorts trade. All things considered, policymakers would be well advised to consider the large distortions created by AD actions before they rush to embrace it.

The remainder of this paper is organized as follows. I will begin by reviewing recent trends in AD activity (section 2). I will document the the rise of AD activity over the past decade and show that the continued growth in AD activity is largely being fuelled by countries that have only recently adopted the statute. It is this spread in AD activity that keeps AD reform a top item on the WTO agenda. In the

594   T.J. Prusa

second part of the paper I estimate the trade impact of AD law (section 3). Here, I will rely on data from the world's heaviest anti-dumping user – the United States – since it is the only country where comprehensive data are available to conduct such a study. Given that most AD adopters have used the U.S. statute as a guide for implementing their own AD statute, the lessons learned from the U.S. experience are likely to carry over to others. Using extremely disaggregated trade data, I find that AD actions have a very large effect on imports. When an AD dispute results in duties or is settled, I estimate that, on average, import quantities fall by almost 70 per cent and import prices rise by more than 30 per cent. It is interesting that even when an AD dispute is ultimately rejected, the scrutiny has a significant impact on trade. The data reveal that AD investigations – regardless of their outcome – harass importers. I find that even when the case is rejected, imports fall by about 20 per cent.

2. The spread of anti-dumping

Until relatively recently AD actions were not not particularly common. For instance, in the 1960s all GATT members filed only about ten anti-dumping petitions per year (Schott 1994). During the 1970s, however, a small set of users began more actively to initiate AD actions, primarily as a way to protect declining industries. Even as recently as the late 1980s AD law was essentially enforced by only five territories: Canada, New Zealand, Australia, the United States, and the European Community. Over the decade of the 1980s, more than 1,600 AD cases were filed worldwide (Finger 1993). As a group, the 'traditional' users accounted for more than 95 per cent of all AD cases during the 1980s.[2]

Demand for AD protection has continued to grow during the 1990s. Over the past ten years, almost 2,200 AD cases have been filed worldwide, a filing rate about 25 per cent greater than during the 1980s (see table 1). While the overall usage has increased, the most noticeable trend is the change in who is using the law. The once exclusive club has now opened its doors. Countries at all stages of development and industrialization have joined the ranks of active AD users, and it is the dozens of new users that have fuelled AD's continued growth.

Over the 1987–97 period twenty-nine countries initiated anti-dumping complaints, about triple the number that had acted during the prior ten years. Over the past ten years there has been a fivefold increase in AD filings by 'new' users.[3] More impressively, as compared with the early 1980s, there has been a fifty-fold increase.

Not only are new users filing more cases than they had previously, but they are also accounting for an increasing share of total complaints. Between 1987 and 1992 new users filed about 20 per cent of the AD cases in each year. By contrast, over the last five years new users account for well over half of AD complaints. The trend is

---

2 This same group similarly dominated AD activity during the 1960s and 1970s.
3 By the term 'new' users I refer to all countries other than the five traditional users of AD.

TABLE 1
AD actions, reporting countries

Reporting country	1987	1988	1989	1990	1991	1992	1993	1994	1995	1996	1997	Total
Traditional users												
United States	15	40	24	34	63	83	32	48	14	22	16	391
Australia	22	16	21	47	68	71	59	15	5	17	42	383
European Community	28	27	18	48	29	42	21	43	33	25	41	355
Canada	31	15	13	15	11	46	25	2	11	5	14	188
New Zealand	0	9	1	1	9	14	0	6	10	4	5	59
TOTAL	96	107	77	145	180	256	137	114	73	73	118	1,376
New users												
Mexico	18	11	7	11	9	26	70	22	4	4	6	188
Argentina	0	0	0	0	1	14	27	17	27	22	15	123
Brazil	0	1	1	2	7	9	34	9	5	18	11	97
South Africa	0	0	0	0	0	0	0	16	16	33	23	88
Others	6	5	11	7	31	21	31	50	31	71	60	324
TOTAL	24	17	19	20	48	70	162	114	83	148	115	820
Overall total	120	124	96	165	228	326	299	228	156	221	233	2,196
Traditional Users	80.0%	86.3%	80.2%	87.9%	78.9%	78.5%	45.8%	50.0%	46.8%	33.0%	50.6%	62.7%
OECD Countries	95.8%	95.2%	96.9%	98.8%	84.6%	89.6%	72.2%	61.8%	51.9%	40.7%	59.7%	74.7%

SOURCE: Author's compilation based on data reported by Miranda, Torres, and Ruiz (1998).

596   T.J. Prusa

even more striking in comparison with trends during the 1980s, when new users accounted for fewer than 5 per cent of AD cases.

It is also striking how quickly AD is embraced once legislation is enacted. Mexico, for instance, signed the GATT/WTO anti-dumping code in 1987 and filed more than thirty cases within three years. Argentina filed its first AD case in 1991 and has since averaged almost twenty cases *per year*. Likewise, South Africa has initiated more than twenty cases per year since it adopted an AD statute. Similar patterns of use – a rush to invoke the new law – are evidenced by India, Indonesia, Turkey, Malaysia, Peru, Israel, Colombia, Costa Rica, and Venezuela. The evidence is overwhelming that AD is not a statute that grows dusty from disuse.

The widespread adoption of AD law has also impacted which countries are targeted. In table 2 I detail AD actions by targeted country. Several interesting trends are evidenced. First, note that over the entire period almost ninety-nine countries were investigated – about twice as many as were investigated during the 1980s. Apparently, AD's expanding reach can be measured equally well by either the number of active users or the number of investigated countries.

Second, note that during the 1980s almost all dumping charges were made by a small number of countries and most targeted a very small set of countries. In particular, during the 1980s two-thirds of AD investigations targeted another traditional user (Finger 1993). By comparison, over the past decade only about one-third of the cases targeted a traditional AD user. In this sense, AD's reach has expanded.

In another sense, however, the targets of AD investigations are much the same as they were during the 1980s. Note that during the 1980s two-thirds of AD investigations involved countries that were fellow AD users. It is interesting that during the 1990s virtually the same percentage of AD cases (1,498 of 2,196) were filed against fellow AD users. In other words, AD is still a policy largely wielded within the club of AD users; the big difference is that now the club is bigger than it was before.

These trends are consistent with Finger's (1993) conjecture that many countries adopt AD, at least in part, to counter the sanctioning of their imports. That is, countries adopt AD not only to protect against unfair imports, but also to defend their exporters against abuse of the law abroad. From this view, AD is a part of a tit-for-tat strategy. In this case, many AD actions are motivated not by a desire to make markets more competitive but rather by a wish to deter other countries from using the law. In other words, by raising the cost of exporting, a government hopes to raise the costs of others using the law.

On the other hand, the trends are also consistent with the view that AD users are primarily the same countries that are subject to AD actions. Perhaps the notion that adopting AD law will deter others from using is incorrect. Rather, it appears that AD activity is better understood as an example of prisoner's dilemma. Each country cannot resist the temptation to protect important import-competing industries. Yet if all countries also use AD law, each country is worse off than they would be under free trade. Under this interpretation, all users would benefit if everyone agreed to stop using the law.

TABLE 2
AD actions, targeted countries

Targeted country	1987	1988	1989	1990	1991	1992	1993	1994	1995	1996	1997	Total
Traditional users												
United States	18	10	8	18	16	26	30	14	12	21	15	188
Australia	0	2	0	0	0	2	3	0	1	0	1	9
European Community	27	23	13	24	68	70	53	31	30	37	57	433
Canada	3	5	1	1	5	8	5	1	2	1	3	35
New Zealand	2	0	0	0	1	1	1	0	1	0	0	6
TOTAL	50	40	22	43	90	107	92	46	46	59	76	671
Other leading targets												
China-PR	1	5	4	12	16	31	45	39	20	43	31	247
Korea	8	12	6	11	12	25	17	8	14	10	16	139
Japan	19	18	10	13	18	14	11	7	5	6	12	133
Brazil	5	6	7	7	7	18	23	9	8	10	5	105
China-Taiwan	6	8	6	11	10	15	11	5	4	8	16	100
Others	31	35	41	68	75	116	100	114	59	85	77	801
TOTAL	70	84	74	122	138	219	207	182	110	162	157	1525
Overall total	120	124	96	165	228	326	299	228	156	221	233	2196
Against traditional users	41.7%	32.3%	22.9%	26.1%	39.5%	32.8%	30.8%	20.2%	29.5%	26.7%	32.6%	30.6%
Against OECD Countries	67.5%	56.5%	42.7%	42.4%	53.9%	47.5%	40.5%	28.1%	43.6%	35.7%	45.5%	44.5%

SOURCE: Author's compilation based on data reported by Miranda, Torres, and Ruiz (1998).

3. Impact of anti-dumping

The filing trends presented indicate that the AD genie is out of the bottle. A multitude of countries have only recently enacted AD statutes, and these new users are now filing a larger and larger number of cases. What do these filings mean for the markets affected? Under the best case scenario I could estimate the impact of AD for each country and sector that has used the law. Unfortunately, the data are not available to perform such an exercise. Instead, I will estimate the effect of AD actions using data from the largest AD user, the United States.

For several reasons the United States is an excellent candidate for understanding the effects of AD protection. First of all, it has filed more AD cases than any other user. Therefore, we have a large sample of cases. U.S. industries filed over 700 AD petitions between 1980 and 1994. About a quarter of the cases were settled; of the remaining cases, about half were rejected and half resulted in duties. Second, as the world's most prominent AD user, the U.S. statute has served as the basis for many countries newly adopting AD law. The GATT AD rules are quite broad and countries have significant latitude in implementing their AD statute, but most have chosen to follow U.S. procedures. Thus, even though the estimates are based on U.S. data, they should reasonably approximate what we can expect for countries with similar AD statutes. Third, the quality of U.S. trade data is excellent. Machine-readable import statistics are available for the entire period and the data are reported at the line-item level.

Several important characteristics of AD protection should be highlighted before we proceed with our estimates. First, AD investigations involve two questions: (1) was there 'unfair' pricing (i.e., price discrimination or below-cost sales) and (2) did the dumped imports cause injury. The former question is almost always answered in the affirmative. Since 1980 fewer than 5 per cent of AD cases were rejected because the domestic industry could not show unfair pricing.[4]

In fact, the estimated margins (a metric of the extent of unfair pricing) averaged about 40 per cent. The median duty levied was 16 per cent. To put these margins in perspective, note that the industries seeking AD protection had MFN tariff levels averaging about 4 per cent. Many cases were subject to seemingly prohibitive levels of protection; for example, 20 per cent of the cases had duties exceeding 50 per cent; 10 per cent of the cases had duties exceeding 100 per cent. Given the size of the dumping margins, one would expect that the typical AD user receives substantial protection.

The second question – existence of injury – is where dumping cases tend to be rejected. At this stage the U.S. International Trade Commission (ITC) must decide if the dumping imports have caused, or threaten to cause, material injury to the

---

4 The rules governing how the Department of Commerce calculates dumping margins are widely considered biased in favour of finding positive margins. See Boltuck and Litan (1991) and Lindsey (1999) for discussions.

domestic industry. Over the sample period, about half of the ITC's final injury determinations were negative (Hansen and Prusa 1996, 1997).

Perhaps the most overlooked feature of AD is that its protection is country specific. AD duties are levied only on imports from countries named in the petition. It would be unusual for a petition to name all import suppliers. Rather, a case usually names only a subset of import competitors. In our empirical analysis, therefore, it will be important to distinguish between countries named in the petition and those not named. For example, if the steel industry alleges that 1/4-inch ball bearings are being dumped from Canada and Brazil, only ball bearings from those two named countries are subject to duties. If Canadian suppliers have 10 per cent of the import market and Brazilian suppliers 15 per cent, the petition would cover 25 per cent of the rival imports. The other countries supplying 1/4-inch ball bearings would not be investigated or subject to duties. Once Canada and Brazil are sanctioned, demand for domestically produced ball bearings should increase. Demand should also increase for similar ball bearings produced by other foreign countries. For instance, Argentina should be able to sell more to the U.S. market and/or raise its price on ball bearings exports destined for the U.S. market. On average, a typical case names about 40 per cent of the total import market.

Therefore, AD actions have the potential to provide substantial protection and also to induce trade diversion. In order to quantify the effect of the petition on trade from named and non-named, I estimate a model of the form

$$y_{it} = \delta y_{i,t-1} + x'_{it}\beta + u_{it}, \quad t = -3, -2, -1, 0, 1, 2, 3, \tag{1}$$

where y_{it} is a variable measuring imports, δ is a scalar, x'_{it} is a $1 \times K$ vector and β is a $K \times 1$ vector. Since AD actions can affect both the price and the quantity of imports, I allow y_{it} to measure either price, quantity, or value of imports, depending upon the specification.

I assume that the u_{it} follow a one-way error component model

$$u_{it} = \mu_i + \nu_{it}, \tag{2}$$

where $\mu_i \sim IID(0, \sigma_\mu^2)$ and $\nu_{it} \sim IID(0, \sigma_\nu^2)$ independent of each other. μ_i denotes the individual-specific residual, differing across cases but constant for a given case. For instance, a country with comparative advantage in ball bearings is likely to have large imports year after year and hence have a large μ_i. Time is normalized so that $t = 0$ denotes the year the petition was filed; hence, $t = -1$ refers to the year *prior* to the filing, $t = +1$ refers to the year following the filing, $t = +2$ refers to the second year following the filing, and so on. Thus, the cross-section is identified by the cases, and the time series variation is driven by annual observations on import trade before and after the AD petition.

The fixed-effects (FE) estimator is a standard way of estimating (1), since it eliminates μ_i. However, in our application the FE estimator will be biased and potentially inconsistent, since $y_{i,t-1}$ will be correlated with the FE-transformed residual. The extent of the inconsistency varies from application to application, but

600   T.J. Prusa

in general the problem will be less serious the longer is the time series (Kiviet 1995). Given the relatively short length of the time series (seven years) it is necessary to account for this potential problem.

To resolve the problem we take first differences of (1), yielding

$$y_{it} - y_{i,t-1} = \delta(y_{i,t-1} - y_{i,t-2}) + (x'_{it} - x'_{i,t-1})\beta + (\nu_{it} - \nu_{i,t-1}),$$

thereby eliminating μ_i. We can rewrite this equation as

$$\Delta y_{it} = \delta\Delta y_{i,t-1} + \Delta x'_{it}\beta + \epsilon_{it}. \tag{3}$$

By construction, $y_{i,t-1}$ will be correlated with the transformed residual $\nu_{it} - \nu_{i,t-1}$, so we need to estimate the transformed equation with instrumental variables (IV). There are a multitude of moment conditions that can be exploited to derive instruments. For all time periods both $y_{i,t-2}$ and lagged values of x'_{it} are valid instruments. For time periods $t = 0, 1, 2, 3$ we can use additional lags of $y_{i,t}$; for instance, for period $t = 0$, $y_{i,t-3}$ can be used as an additional instrument. Additional lags can be added for each forward period.[5]

In the tables presented below, I report estimates for both the FE estimates of (1) and IV estimates of (3). The FE estimates are a useful benchmark and the results for the two estimations procedures do not greatly differ, suggesting the fixed-effect bias is small in this application.

Public sources were used to collect the data. The International Trade Commission's *Annual Report* provides basic case information such as year of filing, outcome, and so forth. Each AD petition also contains information about the industry filing the petition, the country being investigated, the products allegedly dumped, and so on. The products are identified by the line-item tariff codes upon which the duty will be levied. Using these codes, I gathered product level data using import data from Feenstra (1996). Since most cases identify more than one line-item, I sum across all named tariff lines to construct trade for the named products (by country) for each year. Thus, for each case I construct import data for each country (only a subset of which are named).

Let me stress that the duty I use is the final duty for the case.[6] This duty is the best direct measure I have available to quantify the impact of the sanctions. But it should be stressed that the final duty imperfectly measures the actual protective impact. AD duties are reviewed on an annual basis and are often revised. The reason for this is that the AD duty is theoretically designed to establish a 'normal' price for the imported good. The foreign firm can raise its export price in an attempt to have the Commerce Department adjust the assigned AD duty downward (i.e., by raising

---

5 See Hsiao (1986) and Baltagi (1995) for a more complete discussion of the estimation of dynamic panel models and the construction of valid instruments.
6 Individual firms from a named country often (but not always) receive a company-specific duty; trade data, however, are collected only at the country level. It therefore is appropriate to use the average final duty specific to each country. This average tariff is reported for each named country.

its price, the foreign firm's dumping margin falls, and hence the duty can fall).[7] Also, raising the export price also means that the foreign firm earns the higher per unit revenue rather than allowing the duty to be collected by the U.S. government. Unfortunately, the revised duties were not available on a consistent basis, so I was not able to use the revised AD duties in my analysis.[8]

In a given filing, a domestic industry can and often does name more than one source country. In the investigation, if four countries are named, then both the Commerce Department and the ITC make four separate determinations, one for each country. Therefore, in our 'named country' analysis there would be four separate observations. Since the set of 'non-named' countries is the same for each of the four named countries, however, the 'non-named' analysis would have only one observation for this filing. This is the main reason why there are sizeable differences in observations across regressions.[9]

How might an AD investigation affect trade? To get a direct measure of the impact of AD duties, I report a specification with the (log) AD duty in each of the three years following the case ($t = 1,2,3$). Recall, however, that the AD duty is imposed only when the case receives an affirmative final injury determination. This direct measure, then, does not pick up any potential trade restraint when the case is settled or rejected.

It is often argued that AD petitions have a profound impact on imports even if they do not result in duties (Staiger and Wolak 1989; Prusa 1992). Consider, first, that about 20 per cent of U.S. AD cases were settled, and the large majority of these cases were resolved with some type of voluntary restraint agreement. Hence, we would expect these settled outcomes to have a measurable impact on trade. Note, however, that these agreements usually involve explicit quantity restrictions but often do not mandate specific price increases. Thus, settled cases might have a substantial impact on quantities but not on prices.

There is also evidence that imports are significantly restrained when the case is rejected. For example, Staiger and Wolak (1994) find that imports fall dramatically during the investigation period, regardless of the case's ultimate outcome.[10] Legal scholars often refer to this as the 'harassment' effect of an AD investigation. The harassment is due both to the temporary duties that are levied during the investiga-

---

7 Blonigen and Haynes (1999) study the incentives to adjust prices once the AD duties have been imposed. In practice, firms vary in how much they respond to the incentive. In spite of the incentives to raise prices, many firms do not do so.

8 See Gallaway, Blonigen, and Flynn (1999) for an application that uses revised AD duties in its analysis. Note that the task of acquiring revised duties for the Gallaway et al. paper was far smaller than that of this paper, since their analysis required revised duties for only a single year. By contrast, the current application requires revised duties for the entire sample period.

9 The differencing required to perform the IV estimates also leads to fewer observations. In addition, Customs data occasionally have missing values for 'quantity,' thus reducing the number of observations in the unit value and quantity regressions.

10 Staiger and Wolak's (1994) regressions focus on trade during the first year following the filing of the petition and are therefore best interpreted as estimates of the short-run effect of AD investigations. In contrast, the regressions below are best interpreted as longer-run effects.

602   T.J. Prusa

tion and also to the stifling effect of the uncertainty surrounding the cases outcome. It is possible, therefore, that all three outcomes – affirmative decisions (duties levied), settled, and negative decisions – can have a significant impact on imports. In order to quantify the importance of these effects I also report a specification in which dummy variables capture the affect of the case's outcome at time $t = 1,2,3$.

Finally, in all specifications I include (but do not report) year dummies for each regression. Year dummies capture macroeconomic shocks that are common across all cases but vary over time. For instance, the dollar depreciation in 1985 might affect the domestic price of all 1985 imports.[11]

3.1. Named countries
In table 3 I report results for the value of imports. The first (last) four columns report estimates for the named (non-named) countries.[12] According to the FE estimates, the imposition of AD duties significantly restrain trade in each of the first three years following the case.[13] Specifically, a 10 per cent duty causes imports from named countries to fall by about 1.9 per cent during the first year following the AD investigation. The impact is smaller in subsequent years but is still significant. According to the IV estimates, the impact during the first year is somewhat larger than the FE estimates, but the impact in the second and third years is no longer significant.

Given the discussion in Prusa (1997) the estimated elasticities are somewhat smaller than expected. Moreover, given the effort expended to negotiate preferential trade agreements involving tariff cuts far smaller that 10 percentage points, one would think that the estimated elasticities would be larger. More specifically, in competitive markets one would expect a 10 per cent tariff to be a significant barrier. There are several possible explanations for our relatively small estimate. First, as mentioned above in response to the AD duty the foreign firms may raise their price to the U.S. market. In terms of our estimated impact on the value of trade, such price adjustments will diminish the measured impact of AD orders. Second, AD duties vary dramatically from case to case. Although the average duty (in affirmative cases) is 45 per cent, the median duty (in affirmative cases) is 26 per cent, suggesting that there are cases with rather large duties. A review of the data indicates that there were a handful of exceptionally large duty cases: eleven cases had margin exceeding 200 per cent. Ten per cent of the cases had duties exceeding 100 per cent. Such wide disparity in duties might make the constant elasticity specification inappropriate.

For these reasons, from this point on I will primarily emphasize the results from the dummy variable specification. Note that unlike the ln (duty) specification, the parameter estimates for the outcome dummies must be transformed before they can

---

11 Full parameter estimates are available from the author upon request.
12 To keep the table manageable, I abuse notation by denoting the IV parameter estimates without Δ.
13 Using the Davidson-MacKinnon (1993) test, I cannot reject the log-log specification in favour of estimating in levels.

be readily interpreted. At the bottom of the table I report the economic effect of the respective case outcomes. According to both the FE and IV estimates, an affirmative AD determination reduces the value of imports by about 50 per cent in *each* of the three years following the determination. The value of imports falls by about 60 per cent following a settlement agreement. Trade also falls in rejected cases by about 20 percent, although the effect is not statistically significant for the IV estimates.

In tables 4 and 5 I report analogous results for import quantities and prices, respectively. When we compare the tables, it becomes clear that AD has a larger impact on quantities than on prices. In particular, according to the IV dummy results, an affirmative AD determination causes quantities to fall by almost 70 per cent during the first three years following the duty. Prices increase by about half as much. It is interesting to note that the parameter estimates confirm our conjecture that settled cases will primarily entail large restrictions in import quantities but relatively small (and statistically insignificant) price increases. In particular, imported quantities fall about the same when cases are settled or result in duties. However, prices increase far less for settled cases than for affirmative cases.

There are several possibilities for this finding. First, once the final duty is in place, the exporter has an incentive to raise its price. Since the AD duty means that consumers are going to have to pay higher prices for the exporter's product, the foreign firm, rather than the U.S. government, might as well earn the extra revenue. This incentive to offset the duty is not present for settled cases. Second, the finding is consistent with the view that AD law essentially serves as a GATT-consistent tool to manage trade. The logic is that industries can influence when their dispute will be settled (Prusa 1991). For instance, certain industries seem especially proficient at creating political pressure, forcing the government to negotiate a voluntary export restraint. Given this, it appears that industries who opt to settle are primarily interested in managing their import competition rather than desiring to have import prices reflect 'fair' pricing. Third, the settlement-driven voluntary export restraints may not have a large impact on prices if there are many alternative suppliers in the market. Competitive market forces may keep prices low, even though some suppliers have agreed to limit shipments.

3.2. Non-named countries
An AD case should also affect imports from non-named countries. Interestingly, while the FE and IV estimates gave quite similar results for imports from named countries, the two procedures give significantly different results when we analyze imports from non-named countries. As a result, the discussion will concentrate on the IV estimates since they have better theoretical grounding in this application.

Looking first the effect on the value of imports (table 3), we see that the dummy variable specification is not well estimated. However, the ln (duty) specification does find that non-named countries respond to the reduction in trade by named countries by increasing their sales to the U.S. market. This is precisely the effect we expect. The IV elasticity estimates imply that a 10 per cent AD duty raises non-named imports by 6 per cent during the first year, implying that non-named coun-

TABLE 3
Impact of AD Actions on Value of Imports

	Named				Non-named			
	ln Imports (FE)	ln Imports (FE)	ln Imports (IV)	ln Imports (IV)	ln Imports (FE)	ln Imports (FE)	ln Imports (IV)	ln Imports (IV)
ln Imports, $t-1$	0.255 (0.017)**	0.255 (0.017)**	0.386 (0.060)**	0.404 (0.060)**	0.128 (0.014)**	0.136 (0.016)**	0.108 (0.022)**	0.108 (0.023)**
ln Duty, year+1	−0.190 (0.037)**		−0.244 (0.045)**		0.107 (0.029)**		0.065 (0.028)*	
ln Duty, year+2	−0.155 (0.043)**		0.061 (0.052)		0.146 (0.033)**		0.041 (0.029)	
ln Duty, year+3	−0.124 (0.051)*		−0.005 (0.058)		0.183 (0.037)**		0.038 (0.032)	
Aff Dec, year+1		−0.788 (0.138)**		−0.888 (0.156)**		0.352 (0.126)**		0.155 (0.106)
Aff Dec, year+2		−0.651 (0.164)**		−0.656 (0.246)**		0.495 (0.153)**		0.285 (0.166)
Aff Dec, year+3		−0.687 (0.199)**		−0.755 (0.333)*		0.631 (0.184)**		0.398 (0.224)
Neg Dec, year+1		−0.404 (0.139)**		−0.295 (0.159)		0.148 (0.129)		0.009 (0.110)
Neg Dec, year+2		−0.339 (0.162)*		−0.134 (0.245)		0.205 (0.156)		0.024 (0.172)
Neg Dec, year+3		−0.348 (0.195)		−0.126 (0.329)		0.321 (0.188)		0.163 (0.231)

	(1)	(2)	(3)	(4)
Settled, year+1	−0.560 (0.190)**	−0.966 (0.231)**	0.241 (0.172)	0.071 (0.154)
Settled, year+2	−0.475 (0.210)*	−0.835 (0.333)*	0.308 (0.196)	0.106 (0.230)
Settled, year+3	−0.893 (0.249)**	−1.438 (0.439)**	−0.023 (0.223)	−0.219 (0.298)
Observations	3591	2883	1723	1401
R-squared	0.75	—	0.85	—
%Δ in dependent variable per unit change in				
Aff Dec, year+1	−54.95%	−59.36%	41.00%	16.07%
Aff Dec, year+2	−48.53%	−49.65%	62.10%	31.16%
Aff Dec, year+3	−50.66%	−55.53%	84.84%	45.11%
Neg Dec, year+1	−33.87%	−26.51%	14.96%	0.34%
Neg Dec, year+2	−29.67%	−15.13%	21.31%	0.89%
Neg Dec, year+3	−30.70%	−16.45%	35.38%	14.62%
Settled, year+1	−43.93%	−62.93%	25.39%	6.14%
Settled, year+2	−39.14%	−58.96%	33.54%	8.32%
Settled, year+3	−60.29%	−78.44%	−4.68%	−23.19%

NOTES
Standard errors in parentheses; constant and year dummies not reported
* significant at 5% level; ** significant at 1% level

TABLE 4
Impact of AD actions on quantity of imports

	Named				Non-named			
	ln Quantity (FE)	ln Quantity (FE)	ln Quantity (IV)	ln Quantity (IV)	ln Quantity (FE)	ln Quantity (FE)	ln Quantity (IV)	ln Quantity (IV)
ln Quantity, $t-1$	0.134 (0.020)**	0.136 (0.020)**	0.251 (0.061)**	0.250 (0.061)**	0.120 (0.018)**	0.133 (0.019)**	0.201 (0.040)**	0.192 (0.041)**
ln Duty, year+1	−0.271 (0.048)**	−0.294 (0.057)**	0.128 (0.036)**	0.122 (0.038)**				
ln Duty, year+2	−0.237 (0.056)**	0.065 (0.067)	0.182 (0.041)**	0.041 (0.040)				
ln Duty, year+3	−0.195 (0.067)**	−0.003 (0.073)	0.240 (0.046)**	0.053 (0.043)				
Aff Dec, year+1		−1.130 (0.181)**		−1.134 (0.200)**		0.391 (0.155)*		0.356 (0.144)*
Aff Dec, year+2		−0.934 (0.216)**		−0.910 (0.319)**		0.650 (0.187)**		0.615 (0.226)**
Aff Dec, year+3		−0.921 (0.263)**		−1.061 (0.428)*		0.853 (0.226)**		0.816 (0.304)**
Neg Dec, year+1		−0.486 (0.183)**		−0.376 (0.203)		0.265 (0.163)		0.157 (0.154)
Neg Dec, year+2		−0.452 (0.215)*		−0.282 (0.315)		0.123 (0.195)		0.112 (0.239)
Neg Dec, year+3		−0.435 (0.259)		−0.448 (0.425)		0.553 (0.235)*		0.674 (0.324)*

Settled, year+1	−0.628 (0.237)**	−1.100 (0.280)**	0.147 (0.210)	0.027 (0.208)
Settled, year+2	−0.543 (0.265)*	−1.030 (0.406)*	0.282 (0.241)	0.186 (0.313)
Settled, year+3	−1.068 (0.317)**	−1.774 (0.539)**	−0.111 (0.276)	−0.154 (0.407)
Observations	3167	2501	1535	1235
R-squared	0.75	−	0.91	−
%Δ in dependent variable per unit change in				
Aff Dec, year+1	−68.23%	−68.45%	46.02%	41.32%
Aff Dec, year+2	−61.60%	−61.73%	88.16%	80.27%
Aff Dec, year+3	−61.53%	−68.41%	128.73%	116.01%
Neg Dec, year+1	−39.52%	−32.73%	28.58%	15.58%
Neg Dec, year+2	−37.84%	−28.23%	10.92%	8.73%
Neg Dec, year+3	−37.41%	−41.65%	69.12%	86.14%
Settled, year+1	−48.13%	−68.00%	13.31%	0.58%
Settled, year+2	−43.89%	−67.13%	28.71%	14.74%
Settled, year+3	−67.33%	−85.33%	−13.89%	−21.09%

NOTES
Standard errors in parentheses; constant and year dummies not reported
* significant at 5% level; ** significant at 1% level

TABLE 5
Impact of AD actions on unit value of imports

	Named				Non-named			
	ln Unit Value (FE)	ln Unit Value (FE)	ln Unit Value (IV)	ln Unit Value (IV)	ln Unit Value (FE)	ln Unit Value (FE)	ln Unit Value (IV)	ln Unit Value (IV)
ln Unit Value, $t-1$	−0.018 (0.021)	−0.018 (0.021)	0.014 (0.056)	0.008 (0.056)	−0.039 (0.028)	−0.046 (0.028)	−0.076 (0.076)	−0.060 (0.073)
ln Duty, year+1	0.059 (0.020)**		0.051 (0.023)*		0.025 (0.031)		0.030 (0.035)	
ln Duty, year+2	0.044 (0.023)		−0.020 (0.026)		−0.018 (0.035)		−0.046 (0.038)	
ln Duty, year+3	0.094 (0.028)**		0.053 (0.029)		−0.012 (0.040)		0.002 (0.041)	
Aff Dec, year+1		0.297 (0.075)**		0.254 (0.080)**		−0.015 (0.132)		0.069 (0.137)
Aff Dec, year+2		0.250 (0.090)**		0.234 (0.126)		−0.260 (0.159)		−0.197 (0.212)
Aff Dec, year+3		0.398 (0.109)**		0.435 (0.170)*		−0.289 (0.192)		−0.238 (0.288)
Neg Dec, year+1		−0.007 (0.076)		0.013 (0.081)		−0.163 (0.139)		−0.158 (0.148)
Neg Dec, year+2		0.095 (0.089)		0.152 (0.126)		−0.094 (0.166)		−0.102 (0.228)
Neg Dec, year+3		0.176 (0.108)		0.331 (0.170)		−0.403 (0.196)*		−0.325 (0.299)

	(1)	(2)	(3)	(4)
Settled, year+1	0.078	0.116	−0.298	−0.280
	(0.098)	(0.111)	(0.180)	(0.198)
Settled, year+2	0.065	0.144	−0.193	−0.155
	(0.110)	(0.162)	(0.206)	(0.297)
Settled, year+3	0.186	0.286	−0.415	−0.374
	(0.132)	(0.215)	(0.233)	(0.381)
Observations	3167	2501	1535	1235
R-squared	0.89	—	0.90	—
%Δ in dependent variable per unit change in				
Aff Dec, year+1	34.24%	28.54%	−2.37%	6.15%
Aff Dec, year+2	27.93%	25.34%	−23.84%	−19.72%
Aff Dec, year+3	48.05%	52.26%	−26.49%	−24.43%
Neg Dec, year+1	−1.00%	1.01%	−15.86%	−15.55%
Neg Dec, year+2	9.51%	15.46%	−10.23%	−11.97%
Neg Dec, year+3	18.53%	37.31%	−34.47%	−30.90%
Settled, year+1	7.64%	11.58%	−26.96%	−25.89%
Settled, year+2	6.05%	14.02%	−19.28%	−18.06%
Settled, year+3	19.40%	30.10%	−35.74%	−36.01%

NOTES
Standard errors in parentheses; constant and year dummies not reported
* significant at 5% level; ** significant at 1% level

610   T.J. Prusa

tries offset about one-third of the fall from named countries.[14] The IV dummy variable specification also finds that an affirmative determination leads to steadily increasing imports by non-named supplies: imports increase by 16 per cent in year 1, 31 per cent in year 2, and 45 per cent in year 3, but the estimated coefficients are not statistically significant.

Turning next to the price and quantity effects, just as we found for the named countries, we find that the AD has a greater impact on import quantities than on prices. For the price equations, none of the estimated parameters is statistically significant. By contrast, the many of parameters in the quantity equation are significant. For instance, the dummies controlling for an affirmative AD determination are not only significant but also large and positive, implying that non-named suppliers respond to the affirmative duty on named countries by substantially increasing their sales.

4. Concluding comments

In this paper I have documented the spread of AD protection and presented estimates of the trade impact of such protection. Over the past decade the number of countries using AD has dramatically increased. It is now the case that new users more actively pursue AD investigations than traditional users such as the United States and the European Community. In addition, the data suggest that such investigations have a significant impact on import trade, regardless of whether duties are officially levied. Specifically, settled cases are about as restrictive as cases that result in duties. In either event, the value of imports from named countries falls by 50–70 per cent over the first three years of protection, and, even if the case is rejected, I find that imports fall by 15–20 per cent.

Given both the large number of AD users and also the huge impact AD duties have on trade, anti-dumping will surely remain a top issue for the next WTO round. The central issue, of course, is whether the next round will tighten the rules governing AD protection. The estimates presented in this paper should be a sobering reminder to negotiators of the distortions created by AD actions.

References

Baltagi, Badi H. (1995) *Econometric Analysis of Panel Data* (Chichester, England: John Wiley)

Blonigen, Bruce A., and Stephen E. Haynes (1999) 'Antidumping investigations and the pass-through of exchange rates and antidumping duties,' NBER Working Paper No. W7378

Boltuck, Richard, and Robert E. Litan, eds (1991) *Down in the Dumps* (Washington, DC: Brookings Institution)

Davidson, Russell, and James G. MacKinnon (1993) *Estimation and Inference in Econometrics* (New York: Oxford University Press)

14 On average, non-named suppliers have 60 per cent of the import market.

Feenstra, Robert C. (1996) 'U.S. imports, 1972–1994: data and concordances,' NBER Working Paper No. 5515

Finger, J. Michael, ed. (1993) *Antidumping: How It Works and Who Gets Hurt* (Ann Arbor: University of Michigan Press)

Gallaway, Michael P., Bruce A. Blonigen, and Joseph Flynn (1999) 'Welfare costs of U.S. antidumping and countervailing duty laws,' *Journal of International Economics* 49, 211–44

Hansen, Wendy L., and Thomas J. Prusa (1996) 'Cumulation and ITC decision-making: the sum of the parts is greater than the whole,' *Economic Inquiry* 34, 746–69

— (1997) 'Economics and politics: An empirical analysis of ITC decision-making,' *Review of International Economics* 5, 230–45

Hsiao, Cheng (1986) *Analysis of Panel Data* (Cambridge: Cambridge University Press)

Kiviet, Jan F. (1995) 'On bias, inconsistency, and efficiency of various estimators in dynamic panel data models,' *Journal of Econometrics* 68, 53–78

Lindsey, Brink (1999) 'The U.S. antidumping law: rhetoric versus reality,' CATO Institute Trade Policy Analysis No. 7

Miranda, Jorge, Raúl A. Torres, and Mario Ruiz (1998) 'The international use of anti-dumping: 1987–1997,' *Journal of World Trade* 32, 5–71

Prusa, Thomas J. (1991) 'The selection of antidumping cases for withdrawal,' in *Empirical Studies of Commercial Policy*, ed. Robert E. Baldwin (Chicago: University of Chicago Press)

— (1992) 'Why are so many antidumping petitions withdrawn?' *Journal of International Economics* 33, 1–20

— (1997) 'The trade effects of U.S. antidumping actions,' in *The Effects of U.S. Trade Protection and Promotion Policies*, ed. Robert C. Feenstra (Chicago: University of Chicago Press), 191–213

Schott, Jeffrey J. (1994) *The Uruguay Round: An Assessment* (Washington, DC: Institute for International Economics)

Staiger, Robert W., and Frank A. Wolak (1989) 'Strategic use of antidumping law to enforce tacit international collusion,' NBER Working Paper No. 3016

— (1994) 'Measuring industry specific protection: antidumping in the United States,' *Brookings Papers on Economic Activity, Microeconomics*, 51–103

Chapter 4

USA: Evolving Trends in Temporary Trade Barriers*

THOMAS J. PRUSA[1]

1 INTRODUCTION

The USA has long been among the most active seekers of contingent protection. This was true in the 1980s and 1990s and remains true in the first decade of the 2000s. While other policies such as 'buy American' provisions and domestic content rules have received considerably more press attention during the economic crisis of 2007-9, the simple truth is that contingent trade policies remain the primary means of changing the relative cost and/or availability of imports. Under WTO rules, contingent protection policies like antidumping, CVDs, China safeguards and global safeguards should be applied for a limited duration.[2] Consequently, the term 'temporary trade barriers' (TTBs) is a particularly apt description of the policies.

In this chapter the trends in US TTB activity since 1990 are discussed. In order to provide a broad perspective on the issue, the trends are examined using several different metrics. We begin with the traditional case metric. However, Bown (2011b) argues that, for many questions, a product metric provides more insight into the trends and thus both unweighted and trade-weighted product metrics will be used.

These findings indicate that US use of TTBs is evolving. Some of the stylised facts of the past are no longer true. Although the USA continues to be a heavy user of TTBs (as compared with other countries), the number of new TTBs sought by US industries has fallen markedly since 2004. Over 2005-9, the number of new requests for TTBs (case metric) by US industries has fallen by about 60% compared with the late 1990s.

This decrease is especially noteworthy in light of the sharp decline in US economic activity in 2007-9, a development that one would have expected to

---

[1]Department of Economics, New Jersey Hall, Rutgers University, 75 Hamilton St, New Brunswick, NJ 08901-1248, USA. Email: prusa@econ.rutgers.edu.

[2]I discuss what is meant by 'limited duration' later in the chapter.

---

*This article originally appeared in *The Great Recession and Import Protection: The Role of Temporary Trade Barriers*, pp. 53–84.

produce increased calls for protection.[3] Interestingly, using any of the three metrics for TTB activity, little evidence is found that the 2007–9 recession spurred a surge in US protectionism, or at least protectionism in the form of TTBs (Evenett (2010) presents evidence that other forms of protection have increased).

The current level of TTB activity for the USA is even more striking from a longer-run perspective. During 2006–10, the US initiated fewer cases than during any five-year span since 1960.[4] In fact, the two years with the fewest new TTB petitions, 2006 and 2010, have both occurred in this period.

The decline in new TTB activity, however, does not indicate that the USA has turned its back on TTBs. The USA continues to have a large stock of products under existing TTB orders. It seems that the USA is now far more reluctant to remove existing orders than in the pre-Uruguay Round period. In this sense, US TTBs are more onerous than those imposed previously. For example, this study finds that 75% (respectively, 90%) of US TTB orders were removed in the 1980s within five (respectively, ten) years; since 1995 only about 25% (respectively, 50%) of TTB orders were removed within five (respectively, ten) years.

This trend in longer duration is seen in both anti-dumping and CVD orders. Temporary trade barrier measures are far less likely to be removed (or 'sunset' as it is often termed) now than in the past. These trends are particularly noteworthy since the Uruguay Round agreement included a mandatory sunset provision for TTBs. Clearly, what was negotiated and what has happened in practice are two different things.[5] The findings suggest that, in the USA, the term *temporary* trade barrier means something different today from what it did previously. Perhaps the term 'semipermanent' trade barrier is a more accurate description. It is certainly debatable whether the term 'temporary' is an accurate description when a trade barrier is imposed for 20 years.

At least equally as concerning is the discovery that the increased duration of TTBs is especially felt by developing countries. In the post-Uruguay Round period, at the initial sunset review stage, approximately 40% of anti-dumping measures against developed countries are revoked as compared with fewer than 25% of measures against developing countries. The difference between developed and developing countries is even starker for CVD measures. About 10% of CVD measures against developing countries are revoked at the initial review versus 40% of CVD measures against developed countries.

What do these trends mean for the stock of TTBs? The reduced flow of new TTBs should result in a smaller stock of TTBs. On the other hand, longer

---

[3]Levchenko *et al* (2010) provide evidence that the reduction in trade relative to overall economic activity in the 2007–9 period was far larger than in previous downturns. Their findings might partially explain why there was not a surge in contingent protection.

[4]Comprehensive data on worldwide use of anti-dumping prior to 1980 are not available (Bown 2010a; WTO 2010). The statistics presented in Irwin (2005) suggest that the USA has probably been a leading anti-dumping user since the 1950s.

[5]These findings are consistent with those in Moore (1999, 2002).

USA: Evolving Trends in Temporary Trade Barriers   55

duration of existing TTBs means less attrition in existing TTBs and this, in turn, should increase the stock of TTBs. Using either the unweighted measure or trade-weighted measure, the two effects are found to essentially offset each other; as a result, the stock of US TTBs is far more stable than the flow.

There have also been striking developments to the pattern of who is targeted by US TTBs. In the 1980s and 1990s, the majority of TTBs was directed against imports from developed countries. Historically, somewhere between one-half to two-thirds of both the flow and the stock of TTBs were against developed countries. This is no longer the case. By 2009, only about one-third of the US *stock* of TTBs was against developed countries. The change in the flow of TTBs is even more noticeable: more than 80% of the *flow* of TTBs is against developing countries.

While China is the main reason for the shift, China alone does not explain the changing pattern. Even if China were excluded, there would still be a marked increase in the share of US TTBs directed against developing countries. Non-China developing countries accounted for about half of US TTBs by 2009; in comparison, in the mid-1990s, non-China developing countries accounted for about one-third of US TTBs.

Although developing countries are getting greater attention, China is easily the major target of US TTBs. As is the case for many US trade policy issues, China looms large in US TTB activity. With respect to the stock of TTBs, the USA now has more TTBs in effect against China than against all developed countries taken together. China also dominates the flow of new TTBs.

When one accounts for the fact that anti-dumping and CVD protection is often sought against multiple suppliers in a single investigation (*ie* the US industry alleges unfair behaviour against more than one import supplier), it becomes apparent that the attention paid to China is even more intense. In 2006-10, China was involved in about 85% of anti-dumping and CVD investigations. In contrast, in the late 1990s, only about one-quarter of anti-dumping investigations involved China.

The distribution of TTBs by industry is also examined. Not surprisingly, the steel industry dominates US activity throughout the period, consistently accounting for 30-50% of TTBs. The value of the trade-weighted measure of TTB protection is most apparent when examining the pattern of TTBs by industry. When the long-standing Canadian softwood lumber dispute was resolved, the wood product industry went from roughly 20% of all imports subject to TTBs to having less than 5% subject to TTBs. By contrast, when duties were imposed on over $1 billion of warm-water shrimp, the share of all seafood imports covered increased dramatically.

The final section of the chapter considers the impact of the one instance in which the USA levied protection under the China safeguard provision—the 2009 dispute involving Chinese exports of passenger and truck tyres. This has been one of the most widely publicised TTB during 2005-9, garnering significant press attention both in the USA and in China. While Chinese volume

56   *The Great Recession and Import Protection*

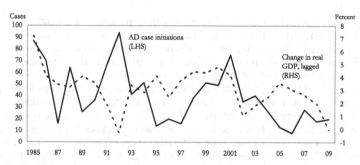

Figure 2.1: *US anti-dumping cases initiated and change in real GDP.*

Source: author's calculations using *Temporary Trade Barriers Database* (Bown 2010a) and US Bureau of Economic Analysis (2010).

and market share had grown in the years prior to the case, China was just one of many countries supplying tyres to the USA. In such circumstances, the country-specific nature of the China safeguard provision is likely to hinder any real change in overall trade flow.

Due to space limitations and because it is rarely invoked, global safeguards are not discussed here.[6] Readers interested in US use of global safeguards should consult Bown (2004, 2011b).

2   CONTEXT FOR CURRENT TRENDS: THE 2007–9 RECESSION

The recent US recession was quite severe by historical standards. The 4.1% peak-to-trough fall in US GDP was greater than any recession since the end of World War II. The 2007–9 recession was certainly far larger than any recession since accurate statistics have been kept on TTBs. For instance, peak-to-trough GDP fell by about 2.7% in the early 1980s recession, by about 1.4% during the early 1990s recession, and by about 0.3% in the 2001 recession.

Knetter and Prusa (2003) show that the flow of new TTB cases is counter-cyclical; typically, TTB activity increases (respectively, decreases) during economic downturns (respectively, expansions). Figure 2.1 depicts this general relationship using anti-dumping cases. In the figure, the number of new anti-dumping cases (solid line) initiated in each year is plotted along with the

---

[6]The USA did not initiate any global safeguards during the 2008–9 economic crisis. In fact, in the first decade of the 2000s there was only a single global safeguard case and that was in 2001. While that case (steel) was broad, received heavy press coverage and resulted in a WTO dispute, the trade impact was muted for several reasons: the largest volume products and suppliers were already covered by existing anti-dumping and countervailing orders; the order was only in place for 18 months; and over 700 product exemptions were granted (Bown 2004).

USA: Evolving Trends in Temporary Trade Barriers   57

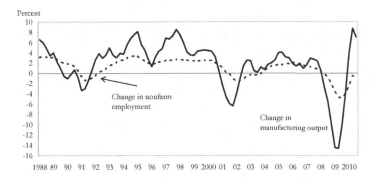

Figure 2.2: *Percentage change in US manufacturing output and non-farm employment.*
Source: US Bureau of Economic Analysis (2010).

lagged change in real GDP (dashed line). The negative correlation between economic activity and the flow of anti-dumping cases is most clearly seen during the recessions in the early 1980s, early 1990s and early 2000s, during which there were large increases in TTB activity (the global safeguard cases triggered by the recessions in the early 1980s and 2000s is not captured in the figure). By contrast, the significant decrease in GDP in 2007–9 was met with only a modest increase in US TTB activity.

Other measures of economic activity reinforce the finding that the level of TTB activity during 2008–9 is quite modest. Figure 2.2 depicts two common measures of US macroeconomic performance, the annual percentage change in manufacturing output and the percentage change in non-farm employment. As can be seen from the figure, the drop during 2008–9 in both measures was deeper than the declines during the 1991 and 2001 downturns. The fall in manufacturing output during the 2007–9 recession was more than twice as large as the 2001 recession and more than three times as large as the early 1990s recession. Only during the recession of the early 1980s has the unemployment level approached the 2007–9 recession's 10%+ level; notably, during the early 1980s recession, there was a large surge in anti-dumping and CVD investigations.

The performance of the steel sector, perennially the heaviest TTB-using industry, further buttresses the view that conditions in 2007–9 were ripe for a surge in TTB activity. In Figure 2.3, steel industry production is shown. Steel output fell by more than 50% during the 2007–9 recession, from a monthly output of over 9 million tons to about 4 million tons. Given a drop of this magnitude, it is not surprising that numerous steel-making facilities were shuttered or operated at unprofitably low rates (Uchitelle 2009). In the previous three downturns, 1982–3, 1991, and 2001, the steel industry used the

58 *The Great Recession and Import Protection*

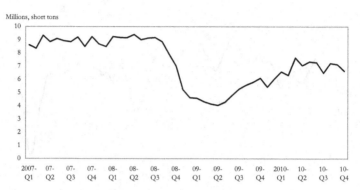

Millions, short tons

Figure 2.3: *US raw steel production (quarterly).*
Source: American Iron and Steel Institute (2010).

recession to justify their need for TTBs. Yet that is not what occurred in the 2007–9 recession.

Given historical TTB trends, one would have expected the 2007–9 recession to have spurred a significant increase in US TTB activity in 2008–9. US antidumping and CVD activity did increase—from 8 anti-dumping initiations in 2006 to 20 in 2009, and from 3 CVD initiations in 2006 to 14 in 2009. Yet this level of activity is quite modest by historical standards. In 1992 there were 94 anti-dumping initiations and in 2001 there were 75 anti-dumping initiations. In fact, the current level of TTB is more akin to the level of activity during previous periods of robust economic activity. Given the severity of the 2007–9 recession, the modest increase in TTB activity is surprising and one of the major findings of this chapter.

This finding will be returned to at various times in the chapter. The fact that US TTBs did not return to previous recessionary levels is important. No matter whether TTBs are measured using a case metric, product metric or trade-weighted metric, there is little evidence that the 2007–9 recession spurred a significant increase in TTB activity. In the final section of the chapter some possible explanations are offered as to why TTBs did not surge during the 2007–9 recession.

3 PATTERNS IN US TEMPORARY TRADE BARRIERS: CASE METRIC

3.1 General Discussion

With this backdrop, let us take an extended look at US TTB activity. In this section, the traditional case metric is used. This metric has several advantages.

USA: Evolving Trends in Temporary Trade Barriers   5S

First, it is consistent with how the USA and the WTO report TTB activity. Second, it is the most convenient metric for a long-run perspective on TTB activity; given changes in product code definitions, it is quite difficult to construct long time series using the product metric. On the other hand, as discussed in the next section, the case metric also has some weaknesses: most notably, the case metric treats a relatively small case (*eg* plastic shopping bags) the same as a very large case (*eg* warm-water shrimp). If the type and size of cases vary over time, the case metric will not adequately capture the changing impact of TTBs on imports.

Tables 2.1 and 2.2 give statistics on anti-dumping and CVD activity since 1990 using the case metric. The data are drawn from Bown (2010a). The tables report activity against developed countries, developing countries, China, and finally, all targets (total cases). The number of cases initiated each year from 1990 to 2009 is listed.[7] The tables also report the number of measures taken, which are the cases that result in duties being levied. Finally, in the last column of each table, the number of conducted investigations is reported. The term 'case' refers to each individual country involved (*eg* warm-water shrimp from Thailand, warm-water shrimp from China) and 'investigation' refers to the set of countries involved (*eg* warm-water shrimp from all source countries). A single investigation often involves multiple countries. On average, a typical anti-dumping or CVD investigation involves two or three countries.[8]

As shown in Table 2.1, between 1990 and 2009 there were 741 anti-dumping cases. Of these, 346 resulted in imposed measures. Table 2.2 gives similar statistics for CVD disputes: there were 187 CVD cases, 82 of which resulted in measures. Put differently, over the entire period, about 45% of anti-dumping and CVD cases resulted in measures.

Figure 2.4 depicts the flow of new anti-dumping and CVD activity (petitions) using the case metric and provides visual evidence of the cyclical nature of TTB filing patterns. Both anti-dumping and CVD cases increased significantly during the economic slowdown in 1991–2 and 2001–2. As discussed above, there was only a modest uptick in activity in the 2007–9 recession.

Tables 2.1 and 2.2 also list the number of measures in effect during each year. If more measures are revoked than imposed in a given year, then the aggregate number of measures in effect will fall. For example, as shown in Table 2.1, the USA had 269 anti-dumping measures in effect during 2000 and 248 measures in effect during 2001. The USA imposed 28 new anti-dumping

---

[7]One caveat when looking at the annual numbers is that investigations typically take 11–14 months, so usually the measure will not be taken until the following calendar year. This makes it quite possible that more measures can be imposed in a given year than new cases initiated.

[8]Distinguishing between a case and an investigation has little impact on the later discussion in this chapter. Nevertheless, it can be important for other questions, such as, for example, Hansen and Prusa's (1996) study of cumulation and Bown and Crowley's (2007) study of trade depression, diversion and deflection.

Table 2.1: *US anti-dumping activity (by case), 1990–2009.*

	Developed			Developing			China			Total cases			
	Cases initiated	Measures Taken	In effect	Cases initiated	Measures Taken	In effect	Cases initiated	Measures Taken	In effect	Cases initiated	Measures Taken	In effect	Total number of investigations
1990	16	11	100	12	3	47	8	7	11	36	21	158	18
1991	30	6	110	31	9	50	6	3	19	67	18	179	24
1992	62	24	116	27	12	57	5	3	21	94	39	194	25
1993	16	6	140	18	7	70	7	4	24	41	17	234	20
1994	17	7	144	22	13	75	12	7	28	51	27	247	23
1995	7	5	141	5	2	86	2	1	33	14	8	260	9
1996	5	2	140	9	4	85	6	6	34	20	12	259	13
1997	12	5	138	4	3	88	0	0	39	16	8	265	7
1998	19	11	139	18	9	92	1	1	39	38	21	270	12
1999	22	11	145	22	6	97	7	4	40	51	21	282	19
2000	19	9	139	23	17	88	7	5	42	49	31	269	12
2001	31	11	110	36	13	93	8	4	45	75	28	248	21
2002	11	3	118	15	2	104	9	7	46	35	12	268	15
2003	12	2	119	18	7	102	10	7	53	40	16	274	20
2004	7	4	120	14	7	108	6	5	59	27	16	287	12
2005	5	2	115	4	3	110	4	3	62	13	8	287	8
2006	1	0	87	3	0	102	4	2	59	8	2	248	5
2007	10	5	75	6	4	93	12	12	61	28	21	229	14
2008	2	1	71	5	4	94	11	10	72	18	15	237	12
2009	0	0	72	8	3	96	12	2	81	20	5	249	13
Total	304	125	—	300	128	—	137	93	—	741	346	—	302
Share (average)	41%	36%	29%	40%	37%	39%	18%	27%	33%	—	—	—	—
Success rate	—	41%	—	—	43%	—	—	68%	—	—	47%	—	—

'Share' denotes average end-of-period share for 'measures in effect'.

Source: author's calculations using *Temporary Trade Barriers Database* (Bown 2010a).

Table 2.2: US countervailing activity (by case), 1990–2009.

	Developed			Developing			China			Total cases			
	Cases initiated	Measures Taken	Measures In effect	Cases initiated	Measures Taken	Measures In effect	Cases initiated	Measures Taken	Measures In effect	Cases initiated	Measures Taken	Measures In effect	Total number of investigations
1990	2	0	18	5	2	46	0	0	0	7	2	64	4
1991	3	2	17	8	3	46	1	0	0	12	5	63	9
1992	32	13	17	12	6	46	1	0	0	45	19	63	9
1993	2	1	30	4	0	52	0	0	0	6	1	82	3
1994	5	2	30	2	0	51	0	0	0	7	2	81	5
1995	1	1	30	1	1	51	0	0	0	2	2	81	1
1996	1	0	27	0	0	23	0	0	0	1	0	50	1
1997	4	1	26	2	0	22	0	0	0	6	1	48	3
1998	9	5	27	4	1	20	0	0	0	13	6	47	7
1999	5	4	32	10	2	17	0	0	0	15	6	49	5
2000	5	4	31	6	6	15	0	0	0	11	10	46	4
2001	9	4	23	6	2	20	0	0	0	15	6	43	8
2002	5	2	30	0	0	22	0	0	0	5	2	52	5
2003	0	0	32	6	2	22	0	0	0	6	2	54	5
2004	1	0	32	3	0	24	0	0	0	4	0	56	3
2005	0	0	29	2	2	24	1	0	0	2	2	53	1
2006	1	0	20	1	0	21	1	0	0	3	0	41	1
2007	0	0	12	0	0	19	7	7	0	7	7	31	7
2008	0	0	10	1	1	19	5	5	7	6	6	36	6
2009	1	0	9	3	1	20	10	2	12	14	3	41	12
Total	86	39	—	76	29	—	25	14	—	187	82	—	99
Share (average)	46%	48%	22%	41%	35%	49%	13%	17%	29%	—	—	—	—
Success rate	—	45%	—	—	38%	—	—	56%	—	—	44%	—	—

'Share' denotes average end-of-period share for 'measures in effect'.

Source: author's calculations using Temporary Trade Barriers Database (Bown 2010a).

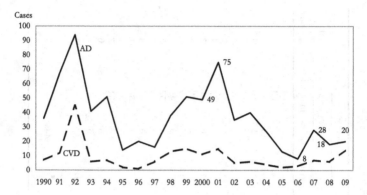

Figure 2.4: *US anti-dumping and CVD case initiations.*
Source: author's calculations using *Temporary Trade Barriers Database* (Bown 2010a).

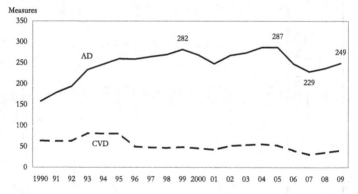

Figure 2.5: *US anti-dumping and CVD measures in effect.*
Source: author's calculations using *Temporary Trade Barriers Database* (Bown 2010a).

measures in 2001. This implies that 49 anti-dumping measures were 'sunset-ted' in 2001.

When using the case metric, 'measures in effect' give the stock of TTB activity. The trends are depicted in Figure 2.5. As can be seen from the figure, there have always been far more anti-dumping measures than CVD measures, but the differential has grown since 1990. Countervailing duty measures have declined modestly, while anti-dumping measures have grown significantly over the period, and, consequently, the relative importance of the two TTBs

USA: Evolving Trends in Temporary Trade Barriers   63

has widened: in 1990 the ratio of anti-dumping to CVD measures was 3:1 and by 2009 it was 5:1.

Figure 2.5 also provides some evidence of the impact of the inclusion of the mandatory sunset provision in the Uruguay Round. In the first two years of its use (1999-2000), mandatory sunset reviews had an appreciable impact on measures in effect; the USA revoked almost 100 orders.[9] Since that initial trove of sunset cases, however, the USA has been disinclined to remove orders (Moore 1999, 2002). This issue will be returned to in Section 6.

The number of CVD measures in effect has been relatively stable. As seen in Figure 2.5, CVD measures declined in the mid-1990s but have since remained nearly constant at 40-50 measures in effect. The impact, if any, of mandatory sunset reviews is not seen in the stock of CVD measures. Table 2.2 reveals that the main development with respect to CVDs is the decrease in the flow. About one-tenth as many CVD cases were initiated during 2000-2009 as during the 1980s.

3.2 Target Countries

It is also interesting to examine TTB patterns after dividing the target countries into development groupings: developed, developing (not including China), and China. China is separated from other developing countries because of the intense trade scrutiny to which it is subject within the USA. There are several important insights gleaned by looking at the targets by development status.

First, developed countries were targeted far less frequently by either anti-dumping or CVD actions over the 2000s relative to the preceding two decades. In the 1980s, about two-thirds of US anti-dumping and CVD cases targeted developed countries. The share of cases targeting developed countries fell throughout the 1990s and even more dramatically over the first decade of the 2000s. Since 2004, the number of cases brought against developed countries has dropped sharply; during 2005-9, fewer than ten cases in any year were aimed at developed countries. Averaging over the 1990-2009 period, 42% of the initiated cases targeted developed countries, but over 2005-9, only 20% of the cases targeted developed countries. The decline in cases brought against developed countries is even sharper for CVDs. Over 2003-9, only three CVD cases involved developed countries and none resulted in measures. By the end of 2009, only nine CVD measures were in effect against developed countries.

Second, the trends against developing countries are more stable. For most of the period, about 40% of US anti-dumping and CVD cases have targeted developing countries.[10] The total number of anti-dumping and CVD measures

---

[9]Moore (1999) points out that the majority of the initial trove of sunset orders involved measures that had been in place for more than 10 years.

[10]There is more volatility in the CVD trends due to the relatively small number of cases in any one year.

64   The Great Recession and Import Protection

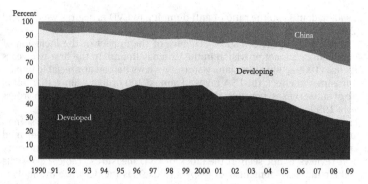

Figure 2.6: *Share of US anti-dumping and CVD measures, by development status (and China).*

Source: author's calculations using *Temporary Trade Barriers Database* (Bown 2010a).

in effect against developing countries has also remained fairly stable during the 1995–2009 period, with 90–100 anti-dumping measures and 20–25 CVD measures in effect in most years.

Third, and very importantly, China has emerged as the single most prominent target of US TTBs over the 2000s. Table 2.1 indicates that the absolute number of anti-dumping cases brought against China is about the same over the 2000s as during the 1990–1995 period. However, given that the number of TTBs targeting all other countries has fallen so sharply, China has emerged as the leading target. In a sense, other targets have taken two steps back while China stood still.

Perhaps the most startling statistic is the growth in the number of measures in effect against China. Over the first decade of the 2000s, the number of US anti-dumping measures in effect against China's exporters increased from 40 to 81. As a result, as of 2009, a full one-third of all US anti-dumping measures in effect are against China.

In addition, China now finds itself under unprecedented CVD scrutiny. Prior to 2007, no US CVD case against China had ever successfully resulted in a measure. This is largely because the US rules made it impossible to levy a CVD against a non-market economy. In 2007, the USA changed its rules and broadened its interpretation of CVDs. Under the new rules, CVDs could be levied on non-market economies like China. Subsequent to this rule change, a remarkable 23 of 30 US CVD cases have involved China.

Figure 2.6 depicts the yearly share of anti-dumping and CVD measures in effect, grouped by development status. The figure highlights the growing importance of China. As can be seen from the figure, over 1990–2009, developing countries accounted for about 40% of all measures. The big difference

USA: Evolving Trends in Temporary Trade Barriers   65

Table 2.3: *US contingent protection against China (number of cases).*

	Cases initiated (%)	China involved (%)	Only China (%)
(a) China's share of US anti-dumping actions			
1980s	4	7	4
1990–94	13	34	16
1995–99	12	27	15
2000–04	18	50	21
2005–09	49	83	42
	Cases initiated (%)	China involved (%)	Only China (%)
(b) China's share of US CVD actions			
1980s	0	1	0
1990–94	3	7	7
1995–99	0	0	0
2000–04	0	0	0
2005–09	72	85	78

Source: author's calculations using *Temporary Trade Barriers Database* (Bown 2010a).

is the diminished role of developed countries and the growing role of China. By the end of the sample period, China accounts for almost one-third of all TTB measures in effect.

While the above trends indicate the growing prominence of China for US TTBs, the focus on China is arguably even greater. As mentioned above, often domestic industries initiate cases against multiple import sources and these cases are almost always considered within a single investigation. While China accounts for a large share of cases, its influence on investigations is even greater. Consider the information in Table 2.3. In panel (a), information for anti-dumping cases is tallied and, in panel (b), CVD cases are considered.

In the first column of panel (a), China's share of anti-dumping cases is reported. China accounted for less than 20% of anti-dumping cases up until 2004. During 2005–9, however, China's share jumped to almost 50% of all cases. Yet, as is argued by Bown (2010b) and Prusa (2010), this statistic does not capture the true extent to which China dominates the action. In the second column, the fraction of *investigations* where China was involved is given. China has been a major target since the early 1990s. From 1990–1999, China was involved in no more than one-third of all anti-dumping investigations. During 2000–2004, China's anti-dumping participation rate jumped to 50%. A remarkable 82% of anti-dumping investigations have involved China since 2005. In the final column, the fraction of investigations that involve only China

66   *The Great Recession and Import Protection*

is reported. Amazingly, over 40% of US investigations target only China. The ascent of China is even more startling for CVDs (panel (b) in Table 2.3). China went from zero CVD activity prior to 2005 to account for 85% of all CVD investigations in 2005–9. To a large extent, US TTB policies have become 'stop China' policies.

4 PATTERNS IN US TEMPORARY TRADE BARRIERS: PRODUCT (HS-06) METRIC

4.1 General Discussion

An issue with the case metric is that it treats each case the same. It does not allow the scope to vary by case. For example, under the case metric, five small cases would be considered to have five times the impact of one large case, even if the one large case covered billions in imports and the small cases involved a few million dollars of imports. Thus, it may be desirable to use a metric that captures the size of each case. Bown (2011b) argues that this 'better' measure can be computed using information on the products involved.[11] For more than 20 years the USA has used the Harmonized System to classify imports. These codes are reported for every TTB case and define the products involved in each dispute.

The advantages of the product measure are two-fold. First, cases rarely involve a single-tariff-line item. A case almost always involves a number of tariff lines. As a result, the scope of a case can be measured by the number of HS products involved (*ie* an unweighted measure of products). Second, the dollar value of trade varies by product. Therefore, the breadth of trade affected by a case may be more accurately measured by the value of trade involved (*ie* a weighted measure of products).

As discussed in Chapter 1 by Bown, constructing a trade-weighted metric is not a trivial task since subject imports fall as a result of the measures. Suppose, for example, that US TTBs completely eliminate subject imports. Since no trade value is measured, a trade-weighted measure of TTBs would imply that no trade is covered by TTBs; given what actually happened, this would be an odd interpretation of TTBs. Instead, here we follow Bown's (2011b) approach and create a measure that adjusts for the trade distortion created by the TTB. Interested readers should consult Chapter 1 for a full discussion of how the trade-weighted product measure is computed.

Despite the product metric's advantages, there are two drawbacks. Both highlight the difficulty in creating accurate time-series trends with the product metric. First, the Harmonized System was only implemented in 1989. While attempts have been made to concord the Harmonized System with the old

---

[11]Until relatively recently, such product information was not available but this information is now publicly available in Bown (2010a).

USA: Evolving Trends in Temporary Trade Barriers 67

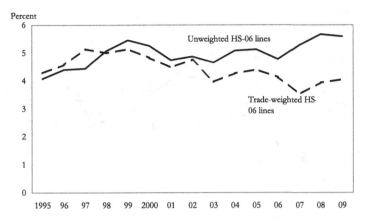

Figure 2.7: *Percentage of HS-06 lines under US anti-dumping/CVD measures (all suppliers).*

Source: author's calculations using *Temporary Trade Barriers Database* (Bown 2010a) and Comtrade.

tariff system, the reality is that measurement error becomes a serious concern if the product measure uses pre-1989 cases. As a result, only measures since 1989 are considered. Consequentially, because TTBs prior to 1989 have been excluded, my product metric will understate the true trade coverage of TTBs. This is likely to be especially problematic prior to the mid-1990s. It becomes less of a concern by the mid-to-late-1990s as more and more of these pre-1989 TTBs were revoked. Consequently, in an attempt to reduce the impact of these pre-1989 codes, results are reported using HS-06 metrics only from 1995. Second, the Harmonized System has undergone regular revisions since it was instituted. As a result, the codes for about one-third of the products have changed since 1990. While an attempt is made to control for these product code changes, some lost coverage is inevitable. In an attempt to balance the desire to use disaggregated data with a desire to minimise the number of code changes, the decision was made to use the HS-06 level to measure products.[12]

With these caveats in mind, let us now turn to examination of TTBs using the product metric. In Figures 2.7–2.9, unweighted and trade-weighted measures are presented. Figure 2.7 summarises the overall trends. In this figure,

---

[12]In most cases the products are identified at the eight-digit or ten-digit level. I opt to do my analysis at the six-digit level because doing so reduces the number of product code changes over time. Code changes occur more frequently at more disaggregated levels. Given that I report the fraction of imports subject to TTBs rather than the absolute level of imports subject to TTBs, I believe the cost of performing my analysis at the higher level of aggregation to be small.

68   *The Great Recession and Import Protection*

Figure 2.8: *Percentage of HS-06 lines under US anti-dumping/CVD measures by development status (and China).*

Source: author's calculations using *Temporary Trade Barriers Database* (Bown 2010a) and Comtrade.

the dashed line depicts the fraction of HS-06 products (unweighted) subject to anti-dumping/CVD orders; the solid line illustrates the fraction of HS-06 import *value* subject to anti-dumping/CVD orders. In terms of the overall picture, the two measures are broadly consistent: both measures indicate that 4–6% of all US imports are subject to TTBs. However, the two metrics differ when it comes to the trends in TTB coverage. The unweighted metric indicates that TTB coverage has increased fairly consistently over 2003–9, and especially over 2006–9. On the other hand, the weighted metric implies that TTB protection has fallen since 2003 and has only risen modestly in 2007–9. The difference in the trends reflects the impact of the removal of TTBs on several large import-value products such as galvanized sheet steel and softwood lumber.

4.2 Unweighted Measure

Figure 2.8 partitions the subject countries by development status. In Figure 2.8, the products covered are measured relative to the entire universe of products (*eg* the number of Chinese products subject to TTBs relative to all US imports of all products from China, the number of developed country products subject to TTBs relative to all US imports from developed countries, *etc*).

USA: Evolving Trends in Temporary Trade Barriers   69

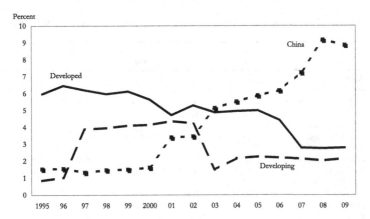

Figure 2.9: *Percentage of import value under US anti-dumping/CVD measures by development status (and China).*

Source: author's calculations using *Temporary Trade Barriers Database* (Bown 2010a) and Comtrade.

Figure 2.8 echoes the trends found using the case metric. First, TTBs against developed countries peaked in about 1998 (solid line) and declined thereafter. At the peak, about 4.5% of imported products from developed countries were subject to US TTBs. Beginning in 1998, the USA conducted its initial trove of sunset determinations, and these early sunset reviews involved a large share of products from developed countries. As is shown by the figure, these revocations resulted in a big decline in TTB coverage. The reduced flow of new TTBs over the 2000s resulted in the coverage ratio steadily declining to about 3% by 2009. Second, TTBs against developing countries (dashed line) rose in the mid-1990s but have remained quite stable at about 2.5% for more than a decade. Third, TTB coverage against China has nearly quadrupled over the 1995–2009 period. In 1995 about 1% of China's products were subject to TTBs; by 2009 China's TTB coverage had risen to more than 4%. As can also be seen when using the case metric, when it comes to TTBs, China is 'wearing the bull's-eye'.

4.3   Trade-Weighted Measure

Figure 2.9 is similar to the previous figure but relies on the trade-weighted metric. While the trends are consistent across the two metrics, the changing incidence of TTBs is much starker under the trade-weighted metric. Using the unweighted metric (Figure 2.8), developed countries' TTB coverage fell from about 4.5% to 3% by 2009. Using the trade-weighted metric (Figure 2.9), developed countries' TTB coverage fell substantially faster, from about 6%

Table 2.4: *Distribution of new US anti-dumping/CVD TTB initiations (case basis, flow).*

	1990-1994 (%)	1995-1999 (%)	2000-2004 (%)	2005-2009 (%)	2007-2009 (%)
Animal and animal products	0.7	4.9	5.3	0.0	0.0
Vegetable products	1.3	3.5	3.3	0.0	0.0
Foodstuffs	1.6	8.3	4.1	3.2	0.0
Mineral products	5.9	0.0	1.2	0.0	0.0
Chemicals and allied industries	17.4	4.9	16.3	24.2	27.0
Plastics/rubbers	1.3	11.1	9.0	8.4	10.8
Wood and wood products	3.0	0.0	1.6	11.6	6.8
Textiles	5.3	2.1	0.0	6.3	5.4
Stone/glass	0.0	0.0	0.8	2.1	2.7
Metals	48.4	55.6	50.6	30.5	29.7
Machinery/electrical	4.9	6.3	3.7	8.4	10.8
Transportation	6.3	1.4	0.8	0.0	0.0
Miscellaneous	3.9	2.1	3.3	5.3	6.8

Source: author's calculations using *Temporary Trade Barriers Database* (Bown 2010a).

to under 3%. The difference is even more pronounced for China. Using the unweighted metric, China's TTB coverage rose from about 1% to 4% by 2009. Under the trade-weighted metric, China's TTB coverage rose from about 1.5% to about 9%.

Taking the two figures together, not only are a very large number of products from China under TTB protection, but as compared with other countries, the TTBs against China (on average) involve larger trade volume than those against other countries.

5   INDUSTRY PATTERNS

Next, let us turn to the question of whether the US industries seeking TTB protection have changed over 1990-2009. We begin by examining the flow of TTBs. In Table 2.4, I use the case metric and report each industry's share of new cases as five-year averages.[13] What is remarkable is how TTB activity is dominated by just a few industries. Very few cases involve food, vegetables, minerals and textiles.

As can be seen from the table, in every subperiod the US steel industry has been the leading seeker of TTB protection. The steel industry was a particularly heavy user during the 1995-2004 period when a large number of

---

[13]Reporting annual filings would produce extremely volatile patterns from year to year.

USA: Evolving Trends in Temporary Trade Barriers 71

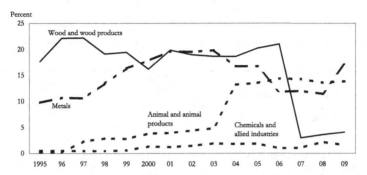

Figure 2.10: *Percentage of import value under US anti-dumping/CVD measures by industry.*

Source: author's calculations using *Temporary Trade Barriers Database* (Bown 2010a) and Comtrade.

firms went through bankruptcy and restructuring. In this ten-year period the industry accounted for more than half of all TTB cases. Throughout the entire 1990-2009 period, chemicals and plastics were the second and third most active industries, respectively.

Filings during the 2007-9 period are also reported in order to examine whether there is any evidence that the recession spurred a significant change in the industry filing patterns. The short-answer is 'no'. The same handful of industries that account for most US TTB activity prior to the crisis are the same industries that account for most TTB activity during the recession.

The stock of TTBs is probably a more revealing metric when considering industry patterns of protection. The lack of new TTB requests (small flow) for a given industry may simply reflect that it already has a large fraction of its import competition subject to TTBs; this pre-existing coverage will be evident when looking at the stock measure. When examining the stock of TTBs by industry, the trade-weighted product metric is used to compute the fraction of each industry's trade value subject to TTBs. The results are given in Figure 2.10 and Table 2.5.

First, consider that, across all industries and suppliers, the USA has about 4-5% of total imports subject to TTBs (see Figure 2.7 and Table 2.5). The average misrepresents the impact at an industry level. For example, the steel industry's persistent use of TTBs has resulted in large coverage. For much of the period, the steel industry had more than 15% of all competing imports subject to TTBs. The industry's coverage peaked at almost 20% during the steel crisis of 1999-2002.[14] It should be noted that a large fraction of steel

---

[14]Temporary trade barrier coverage would be even larger in 2002-3 if the trade effects of the steel safeguard action had been included.

Table 2.5: *Trade impact of US anti-dumping/CVD measures in effect (trade-weighted).*

	1995-99 (%)	2000-2004 (%)	2005-2009 (%)	2007-2009 (%)
All suppliers	4.9	4.5	4.0	3.8
By development status				
Developed	6.1	5.1	3.6	2.8
Developing	2.9	3.3	2.1	2.1
China	1.5	4.1	7.5	8.4
By industry				
Animal and animal products	1.7	6.2	13.9	13.9
Vegetable products	0.7	1.2	0.9	0.4
Foodstuffs	2.6	3.8	6.5	6.5
Mineral products	3.1	2.8	2.5	2.6
Chemicals and allied industries	0.5	1.6	1.5	1.6
Plastics/rubbers	5.3	3.1	3.9	5.1
Wood and wood products	20.1	18.4	11.7	3.5
Metals	12.3	18.5	13.4	13.0
Machinery/electrical	6.8	4.2	2.5	2.6
Transportation	3.9	3.6	4.6	4.9

Source: author's calculations using *Temporary Trade Barriers Database* (Bown 2010a) and Comtrade.

trade is intra-firm trade; one would not expect this trade to be threatened with TTBs. Hence, the industry's TTB coverage on non-affiliated trade is even more impressive. For instance, if one-third of US steel imports is intra-firm trade, then 30% of all unaffiliated imports are covered by TTBs.

Second, other industries have experienced large changes in their stock of imports subject to TTBs. Until 2006, the wood and wood products industry had about 20% of its import competition subject to TTBs. Despite the fact that this industry filed few cases over the period (Table 2.4) it was able to maintain TTBs on a large share of its competition. This was possible because softwood lumber dominates US wood imports and Canada accounts for nearly all of US softwood lumber imports. For this industry, a single dispute against a single supplier can create high coverage. The USA and Canada litigated this dispute for over 20 years. Given the amount of trade involved, neither side was willing to compromise. Finally, after numerous North American Free Trade Agreement (NAFTA) panel and WTO appellate body decisions, the US and Canada agreed to settle the dispute in 2006. The USA revoked the CVDs on softwood lumber and Canada agreed to limit how much softwood lumber it would export to the USA. As can be seen from Table 2.4, the removal of this order reduced the coverage ratio from over 20% to below 5%.

The 'animal products' industry makes for an interesting comparison with the wood industry. Akin to the wood products industry, the animal and animal products industry has not filed a large number of TTB cases (Table 2.4). However, the cases that have been pursued have been large. Most notably,

USA: Evolving Trends in Temporary Trade Barriers 73

in 2004 the USA imposed anti-dumping duties on shrimp from six developing country suppliers, resulting in over $2 billion of trade to be covered in a single TTB. This single case increased industry coverage from about 5% to about 14%.

6 DURATION OF TEMPORARY TRADE BARRIERS

The length of the period that measures remain in effect is vital for understanding the protection afforded by US TTBs. A mandatory sunset provision for anti-dumping and CVD measures was included in the Uruguay Round because developing countries were frustrated by the challenge involved in getting orders removed.[15] As part of the grand bargain to conclude the Uruguay Round, developing countries were able to insert language that required a mandatory sunset review for each TTB every five years. As Moore (1999, 2002) discusses, some users interpreted the language to mean that TTBs were to be removed after five years, while others, including the USA, interpreted the provision to mean that only a mandatory sunset *review* was required. Under US law, the presumption is that the order will be removed unless doing so would lead to a resumption of unfair trade and injury.

The extent to which the new provision matters depends on the basis for determining the likelihood of resumed unfair trade and injury. Moore (1999, 2002) documents that the US procedures make revocation via the sunset review a difficult proposition. With respect to the question of whether there would be a resumption of unfair trade if the order was removed, Moore documents that the USA has *always* found that there would be a return to unfair trading. In every case, no matter how long the order has been in effect, no matter how much evidence administrative reviews have revealed about the changed pricing, the USA always concludes that the affected countries will trade unfairly. With respect to the recurrence of injury, the USA has become far more hesitant to remove orders as it has gained more experience with sunset reviews. In the initial set of reviews covering measures that were in place prior to the 1995, the USA revoked about 50% of the orders.[16] Once these transition orders were finished, the USA adopted a much harder line towards revocation. Only about one-third of the post-Uruguay Round cases have been revoked.

---

[15]While a higher proportion of cases were brought against developed countries pre-1990, developing countries pushed the sunset provision. To begin with, many of the TTB cases brought against developed countries in the 1980s were 'settled'. Second, the accounting requirements to obtain TTBs were particularly difficult for developing countries to master. Hence, developing countries felt that there was a lot to gain by mandatory sunset reviews.

[16]Some of these transition orders were so old that there was no domestic interest in continuing them.

The duration of TTBs is quantified by computing the number of measures that are revoked as a fraction of the total number of measures that are in effect each month/year. Each measure's key calendar dates (date the measure went into effect and date of revocation) are converted into a duration basis. For instance, a measure that went into effect in January 2000 and was revoked in January 2005 would have a duration of 60 months.

Statistically, duration is estimated using the non-parametric Kaplan–Meier survival function. In Figures 2.11 and 2.12, the survival estimates for anti-dumping and CVD measures, respectively, are reported. Both figures are based on the case metric. First, considering panel (a) of each figure, three lines have been graphed: the grey dashed line is the survival experience for cases filed pre-mandatory sunset, the black dashed line is the survival experience for transition cases, and the solid line is the survival experience for cases initiated post-mandatory sunset reviews. Note that these figures use TTB information on cases prior to 1990. Because the case metric is used for the duration analysis, we are not hindered by the fact that the Harmonized System codes are unavailable for these early cases.

The lines depict the fraction of cases that survive through a given time period. As seen, within 36 months, more than half of both anti-dumping and CVD cases during the pre-Uruguay Round period were revoked (grey dashed line). By contrast, in the post-Uruguay Round period, less than 10% were revoked (*ie* more than 90% were still in effect). In the pre-mandatory sunset era, cases ended more or less continuously. In the post-Uruguay Round period, the survival curve is almost constant until the sunset review, and then it drops sharply. About 25–33% of initial sunset reviews result in the order being revoked.[17] In the post-Uruguay Round period, almost all revocations occur during the sunset review.

Mandatory sunset reviews appear to have had two effects on the removal of orders. First, it appears that foreign firms do not seek to have the orders removed via demonstrating multiple years of zero margins. This is not that surprising given the large expense associated with each administrative review. Also, given that the probability of revocation is small (zero unless several prior reviews already demonstrated zero margins), foreign firms seem to have decided to preserve resources for the sunset review.[18]

To get a sense of why they might do so, suppose a TTB was imposed on three firms exporting from a given target country. Each administrative review can cost *each* firm over $1 million. Thus, if all three firms were to pursue an administrative review sunset, they could jointly spend $9 million. By contrast,

---

[17]Due to the time required for the sunset review investigation, the initial sunset review often occurs between 60 and 72 months after the initial order is imposed.

[18]The foreign firms' reluctance to pursue administrative reviews is also possibly due to the 'zeroing' procedures used by the Department of Commerce. We could see more effort on administrative reviews once the USA changes its zeroing policy (Bown and Prusa 2011).

USA: Evolving Trends in Temporary Trade Barriers 75

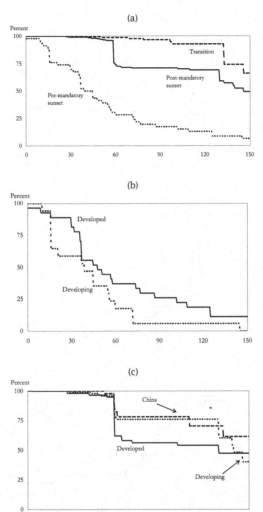

Figure 2.11: *Percentage of US anti-dumping measures in effect by duration (in months): (a) pre- versus post-mandatory sunset review clause; (b) developed versus developing countries (pre-mandatory sunset); (c) developed versus developing countries and China (post-mandatory sunset).*

Source: author's calculations using *Temporary Trade Barriers Database* (Bown 2010a).

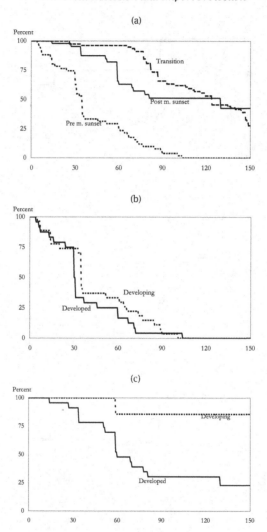

Figure 2.12: *Percentage of US CVD measures in effect by duration (in months): (a) pre-versus post-mandatory sunset review clause; (b) developed versus developing countries (pre-mandatory sunset); (c) developed versus developing countries (post-mandatory sunset).*

Source: author's calculations using *Temporary Trade Barriers Database* (Bown 2010a).

USA: Evolving Trends in Temporary Trade Barriers   77

pursuing a sunset review is a decision common to all three firms and would likely be jointly funded. A sunset review might cost a total of $1 million, about one-ninth the cost of the sunset via the administrative review process.

Second, if countries thought the Uruguay Round's sunset review language would appreciably lower the duration of anti-dumping and CVD orders, they were mistaken. The US implementation of sunset review has produced the opposite effect—measures are now in place longer than they were pre-Uruguay Round. That is, the fraction of measures revoked in two, three, four and five years in the pre-Uruguay Round era far exceed the fraction of measures revoked by four years in the post-Uruguay Round era.

In panels (b) and (c) of Figures 2.11 and 2.12, developed and developing countries' sunset experiences are compared. In panel (b), the duration of orders prior to mandatory sunset is examined. In this period there were sufficiently few cases brought against China that the decision was made not to report China separately. Both Figure 2.11 (anti-dumping) and Figure 2.12 (CVDs) show that, in this early period, developed and developing countries had very similar experiences. The two survival curves are very similar. A log-rank test of equality of the curves cannot reject that they have the same survival experience.

A very different story emerges for the post-Uruguay Round period. Temporary trade barriers against developing countries are far longer lived than those against developed countries. With anti-dumping, developed and developing countries have a similar experience during the first five years. However, at the initial sunset review stage about 40% of measures against developed countries are revoked as compared with less than 25% of measures against developing countries. Moreover, the difference persists for years. About as many cases are revoked against developing countries after 11 years as are against developed countries after 5 years. This is a remarkable result that is especially surprising given that it was developing countries that pushed hardest for mandatory sunset. This observation can be made from Figure 2.11(c), where China is separated from other developing countries as the activity against China becomes significant in the mid-1990s.

The difference between developed and developing countries is even starker when CVDs are considered. As can be seen from the figure, US CVDs imposed against developing countries are rarely revoked. The data indicate that more than 90% of measures against developing countries remain in effect after the initial review. By contrast, measures against developed countries have been removed fairly consistently throughout the period. By year five about 40% of the orders have been removed, and by year ten about 75% of the orders have been removed. The gap in duration is large.

The difference in duration is a serious issue for developing countries. The data indicate that the USA is much more likely to keep an order in place against a developing country than it is against a developed country. This policy issue certainly warrants further analysis.

7 CHINA SAFEGUARD ON PASSENGER AND TRUCK TYRES

Arguably the most publicised TTB during the 2008–9 crisis involved automobile and light-truck tyres imported from China under the 'China safeguard' statute. Prior to the tyre case, US industries had filed six China safeguard petitions between 2002 and 2009. None had resulted in measures being taken. In each case the USA decided that either the imports from China were not a cause of injury to the US industry or that the costs of protection (greater tensions with China, consumer costs) exceeded the benefits (increases in output and/or employment for the domestic industry). In September 2009, the USA announced that it would impose tariffs on tyres from China for three years: 35% tariff in year one, 30% in year two and 25% in year three. The decision not only provoked public criticism and a WTO complaint by China but it was likely a contributing factor in China initiating TTBs on US exports of automotive products and chicken parts. What made this case different from others? Was all the attention warranted?

The primary explanation for the press attention is size: the passenger and truck tyre case involved considerably more trade than any prior China safeguard case. In the last year before the safeguard case was initiated, the USA imported $6.9 billion of tyres—$1.8 billion from China alone. The next biggest China safeguard case involved welded steel piping in 2005. In the last year before the steel piping case was initiated, the USA imported $725 million of steel piping, of which $154 million was sourced from China. Thus, in terms of trade value, the tyres case was about ten times the size of the next largest case.

Yet, there are at least two reasons to believe that too much was made of the involved trade value. First, while the case was easily the biggest China safeguard case, it was not extraordinarily large as far as TTBs go. Figure 2.13 gives information on trade value for other TTB cases in 2009. Trade values for three significant cases initiated earlier in the decade are also included. As can be seen from the figure, the tyre case was not even the biggest TTB case in 2009; the anti-dumping/CVD dispute involving oil-country tubular goods affected almost a billion dollars more of imports (from China alone). The China safeguard on tyres also involved less trade value than earlier TTB cases on shrimp, furniture or dynamic random-access memory, none of which garnered as much of the spotlight as the tyre case. Second, while tyre imports from China were indeed large, the USA also imported almost $5 billion in tyres from other suppliers. The availability of significant alternative suppliers likely diminished the chance that US consumers would experience shortages or significantly higher prices.

Another reason why the tyre case drew so much press was that it was *not* initiated by domestic producers of tyres. In fact, the public record indicates that domestic producers were opposed to the safeguard action. The case was initiated by tyre workers. The argument was that injury from imported tyres

USA: Evolving Trends in Temporary Trade Barriers 79

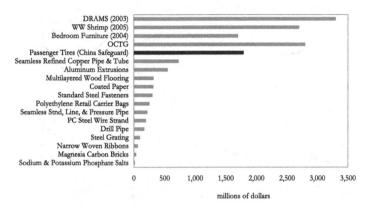

Figure 2.13: *Annual import values of selected products subject to US measures (annual import value corresponds to the year before the case was initiated).*

Source: author's calculations using *Temporary Trade Barriers Database* (Bown 2010a) and Comtrade.

was accruing to workers, not the firms. It might seem surprising that the firms and workers viewed imports so differently before it is understood that the firms accounting for nearly all US domestic production also accounted for most of the tyres imported from China (see United States International Trade Commission (2009, Table II-3)). The vast majority of tyres are produced by large global multinational firms and US tyre facilities are just one part of their global manufacturing base. A trade policy focusing exclusively on China overlooked the many other developing countries who, but for China, would export more tyres to the US market.

Despite the availability of other suppliers, the trade data show that China had indeed gained market share during the late 2000s. Figure 2.14 illustrates imports of tyres, showing both total imports and imports from China alone. As can be seen from the figure, China was selling more than twice as many tyres to the USA in early 2008 than it had just a few years earlier.

The case also highlighted the problem of discerning injury caused by the recession from injury caused by subject imports. Given the lack of support from domestic producers, injury essentially boiled down to evidence of job losses. Nevertheless, blaming imports from China for the losses was confounded by the fact that, during the 12 months prior to the filing of the case, tyre imports from China had fallen. Overall imports were falling, imports from China were receding, tyre demand was plummeting and tyre workers were being laid off, all at the same time. China felt that the case was a prime

80 *The Great Recession and Import Protection*

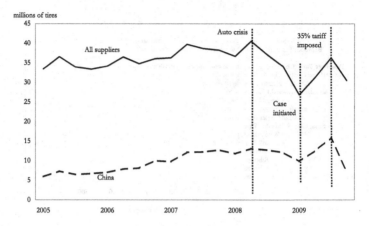

Figure 2.14: *US tyre imports (quarterly).*
Source: author's calculations using *Temporary Trade Barriers Database* (Bown 2010a) and Comtrade.

example of it being made the scapegoat for woes caused by the worldwide recession.

8 CONCLUSION

This review of US TTB activity has yielded a number of interesting insights. One important finding is methodological—most key insights are not sensitive to the metric used to measure TTBs. The different metrics (case, unweighted product, trade-weighted product) are all found to portray similar qualitative results with respect to the flow of new activity. However, the stock of TTBs is sensitive to choice of metric. While the merits of each metric can be debated, it is clear that the weighted metric reveals details on the scope and depth of TTBs that the easier-to-use metrics miss. Exploring these differences is something future research should investigate.

A second key finding is the extraordinary extent to which US TTBs are focused on a single supplier (China). Depending on exactly how the question is framed, the data show that China now accounts for 50–85% of new US TTB activity. China now has a higher fraction of its trade under US TTB measures than all developing countries put together and all developed countries put together. This would be remarkable under any circumstances, but it is even more striking when one realises that China was subject to very few TTBs just a decade ago.

USA: Evolving Trends in Temporary Trade Barriers   81

The relative lack of TTB surge during (and following) the 2007–9 recession is also a key finding. While anti-dumping and CVD filings did increase, the overall level of activity was modest by historical standards. The recession also seemed to have influenced the first (and only) China safeguard measure, but one action cannot reasonably be called a surge.

Why wasn't there a sharp increase in new petition filings in the 2007–9 recession that has been typical in past recessions? Here, four contributing explanations are given. First, the single biggest user of TTBs in the US—the steel industry—already had TTB measures on most of its key products. The efforts by the steel industry to pressurise US authorities into not sunsetting cases meant that most of the usual suspects were already subject to large TTB tariffs. For example, key products such as hot-rolled steel, plate, ball bearings and piping fuelled the surge in TTB activity in the early 1980s, early 1990s, and early 2000s.[19] In the 2007–9 recession, the key foreign suppliers of each of these products (and many other steel products) were already subject to TTBs.

Second, in earlier recessions, the decline in imports appears to have been roughly proportional to the decline in US manufacturing activity. In the 2007–9 recession, imports fell by a greater amount than the decline in US manufacturing activity (Levchenko *et al* 2010). US imports declined by more than 25% in 2009. In earlier recessions, imports declined by about one-quarter that amount. This unusually severe contraction meant that there were not a lot of products where imports were *increasing*, either absolutely or relative to domestic production or consumption. On average, the fall in import market share makes it more difficult to allege that imports 'cause' the domestic industry's injury. In such circumstances, the recession is a more apparent cause of the downturn.

Despite the evidence, it must be stressed that the role of the decline in imports is speculative. Trade cases are filed on specific products that usually make up a very small share of total industry imports, so extrapolating from industry-wide data to a conclusion as to why a particular product within that industry did not seek TTB protection involves a leap of faith that may or may not be warranted. In addition, there is clear evidence that cases were filed and received TTB protection despite large falls in import volume and market share. At least some industries were able to take advantage of the demand fall. Three cases adjudicated in 2010—oil-country tubular goods, drill piping and coated paper—all experienced huge declines in imports. Moreover, in each case the domestic industry was able to remain profitable despite the recession. Consequently, in each case the domestic industry claimed the recession made it vulnerable to imports. The USA was apparently sympathetic to this claim. In each case the US imposed the TTB measure not because the industry was injured but because it was threatened with injury.

---

[19]Moore (1996) discusses the steel industry's surge of cases during the recessions of the early 1980s and early 1990s.

Third, the changing role of manufacturing in the US economy might also be influencing trends. Trade remedy laws like anti-dumping and CVD only apply to goods, not to services. Yet the US economy continues to shift from manufacturing to services. Moreover, an increasing portion of that manufacturing takes place in segments where there is some unique US advantage, or where the industry is highly globalised so that intra-industry trade occurs and each involved country is necessary to the overall functioning. The traditional users of trade remedy laws—industries with large capital costs, and large investments in fixed assets—are becoming a smaller and smaller part of the overall economy.

Fourth, as documented by Knetter and Prusa (2003), the exchange rate plays an even larger role in driving new TTBs than changes in GDP. Since 2001, the US dollar has depreciated relative to other currencies (except the Chinese yuan). This tends to put a damper on import levels, as stronger foreign currencies makes exports to the USA less competitive in US dollar terms. Similarly, China's fixed exchange rate is likely a key contributing factor behind many US TTBs targeting Chinese exporters.

Thomas J. Prusa is Professor at Rutgers, The State University of New Jersey, and Research Associate at The National Bureau of Economic Research.

REFERENCES

American Iron and Steel Institute (2010). Online steel industry resource. URL: www.steel.org.

Bown, C. P. (2011a). Introduction. In *The Great Recession and Import Protection: The Role of Temporary Trade Barriers* (ed. C. P. Bown). London: CEPR/World Bank. (Chapter 1 of this volume.)

Bown, C. P. (2011b). Taking stock of anti-dumping, safeguards, and countervailing duties, 1990–2009. *The World Economy*, forthcoming.

Bown, C. P. (2010a). *Temporary Trade Barriers Database*. World Bank (July). URL: http://econ.worldbank.org/ttbd/.

Bown, C. P. (2010b). China's WTO entry: anti-dumping, safeguards, and dispute settlement. In *China's Growing Role in World Trade* (ed. R. Feenstra and S. Wei). Chicago, IL: University of Chicago Press for NBER.

Bown, C. P. (2004). How different are safeguards from anti-dumping? Evidence from US trade policies toward steel. Econometric Society Report 434 (July).

Bown, C. P., and M. A. Crowley (2007). Trade deflection and trade depression. *Journal of International Economics* **72**(1), 176–201.

Bown, C. P., and T. J. Prusa (2011). US anti-dumping: much ado about zeroing. In *Waiting on Doha* (ed. A. Mattoo and W. J. Martin). Washington, DC: World Bank, forthcoming.

Evenett, S. (ed.) (2010). *Tensions Contained...For Now: The 8th GTA Report*. London: Centre for Economic Policy Research.

Hansen, W., and T. J. Prusa (1996). Cumulation and ITC decision-making: the sum of the parts is greater than the whole. *Economic Inquiry* **34**, 746–769.

USA: Evolving Trends in Temporary Trade Barriers   83

Irwin, D. A. (2005). The rise of US anti-dumping activity in historical perspective. *World Economy* **28**, 651–668.

Knetter, M. M., and T. J. Prusa (2003). Macroeconomic factors and anti-dumping filings. *Journal of International Economics* **61**(1), 1–18.

Levchenko, A. A., L. T. Lewis, and L. L. Tesar (2010). The collapse of international trade during the 2008–2009 crisis: in search of the smoking gun. *IMF Economic Review* **58**(2), 214–253.

Moore, M. O. (2002). Commerce department anti-dumping sunset reviews: a first assessment. *Journal of World Trade* **36**(2), 675–698.

Moore, M. O. (1999). Anti-dumping reform in the US: a faded sunset. *Journal of World Trade* **33**(4), 1–28.

Moore, M. O. (1996). The rise and fall of big steel's influence on US trade policy. In *The Political Economy of Trade Protection* (ed. A. Kreuger). University of Chicago Press.

Prusa, T. J. (2010). Comments on 'China's WTO entry: anti-dumping, safeguards, and dispute settlement', by C. P. Bown. In *China's Growing Role in World Trade* (ed. R. Feenstra and S. Wei). Chicago, IL: University of Chicago Press for NBER.

Uchitelle, L. (2009). Steel industry, in slump, looks to federal stimulus. *New York Times*, 1 January 2009. URL: www.nytimes.com/2009/01/02/business/02steel.html.

US Bureau of Economic Analysis (2010). US Department of Commerce. URL: www.bea.gov/national/index.htm#gdp.

United States International Trade Commission (2009). Certain passenger vehicle and light truck tires from China. Investigation no. TA-421-7. Publication 4085.

World Trade Organization (2010). Anti-dumping statistics. URL: www.wto.org/english/tratop_e/adp_e/adp_e.htm.

Chapter 5

Pricing Behavior in the Presence of Antidumping Law[†]

Thomas J. Prusa*

State University of New York at Stony Brook

Abstract

This paper examines the effect of antidumping (AD) law on the pricing behavior of foreign and domestic firms prior to the filing of an AD action. AD law affects firms in very different ways – almost always distorting the foreign firm's strategy but often not altering the domestic firm's. We show that AD law creates a price floor for the foreign firm and causes it to raise its price. The domestic firm's response is significantly more complicated, in many instances resulting in feigned injury. These diverse effects imply that AD law has important welfare consequences even if duties are never levied.

I. Introduction

Recent years have witnessed a growing interest in the rationale for, and the effects of, antidumping (AD) law. This newfound interest in AD law (as opposed to the more traditional interest in why firm dump) lies primarily in the remarkable worldwide increase in the use of AD law in recent years – between 1980 and 1985 more than 1600 AD actions were initiated worldwide 〈Tharakan [1991]〉.

* Department of Economics, S.U.N.Y. at Stony Brook, Stony Brook, New York 11794-4384, U.S.A. Telephone: (516) 632-7563; Fax: (516) 632-7516; I would like to thank the Japan Foundation Center for Global Partnership and the Harry and Lynde Bradley Foundation for financial support. I received helpful comments from Pradeep Dubey, Rob Feenstra, Jim Hartigan, John Hillas, Mike Leidy, and Bob Staiger.

[†]This article originally appeared in *Journal of Economic Integration*, **9**(2), pp. 260–289.

Bhagwati [1988] was one of the first to raise the possibility that this GATT-sanctioned trade law is being used in an illegitimate manner. He argues that firms can use the AD investigations to harass foreign rivals and, if successful, to restore the protection lost with the multilateral tariff reductions.[1] Hoekman and Leidy [1989] extend Bhagwati's argument claiming that the vagueness of the rules governing AD procedures have made AD actions a substitute for the more difficult to obtain safeguard protection, *i.e.*, that dumping duties are being levied when other forms of GATT-sanctioned protection are more appropriate.[2]

Prusa [1993] argues that receiving protection is only part of the reason why firms file AD actions. He argues that many firms file AD actions without any intent of obtaining duties against their foreign rivals. Rather, it is more desirable if the foreign and domestic industries negotiate a settlement. From this perspective the increase in AD filings is especially disturbing since cases with very dubious merit (*i.e.*, with very small probability of winning protection) can have sizeable affect on welfare.[3] Staiger and Wolak [1991] also use the fact that approximately one-third of AD cases are settled to motivate their model of AD law as a cartel stabilizing punishment mechanism.

All of these papers, however, attempt to explain the effects of AD law once a case has been filed. In this paper, attention is focused on the effects of AD law prior to the filing of a case. We show that the increased incidence of AD petitions should be only one – and possibly the least important – of the concerns about AD law. AD law can have significant effects on firms' strategies, prices, and profits even if duties are never levied. The fact that AD law changes firms' behavior, of course, is not entirely unexpected. In fact, the original intention of AD law was to deter foreign firms from engaging in

---

1. Finger [1981] and Herander and Schwartz [1984] provide early empirical evidence that AD law might be used to harass foreign competitors.
2. Finger, Hall, and Nelson [1982] argue that the rules governing escape clause protection are even more vague than those governing AD protection. Hansen and Prusa [1993] argue that escape clause protection is nonetheless more politically difficult to provide since GATT rules allow foreign retaliation.
3. For another perspective on the welfare implications of antidumping law see Webb [1992].

predatory pricing, so policy makers would likely view the law as a failure unless some response was induced.

In general, however, AD law can have a far more unexpected consequences than expounded in public debates. According to GATT rules, duties can only be levied if two criteria are satisfied "less than fair value" sales (by the foreign industry) and "injury" (to the domestic industry). As it turns out, the likelihood that these criteria are satisfied depend significantly on how domestic governments interpret the GATT guidelines. In fact, given the generous latitude that governments have in implementing the law, it seems clear that AD law is no longer implemented in a way to achieve its original purpose. In many circumstances, the rules are so nebulous that it indeed seems entirely likely that governments are using AD protection as "GATT consistent" protectionism. For example, given current U.S. procedures, foreign firms can be guilty of dumping even if they charge exactly the same prices both at home and abroad.[4]

The cavalier manner which many governments use AD law suggests that foreign firms must be concerned about AD actions, even if they are confident they are not dumping. Foreign firms, however, can influence the likelihood that dumping actions will be brought against them (and the likelihood that such actions will be rejected) by changing their pricing strategy. Not surprisingly, this involves raising the price charged in the domestic market. More interesting, domestic firms can also influence the likelihood of dumping duties by changing their pricing strategies. However, in many circumstances it will not pay the domestic firm to change its behavior. When AD law does influence the domestic firm's behavior, it can result in either higher or lower prices. Either way adversely affects the domestic firm's profits – and increases the likelihood of an affirmative injury determination. In a sense, the domestic firm attempts to induce AD protection by feigning injury.

Both foreign and domestic firms alter their behavior in order to influence the outcome of a (threatened) case. Specifically, the foreign firm attempts to

---

4. Individual export transactions are compared with the foreign firm's mean home market price. Thus, even if the same price is charged in both markets at every point in time, a firm can be found guilty of dumping as long as there is some variance in prices over time.

decrease, and the domestic firm to increase, the probability that duties will be levied. Interestingly, even though both firms' strategies suggest they are willing to sacrifice short-run profit for long-term benefits, there are circumstances when both firms can earn higher current period profit. In this sense, AD law facilitates collusive behavior. The threat of impending legal action reduces the rivals' coordination problem and promotes tacit collusion. As a result, *both* domestic and foreign firms may prefer to operate in an environment where there is the threat of an AD action. Thus, AD law can have a deleterious welfare effect even if duties are never levied.

The approach taken in here is related to several recent papers. Leidy and Hoekman [1990] investigate the foreign firm's production response to AD law under exchange rate uncertainty and show that the different definitions of less than fair value (LTFV) sales can lead to different production responses. Fischer [1992] also focuses on the effects of the LTFV determination on the firms' actions and shows that prices will be driven up. Neither of these papers, however, incorporates the injury criterion into their analysis. Ignoring the injury determination is significant since, in practice, of the two determinations, the LTFV decision involves far less uncertainty. For example, in the U.S. only 6% of AD cases since 1980 have not satisfied the LTFV determination.[5] By contrast, since 1980, 47% of final injury decisions were affirmative and 53% negative, suggesting that the firms' marginal impact on the injury decision could be quite significant. As we will show, AD law has its more prominent effects when there is significant uncertainty over the decision. AD actions can also reveal a great deal of information about the foreign rival. Hartigan [1993a] shows that AD law can either enhance or inhibit the foreign firm's ability to signal its costs. In a related paper, Hartigan [1993b] discusses how an AD action allows foreign and home firms to share information about costs and examines the welfare implications of such information revelation. Finally, Leidy [1993] discusses how the vagueness of the injury criterion can lead to manipulation by the domestic firm. Leidy finds that AD law can lead to "spurious injury". Importantly, Leidy assumes injury is positively related to sales, and thus finds that the domestic firm will

---

5. See Boltuck and Litan [1991] for an excellent discussion of the problems calculating LTFV sales.

264 Pricing Behavior in the Presence of Antidumping Law

always seek to manipulate the injury decision. By contrast, in this paper, AD law has a more subtle effect on the domestic firm's behavior.

The paper is organized as follows. In the next section we present the model and describe the game, relating the modeling assumptions to the actual features of AD actions. In Section III we characterize the Nash equilibrium without AD law while Section IV derives the Nash equilibrium pricing strategies with AD law. The model is extended to incorporate the foreign firm's home market pricing decisions in section V. A few concluding comments are made in section VI.

II. The Model

The section will setup a two period duopoly model which we can use to analyze the strategic aspects of AD law. For expositional convenience, the model will be kept as simple as possible. We begin by assuming that there are two firms, one domestic and one foreign. We will denote foreign values with a star(*). In each period, the firms produce differentiated products which are close, but not perfect substitutes for one another. The domestic firm services the domestic market with local production while the foreign firm exports to the domestic market. Let P_t and $Q_t \equiv Q(P_t^*, P_t)$ denote the domestic firm's price and quantity, respectively, in period t, $t = 1, 2$; P_t^* and $Q_t^* \equiv Q^*(P_t^*, P_t)$ are similarly defined for the foreign firm.

In the first part of the paper we will ignore the foreign firm's behavior in its home market. This simplification can be justified on two grounds. First, it avoids needless complication without much cost. As will be shown in section V, the key strategic effects of AD law are present whether or not the home market is explicitly modeled. Second, in many AD actions, the foreign firm's home market pricing is not directly relevant to the investigation. This is the case, for instance, when a constructed value approach is used to calculate LTFV margin. Under the constructed value approach the government agency will calculate a home market price based upon its estimates of costs and "reasonable" profit rates. Also, when home market sales are too small (or do not exist), or when the exporter operates in a centrally planned economy, the LTFV calculation will be based on sales of a comparable product sold by a third party in another market. Certainly in these cases the foreign firm's home market behavior does not effect the LTFV determination.

When there are no dumping duties, the domestic firm will earn profit $\Pi_t(P_t^*, P_t)$ in period t, while the foreign firm will earn $\Pi_t^*(P_t^*, P_t)$. Without the threat of an AD action the domestic and foreign firms simply maximize their discounted two-period profit. Letting δ denote the common discount factor we can write the domestic firm's problem as

$$\max_{\{P_1, P_2\}} \Pi = \Pi_1(P_1^*, P_1) + \delta \Pi_2(P_2^*, P_2) \tag{1}$$

and the foreign firm's problem as

$$\max_{\{P_1^*, P_2^*\}} \Pi^* = \Pi_1^*(P_1^*, P_1) + \delta \Pi_2^*(P_2^*, P_2) \tag{2}$$

In order to understand how AD law affects the firms' behavior we need to understand how AD law is implemented. GATT rules *require* that two criteria be satisfied before duties be levied, a LTFV determination and an injury determination. However, beyond specifying these criteria, GATT gives domestic governments considerable discretion in implementing the law. In some countries a single agency makes both determinations while in others have two agencies involved. For instance, in the U.S., the Department of Commerce makes the LTFV determination while the International Trade Commission makes the injury determination. In addition, the interpretation of what is meant by "injury" and the rules for calculating LTFV sales vary considerably from country to country, and even from case to case within a given country.[6] What is incorporated in this model, then, is broad characterization of distortions created by AD law, rather than any precise description of any particular country's implementation.

We will say that the foreign firm has sold at LTFV if its price in the domestic market during the first period is less than the "observed" home market price. In other words, LTFV sales are said to have occurred if $P_1 < P_H^*$, where P_H^* denotes the observed home market price (in domestic currency). The observed home market price may not equal the true home market price for a variety of reasons. For instance, in a world with flexible

---

6. Those interested in an excellent summary and cross-country comparison of AD procedures should consult Jackson and Vermulst [1989].

exchange rates there is considerable uncertainty over how currency conversion will affect the *ex post* home market price ⟨Leidy and Hoekman [1990]⟩. Or, as typically happens, adjustments are made to the home market price during the course of the LTFV determination. And, as discussed above, the commonly used "constructed value" method also gives rise to uncertainty over the home market price.

Our analysis of the strategic implications of AD law can be carried out most expeditiously if we assume that P_H^* is determined by a constructed value calculation. In section V we will discuss how the results change if we allow the foreign firm's home market pricing decision to influence P_H^*. At this point, however, we will assume that both the domestic and foreign firms know the general rules by which P_H^* is constructed but do not know P_H^* with certainty. In other words, the distribution governing P_H^*, $F(\cdot)$, is common knowledge. We also assume that $F(\cdot)$ is twice-continuously differentiable on support $[0, \bar{P}^*]$. Note that only the foreign firm can influence the LTFV decision.[7] By raising (lowering) the price it charges during the first period, the foreign firm can decrease (increase) the likelihood of a LTFV determination. While not explicitly modeled here, the upper-bound $\bar{P}^*$ can be thought of as a parameter which is set at some earlier stage of the policy-making process (*i.e.*, $\bar{P}^*$ is exogenous to the play of this game). For instance, in the U.S., $\bar{P}^*$ might be set by Congress when trade legislation is enacted. Over time, amendments to the statute might raise (or lower) the upper-bound.[8]

The probability of a LTFV determination can be written as

$$\rho^L(P_1^*) = \int_{P_1^*}^{\bar{P}^*} F'(x)dx.$$

Clearly, $\rho_1^L(\cdot) \equiv d\rho^L(\cdot)/dP_1^* \leq 0$.

An injury determination must also be made before duties can be levied. In general, many economic factors – profits, market share, employment, capacity utilization, *etc.* – are considered when determining injury; more-

---

7. If the firms competed in quantities, then the domestic firm could influence the LTFV decision by increasing its quantity sold. Fischer's [1991] model highlights the distortions created by the LTFV determination.

8. One sensible interpretation of $\bar{P}^*$ is the price that eliminates the foreign firm from the domestic market (*i.e.*, gives the domestic firm a monopoly).

over, the relative importance of each factor varies from year to year and from case to case.[9] However, the domestic firm's profit level is almost without fail an important element of the injury determination. For simplicity, we will say that the domestic firm has been injured if its profits fall below a specified level, Π^I. That is, injury will be said to have occurred if

$$\Pi_1(P_1^*, P_1) \leq \hat{\Pi}^I = \Pi^I + \mu. \tag{3}$$

The injury criterion specified in (3) establishes a minimum profit level. However, depending on factors beyond the firms' control – the political environment, the current makeup of the agency, the general state of the economy, *etc.* – the precise size of the minimum profit level will vary. In particular, we will assume that the random component of the injury decision is described by an additive stochastic term μ, which is drawn from a twice-continuously differentiable distribution $G(\cdot)$. We assume that $G(\cdot)$ is common knowledge and has zero mean.

Note that both firms can influence the injury determination *via* their ability to influence the size of the domestic firm's first period profit. We can express the probability that injury occurs as

$$\rho^I(\Pi_1(P_1^*, P_1); \ \Pi^I) = \int_{\Pi_1(P_1^*, P_1) - \Pi^I}^{\infty} G'(x)dx.$$

Let $\rho_1^I(\cdot) \equiv \partial \rho^I(\cdot)/\partial \Pi_1$ and note that $\rho_1^I(\cdot) \leq 0$. We will also assume that $\rho_{11}^I(\cdot) \equiv \partial^2 \rho^I(\cdot)/\partial \Pi_1^2 \leq 0$.

Given this set-up, the timing of the game with AD law is as follows: (1) The firms announce their first period prices, $\{P_1^*, P_1\}$. (2) First period sales, $\{Q_1^*, Q_1\}$, and profits, $\{\Pi_1^*, \Pi_1\}$, are realized. (3) If it desires, the domestic firm can initiate an AD investigation at a cost of C. If a petition is initiated, the foreign firm defends itself at cost C^*. (4) If a petition is initiated, the government determines whether or not both criteria are satisfied and announces its decision. (5) If dumping is found, a specific duty of $(P_H^* - P_1^*)$ is charged; the foreign firm collects only P_1^*. (GATT rules restrict the duty

---

9. Boltuck [1991] provides an excellent summary of the factors used by the U.S. International Trade Commission when determining injury.

to only be large enough to offset the LTFV margin.)[10] If dumping is not found, the firms announce their second period prices, $\{P_2^*, P_2\}$. (6) Second period sales, $\{Q_2^*, Q_2\}$, and profits, $\{\Pi_2^*, \Pi_2\}$, are realized.

III. Nash Equilibrium without Antidumping Law

The model developed in the previous section allows a simple characterization of Nash equilibrium without AD law. Without the threat of an AD investigation the firms' optimal strategy is simply to maximize their discounted two-period profit functions, as specified in (1) and (2), respectively. Hence, the firms simply maximize their profit on a period-by-period basis. We will assume that there exists a unique, stable Nash equilibrium in this benchmark scenario and that in equilibrium both firms' prices and output are strictly positive.[11] In particular, assume that profit functions are twice-continuously differentiable and strictly concave in their own price, and that the best response functions are contractions. Denote the domestic firm's best response function as $\beta(P_t^*)$, and let $\beta^*(P_t)$ denote the foreign firm's best response function. The Nash equilibrium is defined by the two-tuple $(\tilde{P}_t^*, \tilde{P}_t)$ which satisfies $\beta^*(\tilde{P}_t) = \tilde{P}_t^*$ and $\beta(\tilde{P}_t^*) = \tilde{P}_t$.

Figure 1 depicts the benchmark equilibrium. The best response function $\beta(P_t^*)$ defines the domestic firm's price that allows the highest iso-profit loci to be reached, given P_t^*. For instance, if the foreign firm charges $\tilde{P}_t^*$ the domestic firm's best response is $\tilde{P}_t = \beta(\tilde{P}_t^*)$, which generates profits of $\tilde{\Pi}_t = \Pi_t(\tilde{P}_t^*, \tilde{P}_t)$. The foreign firm's best response function, $\beta^*(P_t)$, can be interpreted in a similar fashion. In this simple Bertrand game, the reaction functions are positively sloped. That is, a price increase by the one competitor encourages a price increase by the other. The Nash equilibrium is at point N. The shaded region defines the prices which provide both firms with as least as great of profit as they earn under $\{\tilde{P}_t^*, \tilde{P}_t\}$.

---

10. The practice in the U.S. is to set the AD duty equal to the Department of Commerce's calculated dumping margin. In the EC, the AD duty is set equal to the lesser of the dumping margin and a duty sufficient to eliminate injury. It is only a minor extension to the current model to incorporate the EC's duty level.
11. Friedman [1983] discusses the sufficient conditions for these conditions to hold.

Figure 1
Bertrand-Nash Equilibrium – No AD Law

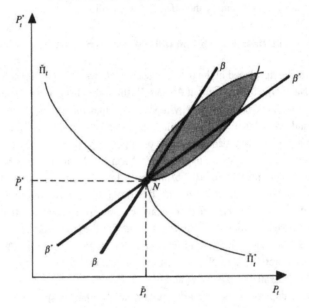

IV. Nash Equilibrium with Antidumping Law

In general, the threat of an AD action implies that the strategy of simply maximizing profit on a period-by-period basis will not be optimal; rather, the firms will want to incorporate their ability to influence expected second period profits in their first period decision.

Solving the model recursively, we begin by analyzing the second period pricing decisions. At the beginning of period two, firms know whether or not duties have been levied. If duties have not been levied, the firms' simply maximize second period profits, just as they did without AD law. Denote this equilibrium as $\{\tilde{P}_2, \tilde{P}_2\}$. In this case, the firms will earn profits $\Pi_2(\tilde{P}_2, \tilde{P}_2)$ and $\Pi_2^*(\tilde{P}_2, \tilde{P}_2)$, respectively. If, on the other hand, dumping duties have been imposed, the foreign firm's price is P_H^*. In this case, the domestic firm sets a price $P_H = \beta(P_H^*)$ and will earn profits $\Pi_2(P_H^*, \beta(P_H^*))$.

If injury is found, then the domestic firm's benefit from filing the AD action depends on the observed home market price, P_H^*. Let $\Delta(P_H^*)$ denote the domestic firm's gain when P_H^* is the calculated home market price,

$$\Delta(P_H^*) \equiv \Pi_2(P_H^*, \beta(P_H^*)) - \Pi_2(\tilde{P}_2^*, \tilde{P}_2) \tag{4}$$

Let $E\Delta(P_1^*)$ denote the expected gain to the domestic firm from an affirmative LTFV determination,

$$E\Delta(P_1^*) \equiv \int_{P_1^*}^{\tilde{P}^*} \Delta(x)F'(x)dx - C. \tag{5}$$

We will assume that $E\Delta(P_1^*) \geq 0$ (*i.e.*, the domestic firm expects to benefit from an affirmative LTFV decision).[12]

We can make similar definitions for the foreign firm. Recall that when dumping duties are levied the foreign firm collects only P_1^* per unit; $(P_H^* - P_1^*)$ is the specific duty. In other words, when dumping duties are levied the foreign firm will earn profits

$$\Pi_2^*(P_H^*, \beta(P_H^*)) - (P_H^* - P_1^*)Q_2^*(P_H^*, \beta(P_H^*)).$$

Let $\Delta^*(P_H^*)$ denote the foreign firm's loss when P_H^* is the calculated home market price, *i.e.*,

$$\Delta^*(P_H^*) \equiv \Pi_2^*(P_H^*, \beta(P_H^*)) - (P_H^* - P_1^*)Q_2^*(P_H^*, \beta(P_H^*)) - \Pi_2(\tilde{P}_2^*, \tilde{P}_2), \tag{6}$$

and let $E\Delta^*(P_1^*)$ denote the expected loss to the foreign firm from an affirmative LTFV determination (inclusive of costs of responding to the petition),

$$E\Delta^*(P_1^*) \equiv \int_{P_1^*}^{\tilde{P}^*} \Delta^*(x)F'(x)dx - C^*. \tag{7}$$

As long as the potential duty is sufficiently large (or as long as C^* is sufficiently large), $E\Delta^*(P_H^*) \leq 0$ (*i.e.*, the foreign firm will be hurt by an affirmative LTFV decision).

Given these definitions, we can write the (AD law-distorted) expected two-period profit functions as

$$E\Pi(P_1^*, P_1) = \Pi_1(P_1^*, P_1) + \delta(1 - \rho^I(\cdot))\Pi_2(\tilde{P}_2^*, \tilde{P}_2)$$

---

12. If C is sufficiently small and if $P_1^* \geq \tilde{P}_2^*$ then it must be the case that $E\Delta(P_1^*) \geq 0$. If, however, the foreign firm's first period price P_1^* is sufficiently low then it is possible that $E\Delta(P_1^*) < 0$. To expedite the presentation we are ruling out this possibility.

$$+ \delta \rho^1(\cdot) \left\{ \int_0^{P_1^*} \Pi_2(\tilde{P}_2^*, \tilde{P}_2) F'(x) dx + \int_{P_1^*}^{\overline{P}^*} \Pi_2(x, \beta(x)) F'(x) dx - C \right\}$$

$$= \Pi_1(P_1^*, P_1) + \delta \left\{ \Pi_2(\tilde{P}_2^*, \tilde{P}_2) + \rho^1(\cdot) E\Delta(P_1^*) \right\}, \qquad (8)$$

and

$$E\Pi(P_1^*, P_1) = \Pi_1^*(P_1^*, P_1) + \delta(1 - \rho^1(\cdot)) \Pi_2^*(\tilde{P}_2^*, \tilde{P}_2)$$

$$+ \delta \rho^1(\cdot) \left\{ \int_0^{P_1^*} \Pi_2^*(\tilde{P}_2^*, \tilde{P}_2) F'(x) dx \right.$$

$$\left. + \int_{P_1^*}^{\overline{P}^*} \left\{ \Pi_2^*(x, \beta(x)) - (x - P_1^*) Q_2^*(x, \beta(x)) \right\} F'(x) dx - C^* \right\}$$

$$= \Pi_1^*(P_1^*, P_1) + \delta \left\{ \Pi_2^*(\tilde{P}_2^*, \tilde{P}_2) + \rho^1(\cdot) E\Delta^*(P_1^*) \right\} \qquad (9)$$

As expressed in equation (8), at the beginning of period 1 the domestic firm's expected two-period profit is just the sum of first period profit, $\Pi_1(P_1^*, P_1)$, and expected second period profit, which is just the weighted sum of the profit when duties are not levied, $\Pi_2(\tilde{P}_2, \tilde{P}_2)$, and profit when duties are levied. After some rearranging, (8) can be written as the domestic firm's expected two-period profit without AD law plus the expected gain from AD law, $\delta \rho^1(\cdot) E\Delta(P_1^*)$. Similarly, the foreign firm's expected two-period profit, equation (8), can be expressed as its profit without AD law plus the expected loss from AD law, $\delta \rho^1(\cdot) E\Delta^*(P_1^*)$.

A. The Foreign Firm's Pricing Decision

We begin by looking at the foreign firm's decision. Differentiating (9) with respect to P_1^* yields

$$\frac{\partial E\Pi^*(\cdot)}{\partial P_1^*} = \frac{\partial \Pi_1^*(\cdot)}{\partial P_1^*} + \delta \left\{ \rho_1'(\cdot) \frac{\partial \Pi_1^*(\cdot)}{\partial P_1^*} E\Delta^*(P_1^*) - \rho^1(\cdot) \Delta^*(P_1^*) F'(P_1^*) \right\} = 0 \quad (10)$$

The first term on the right-hand side of (10) is the marginal change in first period profit while the bracketed expression on the right-hand side of (10) is the marginal change in second period profit. An increase in the first period price decreases the probability that dumping duties will be levied by lowering the probability of injury, $\rho_1'(.)$, and LTFV sales, $F'(P_1^*)$. Therefore, the bracketed expression is nonnegative.

Without AD law, the foreign firm maximizes its profit by setting $\partial\Pi_1^*(\cdot)/\partial P_1^* = 0$. In contrast, with AD law, (10) implies that the foreign firm maximizes profit by setting $\partial\Pi_1^*(\cdot)/\partial P_1^* \leq 0$. In other words, the foreign firm announces a higher first period price than it would without AD law. The foreign firm raises its first period price (relative to the no-AD law level) in order to decreased the probability that the domestic firm will be injured and also to decrease the probability of a LTFV determination. Although raising its first period price beyond its Nash level will lower its first period profit, for any given P_1, the foreign firm is willing to sacrifice first period profit in order to avoid a large profit loss in the second period.

Letting $\beta_d^*(P_1)$ denote the foreign firm's best response function with AD law, we have

Proposition 1: *For any given P_1, the foreign firm will prefer to announce a higher first period price with AD law than without AD law. That is, $\beta_d^*(P_1) \geq \beta^*(P_1)$.*

Figure 2 depicts how the threat of AD duties affects the foreign firm; its best response function, β_d^*, (the shaded curve) shifts up relative to the no-AD law best response function, β^* (the solid curve). From (10) we note that the shift will be larger (i) the greater the marginal decrease in the likelihood of duties and (ii) the more damaging duties will be. For example, $\beta_d^{*'}$ depicts a case when there is a more dramatic increase in the foreign firm's pricing strategy.

From (10) we also know

Corollary 1: *The threat of an AD action will have no effect on the foreign firm's behavior if the domestic firm charges a sufficiently high price. That is, $\beta_d^* = \beta^*$ if $\beta^*(P_1) > \bar{P}$.*

In other words, if the domestic firm charges a sufficiently high price, the foreign firm can charge its profit maximizing first period price, $\beta^*(P_1)$, since there is zero probability of dumping duties being levied (*i.e.*, $\rho^L = 0$). That is, AD law only distorts the foreign firm's behavior if there is some chance of a LTFV determination.

Thus, when $\bar{P}_1$ is relatively small AD law will not distort the foreign firm's

Figure 2
Best Responses – With AD Law

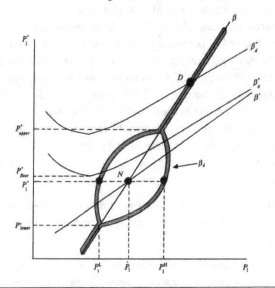

Note: Best response functions without AD law are solid curves;
Best response correspondences with AD law are shaded curves

pricing strategy. In general, however, we would expect AD law to have an effect on prices. In particular, AD law has significant effects on the foreign firm behavior at relatively low prices. In contrast to the best response function without AD law (which slopes upwards in price space) there is a region of price-space where the foreign firm finds it optimal to respond to lower domestic firm prices by *raising* its price. Formally,

Corollary 2: *AD law alters the strategic behavior of the foreign firm. In particular, for sufficiently small P_1 the foreign firm responds by raising its price when the domestic firm cuts its price. Formally, if $0 < \rho^I(\cdot) < 1$, then for P_1 sufficiently small, $\partial \beta_d^* / \partial P_1 \leq 0$.*

Following directly from this result is

Corollary 3: *AD law establishes a price floor for the foreign firm's product.*

Figure 3
Domestic Firm's Profit Function

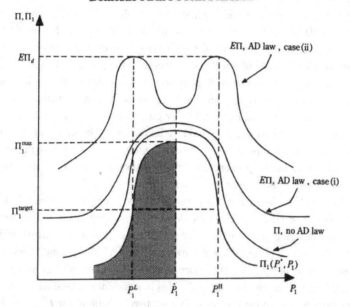

The intuition behind these corollaries is quite sensible. First note that this change in pricing strategy can only occur if the domestic firm is charging relatively low prices, *i.e.*, some $P_1 < \beta(P_1^*)$, *i.e.*, it can only occur in a region to the left of $\beta(P_1^*)$. In this region the domestic firm's first period profits are increasing in its own price. Figure 3, which depicts the *domestic* firm's profit given that the foreign firm sells at price P_1^*, shows why this is the case. The curve labeled $\Pi_1(P_1^*, P_1)$ graphs the domestic firm's strictly concave first period profit function for a given P_1^*. Prices and profits where $P_1 < \beta(P_1^*)$ are depicted by the shaded area in Figure 3.

Consider when the domestic firm charges $\hat{P}_1 \equiv \beta(P_1^*)$. At this price it earns first period profit of $\Pi_1^{max} = \Pi_1(P_1^*, \hat{P}_1)$, which by definition of β is the maximum possible first period profits, given P_1^*. Suppose instead that the domestic firm were charging some price in the shaded region, $P_1 < \hat{P}_1$. In this region, an increase in the domestic firm's price increases its first period profit. However, increasing the first period profit lowers the probability of an injury determination and this allows the foreign firm to be less concerned with an affirmative injury determination, giving the foreign firm an opportunity to focus more on maximizing first period profit (and less on injury).

Since AD law distorts the foreign firm's price upward, the foreign firm can consider lowering its AD-distorted price. However, the foreign firm must weigh the costs (the marginal increase in the probability of a LTFV decision) against the benefits (higher first period profit) from lowering its price. As is shown in the appendix, as P_1 becomes sufficiently small the benefits outweigh the costs, leading the foreign firm to respond to an increase in the domestic firm's price by lowering its own price. In other words, AD law changes the nature of the competition – there is a region where the foreign firm regards the products as strategic substitutes instead of strategic complements ⟨Bulow, Geanakoplos, and Klemperer [1985]⟩.

This result implies that AD law creates a price floor for the foreign firm. The price floor reflects the fact the domestic firm cannot dupe the foreign firm into dumping. Suppose this were not the case. The domestic firm could set its first period price sufficiently low and induce a LTFV finding with certainty because of the fact that the foreign firm will respond with its own low price. However, if the imposition of duties is sufficiently painful for the foreign firm, it will not fall prey to such a strategy; pricing below P^*_{floor} inordinately increases the likelihood of a dumping duties, and the foreign firm will instead prefer to sacrifice first period profits in order to avoid duties.

This is a sensible result and merits at least two comments. First, price floors have well known collusive implications since they clearly alter what prices the foreign firm can threaten to charge ⟨Salop [1986]⟩. Therefore, the creation of a price floor is one example of the potentially deleterious effects of AD law. Second, there has been substantial debate over the U.S.'s use of the Trigger Price Mechanism (TPM) between 1978-1982. Part of this discussion has centered on the effect of the explicit price floor established by the TPM. Note, however, that this result suggests that there is always an implicit price floor created by AD law.

B. The Domestic Firm's Pricing Decision

We can now turn to the domestic firm's problem. We solve for its optimal

276　　　Pricing Behavior in the Presence of Antidumping Law

pricing behavior by differentiating (8) with respect to P_1. The first order condition is

$$\frac{\partial E \Pi(\cdot)}{\partial P_1} = \frac{\partial \Pi_1(\cdot)}{\partial P_1} + \delta \rho_1^I(\Pi_1(\cdot); \Pi^I) \frac{\partial \Pi_1(\cdot)}{\partial P_1} E\Delta(P_1^*) = 0 \tag{11}$$

The first term in (11), $\partial \Pi_1(\cdot)/\partial P_1$, is the marginal change to first period profit while the second term is the marginal change to second period profit. The term $\delta E\Delta(P_1^*)$ represents the expected discounted gain to domestic firm's second period profit when dumping duties are imposed, while $\rho_1^I(\cdot)\partial \Pi_1(\cdot)/\partial P_1$, is the marginal increase in the probability that duties will be levied. Rearranging (11) yields

$$\frac{\partial E \Pi(\cdot)}{\partial P_1} = \frac{\partial \Pi_1(\cdot)}{\partial P_1} \Omega(\Pi_1(P_1^*, P_1); \Pi^1) = 0, \tag{11'}$$

where $\Omega(\cdot) = [1+\delta\rho_1^I(\cdot)E\Delta(P_1^*)]$ can be interpreted as the net effect of a price change on first and second period profit. It may be greater than, less than, or equal to zero. If $\Omega(\cdot) > 0$, the effect on first period profit dominates the effect on second period profit while if $\Omega(\cdot) < 0$, the converse is true. If $\Omega(\cdot) = 0$, the two effects exactly offset one another.

As before, let $\hat{P}_1 \equiv \beta(P_1^*)$ denote the price the domestic firm would charge without AD law. Note that by definition $\partial \Pi_1(P_1^*, \hat{P}_1)/\partial P_1 = 0$ which implies that (11') is satisfied at $\hat{P}_1$. Note also that (11') could be satisfied for some alternative $P_1 \neq \hat{P}_1$ as long as this alternative price implied $\Omega(\cdot) = 0$.

The second order condition will be useful for determining what pricing strategy is optimal. Differentiating (11') yields,

$$\frac{\partial^2 \Pi_1(\cdot)}{\partial P_1^2} \Omega(\cdot) + \delta \left\{ \frac{\partial \Pi_1(\cdot)}{\partial P_1} \right\}^2 \left[\rho_{11}^I(\cdot)E\Delta(P_1^*) \right]. \tag{12}$$

The first term in the first expression is the domestic firm's no-AD law second order condition and is less than zero while $\Omega(\cdot)$ reflects the net effect on first and second period profit. The final expression reflects the change in the marginal likelihood of injury.

From the first order condition it is clear that either $\partial \Pi_1(\cdot)/\partial P_1 = 0$ or $\Omega(\cdot) = 0$ (or both). As it turns out, by focusing on what happens at $\hat{P}_1$ we can determine what the domestic firm's optimal response is.

Case (i) – First Period Effect Dominates: $\Omega(\cdot) > 0$ at $\hat{P}_1$

In this case, (12) evaluated at $\hat{P}_1$ simplifies to

$$\frac{\partial^2 \Pi_1(\cdot)}{\partial P_1^2} \Omega(\cdot) < 0,$$

implying a maximum at $\hat{P}_1$. Moreover, at any alternative $P_1 \neq \hat{P}_1$, $\Omega(\cdot) > 0$. Therefore, $\hat{P}_1$ is the unique maximum.

In this case the domestic firm maximizes profit by announcing price $\hat{P}_1$, just as it did without AD law. This result is easier to understand if one realizes that $\Omega(\cdot) > 0$ evaluated at $\hat{P}_1$ implies that the domestic firm's AD law-distorted objective, $E\Pi$, reaches its maximum at $\hat{P}_1$ and is globally concave. This case is depicted in Figure 3 by the curve labeled "$E\Pi$, case (i)". Not only is this function globally concave but it also lies everywhere above the domestic firm's expected two-period profit without AD law, Π.

Case (ii) – Second Period Effect Dominates: $\Omega(\cdot) < 0$ at $\hat{P}_1$

In this case, the second order condition implies a minimum at $\hat{P}_1$. In other words, the domestic firm's objective, $E\Pi$, is no longer globally concave. The threat of AD duties distorts the profit function because the potential gain from having AD duties levied is so great that the domestic firm seeks to increase the likelihood of an injury determination. Therefore, even though first period profits are maximized at $\hat{P}_1$ the firm does not choose this price since it minimizes the chance of an affirmative injury determination. This case is also depicted in Figure 3 by the curve labeled "$E\Pi$, case (ii)".

In this case, the domestic firm will deliberately lower its first period profit in order to increase the likelihood of having duties levied. It does this by choosing a target level for its first period profit. This target profit level will be chosen in order to balance the marginal loss to first period profit with the marginal gain to second period profit. Let Π_1^{target} denote the target profit level,

$$\Pi_1^{target} = \{\Pi \mid \Omega(\Pi; \Pi^I) = 0\}. \tag{13}$$

The strict concavity of $\Pi_1(\cdot)$ implies that the domestic firm can achieve its target profit by charging a price that is either lower or higher than $\hat{P}_1$. Let P_1^L and P_1^H denote these alternative prices where $P_1^L < \hat{P}_1 < P_1^H$. Formally, P_1^L and P_1^H satisfies

$$\{P_1 \mid \Omega(\Pi_1(P_1^*, P_1); \Pi^I) = 0\}.$$

At P_1^L and P_1^H the second order condition simplifies to

$$\delta \left\{ \frac{\partial \Pi_1(\cdot)}{\partial P_1} \right\}^2 \left[\rho_{11}'(\cdot) E\Delta(P_1^*) \right] < 0.$$

Thus, both P_1^H and P_1^L are local maximums.

Figure 3 depicts the target level of profit, Π_1^{target}, and the prices, P_1^L and P_1^H, that achieve the target. As discussed, the domestic firm's objective function has two maximums but both yield the identical level of profit, $E\Pi_d$. This must be the case since with either price the firm earns the same expected first period profit, Π_1^{target}, and therefore with either price the firm has the same probability of injury. Note however, that P_1^L and P_1^H need not be symmetric about P_1.

Case (iii) – Offsetting Effects: $\Omega(\cdot) = 0$ at $\hat{P}_1$

In this case $\hat{P}_1$ maximizes first period profit and also equalizes the effect on first and second period profit. This also implies that (12) is zero. However, the concavity of $\Pi_1(\cdot)$ implies that $\hat{P}_1$ uniquely solves (11) and maximizes $\Pi(\cdot)$. Therefore, in this case, $\hat{P}_1$ uniquely solves the domestic firm's maximization problem with AD law. The domestic firm's profit function in this case looks similar to the profit function in case (i) in Figure 3.

Summarizing the Domestic Firm's Best Response

Clearly, the domestic firm's best response will depend on whether the first or second period effect dominates. Moreover, the interpretation of the effect of the threat of an AD action varies considerably depending whether the first or second period effect dominates. If the first period effect dominates, the domestic firm does not alter its pricing strategy in order to gain a strategic legal advantage. If, on the other hand, the second period effect dominates, the domestic firm will strategically lower its first period profit in the hope of later winning proving injury, and thus having duties levied against its foreign rival. In this case, we will say the domestic firm feigns injury (or experiences "spurious" injury) since it undertakes actions that decrease its profit.

It is straightforward to show that

Corollary 4: *The domestic firm is more likely to feign injury (i) the larger is the discount factor, (ii) the larger is the benefit from duties, and (iii) the larger is the probability of a LTFV determination.*

The foreign firm also critically influences whether the domestic firm alters its period-by-period profit maximizing behavior. In particular, consider when the foreign firm charges an extremely high first period price. In this case, the domestic firm need not change its behavior since not only does it earn close to monopoly profit in the first period, but it is also highly unlikely that there will be an affirmative LTFV determination. Alternatively, consider when the foreign firm charges a very low first period price. Once again, in this case the domestic firm will simply maximize its first period profit since the foreign firm's unduly low first period price implies that affirmative injury and LTFV determinations will almost certainly follow. Taken together, it is clear that the more extreme the foreign firm prices the more likely will case (i) be the relevant situation. On the other hand, consider when the foreign firm charges an "intermediate" first period price. In this case, whether the first or second period effect dominates depends crucially on the policy parameters. For instance, if the injury level of profit is inordinately high (or low) then there will be no incentive to deviate from the no-AD law behavior. Or, if the AD rules make it particularly difficult to show LTFV then there will once again be no incentive to deviate from the no-AD law behavior. In general, however, we can expect that there will be some range of prices which cause the domestic firm to change its pricing behavior.

In particular, domestic firm changes its behavior depends on the value of $\Omega(\cdot)$ along the no-AD law best response function. Letting P^*_{upper} and P^*_{lower} be defined by

$$\left\{ P^*_1 \mid 1 + \delta\rho^I(\Pi_1(P^*_1,\beta(P^*_1);\Pi^I)E\Delta(P^*_1) = 0, \ 0 \le P^*_1 \le \overline{P}^*_1 \right\},$$

280   Pricing Behavior in the Presence of Antidumping Law

we have

Corollary 5: *If* $P^*_{lower} \le P^*_1 \le P^*_{upper}$ *the domestic firm will feign injury.*

We can now graph the domestic firm's best response correspondence. In Figure 2, the domestic firm's best response function without AD law, β, is depicted as a solid curve. For a given injury level, P^*_{upper} defines the foreign price above which the domestic firm will not choose to deviate from its no-AD law pricing behavior. Similarly, P^*_{lower} defines the foreign price below which the domestic firm will choose to not deviate from its no-AD law pricing behavior. That is, if $P^* \ge P^*_{upper}$ or $P^* \le P^*_{lower}$ then $\beta_d(P^*) = \beta(P^*)$. In other words, the first period effect dominates and case (i) is relevant. If, on the other hand, $P^*_{lower} < P^* < P^*_{upper}$ then the effect on second period profit dominates and domestic firm will choose to deviate from its no-AD law pricing strategy. For any price in this range, the domestic firm will be indifferent between two possible prices. For instance, as depicted in Figure 2 suppose that the foreign firm charges P^*_1. The domestic firm would charge $\hat{P}_1$ if maximizing first period profit were the optimal choice. However, at this price the domestic firm prefers to increase the likelihood of an injury determination, and thus, will be indifferent between charging P^L_1 or P^H_1. Therefore, the domestic firm's best response correspondence bifurcates in this range. Taking the entire price range into account, the domestic firm's best response correspondence, β_d, is depicted by the shaded line in Figure 2.

We can summarize this discussion as follows.

Proposition 2: *Suppose the foreign firm charges* P^*_1. *Let* $\hat{P}_1 = \beta(P^*_1)$ *denote the price the domestic firm would charge without AD law. The domestic firm's best response with AD law,* $\beta_d(P^*_1)$, *can be defined as*

$$\beta_d(P^*_1) = \begin{cases} \beta(P^*_1), & \text{if } [1 + \delta\rho^I_1(\cdot)E\Delta(P^*_1)] \ge 0 \text{ evaluated at } \hat{P}_1, \\ \{P_1 \mid [1 + \delta\rho^I_1(\cdot)E\Delta(P^*_1)] = 0\}, & \text{otherwise .} \end{cases}$$

Figure 4 depicts the equilibria with AD law. If the foreign firm's response is large, say β^*_d, then the domestic firm will not find it in its best interest to deviate from its simple period-by-period profit maximizing behavior. In this case, the AD law equilibrium is depicted by the point D. In this equilibrium,

Figure 4
Bertrand-Nash Equilibrium – With AD Law

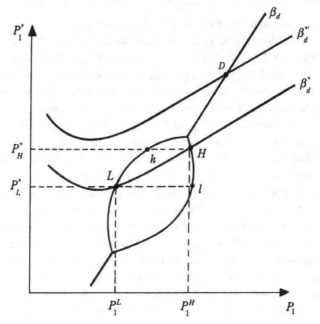

both firms charge higher first period prices than without AD law, but the price increases are driven entirely by the foreign firm's change in behavior. The domestic firm is only moving along its response curve, and therefore we should not interpret the change in the domestic price as a reflection of strategic manipulation of AD law.

If, on the other hand, the foreign firm's response is more moderate, say β_d^*, then the domestic firm may find it desirable to deviate from its period-by-period profit maximizing behavior. In this case, the domestic firm may change its first period behavior in order to induce an affirmative injury determination. For instance, for β_d^* there are two Nash equilibria depicted by the points L and H. When the foreign firm charges P_L^* the domestic firms is indifferent between two prices L and l. However, only L is a Nash equilibrium. At the L equilibrium, the domestic firm strategically attempts to lower first period profit by charging a lower first period price than it would charge

282   Pricing Behavior in the Presence of Antidumping Law

without AD law. Similarly, when the foreign firm charges P'_H the domestic firm is indifferent between two prices h and H, with only H being a Nash equilibrium. At the H equilibrium, the domestic firm strategically attempts to lower first period profit by charging a *higher* first period price than it would charge without AD law.

Interestingly, relative to their no-AD law level of profits, both firms may prefer to compete with the threat of an AD action. In other worlds, the AD law equilibrium at point H may lie in the shaded region in Figure 1. Without AD law, both firms' profits suffer because of the incentive to undercut their rival's price. With AD law, the simple price-cutting motive is only one part of the firms' decision: the desire for high current period profit must be balanced with the goal of high profit next period. Interestingly, even though both firms' strategies suggest they are willing to sacrifice short-run profit for long-term benefits, both firms can earn higher first period profit. In this sense, AD law facilitates collusive behavior.

Note, however, that even if H is a facilitating practice equilibrium, we can not eliminate L as a Nash equilibrium since L might "risk dominate" H. Suppose for example that the price-high equilibrium (H) yields both firms greater profit than the price-low equilibrium (L). From a Pareto dominance perspective, H is the more reasonable equilibria. However, L might be the more reasonable of the two equilibria from a risk dominance perspective ⟨Harsanyi and Selten [1998]⟩. That is, both firms know there are two equilibria. The domestic firm knows that there is some chance (maybe quite small) that the foreign firm will play L and some chance it will play H. The cost (in terms of foregone profit) may quite large if the domestic firm mistakenly conjectures H will be played when in fact L is played. However, the cost may relatively small if the converse happens (*i.e.*, the domestic firm mistakenly conjectures L will be played when in fact H is played). Thus, according to Harsanyi and Selten's [1998] theory of risk dominance, L may be the more reasonable equilibria.

V. Extensions

In this section we demonstrate how the foreign firm's home market pricing decision can be incorporated into the model and show that the equilibria

Economic Effects of Antidumping

do not qualitatively change from that discussed in section IV. To keep this extension as consistent as possible with the analysis in the previous sections, we will use primes to refer to the equations that change with the addition of the home market pricing decision.

We now imagine that the foreign firm sells its product in both its home market and in the domestic market. A prohibitive tariff gives the foreign firm monopoly control at home. Hence, the foreign firm charges P^*_{Ht} and earns $\Pi^H_t(P^*_{Ht})$ in its home market during period t. Thus, the foreign firm's objective function without AD law can be written as

$$\underset{\{P^*_{H1},P^*_1,P^*_{H2},P^*_2\}}{\text{Max}} \Pi^* = \Pi^H_1(P^*_{H1})+\Pi^*_1(P^*_1,P_1)+\delta\{\Pi^H_2(P^*_{H2})+\Pi^*_2(P^*_2,P_2)\}. \quad (2')$$

As before, we will assume that there is a unique equilibrium in the no-AD law case.

With home market sales, we might expect the LTFV calculation to be based upon a comparison of P^*_1 and P^*_{H1}. As discussed in section II there is significant amount of uncertainty surrounding the LTFV decision, and this is true even if the LTFV determination is based on a price comparison. We will say that the foreign firm has sold at LTFV if its price in the domestic market during the first period is less than the "observed" home market price (in domestic currency), $\hat{P}^*_{H1}$. In other words, the foreign firm is considered to have LTFV sales if

$$P^*_1 < \hat{P}^*_{H1} = P^*_{H1} + \varepsilon,$$

where ε captures the uncertainty surrounding the LTFV determination. We will assume that the distribution governing ε, $H(\cdot)$ is common knowledge and twice-continuously differentiable. We can write the probability of a LTFV determination as

$$\rho^L(P^*_1) = \int_{P^*_1-P^*_{H1}}^{\infty} H'(x)\,dx.$$

It is convenient if we reformulate some definitions made earlier in section IV. Let $\Delta(\hat{P}^*_{H1})$ now be defined as

$$\Delta(\hat{P}^*_{H1}) \equiv \Pi_2(\hat{P}^*_{H1},\beta(\hat{P}^*_{H1}))-\Pi_2(\bar{P}^*_2,\bar{P}_2), \quad (4')$$

and $E\Delta(P_1^*, P_{H1}^*)$ as

$$E\Delta(P_1^*, P_{H1}^*) \equiv \int_{P_1^* - P_{H1}^*}^{\infty} \Delta(P_{H1}^* + x) H'(x)\, dx - C. \tag{5'}$$

Let $\Delta^*(\hat{P}_{H1}^*)$ be redefined as

$$\Delta^*(\hat{P}_{H1}^*) \equiv \Pi_2^*(\hat{P}_{H1}^*, \beta(\hat{P}_{H1}^*)) - (\hat{P}_{H1}^* - P_1^*) Q_2^*(\hat{P}_{H1}^*, \beta(\hat{P}_{H1}^*))$$
$$- \Pi_2^*(\tilde{P}_2^*, \tilde{P}_2), \tag{6'}$$

And $E\Delta^*(P_1^*, P_{H1}^*)$ as

$$E\Delta^*(P_1^*, P_{H1}^*) \equiv \int_{P_1^* - P_{H1}^*}^{\infty} \Delta^*(P_{H1}^* + x) H'(x)\, dx - C^*. \tag{7'}$$

Given these definitions, we can now write the domestic firm's expected two-period profit as

$$E\Pi(P_1^*, P_1) = \Pi_1(P_1^*, P_1) + \delta\left\{ \Pi_2(\tilde{P}_2^*, \tilde{P}_2) + \rho^I(\cdot) E\Delta^*(P_1^*, P_{H1}^*) \right\}, \tag{8'}$$

and the foreign firm's expected two-period profit as

$$E\Pi^*(P_{H1}^*, P_1^*, P_{H2}^*, P_2^*) = \Pi_1^H(P_{H1}^*) + \Pi_1^*(P_1^*, P_1) + \delta\Pi_2^H(P_{H2}^*)$$
$$+ \delta\left\{ \Pi_2^*(\tilde{P}_2^*, \tilde{P}_2) + \rho^I(\cdot) E\Delta^*(P_1^*, P_{H1}^*) \right\} \tag{9'}$$

It is clear from (8') that the adding home market sales does not alter the domestic firm's incentives. However, the LTFV determination is now based on both P_1^* and P_{H1}^*, and the foreign firm will find it desirable to alter both prices. In particular, the foreign firm's first order conditions can be written as

$$\frac{\partial E\Pi^*(\cdot)}{\partial P_1^*} = \frac{\partial \Pi_1^*(\cdot)}{\partial P_1^*} + \delta\left\{ \rho_1^I(\cdot) \frac{\partial \Pi_1(\cdot)}{\partial P_1^*} E\Delta^*(P_1^*, P_{H1}^*) \right.$$
$$\left. - \rho^I(\cdot)\Delta^*(P_1^*) H'(P_1^* - P_{H1}^*) \right\} = 0 \tag{14}$$

$$\frac{\partial E\Pi^*(\cdot)}{\partial P_{H1}^*} = \frac{\partial \Pi_1^H(\cdot)}{\partial P_{H1}^*} + \delta\rho^1(\cdot)\left\{ \Delta^*(P_1^*) H'(P_1^* - P_{H1}^*) \right.$$
$$\left. + \int_{P_1^* - P_{H1}^*}^{\infty} \frac{\partial \Delta^*(P_{H1}^* + x)}{\partial P_{H1}^*} H'(x)\, dx \right\} = 0 \tag{15}$$

Equation (14) has the exactly the same form and interpretation as (10); both imply that the foreign firm will raise its price to the domestic market. Equation (15) reflects the effect on profits of a marginal change in P^*_{H1}. Without AD law, the foreign firm simply maximizes home market profits by setting the first term, $\partial \Pi^H_1(\cdot)/\partial P^*_{H1}$ equal to zero. With AD law the foreign firm must balance its desire to maximize home market profit with the incentive to decrease the likelihood of having duties levied. The curly bracketed expression in (15) is negative which implies that the foreign firm will lower the price it charges in its home market.

These is a sensible result. When the LTFV determination is based on the difference $P^*_1 - \hat{P}^*_{H1}$, the foreign firm will in general find it optimal to change both prices, raising P^*_1 and lowering P^*_{H1}. It is clear, then, that for any given P_1, the foreign firm will charge a higher price in the domestic market with AD law than it does without AD law, and thus qualitatively, the equilibria in the domestic market with AD law will be the same as the equilibria discussed in section IV.

This discussion leads us to the following proposition.

Proposition 3: *In a model where the foreign firm has home market sales, AD law induces the foreign firm to (i) announce a higher first period price in the domestic market, for any given P_1, and (ii) announce a lower first period price in the home market.*

VI. Concluding Comments

This paper has presented a model of the effect of domestic AD law on the noncooperative behavior of foreign and domestic rivals. In contrast with most of the previous literature, we have focused on the welfare effects of AD law prior to the filing of an AD action. We have shown that AD law has significant effects even if duties are never levied. First, the foreign firm responds to the law by raising its first period price in order to decrease the chance of LTFV determination and to increase the domestic firm's profit, thereby decreasing the likelihood of an injury determination. This is the intended effect of the law. Second, AD law may distort the domestic firm's pricing decision. In many circumstances, AD will not distort the domestic

286 Pricing Behavior in the Presence of Antidumping Law

firm's strategy, *i.e.*, case (i). In this case, AD raises the domestic firm's price only because it finds it optimal to respond to its rival's higher price by raising its own price. In other words, there is no strategic manipulation of the law.

In other circumstances, however, the domestic firm can have an important marginal impact on the injury determination. In this case, the domestic firm will strategically lower its profits in order to increase the likelihood of an affirmative decision: smaller profits today means a greater chance of an affirmative injury determination and larger profits tomorrow. The domestic firm deliberately injures itself in order to reap the benefits of protection tomorrow. This strategic response involves a distortion to domestic prices. The distortion can either raise or lower prices.

There are several comments to make regarding the robustness of the results. First, unlike many game theoretic models, the choice of strategic variable does not plays an overly important role in the nature of the equilibrium. Although the equilibria will differ under Cournot competition, the two key insights of the model – that the domestic firm has incentives to injury itself and that AD law can lead to collusive outcomes – would be robust to such a change. Moreover, if the injury determination continues to be a function of domestic profits, there will continue to be a region where the domestic firm chooses not to deviate from its no-AD law quantity strategies. And, when it does deviate, the distortion can again involve either increasing or decreasing its quantity.

Second, in practice other factors, such as employment, shipments, investment, *etc.* are often incorporated into the injury decision, which might lead us to broaden how we model the injury criterion.[13] In general, changing the injury criterion will not only alter the domestic firm's response, but also change how and when the domestic firm chooses to respond. For instance, if the domestic firm's investment is a part of the injury criterion, then the domestic firm will clearly choose to decrease its current period investment. Such strategic under-investment can have drastic welfare consequences, especially if protection is not granted.[14] Shipments are also often used to

---

13. It is not obvious, however, that the weight attached to these criteria is done in any consistent way.

determine the status of the domestic industry. Typically, one would expect a decrease in shipments to reflect injury. This suggests that the "price low" strategy might be dominated by the "price high" strategy, and thus that the bifurcation result to be eliminated. However, if the LTFV determination is based on the "sales below cost" definition, then the domestic firm may prefer the "price low" strategy. Without more extensive model development, it seems possible that either strategy could dominate.

All in all, the results of the model appear quite intuitive and have important policy implications. Due largely to the historical preeminence of tariffs and quotas, analysts have tended to focus only on the effects of trade policy once the duty/restriction was imposed. Given the emergence of administered protection, it especially important for trade theorists to examine not only the administered outcome but also the incentive to influence the outcome. This paper suggests, for instance, that since government's use standard economic criteria (*e.g.*, profits, employment, capital utilization, *etc.*) to assess injury, they should try to separate the avoidable injury (due to suboptimal firm decisions) from injury due to foreign competition.

Appendix
Proof of Corollaries 2 and 3

The slope of the foreign firm's best response function is

$$\frac{d\beta_d^*}{dP_1} = -\frac{-\partial^2 E\Pi^* / \partial P_1^* \partial P_1}{\partial^2 E\Pi^* / \partial P_1^{*2}}.$$

The denominator is merely the second order condition and is less than zero. The numerator can be rewritten as

$$-\frac{\partial^2 E\Pi^*}{\partial P_1^* \partial P_1} = \frac{\partial^2 \Pi_1^*(\cdot)}{\partial P_1^* \partial P_1} + \delta\left\{\frac{\partial \Pi_1(\cdot)}{\partial P_1}\left[\rho_{11}^I(\cdot)\frac{\partial \Pi_1(\cdot)}{\partial P_1^*}E\Delta^*(P_1^*) - \rho_1^I(\cdot)\Delta^*(P_1^*)F'(P_1^*)\right]\right\}$$

$$+ \delta\left\{\rho_1^I(\cdot)\frac{\partial^2 \Pi_1(\cdot)}{\partial P_1^* \partial P_1}E\Delta^*(P_1^*)\right\}$$

---

14. Krugman [1982] discusses the important dynamic effect current investment strategies play in long-run profitability.

The first and last terms are positive. However, note that the square bracketed expression is negative; for $P_1 < \beta^*$ the curly bracketed expression is negative since $\partial\Pi_1/\partial P_1 > 0$. The strict concavity of Π_1 implies that for P_1 sufficiently small, $\partial^2 E\Pi^*/\partial P_1^*\partial P_1$ will become negative. The continuity of all functions implies corollary 3.

References

Bhagwati, Jagdish [1988], *Protectionism*, Cambridge: The MIT Press.

Boltuck, Richard [1991], "Assessing the Effects on the Domestic Industry of Price Dumping," in P.K.M. Tharakan (ed.), *Policy Implications of Antidumping Measures*, Amsterdam: North-Holland.

Boltuck, Richard and Robert E. Litan [1991], *Down in the Dumps*, Washington, D.C.: The Brookings Institution.

Bulow, Jeremy I., John D. Geanakoplos, and Paul D. Klemperer [1985], "Multimarket Oligopoly: Strategic Substitutes and Complements," *Journal of Political Economy* 93; 488-511.

Finger, J.M. [1981], "The Industry-Country Incidence of LFV Cases in U.S. Import Trade," *Quarterly Review of Economics and Business*; 260-279.

Finger, J.M., H. Keith Hall, and Douglas R. Nelson [1982], "The Political Economy of Administered Protection," *American Economic Review* 72; 452-466.

Fischer, Ronald D. [1992], "Endogenous Probability of Protection and Firm Behavior," *Journal of International Economics* 32; 149-163.

Friedman, James [1983], *Oligopoly Theory*, Cambridge: Cambridge University Press.

Hansen, Wendy L. and Thomas J. Prusa [1993], "The Road Most Traveled: The Rise of Title VII Protection," unpublished manuscript, S.U.N.Y. at Stony Brook.

Harsanyi, John C. and Reinhard Selten [1988], A *General Theory of Equilibrium Selection in Games*, Cambridge: The MIT Press.

Hartigan, James C. [1993a], "Dumping and Signaling," forthcoming *Journal of Economic Behavior and Organization*.

Hartigan, James C. [1993b], "Collusive Aspects of Cost Revelation through Antidumping Complaints," unpublished manuscript, University of

Oklahoma.

Herander, Mark G. and J. Brad Schwartz [1984], "An Empirical Test of the Impact of the Threat of U.S. Trade Policy: The Case of Antidumping Duties," *Southern Economic Journal* 51; 59-79.

Hoekman, Bernard M. and Michael, P. Leidy [1989], "Dumping, Antidumping, and Emergency Protection," *Journal of World Trade Law* 23; 27-44.

Jackson, John H. and Edwin A. Vermulst [1989], *Antidumping Law and Practice*, Ann Arbor: University of Michigan Press.

Krugman, Paul [1982], "Import Competition as Export Promotion: International Competition in the Presence of Oligopoly and Economies of Scale," in H. Kierzkowski (ed.), *Monopolistic Competition and International Trade*, Oxford: Clarendon Press.

Leidy, Michael P. [1993], "Quid Pro Quo Restraint and Spurious Injury: Subsidies and the Prospect of CVDs," in Alan Deardorff and Robert Stern (eds.), *Analytical and Negotiating Issues in the Global Trading System*, Ann Arbor: University of Michigan.

Leidy, Michael P. and Bernard M. Hoekman [1990], "Production Effects of Price- and Cost-based Antidumping Laws under Flexible Exchange Rates", *Canadian Journal of Economics* 23; 873-895.

Prusa, Thomas J. [1993], "Why are so Many Antidumping Petitions Withdrawn?," *Journal of International Economics* 33; 1-20.

Salop, S.C. [1986], "Practices that (Credibly) Facilitate Oligopoly Coordination," in J. Stiglitz and G.F. Matthewson (eds.), *New Developments in the Analysis of Market Structure*, Cambridge: The MIT Press.

Staiger, Robert W. and Frank A. Wolak [1991], "Strategic Use of Antidumping Lwa to Enforce Tacit International Collusion," unpublished manuscript, Stanford University.

Tharakan, P.K.M., (ed.) [1991], *Policy Implications of Antidumping Measures*, Amsterdam: North-Holland.

Webb, Michael A. [1992], "The Ambiguous Consequences of Antidumping Law," *Economic Inquiry* 30; 437-448.

Chapter 6

DUMPING AND DOUBLE CROSSING: THE (IN)EFFECTIVENESS OF COST-BASED TRADE POLICY UNDER INCOMPLETE INFORMATION*

BY DOBRIN R. KOLEV AND THOMAS J. PRUSA[1]

*Union Square Associates, Inc., U.S.A.; and
Rutgers University and NBER, U.S.A.*

We argue that the rise of antidumping protection and the proliferation of voluntary export restraints (VERs) are fundamentally interrelated. We show that both can be explained by a cost-based definition of dumping when the domestic government has incomplete information about the foreign firm's costs. Given that its costs are only imperfectly observed and knowing the government's incentives to protect, efficient foreign firms will voluntarily restrain their exports prior to the antidumping investigation. In turn, the VER distorts the government's perception of the foreign firm's efficiency and leads to undesirably high duties regardless of the foreign firm's efficiency.

1. INTRODUCTION

In this article, we show that the two most widely given explanations for the rise of protection over the past 20 years—antidumping (AD) protection and voluntary export restraints (VERs)—are fundamentally interrelated.[2] We argue that VERs are a natural consequence of cost-based AD legislation. Specifically, when governments implement cost-based AD under incomplete information about foreign costs, foreign firms undertake VERs in an attempt to convince domestic authorities that they are not competitive threats. In fact, we show that although cost-based AD raises welfare under complete information, the distortions inherent with implementing it under incomplete information make it an undesirable policy.

Three important institutional characteristics of AD law motivate our approach. First, cost-based AD petitions have become "the dominant feature of U.S. antidumping law" (Horlick, 1989, p. 136). Traditionally, dumping was defined as

*Manuscript received January 1999; revised May 2000.

[1] We would like to thank the seminar participants at Princeton University, Columbia University, and Syracuse University and also Kyle Bagwell, Pradeep Dubey, John Hillas, Rich McLean, and Daijiro Okada for their many helpful comments and discussions. The paper also benefited greatly from the comments of three anonymous referees. E-mail: *dkolev@unionsq.biz* and *prusa@ econ.rutgers.edu.*

[2] Almost 10 percent of U.S. imports were covered by antidumping orders in 1990, almost triple the coverage in 1980. During the same period, the number of VERs doubled (Krueger, 1995; Low, 1993).

*This article originally appeared in *International Economic Review*, **43**, pp. 895–918.

international price discrimination, but in 1974 the definition was broadened to include sales below cost. According to Clarida (1996), since 1980 between one-half and two-thirds of U.S. AD cases have been conducted using the cost-based definition of dumping.[3] Not coincidentally, Bhagwati (1988) and Krueger (1995) both date the rapid increase in high-track (VERs) and low-track (AD duties) restraints to the mid-1970s. From this perspective, if one seeks to understand the rise of AD protection and the proliferation of VERs, cost-based AD policy is a sensible place to start.

Second, governments implement cost-based dumping under incomplete information. Under cost-based dumping, the domestic government estimates the foreign firm's production costs and then constructs an AD duty designed to insure that the exporter's price is "fair." Not surprisingly, the ambiguous nature of estimating the foreign firm's costs is the source of numerous complaints. Foreign defendants often claim that estimated costs have nothing to do with their actual costs. Rules such as the use of "best information available," which bases the cost estimate on the *domestic* firm's estimate of foreign costs, and *ad hoc* methods such as basing cost estimates on third market surrogates make AD procedures quite capricious.

Third, foreign firms often undertake VERs prior to any AD investigation hoping to appease domestic cries for protection. For instance, the 1981 automobile VER, perhaps the best-known VER, was negotiated under the threat of an AD action. Similarly, many of the steel restraints undertaken in the mid-1980s were negotiated under the threat of imminent AD action. Krueger (1995, p. 35) states that "*threats* of administered protection have induced trading partners to accept other bilateral measures, such as VERs" (emphasis added). A senior negotiator in the semiconductor dispute stated that the U.S. industry used "the *threat* of the dumping case to stimulate broad negotiations on all aspects of the problem" (Prestowitz, 1988, p. 196, emphasis added). Recently it was noted that the "threat of U.S. antidumping duties" caused U.S. steel imports to sharply fall (Lawrence, 1999, p. 9). In all of these cases, the VER was conceived of as a "pressure-release valve," where foreign firms reduce exports until protectionist sentiments subside.[4]

The starting point for our analysis is the long understood insight that governments have an incentive to implement cost-contingent protection (Brander and Spencer, 1984). We interpret cost-based AD as a GATT/WTO-sanctioned vehicle for implementing a cost-contingent tariff policy. Although this interpretation of cost-based procedures differs from GATT guidelines, many Department of Commerce (DOC) decisions are so perplexing that our interpretation is a plausible view of how AD is implemented in practice (Boltuck and Litan, 1991).

---

[3] Note also that the European Community (EC), the other major user of AD, has similarly embraced cost-based methodology. Messerlin (1989) estimates that over 90 percent of EC cases against developing countries are based on constructed costs.

[4] The view that AD actions are often motivated to restrain imports rather than offset unfair trade is widely held. In describing the United States' reluctance to amend AD rules, it was reported that "antidumping is the most convenient way of controlling the influx of low-priced goods" (*Korea Times*, 11/26/1999) In fact, the U.S. Trade Representative conceded that "antidumping rules are not intended as a remedy for predatory pricing practices." (*New Republic*, 11/01/1999, p. 16). Another expert estimated that "95 percent of AD investigations initiated resulted from irregular trade volume and only 5 percent due to pricing irregularities" (*The Nation*, 09/07/1999).

We also suppose that the home government cannot observe the foreign firm's costs; we show that this induces the foreign firm to announce a VER in order to signal its (in)efficiency in an attempt to reduce the size of the potential duty. Interestingly, as is often the case in practice, we find that the VER fails to release the protectionist pressures, and domestic industries clamor for more protection. A review of AD cases suggests that preemptive export restraints have only had mixed success at averting AD investigations. As a noted AD expert stated, VERs "have certainly been instrumental in preventing a number of antidumping proceedings from arising, but (they are not) ... a substitute for relief" (Bellis, 1989, p. 54).

Our approach differs from Harris (1985) and Krishna (1989), who emphasize the collusive and cartel-enhancing features of VERs.[5] Although the facilitating practice explanation is a powerful ex post justification for VERs, we have found no evidence that collusion was the original motivation for a VER at the outset of any trade dispute.

Our article complements the recent work by Yano (1989), Anderson (1992), and Rosendorff (1996). Yano's and Anderson's models show that the expectation of a VER can intensify competition. Rosendorff assumes that the domestic government has a political incentive to increase the profits of the domestic firm and hence, is willing to offer a lower AD duty in return for a VER.[6] Our article also complements a growing body of work incorporating incomplete information in strategic trade policy models (Qiu, 1994; Collie and Hviid, 1993, 1994; Brainard and Martimort, 1997).

Our analysis is also of interest from a technical viewpoint. We show that the standard "single crossing" property (also referred to as the Spence–Mirrlees sorting condition) does not hold globally in our model. In our context, a key issue is the extent to which producers are willing to restrain exports in order to avoid the AD duty. For a given duty, if at every quantity level inefficient producers were more willing to restrain output than more efficient producers, then the single crossing condition would be satisfied. We demonstrate that single crossing does not hold for all parameter values and that producers' preferences are characterized by a "double crossing" property.

If the model were characterized by single crossing, it is well known from the work of Cho and Sobel (1990) that the stable equilibrium involves separation, albeit with some distortion to trade. If this were the case, then cost-based AD could be justified, at least to the extent that duties were being levied optimally. We show that double crossing inhibits firms' ability to separate and leads to pooling. This in turn implies AD duties are levied suboptimally. Thus, distortions occur before and after the investigation, making cost-based AD a particularly futile policy.[7]

---

[5] Staiger and Wolak (1989, 1992) and Prusa (1992) also emphasize AD's role for maintaining cartels.

[6] In his model, not only does the informational structure of the game differ from ours, but the policy choices available to each player are different. In terms of policy choices, Rosendorff (1996) is similar to Qiu (1994).

[7] For models where single crossing fails, see Bernheim (1991, 1994). The properties of our model are closest to those of Cho (1994) who revisits the limit pricing argument of Milgrom and Roberts (1982).

The article proceeds as follows. In Section 2, we describe the extensive form of the game and in Section 3, we solve for the unique equilibrium behavior of the players once the dumping case is completed. In Section 4, we provide the solution to the model and in Section 5, we show that a pooling outcome emerges under most reasonable demand and cost parameter values. The welfare implications of cost-based AD are discussed in Section 6. Policy implications and the applicability of our findings to other economic issues are discussed in Section 7.

2. THE MODEL

We describe a scenario where a single foreign producer competes against a home firm under the scrutiny of the home government. Broadly speaking, the game can be thought of as occurring in two distinct phases: pre-AD and post-AD determination. During the first part of the game, the foreign firm is aware of the build-up of protectionist pressure. It also understands the home country's rent-extracting and profit-shifting incentives for implementing an AD policy where lower cost firms will be subject to higher AD duties. Thus, during the first part of the game, the foreign firm's export decision is strategic since it can influence the government's posterior beliefs about the foreign firm's efficiency. We will show that the export decision involves a choice of either myopic profit maximization or a VER that might conceal the firm's true type and alleviate protectionist sentiments.

The extensive form of the game has the following structure. The foreign firm's constant marginal cost is drawn from the set $T = \{C_1, \ldots, C_T\}$, with $C_i < C_j$ for $i < j$, according to a commonly known probability distribution, μ. The realization of the cost is private information for the exporter and will be referred to as its type. For simplicity, we will use i to denote the type of exporter with true cost C_i.

In the first period, we assume that the foreign firm's exports are subject to a specific tariff of $\tau_0 \geq 0$. Given this information, the foreign firm chooses and announces its first period export quantity, Q. Following the decision of its rival, the home firm chooses its first period quantity, q.

At the conclusion of the first stage, the government observes the level of imports and home production and then forms beliefs about the efficiency of the foreign firm. If an AD petition is filed, the government selects a per unit AD duty, $\tau_D \geq 0$, which will remain in effect during the next N periods of trade. Given the level of the AD duty, the two firms compete simultaneously in quantities for the remainder of the game.

A couple of comments about the design of the game are in order. First, we are modeling a situation where the home government has an AD statute and the home firm has an opportunity to file an AD petition at the end of the first period. As discussed above, it is not the foreign firm's costs per se that are the impetus for the investigation, but rather the high level of trade associated with an efficient firm. Thus, the foreign firm has an incentive to voluntarily restrict its exports in order to reduce the potential duty. Moreover, it is common knowledge that the foreign firm is likely to announce a VER; therefore it is natural to assume that the home firm will wait to observe the foreign firm's actions before proceeding with first period sales and its filing decision. Thus, we model the home firm as a Stackelberg follower.[8]

Second, as is common in the signaling literature, we assume that the home firm learns the true costs of the foreign firm after the AD investigation.[9]

Third, demand in the home country is assumed to be linear $p = a - Q - q$. This simple functional form will allow us to describe the behavior of the players without resorting to abstract arguments.

Fourth, our model is a signaling game with three players. The foreign firm (the sender) signals its type through its export choice; the home firm then chooses its output level and whether to file a petition; finally, the government (the receiver) levies an AD duty based on its beliefs about the type of the exporter. One can show that a strategy that is not a best reply for the government and the home firm to a given level of exports is strictly dominated, and also that the best reply function of the government is independent of the first period strategy of the home firm. As a result, our analysis essentially reduces to a two-player signaling game.

Finally, we will refine the set of sequential equilibria by eliminating those which assign unreasonable beliefs at null events (Cho and Kreps, 1987; Banks and Sobel, 1987). In particular, we will require the government to perceive each out-of-equilibrium quantity as a possible signal by the exporter and place probability zero on a type which is unlikely to send it. We thus use the D_1 refinement, and throughout the remainder of the article, when we use terms like "equilibrium" and "outcome" we mean "D_1 equilibrium" and "D_1 outcome."[10]

3. ANALYSIS OF THE SUBGAME FOLLOWING THE AD PETITION

3.1. *Firm Decisions.* Since the subgame starting after the government chooses an AD duty has a finite number of periods, N, the linear structure of the model guarantees that it has a unique path which is part of a subgame perfect equilibrium.

In any stage n of this proper subgame, a type i foreign firm takes the total per unit levy, $t = \tau_0 + \tau_D$, as given and maximizes its (variable) profit function

$$\pi_i(Q, q, t) = Q(a - Q - q) - tQ - C_i Q$$

The per-period payoff for the domestic firm is

$$\phi(Q, q) = q(a - Q - q) - c_d q$$

where c_d denotes the domestic firm's marginal costs.

---

[8] Modeling the home firm as a Stackelberg follower is not uncommon (Rosendorff, 1996). Since there is no obvious reason to give any firm the advantage of a first mover in subsequent periods, we model the competition à la Cournot. Furthermore, the mode of competition is inessential for the analysis of the postduty subgame.

[9] If costs are not revealed after the determination is made, we would enter a typical limit-pricing game in which the efficient types would try to prove themselves. This would shift the analysis away from the issue at hand. Of course, such problems would not arise if competition continues to be sequential in future periods.

[10] Readers interested in a more extensive discussion of the equilibrium should consult the working paper version of this article, Kolev and Prusa (1999).

Economic Effects of Antidumping

At each stage, the resulting optimum quantity for a type i exporter is

(1) $$\tilde{Q}_i^n = (a + c_d - 2C_i - 2t)/3$$

and for the domestic firm is

(2) $$\tilde{q}^n(i) = (a + C_i + t - 2c_d)/3$$

where we use the superscript n to denote that these are solutions to the subgame following the AD duty.

The total profit (over all N periods following the AD duty) for the foreign and domestic firms, respectively, is

(3) $$N \cdot \tilde{\pi}_i^n = (N/9)(a + c_d - 2C_i - 2t)^2 \quad \text{and} \quad N \cdot \tilde{\phi}^n(i) = (N/9)(a + C_i + t - 2c_d)^2$$

3.2. *Optimal AD Duty.* As discussed earlier, we will assume that the government uses its cost-based policy to implement a duty that maximizes host country welfare. Although this assumption does not follow official AD procedures, it is consistent with the widespread opinion that the DOC levies AD duties in an arbitrary fashion (Boltuck and Litan, 1991), and is consistent with the desire for governments to devise efficient protection schemes.

Assuming for the moment that the host government could observe the true cost of the exporter, its payoff for the N period subgame would be the sum of consumer surplus, profit of the domestic producer and tariff revenue

(4) $$w = N\left[(Q+q)^2/2 + \phi(Q,q) + tQ\right]$$

Using the unique subgame outcomes, the welfare can be expressed as

(5) $$w(i,t) = N[(2a - C_i - c_d - t)^2/18 + (a + C_i + t - 2c_d)^2/9 + t(a + c_d - 2C_i - 2t)/3]$$

When an AD petition is filed, the government chooses τ_D to maximize (5), yielding a total levy of

(6) $$\tilde{t}_i = (a - C_i)/3$$

The above expression makes it clear that higher duties are levied against more efficient exporters. If an efficient exporter does not voluntarily restrict first period exports and behave like a more inefficient exporter and if a petition is filed, the home government would levy an AD duty in the amount of $\tau_D = \tilde{t}_i - \tau_0$. From this point on, a total tariff $t > \tau_0$ is to be understood as the initial tariff plus an AD surcharge equal to $t - \tau_0$. Hence we will use the terms tariff and duty interchangeably to describe the total level of protection. To keep the model as simple as possible, we will assume that $\tau_0 \le \tilde{t}_T$, which implies that an AD petition will be filed against all types.[11]

---

[11] This is not a restrictive assumption since the most frequent users of cost-based AD, the United States and the EC, also have very low tariffs. In addition, a higher initial tariff would introduce another stage to the game without providing additional insight. At this stage, the domestic firm would make a decision whether to file a petition. Since the beliefs of the government are common knowledge in equilibrium, the firm would obviously file a petition if the beliefs entail a positive AD duty.

Finally, we note that the marginal benefit to the home country from lowering the AD duty is increasing in C_i. This implies that the government's best response is monotonically decreasing in the posterior likelihood of a more inefficient exporter. This explains the desire of each type to be considered type T.

4. SOLUTION OF THE SUBGAME PRIOR TO THE AD PETITION

We will solve for the first stage equilibrium by breaking the problem into several steps. First, we will characterize the foreign firm's isoprofit curves and show that the game falls into a subclass of signaling games with double crossing. Next, we will establish two conditions: a mimicking condition and a condition that in conjunction with the double crossing property implies that the most natural outcome is for all types to pool. Finally, we will describe the behavior of each type in the pooling outcome.

4.1. *Isoprofit Curves and the Double Crossing Property.* In the first period, a type i exporter knows that upon observing Q, the home firm will produce according to its best response function

$$(7) \qquad \tilde{q} = (a - Q - c_d)/2$$

From this point on, we adopt the convention that if there is no time superscript, we are referring to first period variables.

The equilibrium first period profit of the foreign firm when producing Q is

$$(8) \qquad \pi_i(Q) = Q(a - Q - 2C_i - 2\tau_0 + c_d)/2$$

The incentive compatible constraint for type i can be constructed by defining an isoprofit curve consisting of combinations of quantities Q and duties t which yield the same total profit, $\bar{\Pi}_i$, given that the home firm produces according to its best response, (7). From (8) and (3), the isoprofit curve is implicitly given by

$$(9) \qquad \bar{\Pi}_i = \Pi_i(Q, t) \equiv \pi_i(Q) + (N/9)(a + c_d - 2C_i - 2t)^2$$

Consider the case when the government has full information. In this case, each type i knows that a petition will lead to an AD duty, $\tilde{t}_i - \tau_0$. Hence, each type will myopically maximize its first period profit yielding

$$(10) \qquad \tilde{Q}_i = (a - 2C_i - 2\tau_0 + c_d)/2 \qquad \text{and} \qquad \tilde{\pi}_i = (a - 2C_i - 2\tau_0 + c_d)^2/8$$

and an equilibrium profit over all periods

$$\Pi_i^s \equiv (a + c_d - 2C_i - 2\tau_0)^2/8 + (N/81)(a + 3c_d - 4C_i)^2$$

In Figure 1 we depict the isoprofit curves for three types under the full information outcome. Note that as graphed, each firm's preferred set lies to the south of its respective isoprofit curve—for a given quantity, profit increases as the tariff falls.

In standard signaling games, it is assumed that one type always has a greater incentive to deviate from a given outcome than another type. This is referred to as

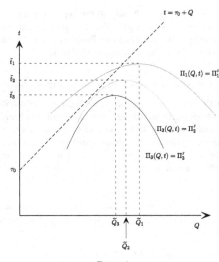

FIGURE 1

ISOPROFIT CURVES UNDER FULL INFORMATION

the single crossing property since it implies that the isoprofit curves cross only once. We will now show that the isoprofit function of the exporter does not exhibit the single crossing property. As will become apparent, this fact will play a key role in solving for the equilibrium of the model.

LEMMA 1. *For any two isoprofit curves* $\{\bar{\Pi}_i, \bar{\Pi}_j\}$, $i < j$, *the graph of the function* $t = \tau_0 + Q$ *divides* (Q, t)-*space in such a way that at any* (Q, t) *the slope of* $\bar{\Pi}_j$ *is bigger (smaller) (the same as) the slope of* $\bar{\Pi}_i$ *whenever* $t > (<)(=)\tau_0 + Q$.

All proofs are in the Appendix.

Lemma 1 implies that the isoprofit curves can cross at most once in either of the two half-spaces defined by $t = \tau_0 + Q$. If they cross in the half-space $t < \tau_0 + Q$, then j's curve crosses i's from below; if they cross in the half-space $t > \tau_0 + Q$, then j's curve crosses i's from above. This implies that the incentives for any two types to deviate from a given outcome differ depending on the relative sizes of t and Q. Furthermore, if the isoprofit curves have a point in common along $t = \tau_0 + Q$, then they are tangent at that point. We will refer to this property as "double" crossing.

Intuitively, the double crossing property reflects the varying incentives to lower current quantity in order to receive a lower duty in the future. On the one hand, high-cost firms already produce less than low-cost firms, and, hence, do not have to distort their sales as much as low-cost firms. Thus, in this respect, high-cost firms find it easier to deviate from a given outcome (by lowering quantities). On the other hand, low-cost firms have more to gain if future duties are lower, and, hence, they benefit more when today's lower exports result in lower duties tomorrow. Thus, in this respect, low-cost firms find it easier to deviate from a given outcome. Which incentive dominates depends on the relative sizes of t and Q. If t is relatively small, the former effect dominates, while if t is relatively large, the latter effect dominates.

The double crossing property is graphically depicted in Figure 2. Consider first the case when $Q > t - \tau_0$ (i.e., relatively high quantity levels). This case is depicted graphically by point X in Figure 2. At the point of intersection (X), the slope of isoprofit curve for the more efficient type (type 1) is bigger than the slope of inefficient type's isoprofit curve. This relationship can simply be interpreted as implying that at X, a decrease in exports by 1 is *less* profitable than a decrease by 2.

Consider the other case, when $Q < t - \tau_0$. This case is depicted by the point Y in Figure 2. At the point of intersection, the slope of the isoprofit curve for the efficient type is smaller than the inefficient type's, implying that at Y, a decrease in exports by 1 is *more* profitable than a decrease by 2.

Finally, if the two isoprofit curves have a point in common along the locus $Q = t - \tau_0$, they must be tangent at that point. This case is depicted by the point Z in Figure 4 and will be discussed at greater length in Section 4.3. Hereafter, we will refer to the line $t = \tau_0 + Q$ as the tangency locus.

Another property of the isoprofit curve is:

COROLLARY 1. *Any isoprofit curve can cross the tangency locus at most once.*

Corollary 1 implies that an isoprofit curve either never crosses the tangency locus or only crosses the tangency locus once. As will become clear, whether an isoprofit curve crosses the tangency locus depends primarily on the duration of the AD duty.

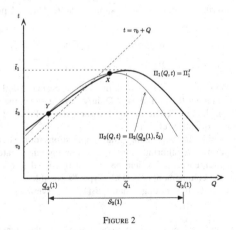

FIGURE 2

INCENTIVE COMPATIBILITY CONSTRAINT FOR 2 DEFINED BY 1

4.2. *The Unique Candidate for a Pure Strategy Separating Equilibrium Outcome.* We begin by deriving the unique candidate for a pure strategy separating equilibrium outcome. In order to support such a solution, we must provide each type with a quantity, Q_i^s, which is exported with probability one.

If the outcome is a pure strategy separating equilibrium, then the government is able to infer each type's true cost and will in turn levy the optimal duty, $\tilde{t}_i$. This implies that type 1's unique separating sequential equilibrium strategy is to maximize its first period profit myopically, yielding exports of $Q_1^s = \tilde{Q}_1$ and profit over all periods of Π_1^s.

The extent to which types $j > 1$ distort exports depends on whether others have a desire to mimic them. If the game is not to be trivial, we must assume that some i is willing to mimic some type j, $i < j$. In general, this means $\Pi_i^s < \Pi_i(\tilde{Q}_j, \tilde{t}_j)$. Since we are interested in explaining why the most efficient firms restrain their exports, we require that type 1 be willing to mimic 2,

(11) $$\Pi_1^s < \Pi_1(\tilde{Q}_2, \tilde{t}_2)$$

In Figure 1 we depict a game where (11) is satisfied. As depicted, 2's full information outcome, $(\tilde{Q}_2, \tilde{t}_2)$ lies in 1's strictly preferred region. In other words, as depicted, 1 has an incentive to mimic 2, if doing so could induce an AD duty of only $\tilde{t}_2$.

Since Π_1^s is the minimum profit type 1 will earn in any sequential equilibrium, the incentive-compatible constraint for type 1 can be defined by the locus of quantity–duty pairs in (9), yielding at least Π_1^s

(12) $$\Pi_1^s \leq \Pi_1(Q, t)$$

In Figure 1, (12) is satisfied for all (Q, t) lying below $\Pi_1^s = \Pi_1(Q, t)$.

It is easy to verify that the equation in (12) implicitly defines a function which is strictly concave in Q and symmetric around $\tilde{Q}_1$. For each $i > 1$, (12) defines an open set of quantities around $\tilde{Q}_1$, $S_i(1) = (\underline{Q}_i(1), \bar{Q}_i(1))$, which type 1 would strictly prefer to its equilibrium strategy if the response was $\tilde{t}_i$. The end points of these intervals are

$$\underline{Q}_i(1) = \tilde{Q}_1 - (2/9)\sqrt{2N(C_i - C_1)(C_i + 3c_d + a - 5C_1)}$$
$$\bar{Q}_i(1) = \tilde{Q}_1 + (2/9)\sqrt{2N(C_i - C_1)(C_i + 3c_d + a - 5C_1)}$$

Since $C_1 < C_i$, the above quantities are real. In addition, $S_i(1)$ is strictly increasing in N, implying that the longer the period the AD duty stays in effect, the more type 1 is willing to sacrifice if doing so could insure a lower duty. In Figure 2, we depict an incentive compatible quantity set, $S_2(1)$.

Incentive compatibility has several important implications for the behavior of each type $i > 1$ in a separating equilibrium. For instance, in any pure strategy sequential separating equilibrium, each $i > 1$ would be at least restricted to $Q \in S_i^c(1)$, where $S_i^c(1)$ is defined as the complement of $S_i(1)$.[12] Type 2's possible quantity choices can be further restricted by noting that: $S_2(1)$ is symmetric around $\tilde{Q}_1$;

---

[12] The strategy set of type i, $S_i(h)$, may be further restricted by the incentive compatibility constraint of other types h, $h < i$.

$\underline{Q}_2(1) \leq \tilde{Q}_2 < \tilde{Q}_1 < \bar{Q}_2(1)$; and, given $\tilde{t}_2$, the profit function of type 2 is symmetric about $\tilde{Q}_2$. These observations imply that the payoff for 2 at $\underline{Q}_2(1)$ is higher than at $\bar{Q}_2(1)$. Moreover, the fact that 2's profit is monotonically increasing up to $\tilde{Q}_2$ and decreasing thereafter implies that $\underline{Q}_2(1)$ is the unique maximizer among the set of quantities available to 2 in a separating equilibrium. Not surprisingly, then, it is the unique candidate to be a part of a self-enforcing separating equilibrium outcome.

PROPOSITION 1. *If there exists separating equilibria, then their outcome is unique and must contain type 2 exports of* $Q_2^s = \underline{Q}_2(1)$.

Denote by $\underline{Q}_j(i)$ and $\bar{Q}_j(i)$ the end points of the interval $\mathcal{S}_j(i)$, $1 \leq i < j$. $\mathcal{S}_j(i)$ is the set of quantities in combination with $\tilde{t}_j$ that type i would prefer to Π_i^s. We can also show:

COROLLARY 2. *There exists a unique candidate for a separating equilibrium outcome. The export quantity for type j in this outcome is* $Q_j^s = \min\{\underline{Q}_j(i)\}$, $1 \leq i < j$.

We depict this outcome in Figure 3. The outcome has several nice properties. First, the most efficient exporter does not restrain its exports. Rather, the potential AD duty distorts trade from the less efficient types who voluntarily restrain their exports in order to separate themselves. Second, this outcome involves the least amount of trade restraint, and, as such, is the best outcome in the sense of Riley

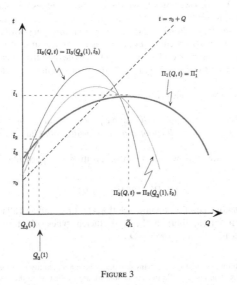

FIGURE 3

THE UNIQUE CANDIDATE FOR A SEPARATING EQUILIBRIUM

(1979). Finally, the outcome has the desirable characteristic that the optimal duties are levied.

4.3. *The Unique Pooling Equilibrium.*   Now we explore the possibilities for pooling.[13] The next two lemmas will provide a candidate for an equilibrium in which more than one type exports the same quantity and characterize the foreign firm's isoprofit function in the equilibrium.

LEMMA 2.   *Fix a pooling outcome in which more than one type exports Q^p with positive probability in the first period, and the response of the government is t^p. Then it must be that $Q^p = t^p - \tau_0$.*

Lemma 2 states that any export-duty pair that does not lie on the tangency locus cannot be a part of a pooling outcome.

We now show that if the indifference curves of two types have a point in common along the tangency line, then everywhere else the isoprofit line of the lower type lies above that of the higher type.

LEMMA 3.   *Let $i < j$ and let $\hat{Q} = \hat{t} - \tau_0$. Then $\Pi_i(\hat{Q}, \hat{t}) = \Pi_i(Q', t_i)$ and $\Pi_j(\hat{Q}, \hat{t}) = \Pi_j(Q', t_j)$ imply $t_j < t_i$.*

Figure 4 is useful for clarifying Lemma 3. Consider a point, say Z, on the tangency locus. By Lemma 1 we know that any two isoprofit curves through Z must be tangent. For example, in Figure 4 we have drawn three isoprofit curves containing Z. Lemma 3 implies that the isoprofit curves of the higher types are nested within the isoprofit curve of the lower types. For instance, 3's isoprofit curve lies within 2's which, in turn, lies within 1's isoprofit curve. Lemma 3 is important since it implies that the government can clearly rank each type's incentive to deviate from a candidate on the tangency locus. In particular, at Z, type 1 has the strongest incentives to make a small deviation.

Using Lemma 3 we can also show:

COROLLARY 3.   *If type i pools with positive probability in a sequential equilibrium then every type $j > i$ exports the pooled quantity with probability one.*

We are now ready to prove our main proposition. In particular, we now show that if

$$(13) \qquad\qquad \Pi_1^r \leq \Pi_1(\hat{t}_2 - \tau_0, \hat{t}_2)$$

then there is a unique equilibrium in which the AD threat induces all types to sell the same quantity. In this equilibrium, the most efficient types voluntarily restrain their exports in order to receive a lower AD duty.

---

[13] We use the term pooling to refer to any outcome wherein a quantity is exported with positive probability by more than one type. In our discussion, we are explicit when the pooling is partial or full, and which types participate in the pool.

DUMPING AND DOUBLE CROSSING 907

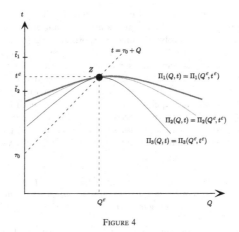

FIGURE 4

THE UNIQUE POOLING EQUILIBRIUM

PROPOSITION 2. *If (13) is satisfied, then there exists a unique equilibrium. In it, type 1 produces the pooled quantity with positive probability and all other types pool with probability one.*

Figure 4 depicts the unique pure pooling equilibrium. Several comments are warranted. First, unlike the separating candidate, in the pure pooling equilibrium, the most efficient firm voluntarily restricts its output prior to the AD investigation. In fact, it is generally the case that exports are restrained not just by 1 but by many of the more efficient types. Thus, the pooling equilibrium is consistent with the empirical evidence that the threat of an AD duty induces VERs by most efficient foreign competitors.

Second, depending on the probability distribution μ, cost-based AD can easily result in the perception that inefficient exporters are more threatening than they actually are. For instance, as depicted, all types $i > 1$ will receive a higher duty than is optimal. This prediction is again consistent with the empirical evidence. In the steel industry, for instance, a large number of cases have been filed against relatively inefficient producers. This perception was most forcefully asserted during the Uruguay Round negotiations as representatives from developing countries (i.e., relatively inefficient firms) vigorously negotiated for changes in the rules governing cost-based AD.

Third, these distortions imply that domestic consumers get the worst of both worlds. Prior to the AD investigation, consumers suffer as the efficient firms restrict output. Following the investigation, consumers bear the burden of having overly large AD duties being levied on inefficient firms.

4.4. *A Necessary and Sufficient Condition.* Before concluding this section, we would like to relax condition (13) and give a necessary and sufficient condition for the unique equilibrium to involve pooling in exports (not necessarily by all types) and characterize the outcome. The condition requires type $T - 1$ to prefer the point $(Q = \tilde{\imath}_T - \tau_0, \tilde{\imath}_T)$ to its unique candidate separating equilibrium strategy.

Intuitively, this is the case because Lemma 1 guarantees that if $T - 1$ prefers to separate rather than mimic T at $(Q = \tilde{\imath}_T - \tau_0, \tilde{\imath}_T)$, then so will every lower type. Consequently, the separating equilibrium isoprofit curves of each lower type lie in the right half space defined by the tangency locus. In the proposition below, we establish that if this necessary and sufficient condition does not hold, then the candidate for a separating equilibrium outcome defined in Corollary 2 arises from a unique equilibrium.

PROPOSITION 3. *There exists a pooling equilibrium if and only if* Π_{T-1}^s $\leq \Pi_{T-1}(\tilde{\imath}_T - \tau_0, \tilde{\imath}_T)$. *Moreover, this equilibrium is unique and involves all but (possibly) the lowest types exporting the same quantity with positive probability.*

Proposition 2 gives a sufficient condition for type 1 to voluntarily restrict exports in equilibrium. Proposition 3 provides a necessary condition for a type i to participate in a pool. By replacing i with 1 in the construction of the unique pooling equilibrium, we see that the most efficient type will restrict exports only if $\Pi_1^s > \Pi_1(\tilde{\imath}_T - \tau_0, \tilde{\imath}_T)$.

5. CHARACTERIZATION OF THE POOLING CONDITION

We have argued above that if (13) holds, then pooling is the unique equilibrium. In this section we will relate this condition to the underlying primitives of the model. For analytical convenience we will now assume that the foreign firm is one of two possible types, 1 and 2. We will also assume that $c_d = C_2$ and that $\tau_0 = \tilde{\imath}_2$.

First, we want to establish that the mimicking condition (11) holds. Substituting, we can show that 1 would like to mimic 2 if

$$N > N^m \equiv \frac{81(A - 1)}{8(5A - 4)}$$

where we have defined relative costs as

(14) $$A \equiv \frac{a - C_1}{a - C_2} > 1$$

In Figure 5, we graph the mimicking condition in $A - N$ space. The mimicking condition is satisfied for all points lying above the N^m contour. As the graph makes clear, for all $N > 1$ the mimicking condition holds for all reasonable values of A. For $N = 1$ the condition only holds for $A \in (1, 49/41)$. Recall that when a firm restrains exports to $\tilde{Q}_2$, some first period profit is sacrificed. If the game is sufficiently short, the gain from the lower duty is insufficient to induce mimicking. In current U.S. practice, duties are rarely removed sooner than 2 years after being imposed. Given

DUMPING AND DOUBLE CROSSING 909

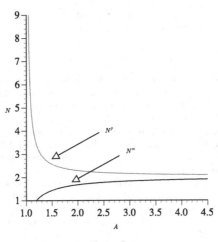

FIGURE 5

N^m AND N^p CONTOURS

this practice, we believe that the relevant scenario is when the AD duty stays in effect for longer than one period, and thus that the mimicking condition holds for all values of A.

Conditional on (11), the question now is whether (13) is satisfied. Substituting, we can show that the pooling condition holds if

$$N > N^p \equiv \frac{9(6A - 5)^2}{32(5A - 4)(A - 1)}$$

This sufficient condition is also graphed in Figure 5 and is satisfied for all points lying above the N^p contour. The graph shows that the pooling condition is likely to hold for most reasonable parameter values. In particular, if the duty is levied for at least several periods, the condition is satisfied for almost all A. For instance, if $N = 3$, the condition holds for all $A > 1.284$, if $N = 5$, the condition holds for all $A > 1.093$, . and if $N = 10$, the condition holds for all $A > 1.035$.

Although the precise values are clearly specific to this example, this exercise does illustrate the two general insights. First, pooling is most likely to occur the larger the cost differential among types. Second, the longer is the duration of the postduty game, the more likely will the pooling outcome emerge. Note that the postduty game does not have to be particularly lengthy for pooling to emerge. A review of the United States' experience reveals that AD duties are often quite long-lived. For instance, in the United States, the duties have been in place for at least 10 years in more than 20 percent of (affirmative) AD cases; in fact, according to International Trade Commission (1995), more than half of the AD duties levied between 1955 and

1991 were still in effect in 1991. Thus, the model's prediction that foreign firms restrain exports in order to reduce potential AD duties seems plausible.

6. WELFARE IMPLICATIONS

We would like to conclude our discussion by conducting a simple welfare analysis. As we did in the previous section, we will assume that the foreign firm is one of two possible types, 1 and 2. The prior probability of type 1 is μ. We will continue to assume that $c_d = C_2$ and that $\tau_0 = \bar{t}_2$.

We compare the expected welfare in the pure strategy pooling equilibrium with a situation in which the government does not have a cost-based AD mechanism. In keeping with GATT rules, we thus consider an alternative where exporters are subject to a uniform tariff.[14]

In a pure strategy pooling equilibrium, the government levies a duty equal to $t^e - \tau_0$ where $t^e = \mu\bar{t}_1 + (1 - \mu)\bar{t}_2$. Regardless of the firm's type, first period exports are $Q^e = t^e - \tau_0$ and the domestic firm maximizes its profit taking Q^e as given. In subsequent periods, the welfare results from the unique Cournot equilibrium with the AD duty imposed.

If the government does not have AD law and commits to τ_0, the welfare would be calculated from the unique Stackelberg and Cournot equilibria in first and later periods, respectively. Using our expression for relative costs (A), the difference between the expected equilibrium welfare and the ex ante expected welfare from precommitment can be shown from (4) and (5) to be

$$\Delta(N, A, \mu) = (1/72)(4N + 11)(A - 1)^2\mu^2 - (1/72)(27A - 14)(A - 1)\mu - 7/288$$

$\Delta(\cdot)$ is increasing with N, implying that the longer the duration of the duty the larger are the losses due to a commitment to a suboptimal duty.

In Figure 6, we depict the zero contours of $\Delta(\cdot)$ for $N = 5$ and $N = 10$. Cost-based AD raises welfare in the region lying above the contour. The intuition is quite clear: Cost-based AD raises welfare the more likely the firm is type 1 (higher μ) and the longer the duration of the duty (larger N). However, note that if the duty stays on for five periods, the cost difference between the firms must get quite large before the AD policy raises welfare. $\Delta(\cdot)$ is positive for a substantial region of the parameter space only for $N = 10$.

A couple of comments about the effect of the duration of the game are in order. First, our model does not endogenously derive the duration of AD duties. The long-standing nature of AD duties could be explained by factors such as political influence, bureaucratic inertia, and so on. Be that as it may, given that in practice antidumping duties remain in place for a long time and also that they are in most cases cost based, our analysis shows that pooling is likely to emerge, and hence that AD policy is inefficient. Second, we assume that N is known. Adding uncertainty

---

[14] The unique ex ante optimum duty is easily seen to be $\mu\bar{t}_1 + (1 - \mu)\bar{t}_2$. We can perform the welfare analysis with this tariff imposed in all periods, but we want to emphasize that even with suboptimal tariffs (and maybe even the worst ex ante tariff), the country is still better off without an AD law.

DUMPING AND DOUBLE CROSSING 911

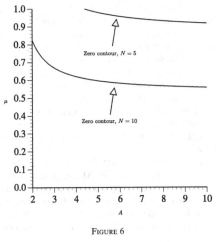

FIGURE 6

ZERO CONTOUR OF $\Delta(N,\mu,A)$

about the duration of the game will not yield significant insights; the firms will simply maximize their expected profits given the distribution of N.

The example suggests that pooling is likely for almost all N. Nevertheless, expected welfare and realized welfare may differ. Our findings make the Uruguay Round's sunset amendment particularly relevant. This provision mandates that AD duties must be reviewed after 5 years and the duty should be removed unless there is evidence that doing so will result in injury. The sunset amendment was designed to limit the attractiveness of AD actions (to domestic industries), and, as such, this provision should raise welfare. Surprisingly, we find that it may well exacerbate the costs of cost-based AD policy.

7. CONCLUDING COMMENTS

By most accounts, the downward trend in trade restrictions was halted (or at least slowed) in the mid-1970s (Bhagwati, 1988; Krueger, 1995). Blame is usually pointed to the combination of high-track (VERs) and low-track (AD duties) restraints. In this article, we have demonstrated that both phenomena can be explained by the fact that AD laws were broadened to allow for cost-based allegations in the mid-1970s. We have shown that VERs are undertaken to discourage cost-based AD complaints. However, we find that in general, the VER does not completely release the protectionist pressures but rather causes the duties to be clumsily levied.

Our results also help explain why all concerned parties—domestic firms, foreign firms, and consumers—are unhappy with AD protection. Domestic industries complain that AD does not sufficiently protect them against their most feared foreign competitors (Stewart, 1991). At the same time, foreign firms often gripe that the duties are excessive. Our model shows that both charges have validity. The VER distorts the government's perception of the foreign firm's efficiency and leads to undesirably low (high) duties on efficient (inefficient) competitors. Cost-based duties would be more efficiently levied if the VERs did not interfere with the government's ability to perceive costs. Finally, consumers suffer due to both the anticipatory VER and to the ineptly determined duty. Our results provide additional evidence that AD law creates a heavy burden on consumers. All in all, even though cost-based AD raises welfare under complete information, the distortions inherent with implementing it under incomplete information make it an undesirable policy—especially if the duties are levied for relatively short durations. Thus, GATT/WTO parties would be well served to couple the recent sunset provision with additional restrictions on cost-based allegations.

From a technical perspective, our results highlight the importance of the single crossing assumption in economic models. Although this assumption is usually imposed, our model suggests that those interested in accurately depicting the outcomes in signaling games should formally model agents' payoffs, that is, derive payoffs from more basic economic primitives. As we have shown, the equilibrium depends crucially on whether the payoffs satisfy single crossing or double crossing.

APPENDIX

PROOF OF LEMMA 1. Implicit differentiation of (9) at any (Q, t) yields a slope of an isoprofit curve given by

$$\sigma(Q, t) = \frac{dt}{dQ} = \left(\frac{9}{8n}\right)\left(\frac{a - 2Q - 2C_i - 2\tau_0 + c_d}{a - 2t - 2C_i + c_d}\right)$$

The first part of the claim follows directly from the definition of $\sigma(Q, t)$ and monotonocity of the profit function. The second part of the claim follows from differentiating $\sigma(Q, t)$ with respect to C_i at any (Q, t).   □

PROOF OF COROLLARY 1. If the isoprofit curve of type i crossed the tangency locus twice, then continuity would imply that i must have another isoprofit curve tangent to $t = \tau_0 + Q$ at a point $(\hat{Q} = \hat{\imath} - \tau_0, \hat{\imath})$. Lemma 1 shows that an isoprofit curve of any i' through $(\hat{Q} = \hat{\imath} - \tau_0, \hat{\imath})$ would be tangent also and both curves would lie in the same half space defined by $t = \tau_0 + Q$ at least in an ϵ-neighborhood of $(\hat{Q} = \hat{\imath} - \tau_0, \hat{\imath})$. Since profit is continuous, we can always find a sufficiently small δ-perturbation of the payoff of one type so that the isoprofit curves cross twice within ϵ of $(\hat{Q} = \hat{\imath} - \tau_0, \hat{\imath})$. This would violate Lemma 1.   □

PROOF OF PROPOSITION 1. Before we proceed with the proof of the proposition, we introduce some notation and concepts relevant to applying the D_1 refinement in this proof and others that follow.

Fix a probability distribution over the end points of the signaling subgame induced by a sequential equilibrium in which an exporter of type i obtains a profit (over all periods) of Π_i^*. Call this probability the outcome of the game associated with the given equilibrium. Fix also an out-of-equilibrium export level, Q'. Let $BR(\eta, Q')$

denote the set of best responses of the government at Q' given that: (a) the induce beliefs about the types exporting this quantity are η, and (b) the home firm produce its unique maximizer when it observes Q'. Write element i of η as $\eta(i|Q')$. Then

$$BR(\eta, Q') \equiv \arg \max_{t \in [\tau_0, \bar{t}_1]} \sum_{i=1}^{T} w(i, t)\eta(i|Q')$$

Let $\Pi_i(Q, t)$ denote the foreign firm's profit over all periods when it exports Q i: period 1 and is thereafter subject to a total duty, t. Define

$$E_i^0(Q') \equiv \{t \in BR(\eta, Q') : \Pi_i(Q, t) = \Pi_i^*\}$$

to be the set of best responses of the government that would leave i indifferen between his/her equilibrium strategy and exporting Q'. Similarly, the set c sequentially rational AD duties that would make i strictly better off is denoted by

$$E_i(Q') \equiv \{t \in BR(\eta, Q') : \Pi_i(Q, t) > \Pi_i^*\}$$

We say that a sequential equilibrium outcome is D_1 if and only if there exists a: equilibrium giving rise to this outcome which can be supported with belief $\eta(i|Q') = 0$ at each off equilibrium quantity Q' whenever

(A.1) $$E_i^0(Q') \cup E_i(Q') \subseteq E_{i'}(Q')$$

for $E_{i'}(Q') \neq \{\emptyset\}$. Thus, D_1 requires the beliefs of the government to place probabilit zero on type i if whenever i wants to deviate from a particular equilibrium so does i Intuitively, this makes i' the more likely type to break the equilibrium.

Fix a sequential separating equilibrium outcome obtained from 2 exportin $Q^* \in S_2^c(1)$, $Q^* \neq \underline{Q}_2(1)$, and 1 exporting $\tilde{Q}_1$. Take an out of equilibrium messag $Q' \in S_2^c(1)$ such that $|Q^* - \tilde{Q}_1| > |Q' - \tilde{Q}_1|$.

Let us construct the sets of sequentially rational responses of the government t Q' which would make each type break the equilibrium. By the definition (incentiv compatibility) of $S_2(1)$, no duty $t \in [\tilde{t}_2, \tilde{t}_1]$ would make 1 deviate from $\tilde{Q}_1$ to Q Continuity and monotonicity of 2's profit function guarantee that exporting Q' woul be strictly preferred to Q^* if that would make the country impose $\tilde{t}_2$ (or any lowe duty). Hence,

$$E_1^0(Q') \cup E_1(Q') \subseteq E_2(Q')$$

and the D_1 criterion requires the beliefs of the government to place probability zer on 1 at Q'. Hence, at Q', we must have the posterior restricted to $\eta|_{i \geq 2}$, where

$$\eta|_{i \geq j}(i'|Q) = \begin{cases} \frac{\eta(i'|Q)}{\sum_{i \geq j} \eta(i|Q)}, & \text{if } i' \geq j \\ 0, & \text{otherwise} \end{cases}$$

Since the best reply of the government is decreasing in its beliefs, this would make defect from the equilibrium.

We could make the same argument for all $Q^* \neq Q_2(1)$. Hence, the unique candidate separating D_1 equilibrium outcome is the one arising from type 2 exporting $Q_2(1)$. $\square$

PROOF OF COROLLARY 2. Note that the strict concavity of the separating equilibrium isoprofit curve for type 1 implies that $\bar{Q}_j(1) > \bar{Q}_i(1)$ for $j > i > 1$. On the other hand, Lemma 1 implies that $\Pi_i(\bar{Q}_i(1), \tilde{t}_i) > \Pi_i(\bar{Q}_j(1), \tilde{t}_j)$. Hence, $\bar{Q}_j(1) > \bar{Q}_j(i)$, $\forall j > i > 1$ and each type j is constrained only by type 1 at high quantity levels.

Starting with type 3, for each type $j \geq 3$, apply the arguments used in Proposition 1 to show that any quantity $Q' > \bar{Q}_j(1)$ in combination with $\tilde{t}_j$ is inferior to $\bar{Q}_j(1)$. This is the case because the D_1 criterion concentrates the beliefs of the government on $k \geq j$ and the corresponding best response would make j deviate from Q'.

Fix a candidate equilibrium in which each type j exports $\bar{Q}_j(1)$. To see that $\bar{Q}_j(1)$ is not a stable equilibrium, we use Lemma 1 once again to claim that

$$E_1^0(\bar{Q}_j(1) - \epsilon) \cup E_1(\bar{Q}_j(1) - \epsilon) \subseteq E_j(\bar{Q}_j(1) - \epsilon)$$

Since $\Pi_j(\bar{Q}_j(1), \tilde{t}_j) > \Pi_j(\bar{Q}_{j-1}(1), \tilde{t}_{j-1})$, D_1 requires that the response of the government at $\bar{Q}_{j-1}(1) - \epsilon$ be at most $\tilde{t}_{j-1}$, which is sufficient to discard $\bar{Q}_{j-1}(1)$ as a candidate equilibrium.

Proposition 1 showed that the unique candidate for a D_1 strategy for 2 is $Q_2^s = Q_2(1)$. Let $\hat{Q} = \min\{Q_3(1), Q_3(2)\}$. Then both type 1 and type 2 are content with separation rather than mimic type 3 at $Q' < \hat{Q}$ and get $\tilde{t}_3$. Hence, D_1 would restrict the beliefs of the government to $i \geq 3$ at $Q' + \epsilon < \hat{Q}$ and the sequentially rational tariff would make 3 deviate from Q'. The arguments for all other types are identical. $\square$

PROOF OF LEMMA 2. Without loss of generality, assume that $Q^p < t^p - \tau_0$. Let i be the highest type in the pool. Then $t^p > \tilde{t}_i$. Lemma 1 guarantees that in a D_1 equilibrium, the beliefs of the government at Q', ϵ-smaller than Q^p should place $\eta(i' | Q') = 0$ for all $i' < i$. Hence, the response of the government at Q' should be less than or equal to $\tilde{t}_i$. Continuity of the exporter's payoff in Q' would make i strictly better off deviating from the pool for sufficiently small ϵ. $\square$

PROOF OF LEMMA 3. In Corollary 2, we established that any point $(\hat{Q} = \hat{i} - \tau_0, \hat{t})$ is the unique intersection of the tangency locus with the isoprofit function $\Pi_j(\hat{Q}, \hat{t}) = \Pi_j(Q, t)$ so that any $Q' < \hat{Q}$ and t' such that $\Pi_j(\hat{Q}, \hat{t}) = \Pi_j(Q', t')$ implies $t' > Q' + \tau_0$.

Assume that at $Q' < \hat{Q}$, $\Pi_i(\hat{Q}, \hat{t}) = \Pi_i(Q', t_i)$ and $\Pi_j(\hat{Q}, \hat{t}) = \Pi_j(Q', t_j)$ with $t_j > t_i$, so that the isoprofit curve of j through $(\hat{Q}, \hat{t})$ is above that of i. We will show that this assumption leads to a contradiction. By monotonicity of the profit in t we have

(A.2) $\Pi_i(\hat{Q}, \hat{t}) = \Pi_i(Q', t_i) > \Pi_i(Q', t_j)$

On the other hand, since $t_j > \tau_0 + Q'$, Lemma 1 shows that the slope of j's isoprofit curve through (Q', t_j) is bigger than the corresponding slope for i. This implies that

$$\Pi_i(\hat{Q}, \hat{t}) \geq \Pi_i(Q', t_j) \Rightarrow \Pi_j(\hat{Q}, \hat{t}) > \Pi_j(Q', t_j)$$

The last statement contradicts (2) and the construction of t_j as $\Pi_j(\hat{Q}, \hat{t}) = \Pi_j(Q', t_j)$. Similar arguments hold for $Q' > \hat{Q}$. $\square$

PROOF OF COROLLARY 3. Suppose that i is the lowest type in the pool and $j > i$ randomizes in equilibrium between some Q^* and the pooled quantity Q^p. Then j must be indifferent between Q^* and Q^p. Since the equilibrium isoprofit curve of i is everywhere above that of j according to Lemma 3, it must be that $\forall Q \neq Q^*$ and $j > i$

$$E_j^0(Q) \cup E_j(Q) \subseteq E_i(Q)$$

Hence, in a D_1 equilibrium, the beliefs of the government at $Q \neq Q^*$ must place probability one on i and the corresponding duty should be $\tilde{t}_i$. As shown above, every type j, $j > i$, is strictly better off with Q^p than producing Q in combination with $\tilde{t}_i$; hence, every $j > i$ exports Q^p with probability one. $\square$

PROOF OF PROPOSITION 2. Note first that $\underline{Q}_2(1)$ is not a D_1 strategy for 2. Let us fix the outcome arising from 2 exporting $\underline{Q}_2(1)$. By construction, $\underline{Q}_2(1) < \tilde{t}_2 - \tau_0$, which guarantees that the isoprofit curve of 2 through $(\underline{Q}_2(1), \tilde{t}_2)$ has a slope that is bigger than the corresponding slope for type 1 (by Lemma 1). This implies that for Q' ϵ-bigger than $\underline{Q}_2(1)$, the set of sequentially rational duties weakly preferred to $(\underline{Q}_2(1), \tilde{t}_2)$ by 1 in combination with Q' is a subset of the best responses, which 2 strictly prefers to its equilibrium action. If the given equilibrium produces a D_1 outcome, we should be able to support it with beliefs $\eta|_{i \geq 2}$ at Q'. Hence, the best response of the government is at most $\tilde{t}_2$. Since, with any $t \leq \tilde{t}_2$ fixed along with the fact that the profit of 2 is monotonically increasing in Q at $\underline{Q}_2(1)$, type 2 would deviate to Q'. Hence, if (13) holds, there are no pure strategy separating equilibria.

Let us fix a pooling equilibrium in which all types produce the pooling quantity with positive probability. By Corollary 3, all $i \geq 2$ export the pooled quantity with probability one. We now consider the government's and type 1's equilibrium strategies. Let $t^e \equiv \arg\max_t w(\mu, t) \geq \tau_0$ denote the ex ante optimal duty and let $Q^e = t^e - \tau_0$.

First suppose that the prior probability, μ, is such that $\Pi_1^s \geq \Pi_1(Q^e, t^e)$. We claim that in this case, type 1 cannot pool with probability one in any sequential equilibrium. This follows from the fact that if 1 pools with probability one, then the unique best response of the government would be t^e to the quantity Q^e. The point (Q^e, t^e) is strictly inferior for 1 compared to full separation at $\tilde{Q}_1$. This implies that the only possible solution must involve partial pooling.

As argued above, in any D_1 pooling equilibrium, all disequilibrium beliefs will induce the government to impose $\tilde{t}_1$. The strict concavity of 1's profit function will then guarantee that the only quantity produced with positive probability and met with $\tilde{t}_1$ is the unique maximizer, $\tilde{Q}_1$. Moreover, the payoff from such an action must be equal to the payoff at the pooled message if 1 is to randomize. This implies that the pool must occur at the point of intersection of 1's complete information isoprofit curve (9) and the tangency locus. Denote this quantity Q^p. Since $\Pi_1(Q, BR(Q^p, \rho\mu|_{i\geq2} + (1 - \rho)\mu))$ is a continuous strictly increasing function of ρ, there exists a unique solution to

$$\Pi_1^s = \Pi_1(Q^p, BR(Q^p, \rho\mu|_{i\geq2} + (1 - \rho)\mu))$$

such that if 1 puts weight ρ on Q^p and $1 - \rho$ on $\tilde{Q}_1$, t^p would be the unique best response to Q^p.

Second, suppose now that the prior probability, μ, is such that $\Pi_1^s < \Pi_1(Q^e, t^e)$. In this case, type 1 would rather pool at Q^e than separate. The partial pooling equilibrium described in the preceding paragraph is not even sequential in this case, since the posterior making t^e a sequential best response would require 1 to export Q^p with probability larger than one. (Keep in mind that in any D_1 pooling equilibrium $i \geq 2$ must pool with probability one.) This shows that the only D_1 equilibrium is in pure strategies at exports Q^e and duty level t^e. The beliefs of the government for any off-equilibrium quantity are uniquely defined as concentrated on type 1 regardless of the prior. The off-equilibrium response is $\tilde{t}_1$, $\forall Q \neq Q^e$. The domestic firm produces according to (7) in response to Q^e.

Finally, note that if $t^e < \tau_0$, then no AD petition will be filed in equilibrium and the firms simply maximize profits myopically and the tariff remains at τ_0.   □

PROOF OF PROPOSITION 3.   Let Q_i^s, as defined in Corollary 2, be the unique candidate for a D_1 separating equilibrium strategy for i. Then $\Pi_i^s = \Pi(Q_i^s, \tilde{t}_i - \tau_0)$.

To show necessity observe that $\Pi_{T-1}^s > \Pi_{T-1}(\tilde{t}_T - \tau_0, \tilde{t}_T)$ implies $\Pi_i^s > \Pi_i(\tilde{t}_T - \tau_0, \tilde{t}_T)$ by Lemma 1. It follows that $Q_i^s > \tilde{t}_i - \tau_0$ for all i, and $Q_i^s < Q_{i-1}^s$. Hence, by Lemma 1 the isoprofit curve for i through $(Q_i^s, \tilde{t}_i)$ has a slope smaller than the isoprofit curve of type $i - 1$ through the same point. In fact, the isoprofit curve for type i is below the curve for type $i - 1$ for export levels higher than Q_i^s and above the curve for $i - 1$ at quantities smaller than Q_i^s. Hence, D_1 requires that the beliefs of the government be placed on type $i - 1$ at off-equilibrium exports $Q \in (Q_i^s, Q_{i-1}^s)$ for all i. Above $\tilde{Q}_1$, the government levies a duty of $\tilde{t}_1 - \tau_0$, and below Q_T^s, the response is $\tilde{t}_T - \tau_0$. These are the unique D_1 beliefs, and they support the outcome in which every type i exports a distinct quantity Q_i^s with probability one as the unique outcome of the game. By Lemma 2 no pooling equilibria exist.

We now show that if the condition of the proposition holds, there exists a unique D_1 equilibrium, and that in its outcome, all but possibly the lowest types export the same quantity with positive probability.

Assume that $\Pi_{T-1}^s > \Pi_{T-1}(\tilde{t}_T - \tau_0, \tilde{t}_T)$ and let type i be the smallest type such that $\Pi_i^s > \Pi_i(Q = \tilde{t}_T - \tau_0, \tilde{t}_T)$. According to Corollary 1, for each $j \geq i$ there exists a unique point $(\hat{Q}_j = \hat{t}_j - \tau_0, \hat{t}_j)$ such that $\Pi_j^s = \Pi_j(\hat{Q}_j, \hat{t}_j)$. Recall that if a type prefers a point along the tangency locus to its separating strategy, so does every higher type. Hence, if a type pools, every higher type produces the pooled quantity with probability one by Corollary 3. Every type lower than i separates with a pure strategy. We now construct the unique equilibrium by induction on j.

1. Suppose that $t(\mu|_{j \geq i}) \leq \hat{t}_i$. In this case all $j \geq i$ pool with probability one at $Q = t(\mu|_{j \geq i}) - \tau_0$. The unique sequentially rational response to the pooled quantity is $t(\mu|_{j \geq i})$.

2. If $t(\mu|_{j \geq i}) > \hat{t}_i$, we have two possibilities.

   (a) Assume that $t(\mu|_{j \geq i+1}) < \hat{t}_i$. In this case, there exists a unique mixed strategy for type i in which it randomizes between Q_i^s and $\hat{Q}_i$ in a way that makes $\hat{t}_i$ a sequential response for the government. (The construction of the mixed strategy for i is the same as the one for type 1 in Proposition 2.) All $j \geq i$ export $\hat{Q}_i$ with probability one.

   (b) Let $t(\mu|_{j \geq i+1}) \geq \hat{t}_i$. If type i pools, we know that all $j \geq i$ would pool with probability one. Hence, the equilibrium response of the government must be bigger than $t(\mu|_{j \geq i+1})$. This implies that i would separate at Q_i^s.

Suppose now that all types smaller than a type $r > i$ separate. From the preceding analysis, it must be that $t(\mu|_{j \geq r}) \geq \hat{t}_{r-1}$.

1. If $t(\mu|_{j \geq r}) \leq \hat{t}_r$, then all $j \geq r$ produce $Q = t(\mu|_{j \geq r}) - \tau_0$ with probability one.

2. If $t(\mu|_{j \geq r}) > \hat{t}_r$, we are facing two scenarios.

   (a) Let $t(\mu|_{j \geq r+1}) < \hat{t}_r$. In this case, r mixes between Q_r^s and $\hat{Q}_r$, all $j \geq r$ export $\hat{Q}_r$ with probability one, and the equilibrium duty is $\hat{t}_r - \tau_0$.

   (b) If $t(\mu|_{j \geq r+1}) \geq \hat{t}_r$, type r separates at Q_r^s with probability one.

This completes the induction.

Since by assumption $\hat{t}_{T-1} > \tilde{t}_T$, separation is not feasible for $T - 1$ by the above construction. Hence, in any D_1 equilibrium, at least types T and $T - 1$ export the same quantity with positive probability.

It is easy to see that if i is the lowest type in a pool, D_1 restricts the off-equilibrium response of the government to $\tilde{t}_i$ in the neighborhood of the pool where the equilibrium isoprofit curve for i is above that of $i - 1$. For lower quantity levels, the beliefs are concentrated on the type willing to break the equilibrium at the highest duty. By Lemma 1, this is necessarily a type smaller than i. For export levels where the equilibrium isoprofit curve of i is below the isoprofit curve for $i - 1$ but (necessarily) lower than Q_{i-1}^s, the beliefs are concentrated on $i - 1$. For any $j \leq i - 1$, the beliefs of the government are placed on $j - 1$ between Q_j^s and Q_{j-1}^s. For export levels higher than the equilibrium quantity of type 1, the response is $\tilde{t}_1$. This is the unique system of beliefs that satisfy D_1 and they trivially support the pooling outcome of the game. □

REFERENCES

ANDERSON, J. E., "Domino Dumping I: Competitive Exporters," *American Economic Review* 82 (1992), 65–83.

BANKS, J., AND J. SOBEL, "Equilibrium Selection in Signaling Games," *Econometrica* 55 (1987), 647–61.

BELLIS, J.-F., "The EEC Antidumping System," in J. H. Jackson, and E. A. Vermulstt, eds., *Antidumping Law and Practice* (Ann Arbor, MI: The University of Michigan Press, 1989).

BERNHEIM, B. D., "Tax Policy and the Dividend Puzzle," *RAND Journal of Economics* 22 (1991), 455–76.

———, "A Theory of Conformity," *Journal of Political Economy* 102 (1994), 841–77.

BHAGWATI, J., *Protectionism* (Cambridge, MA: The MIT Press, 1988).

BOLTUCK, R., AND R. E. LITAN, eds., *Down in the Dumps* (Washington, DC: The Brookings Institution, 1991).

BRAINARD, S. L., AND D. MARTIMORT, "Strategic Trade Policy with Incompletely Informed Policymakers," *Journal of International Economics* 42 (1997), 33–66.

BRANDER, J. A., AND B. J. SPENCER, "Tariff Protection and Imperfect Competition," in H. Kierzkowsky, ed., *Monopolistic Competition and International Trade* (Oxford: Clarendon, 1984).

CHO, I.-K., "Separation or Not: A Critique of 'Appearance-Based' Selection Criteria," *Seoul Journal of Economics* 7 (1994), 249–68.

———, AND D. M. KREPS, "Signaling Games and Stable Equilibria," *Quarterly Journal of Economics* 42 (1987), 179–221.

———, AND J. SOBEL, "Strategic Stability and Uniqueness in Signaling Games," *Journal of Economic Theory* 50 (1990), 381–413.

CLARIDA, R. H., "Dumping in Theory, in Policy, and in Practice," in J. Bhagwati and R. Hudec, eds., *Fair Trade and Harmonization* (Cambridge, MA: The MIT Press, 1996).

COLLIE, D. AND M. HVIID, "Export Subsidies As Signals of Competitiveness," *Scandinavian Journal of Economics* 95 (1993), 327–39.

———, AND ———, "Tariffs for a Foreign Monopolist Under Incomplete Information," *Journal of International Economics* 37 (1994), 249–64.

HARRIS, R., "Why Voluntary Export Restraints Are 'Voluntary'," *Canadian Journal of Economics* 18 (1985), 799–809.

HORLICK, G. N., "The United States Antidumping System," in J. H. Jackson and E. A. Vermulst, eds., *Antidumping Law and Practice* (Ann Arbor, MI: The University of Michigan Press, 1989).

INTERNATIONAL TRADE COMMISSION, *The Economic Effects of Antidumping and Countervailing Duty Orders and Suspension Agreements*, Publication No. 2900, 1995.

KOLEV, D. R., AND T. J. PRUSA, "Dumping and Double Crossing: The (In)Effectiveness of Cost-Based Trade Policy under Incomplete Information," NBER Working Paper 6986, 1999.

KRISHNA, K., "Trade Restrictions As Facilitating Practices," *Journal of International Economics* 26 (1989), 251–70.

KRUEGER, A. O., *American Trade Policy: A Tragedy in the Making* (Washington, DC: The AEI Press, 1995).

LAWRENCE, R., "Outlook is Mixed for US Steel Manufacturers," *Journal of Commerce* 5 (1999), 9.

LOW, P., *Trading Free: The GATT and U.S. Trade Policy* (New York: The Twentieth Century Fund Press, 1993).

MESSERLIN, P. A., "The EC Antidumping Regulations: A First Economic Appraisal 1980–85," *Weltwirtschaftliches Archiv* 125 (1989), 563–87.

MILGROM, P., AND J. D. ROBERTS, "Limit Pricing and Entry under Incomplete Information: An Equilibrium Analysis," *Econometrica* 50 (1982), 443–59.

PRESTOWITZ, C., *Trading Places: How We Are Giving Our Future to Japan and How to Reclaim It* (New York: Basic Books, 1988).

PRUSA, T. J., "Why Are So Many Antidumping Petitions Withdrawn?" *Journal of International Economics* 33 (1992), 1–20.

QIU, L., "Optimal Strategic Trade Policy under Asymmetric Information," *Journal of International Economics* 36 (1994), 333–54.

RILEY, J., "Informational Equilbrium," *Econometrica* 47 (1979), 331–59.

ROSENDORFF, B. P., "Voluntary Export Restraints, Antidumping Procedure, and Domestic Politics," *American Economic Review* 86 (1996), 544–61.

STAIGER, R. W. AND F. A. WOLAK, "Strategic Use of Antidumping Law to Enforce Tacit International Collusion," NBER Working Paper No. 3016, 1989.

———, AND ———, "The Effect of Domestic Antidumping Law in the Presence of Foreign Monopoly," *Journal of International Economics* 32 (1992), 265–87.

STEWART, T., "Administration of the Antidumping Duty Law: A Different Persective," in R. Boltuck and R. E. Litan, eds., *Down in the Dumps* (Washington, DC: The Brookings Institution, 1991).

YANO, M., "Voluntary Export Restraints and Expectations: An Analysis of Export Quotas in Oligopolistic Markets," *International Economic Review* 30 (1989), 707–23.

Chapter 7

Macroeconomic factors and antidumping filings: evidence from four countries[†]

Michael M. Knetter[a], Thomas J. Prusa[b],*

[a]*University of Wisconsin and NBER, Madison, WI 53706-1393, USA*
[b]*Department of Economics and NBER, Rutgers University, New Brunswick, NJ 08901, USA*

Received 30 November 2001; received in revised form 25 February 2002; accepted 6 June 2002

Abstract

This paper examines the relationship between antidumping filings and macroeconomic factors. Real exchange rate fluctuations affect the two criteria for dumping in opposite ways, making the overall effect on filings ambiguous in theory. Examining the filing patterns of the four major users of AD law during the 1980–98 period we find that real exchange rates and domestic real GDP growth both have statistically significant impacts on filings. Bilateral filing data indicate that a one-standard deviation real appreciation of the domestic currency increases filings by 33%. We also find one-standard deviation fall in domestic real GDP increases filings by 23%. © 2002 Elsevier B.V. All rights reserved.

Keywords: Antidumping law; exchange rate pass-through

JEL classification: F13

1. Introduction

The GATT/WTO antidumping (AD) statute requires two criteria to be met in order to impose duties on foreign suppliers named in antidumping suits. First, there must be evidence that the domestic industry has suffered "material injury" (e.g., a decline in profitability) as a result of foreign imports. Second, the foreign suppliers must be found to be pricing at "less than fair value" (LTFV). This latter

---

*Corresponding author. Tel.: +1-732-932-7670; fax: +1-732-932-7416.
E-mail address: prusa@econ.rutgers.edu (T.J. Prusa).

[†]This article originally appeared in *Journal of International Economics*, **61**(3), pp. 1–17.

2   *M.M. Knetter, T.J. Prusa / Journal of International Economics 61 (2003) 1–17*

criterion can be determined in either of two ways: (1) by showing that the price charged in the domestic market by the foreign suppliers is below the price charged for the same product in other markets (i.e., the "price-based" method) or (2) by showing that the price charged in the domestic market is below an estimate of cost plus a normal return (i.e., the "constructed-value" method).

The focus of this paper is on how macroeconomic factors in general, and fluctuations in real exchange rates in particular, can affect the determination of each of these criteria. As we will explain, a foreign firm's response to a real exchange rate changes increases the likelihood that at least one of the AD criteria will be satisfied. At a theoretical level real exchange rate changes can either increase or decrease filings, depending on which AD test is most responsive to pricing changes. Empirically which effect is more important is also an open question. Within the business community there appears to be a belief that a strong domestic currency precipitates filings. For example, in its March 26, 1999 *Economic Analyst* publication, Goldman Sachs documents a rise in AD cases associated with an increase in the value of the trade-weighted U.S. dollar. Interestingly, the existing empirical literature reaches the opposite conclusion. In particular, using a dataset based on U.S. AD filings from 1982 to 87 Feinberg (1989) finds that filings increase with a weaker dollar.

Fluctuations in economic activity, both in the importing country and the exporting country, might also affect filing decisions. Clearly, a slump in economic activity in the importing country makes it more likely domestic firms perform poorly which may facilitate a finding of material injury. Also, a weak economy in the importing country might naturally lead foreign firms to reduce prices on shipments to the importing country. This could increase the likelihood of pricing below fair value. Thus we would expect that import country GDP will be negatively related to filings. It is less clear how export country GDP is related to filings. One possibility is that a weak foreign economy increases the likelihood that foreign firms will cut prices to maintain overall levels of output. While such behavior might cause injury to domestic firms, it is not clear that it would trigger pricing below "fair value" in the price-based sense, since foreign firms would presumably be lowering prices to all markets (especially their own home market). It is possible, however, that generally low prices would increase the chance of LTFV using the "constructed-value" method.

Our goal in this paper is to examine the relationship between AD filings, real exchange rates, and economic activity using data for four of the primary AD users (Australia, Canada, the European Union, and the U.S.).[1] Interestingly, despite the

---

[1] Several recent papers study issues related to those examined in this paper. Hens et al. (1999) study pricing-to-market in a reciprocal duopoly model. However, they do not address the issue of how pricing-to-market is affected by AD law. Blonigen and Haynes (1999) study the pricing behavior of firms following the imposition of AD duties. We are interested in the pricing behavior prior to an AD investigation. Finally, a number of papers including Baldwin and Steagall (1994) and Krupp (1994) examine how various factors influence the ITC injury decision. We focus not on the injury determination but on the number of filings in this work.

M.M. Knetter, T.J. Prusa / Journal of International Economics 61 (2003) 1–17 3

theoretical ambiguity we find unambiguous support in both the aggregate and bilateral filing data that a real appreciation of the filing country's currency will lead to a significant increase in AD filings. For instance, in our bilateral data we find that a one standard deviation real appreciation of the filing country currency leads to a 33% increase in AD filings. We also find that a one standard deviation fall in domestic real GDP growth leads to a 23% increase in AD filings.

We believe that these findings are further evidence that antidumping law is not primarily used to combat unfair trade, but rather is often simple protectionism. While fluctuations in real GDP and real exchange rates are certain to affect industry equilibria, they are unlikely to be systematically associated with malevolent behavior by foreign firms. Our results suggests that foreign firms are being held responsible for the impact of factors beyond their control.

2. Exchange rates and antidumping filings

From a theoretical perspective, a foreign firm's response to a real exchange rate change will exacerbate either the injury or LTFV test. This point can be made simply by considering the case of a foreign firm servicing the domestic market.[2] In Fig. 1 we graph the foreign supplier's response to a real depreciation in its home currency (e.g., Japanese exporter's response to a weakening of the yen). As the firm is servicing the domestic market, the demand curve represents domestic demand (e.g., demand in the U.S. market).

When the foreign currency weakens, the firm's costs (denominated in domestic currency units) fall from MC_0 to MC_1. Therefore, normal response of foreign firms is to lower the domestic currency price of foreign goods. This would be expected to reduce the profits of domestic producers in the same industry by lowering their margins or market share.[3]

In general, however, this price response (in terms of its own home currency) implies that the foreign firm has increased the foreign currency price of shipments to the domestic market relative to other destinations, but by less than the appreciation of the domestic currency.[4] An increase in the foreign currency price

---

[2] The informal verbal arguments made here are thoroughly derived in the working paper version of this paper (Knetter and Prusa, 2000).

[3] Note that the dollar price of imported goods will fall relative to domestic goods with a real appreciation of the dollar provided the foreign firm does not completely offset the relative cost change with a markup change. The special case in which markups are adjusted to fully offset the effects of currency movements is known as "complete pricing-to-market" in the literature. The opposite case, in which exchange rate changes are fully passed-through to foreign buyers is known as "full pass-through."

[4] The relationship between exchange rate fluctuations and destination-specific pricing of exports is known as pricing-to-market behavior. The evidence on pricing-to-market varies by industry (see Goldberg and Knetter, 1997), but the median price response to a real exchange rate change across industries studied in the literature is close to 50%—i.e., half of the movement in the real exchange rate is offset by destination-price adjustment.

Economic Effects of Antidumping

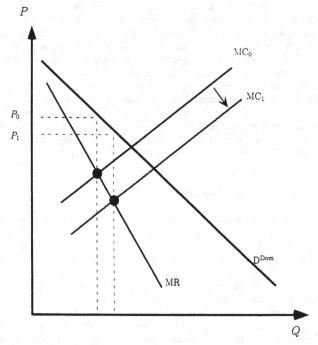

Fig. 1. Reaction of foreign supplier when its home currency weakens.

of shipments to the domestic market obviously reduces the chance that the foreign firm is guilty of LTFV pricing.

Thus, with typical pricing-to-market behavior, a strong (weak) domestic currency will increase (decrease) the chance of injury and make it less (more) likely that the foreign firm is guilty of LTFV pricing. If we presume that the incentive to file an AD case is positively related to the likelihood of affirmative decisions on the injury and LTFV criteria then in theory it is entirely possible that either exchange rate appreciations or depreciations can precipitate AD filings.

As an empirical matter, the issue is further clouded by the fact that the four major users of AD protection all have their own specific implementation of the GATT/WTO rules. The conventional wisdom for the world's heaviest user of AD protection—the United States—is that the material injury criterion is the more difficult test to satisfy. For instance, over the past 20 years only 28 of 800 U.S. cases received negative LTFV determinations; by contrast, there have been over 300 negative injury determinations. This track record suggests that more an-

M.M. Knetter, T.J. Prusa / Journal of International Economics 61 (2003) 1–17 5

tidumping cases would be filed when exchange rates or output fluctuations improve the odds of an affirmative material injury decision—i.e., when the domestic currency is strong in real terms or when the domestic country is in recession.

The other countries implement AD protection somewhat differently and so this presumption that injury drives the filings is not obvious. To begin with, the EU uses a single agency to make both determinations while Canada, Australia, and the U.S. all use two agencies. This could make the EU results more muddled. Second, EU and Australian AD regulations likely make the injury criterion easier to satisfy than in the U.S. (Santos, 1998). Both have very restrictive rules for accessing information so foreign firms have a more difficult time defending themselves. Third, Australia and the EU both use the "lesser duty" rule which dampens the importance of large margins; the U.S. has no such rule. Finally, ministerial oversight in both Australia and the EU mean their AD determinations are subject to more direct political interference. Depending upon whether political pressure is greater when injury or dumping margins are larger, this oversight could make either criterion more important.

3. Data

To investigate the relationship between antidumping filings and macroeconomic conditions, we collected data on AD filings by the four largest users: Australia, Canada, the United States, and the European Union. The filing data is available from the GATT/WTO annual reports.

These four users accounted for more than two-thirds of all AD actions filed worldwide since 1980. For each of these four reporting regions (henceforth referred to as "reporting" or "filing" countries), we have aggregate filing data on an annual basis from 1980 to 98.[5] For each filing, we know the filing country, the industry, the country named in the filing (i.e., the defendant), and the ultimate determination (injury or no injury). The GATT/WTO reports do not include any information on the dumping margin which precludes us from directly looking at how exchange rate changes affects margins.

Fig. 2 displays the number of filings by filing country for our 1980–98 sample period. The figures show there is considerable variation in the number of filings from year-to-year. Furthermore, it is clear that filings are related to the business cycle, especially for the United States and Australia. The recessions that began in the early 1980s and early 1990s (the only two in our sample) are associated with large spikes in the number of filings.

The level and variation of filings across filers is summarized in Table 1.

---

[5]Changes in antidumping law in 1979 preclude us from using filing data prior to 1980. Also, due to reporting problems we do not have Australian filings in 1980 and 1981.

6   M.M. Knetter, T.J. Prusa / Journal of International Economics 61 (2003) 1–17

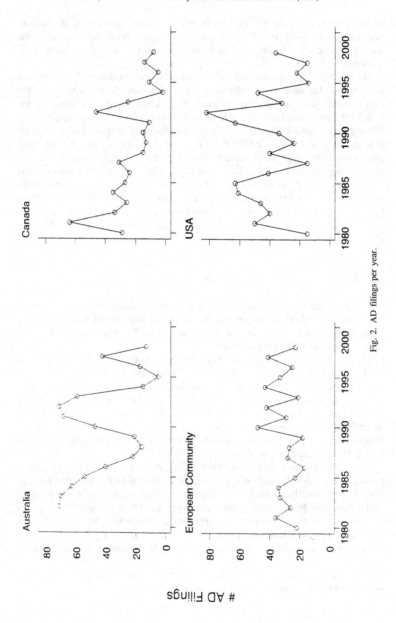

Fig. 2. AD filings per year.

M.M. Knetter, T.J. Prusa / Journal of International Economics 61 (2003) 1–17   7

Table 1
Mean and standard deviation of filings by source country, 1980–98

	Avg. filings per year	Std. Dev.
Australia*	41	24
Canada	23	15
EU	30	9
USA	39	19

*1982–98.

Adjusting for the fact that its filing data is missing for 1980–81, we find that Australia is the heaviest filer of the four regions. This is surprising given that it is the smallest of the four countries by a fairly large margin (e.g., Canada has a population about 50% greater than Australia, while the U.S. and EU are about 10 times the size of Canada). Table 2 shows the pattern of bilateral filings across countries. As is readily apparent there is substantial variation in filing across countries. The US and EU have frequently targeted Japanese products while Australia and Canada have both made the US a prime target.

The International Monetary Fund *International Financial Statistics* CD-ROM provided real GDP data for both the filing countries and the named countries. In our empirical work we perform tests using both aggregate filings and also the number of filings against individual countries. For the aggregate filing behavior, we use the real effective exchange rate index (based on labor costs) for the filing country as reported by the IMF. In our examination of filings against individual foreign countries (i.e., "bilateral filings"), we used bilateral real exchange rates between each of the four filing countries and each country named in at least one antidumping case since 1980. The Economic Research Service of the U.S. Department of Agriculture was a convenient source for bilateral real exchange rates since they report exchange rates in a consistent fashion for virtually all countries in the world. The exchange rate is defined as foreign currency per unit of domestic currency so that an increase in the exchange rate reflects an appreciation of the filing country's currency. Also, we normalize each country's exchange rate by dividing by the sample average.

4. Empirical specification and results

The preceding discussion motivates how filings might be affected by real exchange rates, filing country GDP, and rest of world GDP. The dependent variable in our econometric work will be the number of filings occurring in a year.

Since the number of filings is a non-negative count variable, we will estimate the relationship between number of filings and macroeconomic factors using negative binomial regression which is essentially a Poisson model with a more flexible error structure.

8 *M.M. Knetter, T.J. Prusa / Journal of International Economics 61 (2003) 1–17*

Table 2
Bilateral filing patterns

Affected country	Reporting country				
	Canada	USA	European union	Australia	Total
Japan	26	88	53	45	212
USA	83	0	30	63	176
South Korea	25	47	37	47	156
PR-China	14	60	45	37	156
Taiwan	16	50	11	49	126
Germany	31	43	0	47	121
Brazil	15	43	20	23	101
Italy	22	35	0	28	85
United Kingdom	25	27	0	31	83
France	24	29	0	28	81
Spain	18	18	18	9	63
Canada	0	41	8	11	60
Thailand	2	10	17	25	54
Czechoslovakia	8	1	37	7	53
Poland	8	8	28	6	50
Belgium–Luxembourg	11	16	0	22	49
India	5	14	21	7	47
Romania	9	9	25	2	45
Mexico	6	21	8	4	39
Singapore	5	5	6	21	37
Sweden	10	8	7	11	36
Hungary	1	5	22	6	34
Netherlands	5	12	0	16	33
Malaysia	5	3	11	13	32
Indonesia	2	3	11	15	31
South Africa	3	6	5	15	29
Hong Kong	5	4	10	10	29
Turkey	0	6	14	4	24
Argentina	3	13	1	6	23
Austria	3	7	5	8	23
New Zealand	2	3	0	17	22
Venezuela	1	17	1	2	21
All other countries	24	58	58	56	196
Total	417	710	509	691	2327

The Poisson regression model assumes that the incidence rate v (the rate per unit time at which happenings occur) is a function of some underlying variables as follows:

$$v_j = e^{\beta_0 + \beta_1 x_{1j} + \beta_2 x_{2j} + \cdots + \beta_k x_{kj}}$$

The expected number of occurrences is equal to this incidence rate multiplied by the exposure (the number of units of time over which observations are measured).

M.M. Knetter, T.J. Prusa / Journal of International Economics 61 (2003) 1–17 9

The exposure is uninteresting in our case since each observation in the data set is the number of AD filings in a 1-year interval. We believe that the incidence rate is a function of GDP growth in the home and foreign countries, the real exchange rate, and possibly other factors.

One feature of the Poisson model that is frequently violated in applications is the equivalence of the expected value and variance of a Poisson random variable. Often, count data exhibit overdispersion with respect to the Poisson model—i.e., the variance of the observed counts exceeds their mean. This is certainly true regarding the data reported in Table 1. In such cases, an alternative is to assume that the data are generated by a negative binomial random variable, which allows for a variance that is greater than the expected value of the distribution. While we present conclusions based on the negative binomial (NB) regression model, we also estimated the models using Poisson and found similar results in terms of the statistical and economic significance of the macroeconomic factors on AD filings.

In addition to method of estimation, another important specification issue is the lag structure of the regressors. The legal framework for determining LTFV and material injury offers some guidance here. While not specified under WTO rules, all of the reporting countries generally analyze pricing behavior over the year prior to the filing of the case in order to assess LTFV. By contrast, all of the reporting countries evaluate injury over a longer time horizon. In general, injury is determined over the 3 years preceding the filing. Given these features of the law, it seems plausible to consider lags from 1 to 3 years for our variables. We report results with a 1-year lag on the real exchange rate (since we conjecture that exchange rates may be more important for LTFV which is assessed over the 1-year period) and 3-year lags on real GDP growth. We have experimented with other lag structures (and contemporaneous values) and are confident that none of our main results is affected by the choice of lag structure.

4.1. Annual data on aggregate filings

Our first set of results is based on the annual number of filings for each of our four reporting units (Australia, Canada, EU, and US). We estimate the number of filings as a function of the real exchange rate, domestic real GDP growth, and rest of world real GDP growth using the NB regression. The real exchange rate variable is normalized by dividing each exchange rate series by its sample mean before taking logs. The real GDP growth variable is the 3-year growth rate from $t-3$ to t (i.e., the 3 years prior to the filing date).

In Tables 3–5, we report "incidence rate ratios" associated with the parameter estimates. The incidence rate ratio (IRR) is the ratio of the counts predicted by the model when the variable of interest is one unit above its mean value and all other variables are at their means to the counts predicted when all variables are at their means. Thus, if the IRR for the real exchange rate is 1.50, then a one unit increase in the real exchange rate (a 100% real appreciation given that we use the log of the

10   M.M. Knetter, T.J. Prusa / Journal of International Economics 61 (2003) 1–17

Table 3
Negative binomial estimation of aggregate filings

Model	(1)	(2)	(3)	(4)
rxr (−1)	4.18	4.69	3.67	3.91
	(2.75)	(3.40)	(2.80)	(2.96)
FGDP (avg)			0.93	0.97
			(−2.05)	(−0.61)
WGDP (avg)				0.89
				(−1.21)
Random effects	NO	YES	YES	YES

Notes: rxr (−1) is the log of the real exchange rate, lagged 1 year; FGDP (WGDP) is percentage growth in real GDP of filing country (rest of world) over prior 3 years. Estimates are reported as "incidence rate ratios". *t*-statistics reported for a test of no effect on filings (which corresponds to an IRR value of 1.0). Number of observations = 74.

Table 4
Negative binomial estimation of aggregate filings-country specific exchange rate and domestic GDP response

Model	(1)	(2)	(3)	(4)	(5)
rxr (Australia)	51.6	30.4	38.2		36.2
	(4.46)	(3.58)	(4.09)		(4.43)
rxr (Canada)	2.22	0.93	1.17		0.11
	(0.55)	(−0.05)	(0.11)		(−1.33)
rxr (EU)	2.16	2.04	1.68		1.98
	(0.56)	(0.55)	(0.39)		(0.55)
rxr (US)	2.51	2.62	2.60		2.61
	(1.57)	(1.67)	(1.70)		(1.79)
FGDP (avg)		0.94	1.00		
		(−1.56)	(0.08)		
WGDP (avg)			0.86		
			(−1.73)		
rxr				3.56	
				(2.75)	
GDP (Australia)				0.97	0.96
				(−0.99)	(−1.01)
GDP (Canada)				0.82	0.79
				(−2.99)	(−3.50)
GDP (EU)				0.92	0.90
				(−1.28)	(−1.67)
GDP (US)				0.97	0.95
				(−0.63)	(−0.90)

Note: All regressions include random effects. All variables defined as in Table 3. Estimates are reported as "incidence rate ratios". *t*-statistics reported for a test of no effect on filings (which corresponds to an IRR value of 1.0). Number of observations = 74.

M.M. Knetter, T.J. Prusa / Journal of International Economics 61 (2003) 1–17 11

Table 5
Negative binomial estimation of bilateral filings

Model	(1)	(2)	(3)	(4)	(5)
rxr (−1)	3.28	3.30	3.37		
	(7.98)	(8.14)	(8.02)		
rxr (Australia)				7.80	7.57
				(6.29)	(6.14)
rxr (Canada)				2.37	2.37
				(2.54)	(2.55)
rxr (EU)				4.23	4.22
				(4.47)	(4.43)
rxr (US)				2.09	1.97
				(2.93)	(2.66)
FGDP (avg)		0.97	0.97	0.97	
		(−6.12)	(−5.93)	(−5.36)	
AGDP (avg)			1.00	1.00	1.00
			(−0.43)	(−0.48)	(−0.56)
GDP (Australia)					0.96
					(−5.01)
GDP (Canada)					0.98
					(−1.81)
GDP (EU)					0.96
					(−1.74)
GDP (US)					0.98
					(−1.71)
No. Obs.	3469	3469	3397	3397	3397

Note: All specifications include random effects for each reporting country-affected country pair. Estimates are reported as "incidence rate ratios". *t*-statistics reported for a test of no effect on filings (which corresponds to an IRR value of 1.0). The number of observations falls in specifications (3)–(5) due to missing values for affected country GDP.

real rate) would increase counts by 50% when all other variables are at their means. The *t*-statistics are reported for a test of the null hypothesis that the IRR = 1, which would imply no relationship between the dependent variable and the regressor.

The most basic results based on aggregate filings are presented in Table 3. In all of the models the exchange rate has a statistically significant impact at the 1% level. The aggregate filing data unambiguously indicate that AD filings increase substantially when the filing country currency strengthens in real terms, which contrasts with Feinberg's (1989) result that U.S. filings rise with a weakening currency. We will analyze the sources of this difference later in the paper.

Domestic GDP growth is negatively related to filings when it is included alone, but when domestic and world GDP growth are both included, neither variable is statistically significant, although both have the expected negative relationship.

In Table 4 we report results on aggregate filings that include a filing-country specific real exchange rate effect. This allows us only 19 annual observations (17

12   *M.M. Knetter, T.J. Prusa / Journal of International Economics 61 (2003) 1–17*

for Australia) with which to detect a relationship, and more importantly, only a few big swings in the real exchange rate series for each filing country. Here we find that Australia has by far the most pronounced exchange rate effect. The IRR values exceed 50 in some cases and the coefficients are significant at the 1% level. The U.S. results are "borderline significant" with *t*-values ranging from 1.6 to 1.8 and IRRs between 2.5 and 2.6. Canada and the EU are never close to being statistically significant and the IRRs tend to be quite small. Part of the problem may be the limited number of observations, which we can rectify by examining filings by "affected country" (i.e., those countries named in a suit as "defendants") for each of our filing countries. These results are discussed below. All of the countries have the expected negative relationship between own GDP growth and filings, but only Canada's is statistically significant.

Our findings in Tables 3 and 4 are based on pooling all data on AD filings across our four filing countries for all industries. Given that the steel industry files a large fraction of U.S. and Canadian cases, we felt is was important to verify that our findings are not being driven by the steel industry's behavior. Unfortunately, the GATT/WTO reports have only identified industry since 1987, thereby limiting our ability to drop steel cases from the entire dataset. Using the data available, we performed the above analysis eliminating the steel industry and we find that the statistical significance of the real exchange rate effects is similar and the economic significance (given by the magnitude of the IRR in NB regression) is much greater. The real GDP growth effects become insignificant (although the point estimates are still negative) when steel cases are excluded from the data. The impact on exchange rates and GDP from excluding steel suggests that AD filings in steel are heavily influenced by the business cycle, but not so much by exchange rates.[6]

4.2. Annual data on bilateral filings

In constructing the database with filings broken down by affected country, we lost a relatively small number of observations due to the inability to construct real exchange rates or real GDP growth over the sample period. Most of the cases involved countries that were part of the former Soviet Union. Once these observations were eliminated, we had a panel dataset with 4 filing countries, 48 affected countries (47 for each filing country), and 19 years (17 for Australia).[7] We model the number of cases against an affected country by a filing country in each year as a function of the bilateral real exchange rate, filing country real GDP growth, and affected country real GDP growth. The advantage of this dataset, which we believe is substantial, is that the exchange rate and foreign GDP growth variables are more precisely targeted to match the country named in the filings.

---

[6]These results are available upon request.

[7]There are still a small number of missing observations for certain affected countries due to missing GDP data.

M.M. Knetter, T.J. Prusa / Journal of International Economics 61 (2003) 1–17 13

Following the findings with aggregate filing data, we apply the negative binomial regression model to the data.

The main results are presented in Table 5. These regressions use random effects for each filing-affected country pair. When we estimate a common response to exchange rates across all filing countries, we find the real exchange rate variable is significant at the 1% level in all models, with an IRR ranging from 3.28 to 3.37. Although the estimated IRR values are somewhat lower than with aggregate filings, one must keep in mind that the bilateral exchange rate series are much more volatile than the trade-weighted exchange rates used in the aggregate filings (e.g., the standard deviation tends to be about twice as big).

The results when we allow for a filing-country specific response to the real exchange rate with random effects and real GDP growth are reported in column (4). We find that the real exchange rate impact is significant at the 1% level for Canada (with an IRR of 2.37), the U.S. (IRR equal to 2.09), the EU (IRR equal to 4.23) and Australia (IRR equal to 7.80). The increased detail of the observations has the greatest impact on our results for the EU, which with the aggregate data showed no indication of increased filings when the trade weighted real exchange rate appreciated. In the bilateral data, it is clear that filings rise systematically against countries whose real exchange rates have depreciated against the countries of the EU. The exchange rate impacts are very similar when we allow reporting country-specific real GDP growth effects (column 5). It is worth noting that the country that has filed the most AD cases, Australia, also has the greatest estimated increase in filings in response to a currency appreciation.

In the bilateral filings database, it is also apparent that filing country real GDP growth is negatively and significantly related to the number of filings. In the model with random effects and a common real exchange rate response in column (2), we find that a one percentage-point increase in filing country 3-year real GDP growth leads to a 3% decrease in the number of filings (i.e., the IRR is 0.97). Adding real GDP growth of the affected countries in column (3) does not affect this estimate. Affected country real GDP growth now appears to be unrelated to the number of filings. The IRR estimates are very close to 1.00 and are never close to being statistically significant. This change in the impact of reporting country and affected country real GDP growth on the number of filings is the main difference from the results obtained with the aggregate filings data. It appears that domestic, but not foreign, recessions systematically provoke more filings.

In terms of the economic significance of the macro factors in the bilateral filings data, we find that for the specifications in columns (1) and (2) of Table 5, a one-standard deviation real appreciation of the domestic currency leads to a 33% increase in filings, while a two-standard deviation real appreciation results in a 77% increase. In column (2), the estimated real GDP impact implies that a one standard deviation reduction in real GDP growth leads to a 23% increase in filings. Based on these estimates, we conclude that both variables are economically significant in explaining the pattern of filings across countries and over time, and that real exchange rates are somewhat more important.

Table 6
Tobit estimation of bilateral filings

Model	(1)	(2)	(3)	(4)	(5)	(6)	(7)
Years	1982–1987	All	1982–1987	All	All	1982–87	All
Reporting countries	U.S.	U.S.	U.S.	U.S.	All	All	All
Affected countries	Feinberg 4	Feinberg 4	All	All	Feinberg 4	All	All
rxr	−1.94	2.09	2.44	1.63	3.59	3.82	2.05
	(−0.46)	(1.21)	(2.52)	(2.87)	(3.61)	(6.46)	(6.13)
Constant	3.55	2.35	−0.87	−1.22	0.97	−1.65	−2.05
	(3.91)	(7.36)	(−3.39)	(−7.51)	(5.34)	(−9.65)	(−18.89)
No. Obs.	24	76	281	890	304	1094	3465

Note: t-statistics in parentheses.

M.M. Knetter, T.J. Prusa / Journal of International Economics 61 (2003) 1–17 15

The more robust link between filings and macro factors (especially for filing country specific responses to exchange rates) in the bilateral data is no doubt attributable to the increased number of observations and the reduction in noise associated with the real exchange rate. The latter results from the fact that the real exchange rate is matched to a specific affected country, rather than being a trade-weighted average rate as it was for the regressions based on aggregate filings. This appears to be a case where aggregation over the affected countries and studying total filings in relation to a trade-weighted exchange rate obscures some interesting information. We place more faith in the bilateral results.

Given the robustness of our findings we want to address the discrepancy between our results and Feinberg's finding that U.S. AD filings increase when the dollar is weak. Feinberg's analysis differs from ours in two important ways. First, he uses a Tobit model. Second, his sample is much smaller than ours. He uses quarterly data to analyze U.S. filings against Korea, Mexico, Brazil, and Japan for the 1982–87 period. Either the estimation approach or some aspect of his sample selection could explain the difference in our findings.

In order to identify why our findings differ, we estimated the impact of the exchange rate on filings using Tobit analysis with our annual bilateral filings sample. We report results in Table 6. In column one we report results using only U.S. filings against the same four countries for the same time period Feinberg studied. Although the results are not statistically significant, we find the same qualititative result as Feinberg—namely, filings increase when the dollar is weak. This suggests that the difference in our findings is not being driven by estimation procedure. In columns 2–7 we expand the sample, allowing more affected countries, more years, and more filing countries. The results are quite striking. In *all* cases we find that filings increase when home currency is strong. In other words, Feinberg's finding is very sensitive to the sample chosen. For instance, in column two we study U.S. filings against the countries in Feinberg's study but for the entire time period. We find that Feinberg's result is reversed, albeit the estimate is statistically insignificant in both samples. In column three we examine U.S. filings against all affected countries for the Feinberg time period, 1982–87. Again, we find that Feinberg's result is reversed. In the other columns we progressively broaden the sample and we continue to find strong support for the finding that AD filings increase when the home currency is strong. We interpret these results as indicating that our finding is highly robust.

5. Conclusion

Antidumping suits have become an increasingly popular form of protection for firms engaged in international markets. This paper has examined how macroeconomic factors in general and the real exchange rate in particular, can influence the probability of affirmative findings for the LTFV and material injury criteria.

168   *Economic Effects of Antidumping*

16   *M.M. Knetter, T.J. Prusa / Journal of International Economics 61 (2003) 1–17*

Our empirical work uses data on AD filings from Australia, Canada, the European Union, and the United States. We find that a real appreciation of the filing country's currency will lead to a significant increase in AD filings. This result is at odds with existing research on the subject, but is robust to the method of estimation, to the inclusion of other macroeconomic variables such as real GDP growth, and to the elimination of steel cases in the filing data. The results are strongest when we examine bilateral filings. The economic significance is substantial—a one (two) standard deviation real appreciation of the filing country currency leads to a 33% (77%) increase in AD filings in our specification that constrains the response to be common across filing countries. We also find that a one standard deviation fall in domestic real GDP growth leads to a 23% increase in AD filings.

In addition, our research resolves the tension between Feinberg's result that a weak domestic currency encourages filings and the belief within the business community that a strong domestic currency precipitates filings. We find that Feinberg's result is quite fragile, severely dependent on the particular sample he used.

The link between real exchange rates and filings suggests that either foreign firms are being held responsible for factors outside of their control or that foreign firms behave in a "predatory" manner when conditions favor them most.[8] Given the findings of other related literature (Boltuck and Litan, 1991) we are more inclined to believe the former hypothesis, which casts further doubt on the fairness of AD law.

The fact that we find that filings for all four major users of antidumping protection are significantly influenced by exchange rate fluctuations suggests that the problem with countries abusing antidumping rules is not simply a U.S. or EU problem. Rather, it indicates that GATT/WTO rules governing antidumping law allow abuses of the statute. Our findings support the notion that current (and perhaps future) rounds of the WTO must include antidumping reform on the negotiating agenda.

Acknowledgements

We would like to thank Andy Bernard, Bruce Blonigen, Mendy Rudolph, and seminar participants at the NBER ITI Summer Institute, Tokyo University, and Penn State University for useful comments and discussion. The paper also benefitted from the comments of two anonymous referees. We are especially

---

[8]This view is echoed in the Goldman Sachs *Economic Analyst* which claims that "the correlation between the number of AD cases initiated and the change in the G7 trade-weighted dollar index suggests that domestic producers have been seeking protection against adverse market conditions, not against anti-competitive dumping."

M.M. Knetter, T.J. Prusa / Journal of International Economics 61 (2003) 1–17 17

appreciative of the assistance of Jorge Miranda in compiling the AD filing database. Finally, we thank Tara Nells for her excellent research assistance.

References

Baldwin, R.E., Steagall, J.W., 1994. An analysis of ITC decisions in antidumping, countervailing duty, and safeguard cases. Weltwirtschaftliches Archiv 130 (2), 290–308.

Blonigen, B.A., Haynes, S.E., 1999. Antidumping Investigations and the Pass-Through of Exchange Rates and Antidumping Duties, NBER Working Paper No. W7378.

Boltuck, R., Litan, R.E., 1991. Down in the Dumps. The Brookings Institution, Washington, DC.

Feinberg, R.M., 1989. Exchange Rates and Unfair Trade, Review of Economics and Statistics, 71, 704–707.

Goldman Sachs, 1999. Economic Analyst, March 26.

Goldberg, P., Knetter, M.M., 1997. Goods prices and exchange rates: What have we learned? Journal of Economic Literature 35, 1243–1272.

Hens, T., Jäger, E., Kirman, A., Phlips, L., 1999. Exchange rates and oligopoly. European Economic Review 43, 621–648.

Knetter, M.M., Prusa, T.J., 2000. Macroeconomic factors and antidumping filings: Evidence from four countries, NBER Working Paper No. 8010.

Krupp, C., 1994. Antidumping cases in the U.S. chemical industry—A panel data approach. Journal of Industrial Economics 42 (3), 299–311.

Santos, L.E. (Ed.), 1998. The Compendium of Foreign Trade Remedy Laws. The American Bar Association, Washington, DC.

Chapter 8

CUMULATION AND ITC DECISION-MAKING: THE SUM OF THE PARTS IS GREATER THAN THE WHOLE†

WENDY L HANSEN and THOMAS J PRUSA*

In 1984 Congress amended the antidumping and countervailing duty laws, mandating that the International Trade Commission (ITC) "cumulate" imports across countries when determining injury. We estimate that cumulation increases the probability of an affirmative injury determination by 20 to 30 percent and has changed the ITC's decision (from negative to affirmative) for about one-third of cumulated cases. We also show that the protective effect of cumulation increases as the number of countries involved increases, holding import market share constant. That is, cumulated imports have a super-additive effect on ITC decision-making.

I. INTRODUCTION

In recent decades, the rise in international competition has led many U.S. firms to seek protection from foreign imports. Particularly noteworthy in the 1980s was the increased use of the U.S. "unfair" trade laws. Two popular trade statutes, the antidumping law and the countervailing duty law, allow U.S. firms or industries to seek protection from alleged unfair trade practices, namely dumping and subsidization.

Under these laws, U.S. firms or industries apply simultaneously to the Department of Commerce and the U.S. International Trade Commission (ITC); these agencies have the authority granted by Congress to determine, respectively, whether or not an unfair practice has occurred and whether or not the unfair practice has caused injury to the U.S. industry. Affirmative decisions by both of these bodies generally result in the imposition of higher tariffs designed to counter the alleged unfair practice.

* Department of Political Science, University of New Mexico and Department of Economics, Rutgers University, and NBER. We would like to thank Se Park for excellent research assistance This paper benefited from the comments of participants in the NBER International Trade and Investment group and also two anonymous referees.

Since 1974, the U.S. Congress has made a number of major changes to the antidumping and countervailing duty laws, largely in response to domestic industry pressures. These amendments were intended to either increase the applicability of the laws or to make the unfair practice and injury requirements easier to satisfy. Although Hansen [1990], Moore [1992], and Baldwin and Steagall [1994] have all analyzed the decision-making process of the ITC, none have incorporated the fact that Congress often amends the rules that define how decisions are to be made. There is no empirical evidence of the impact of the *changes* in the statutes on trade policy. Authors such as Bello and Holmer [1985], Lande and VanGrasstek [1986], and Horlick and Oliver [1989] who do discuss the amendments tend to focus on legal issues and only offer conjectures as to the consequences of the revisions. Although some observers cite the increased incidence of affirmative antidumping and countervailing duty decisions as de facto evidence of the effect of the amendments, this type of casual empiricism is not reliable. Many possible explanations for changes in ITC behavior—macroeconomic slowdown, election year political pressures, etc.—have nothing to do with the changes in the statutes. Without careful

†This article originally appeared in *Economic Inquiry*, **34**(4), pp. 746–769.

econometric analysis, attributing observed changes in protection to statutory changes will almost surely misrepresent the true effect of the amendments.

The main purposes of this paper are to provide such an econometric analysis and to quantify the protective effect of perhaps the most important amendment to the antidumping and countervailing duty statutes during the 1980s: mandatory cumulation. Enacted in the Trade and Tariff Act of 1984, this provision requires the ITC to cumulate imports when a trade dispute involves imports from multiple sources. Without cumulation, imports are evaluated on a country-by-country basis; when cumulation is applied, the ITC aggregates all "like" imports from all countries under investigation and assesses the combined impact upon the domestic industry. Without cumulation, the volume from any one country is less likely to comprise a significant share of the domestic market and therefore is less likely to cause injury. On the other hand, if the imports from individual foreign competitors are aggregated, the impact of foreign competition will be more significant, making it more likely that the ITC will decide that the domestic industry has suffered material injury by reason of unfairly traded imports.

In order to measure the impact, if any, of the cumulation provision we must control for any other economic and political factors that also explain ITC decision making. Therefore, in addition to empirically analyzing the impact of cumulation, we offer a broad characterization of the factors that determine antidumping and countervailing duty outcomes. Thus, our results have general implications for evaluating the efficacy of the ITC's decision making. For example, our estimates allow us to compare the importance of statutorily mandated requirements, such as economic measures of injury, with unofficial influences, such as political pressure from members of Congress who have a vested interest in seeing an industry receive a favorable ITC decision.

Our explicit consideration of political pressure is another unique aspect of our research. Most previous research has focused solely on the impact of statutory requirements on ITC outcomes (Finger et al. [1982], Moore [1992], Baldwin and Steagall [1994]). By contrast, our estimates show that political pressure, via both direct representation and PAC contributions, significantly influences decisions made by the ITC, a supposedly apolitical decision-making agency.

However, while our model allows us to address these broader issues, our primary goal is to measure the significance of cumulation on trade policy outcomes. Using data on antidumping and countervailing duty cases filed between 1980 and 1988, we find that cumulation has had a dramatic impact on ITC decision making. Specifically, after controlling for other economic and political factors we find that cumulated cases are 20–40 percent more likely to result in duties than non-cumulated cases. Our results also imply that one-third to one-half of the cumulated cases that resulted in duties would have been denied protection were cumulation not mandated.

Most interestingly, our results imply that cumulated imports have a super-additive effect on ITC decisions. That is, the ITC perceives cumulated imports as more injurious than an equivalent amount of named country imports. In other words, under cumulation the domestic industry has a greater chance of protection by filing against two countries each with, say, 20 percent of the import market than against a single country with a 40 percent import market share. Further, the super-additive effect of cumulation becomes more pronounced the larger the number of countries being cumulated. Holding the total import share under investigation constant, the probability of an affirmative decision when imports from five countries are cumulated is greater than the probability when imports from only two countries are cumulated, which in turn is greater than the probability when a single country is being investigated. At least with respect to ITC decision making, it appears that the sum of the parts is greater than the whole.

The remainder of the paper is organized as follows. In the next section, we examine ITC decision making and its use of the cumulation provision both before and after the 1984 mandate. In sections III and IV, we econometrically analyze the decision-making behavior of the ITC. In section V we provide a variety of quantitative measures of the impact of mandated cumulation on ITC decision making. In section VI we conclude with some additional interpretations and extensions of our results.

II. BACKGROUND

Generally speaking, there are three possible outcomes for an antidumping or countervailing duty petition. First, a case can be rejected. For instance, if the Department of Commerce makes a negative ruling in its final investigation, the case is dismissed; no protection is granted and no final ITC determination is made. A case is also dismissed if either the ITC's preliminary or final investigation is negative. Second, if both bureaucratic agencies' final determinations are affirmative, then a duty (tariff) is levied on the named country's imports; the size of the duty is determined by the Department of Commerce in its investigation of the alleged unfair practice. Finally, a case can be withdrawn. As discussed in Prusa [1992] and Finger and Murray [1990], cases are generally withdrawn only after some type of agreement (e.g., an orderly marketing arrangement, the foreign firms agree to raise their prices and stop dumping, the foreign government agrees to remove the subsidy, etc.). Note that since the focus of this paper is actual ITC decision making, we exclude withdrawn cases from our analysis.

If the ITC makes an affirmative decision, duties are only levied against country named as an unfair trader in the petition. As Hansen and Prusa [1995] document, such protection is quite porous; 90 percent of the reduction in trade from the named country is merely diverted to other foreign suppliers. As a result, a domestic industry often files petitions against multiple exporting countries. Note, however, that the ITC always makes its decisions on a country-by-country basis, even if imports from a set of countries are cumulated. For example, if seven countries are named in the petition, the ITC makes seven separate injury decisions.

Prior to 1984, it was left to the ITC commissioners' discretion whether or not to cumulate. However, by incorporating the cumulation provision into the Trade and Tariff Act of 1984 (P.L. No. 98-573), Congress required that the ITC cumulate whenever like products from multiple countries were subject to investigation. In particular, the 1984 amendment stipulates that imports from multiple sources must be cumulated when three criteria are satisfied: (1) the imports must compete with one another and the domestic product, (2) the imports must be marketed within a reasonably coincidental period, and (3) the imports must be under investigation. Thus, the 1984 amendment clearly defined when cases should be cumulated, and thereby removed almost all of the ITC's discretion regarding cumulation.

Table I gives an example of how the cumulation provision works in practice. In March 1986, the U.S. brass sheet and strip industry filed an antidumping petition against firms located in seven different countries. West German firms dominated the U.S. import market, accounting for over 20 percent of all U.S. brass sheet and strip imports and more than half of the allegedly dumped imports. The next largest named country, Brazil, accounted for less than 5 percent of the overall import market. In January 1987 the Department

TABLE I
Example of Cumulation
Brass Sheet and Strip (Cases #311–317)

Country	Import Market Share	Cumulated Market Share	Market Share of Other Named Countries	Less-Than-Fair-Value Duty
West Germany	21.27%	38.35%	17.08%	8.87%
Brazil	4.81%	38.35%	33.54%	40.62%
France	3.78%	38.35%	34.57%	42.24%
Italy	3.27%	38.35%	35.08%	12.08%
South Korea	2.20%	38.35%	36 15%	7.17%
Canada	1.83%	38.35%	36.51%	8.10%
Sweden	1.20%	38.35%	37.15%	9.49%

of Commerce determined that each of the countries had indeed engaged in "less than fair value" sales, implying that duties would be levied against any country whose imports were deemed by the ITC to have materially injured the U.S. industry. Since the cases were subject to cumulation, the ITC was required to assess the injurious impact of the imports from all named countries. For example, when determining whether dumped imports from France materially injured the U.S. industry, the ITC could not merely evaluate the injurious effects of France's 3.78 percent market share, but was required to factor in the additional 34.57 percent market share from the other named countries. In February 1987, the ITC found that imports from each of the seven countries had injured the U.S. industry.

The central issue in this study is whether or not cumulation alters the outcomes. For example, in the brass sheet and strip cases above, had cumulation not been mandated, would any of the seven injury decisions have been negative? Between 1980 and 1984, fifty-one antidumping cases were filed where the named country had an import market share of less than 5 percent; in only seven of these cases (14 percent) did the ITC find material injury. In contrast, during the same time period approximately 30 percent of cases filed against countries with import

market shares greater than 5 percent resulted in duties. This discrepancy suggests that cumulation may have changed the outcome for six of the seven countries in the brass sheet and strip petition. On the other hand, it is also possible that cumulation simply strengthened the U.S. industry's already strong hand. With its large workforce and with production facilities located in a number of trade oversight committee members' districts, the steel industry's political clout is legendary. Moreover, profits and employment in the industry had fallen during the years preceding the petition, indicating possible injury. Finally, the large less-than-fair-value margins also may have contributed to the ITC's determination. Together these factors suggest that injury would have been found without cumulation.

In Table II we give a breakdown of cases by outcome and whether or not cumulation was used both before and after the 1984 Trade Act. Title VII cases include both antidumping and countervailing duty petitions ("Title VII" refers to the section of trade law where the statutes appear). In addition, we report the breakdown for antidumping cases alone, where cumulation seems to have had a disproportionate impact.

A review of the data makes it clear that once Congress mandated cumulation, cases involving cumulation became the

ECONOMIC INQUIRY

TABLE II
Title VII Case Summary
Number of Cases Filed with and without Cumulation, 1980–1988*

Outcome	Pre-1984 Cum.	Pre-1984 No Cum.	Title VII Cases Post-1984 Cum.	Post-1984 No Cum.	All Years Cum.	All Years No Cum.
Negative DOC	2 (3%)	32 (8%)	8 (5%)	9 (7%)	10 (5%)	41 (7%)
Negative ITC	37 (62%)	126 (29%)	30 (20%)	45 (35%)	67 (32%)	171 (31 %)
Affirmative	9 (15%)	123 (28%)	95 (64%)	41 (32%)	104 (50%)	164 (29%)
Withdrawn	12 (20%)	152 (35%)	16 (11%)	33 (26%)	28 (13%)	185 (33%)
Total	60	433	149	128	209	561
Antidumping Cases						
Negative DOC	2 (7%)	15 (7%)	3 (3%)	4 (6%)	5 (4%)	19 (7%)
Negative ITC	10 (33%)	65 (32%)	21 (19%)	33 (46%)	31 (22%)	98 (36%)
Affirmative	9 (30%)	43 (21%)	78 (71%)	18 (25%)	87 (62%)	61 (22%)
Withdrawn	9 (30%)	81 (40%)	8 (7%)	16 (23%)	17 (12%)	97 (35%)
Total	30	204	110	71	140	275

*Numbers in parentheses denote percent of column total

norm rather than the expectation. Between 1980 and 1984 (i.e., prior to mandated cumulation) only 60 cases out of 493 Title VII petitions (12 percent) involved cumulation. And, of the 60 cumulated cases, only 15 percent resulted in affirmative ITC decisions. In contrast, of the 433 petitions that were not cumulated, 28 percent received an affirmative ITC decision. Thus, prior to 1984, not only was cumulation rarely used, but when it was used it apparently did not enhance an industry's chance of receiving protection.

Compare the pre-1984 Trade Act numbers with the patterns post-1984. Between 1985 and 1988, 149 of 277 Title VII cases (54 percent) involved cumulation. And, of the 149 cumulated cases, a remarkable 64 percent were granted relief; in contrast, only 32 percent of the non-cumulated cases received favorable ITC decisions. From 1985 onwards, it appears that cumulation was leading the ITC to be more protective.

The patterns in Table II warrant several comments. Most notable is the fact that prior to the 1984 Trade Act cumulated cases seem to fare worse than non-cumulated cases. Given the near unilateral support that the cumulation provision received from import-competing industries in congressional hearings and debates leading up to the passage of the 1984 Trade Act, this appears somewhat anomalous. This paradox can be attributed to several factors. First, prior to the 1984 Trade Act the decision of whether or not cumulate was left to the discretion of ITC commissioners. Wilson [1989, 277–94] and Shapiro [1988] have argued that ITC commissioners prefer not to have their decision overturned by the Court of International Trade. Given that during the 1980s the court reversed nearly 50 percent of antidumping appeals, and over one-third of all cases appealed (Hansen, Johnson, and Unah [1995]), agency concerns about reversal are well founded. Given the uncertainty surrounding the legal status of cumulating imports, it may be that the ITC commissioners chose to cumulate only when it was clear that doing so would not affect the ultimate outcome, and therefore would not be the basis for a Court of International Trade reversal.

A closer examination of the voting and cumulation decisions of the individual commissioners on the cases cumulated prior to 1985 seems to support this conjecture. Among the sixty cases involving cumulation, two cases ended with negative Department of Commerce final decisions and twelve cases were withdrawn. These cases are excluded from our analysis since they did not involve ITC decisions. Of the remaining forty-six cases, forty-one were unanimous decisions (thirty-seven negative), and only five cases involved split voting behavior. Clearly, the vast majority of cumulated cases prior to the 1984 amendment were unanimous decisions, supporting the hypothesis that cumulation occurred almost always in clear-cut cases where the outcome was determined by other factors.

Second, even when the ITC chose to cumulate, individual commissioners often disagreed over whether a set of petitions should be cumulated. Often, several commissioners would cumulate while the others would not. Since the ITC makes an affirmative determination if at least half of the commissioners find injury, it may be the case that cumulation did not have any measurable impact on the official outcome in these "split" cases.[1] On the other hand, the fact that only one or two commissioners cumulated imports does not imply that cumulation did not have an important effect on the outcome. For instance, if the other commissioners were split on injury, the overall ITC decision could change if a single commissioner cumulated, since a single vote can change the majority deci-

sion.[2] We believe that the most sensible (and conservative) approach is to classify a case as being cumulated if at least one commissioner cumulated imports. If there is a bias inherent in this classification scheme, it would be that we understate the significance of cumulation (since we may be classifying some non-cumulated cases as cumulated) and this may be what we are seeing in Table II.[3]

Comparing cumulated cases pre- and post-1984 suggests that Congress's mandating of cumulation did indeed change ITC behavior. In particular, only 15 percent of cumulated cases were affirmatively decided when cumulation was discretionary as compared with 64 percent once cumulation was mandated. In addition to the possible explanations discussed above, this result might also simply reflect that ITC commissioners viewed Congress's mandate as a signal to be more protectionist.

The data also indicate that cumulation has been a more important provision for antidumping cases. Pre-1984 antidumping cases account for one-half of cumulated Title VII cases, while post-1984, antidumping cases account for almost three-quarters of cumulated cases. Note however that antidumping cases account for about half of non-cumulated Title VII cases both pre- and post-1984. It is not clear why cumulation would be more important for antidumping cases, although part of the explanation lies in the fact that an injury determination is not required for counter-

---

1. If the commissioners are evenly divided on a case, the determination of the Commission is affirmative.

2. See Moore [1992] and Baldwin and Steagall [1994] for discussions of individual commissioner voting.

3. In particular, Mock [1986] states that there were no cumulated countervailing duty cases prior to the 1984 Trade Act. In contrast, our review of ITC proceedings indicates that thirty countervailing duty cases involved at least one commissioner cumulating imports. However, twenty-seven of the thirty pre-1984 countervailing duty cases that we classify as cumulated were rejected by the ITC. While it is not entirely clear from the text, Mock's discussion suggests that he considers a case to be cumulated only if a majority of ITC commissioners cumulated imports

vailing duty cases filed against countries that have not signed the GATT subsidy code. Since there is no need to prove injury against firms from these countries, there is less of a need to rely on cumulation. Cumulation also seems to have had a more significant effect on antidumping outcomes. Cumulated antidumping cases are almost three times as likely to result in duties as non-cumulated cases; in contrast cumulated and non-cumulated countervailing duty cases were about equally likely to receive protection (especially after 1984).

When Congress was debating whether or not to mandate cumulation, one argument repeatedly made was that the source of the dumped or subsidized imports was irrelevant. What mattered was that the cumulated volume was injurious. This argument in favor of cumulation has been referred to as the "hammering effect" hypothesis, since according to industries and their representatives,

> a domestic industry that suffers material injury by reason of 100,000 tons of unfairly traded imports from a single country is injured to the same degree by 20,000 tons of unfairly traded imports from each of five different countries. (Suder [1983])

Whether or not the "hammering effect" theory is valid, one could hypothesize that industries would respond to mandated cumulation by (a) filing more multiple-country petitions and (b) filing more cases against countries with smaller import market shares.

In order to address the first issue we tallied the number of multiple-country petitions and found that 22 percent of pre-1984 petitions and 33 percent of post-1984 petitions involved firms located in more than one country, suggesting that mandated cumulation has led to a 50 percent increase in multiple petition filings. On the other hand, there is virtually no difference in the average number of countries per filing pre- and post-1984. Of course, the large scale steel industry filings in 1982

and 1984 might explain the similarity. If we exclude the steel industry filings in 1982 and 1984, we find that the average Title VII pre-1984 petition involved 1.3 countries while post-1984 petitions involved an average of 1.8 countries—about a 40 percent increase. Thus, there is some support for the claim that cumulation increases the number of multiple-country petitions.

To address the second issue, we calculated the average import market share held by the country named as the unfair trader in the Title VII petition. Overall, we found an average import market share of 11 percent when cumulation was used, as compared with 17 percent when cumulation was not used. This suggests that cases involving cumulation are indeed filed against countries with smaller market shares.

Of course, these cross tabulations alone do not adequately measure the effect of cumulation since they do not control for a wide variety of other economic and political variables that might also be influencing the ITC's decision making. For instance, if cases with cumulation were also cases where the domestic industry had experienced significant loss in profits, large layoffs, decreased capital utilization, and the like, one should not attribute changing patterns of protection to cumulation alone. In order to more fully address these concerns, we develop a more formal model of bureaucratic decision making in the next section.

III MODELLING ITC DECISION MAKING

In this section we model the decision-making behavior of the ITC. During the past decade the ITC has been the subject of a growing body of empirical research. Takacs [1981], Hansen [1990], and Finger et al. [1982] focused on determinants of the annual number of petitions filed with the ITC, either in conjunction with or instead of the determinants of ITC decisions, while Baldwin [1985], Moore [1992], and Baldwin and Steagall [1994] more narrowly focus on ITC decision making. However, none of the previous research has analyzed how a specific amendment affects decision making nor do these papers offer as precise measures of political pressure as we do.

We incorporate both economic and political factors that may affect whether or not a Title VII petition receives protection. Clearly, we expect measures of economic injury to be positively related to affirmative ITC decisions, since this is stipulated in the statutes. However, it is widely agreed that political and more general economic pressures also influence ITC decision making. For instance, the U.S.'s large and growing trade deficit might raise the public's ire over trade-related problems, and thereby create substantial pressure for more affirmative ITC decisions, regardless of whether or not the less-than-fair-value imports have statutorily caused injury. Or, a petition filed by an industry with production facilities located in districts of representatives who sit on trade oversight committees might have more success than a petition filed by an industry that does not have a representative who will lobby the commission on its behalf. Below we discuss the variables used to measure these influences. A more detailed description of the variables used in our model is provided in the appendix.

Economic Measures of Injury

By statute, the ITC is directed to take into account the economic situation of an industry in determining injury. Thus evidence of economic hardship or decline should be important to the decision-making behavior of the Commission. In our model, percentage changes in industry capacity utilization and shipments are used to measure recent industry performance.[4]

One would expect that the greater the fall in each variable, the greater the likelihood of an affirmative decision.

Even though ITC commissioners are not required to consider the less-than-fair-value margin when making their injury determination, it would not be surprising to find a relationship between the less-than-fair-value margin and the likelihood of injury. Palmeter [1987] argues that the ITC relies more on the volume of less-than-fair-value imports rather than the less-than-fair-value margin. We investigate both hypotheses and include both the less-than-fair-value margin and the named country's import market share as independent variables.[5]

Cumulation is the economic criterion in which we are most interested. We use two different measures of the cumulation provision. One measure is a dummy variable (= 1 when the case is cumulated). While this is a straightforward measure, it does not capture the fact that cumulation is likely to have a more significant effect on the outcome for named countries with small market shares. For instance, in the brass sheet and strip example discussed above, West German firms had over 20 percent of the import market, and it is likely that they would have been found to have caused injury with or without cumulation. On the other hand, Canada and Sweden, with tiny market shares, would more likely have not been found to have caused injury. In other words, one would expect the market share contributed by the *other* named countries to be important in their injury decision. Our second measure, the market share of the other named countries, captures the fact that cumulation is likely to be more important for countries with small import market shares.

---

4. We could have also included the percentage change in employment, but did not do so because it is highly correlated with the change in shipments.

5 We use the term "less-than-fair-value" margin to refer to both the dumping margin and also the subsidy margin.

Title VII Protection As Compensation for Lost Protection

Baldwin [1985], Hoekman and Leidy [1989], and Hansen and Prusa [1995] have argued that administered protection often serves to substitute for the more traditional, but GATT-constrained mode of protection, namely tariffs. Formally, there is no statutory requirement that there be a connection between increased imports and tariff concessions. However, following Finger, Hall, and Nelson's [1982] argument that administered protection serves as a "poor man's escape clause," we hypothesize that the pleas of industries that have low levels of protection—or have lost protection—will be more successful. In other words, the lower the current tariff, the more likely bureaucrats will use Title VII duties to compensate for lost protection.

Similarly, while Title VII protection is supposed to be granted in response to injury caused by a particular unfair trade action, it may be more appropriately thought of as compensation for overall market share gains by foreign rivals. In other words, Title VII may serve to protect those industries that have experienced the greatest overall import competition. As a measure of general import gains, we construct an industry-level measure of foreign penetration [imports/(output + imports − exports)]. Note that foreign penetration is a far more aggregated index than the measures of import gains reported in the ITC's reports and thus is capturing general industry-wide trends rather than the market share gains by the named importers. If this hypothesis is correct, increased foreign penetration makes it easier for the ITC to make an affirmative injury decision.

Macroeconomic Influences

Trends in the aggregate economy are also likely to influence the ITC. We use the percentage change in the U.S. trade deficit to capture macroeconomic trends in the flow of imports and exports. We expect a positive relationship between the change in the deficit and ITC decisions.[6]

We also control for additional aggregate trends with dummy variables for each of the years included in our data (with 1980 as the base year of comparison). For instance, changes in the composition of the ITC might lead all cases filed in some years to be more successful.

Political Pressure

Besides the condition of U.S. industries and the overall economy, research has also demonstrated the importance of political factors in explaining ITC decisions. One manifestation of political impact on bureaucratic decision making is the principal-agent relationship between Congress and the ITC (Weingast [1984]). As discussed in Baldwin [1985] and empirically examined in Hansen [1990], congressional oversight committees can exert a great deal of pressure on ITC commissioners not only via direct lobbying but also through budgetary control. If this notion is correct, and if members of Congress take actions in order to keep their constituencies happy, then industries located in districts (or states) of oversight committee members would be more likely to receive trade relief than those that do not have such representation.

The House Ways and Means Committee and Senate Finance Committee have jurisdiction over the ITC in their respective houses. In order to measure these committees potential political influence, we first determined which SIC industries had operations in oversight members' districts. Our first measure is simply the number of oversight committee members' districts in which the domestic industry operates. Our second measure weights each committee member by the number of employ-

---

6. We also included the national unemployment rate as a control. Since the regression results are virtually identical with either measure, we only report regressions with the trade deficit.

ees in the industry in each district. Thus with this second measure, (i) large industries and (ii) industries located in many oversight districts are more influential.

A second manifestation of political impact on ITC decision making is interest group influence. As a measure, we use Political Action Committee (PAC) contributions to congressional oversight members.[7] The hypothesis is that industries (via their PACs) contribute to the oversight members' campaigns and that more pressure will be exerted on the ITC on behalf of those industries that made larger contributions.

Another measure of interest group influence is an industry's size. For any Title VII case, the larger the petitioning industry is, the greater its electoral impact may be; hence, larger industries can exert greater political pressure either directly on the ITC or indirectly through powerful senators and representatives. Employment and output are two alternative measures of industry size. Since the variables are highly correlated and the estimation results are quite similar using either measure, we present the estimates using employment as the measure of industry size.

The ability of an interest group to influence policy may also be affected by its ability to effectively organize. An industry with a large number of small producers may find the benefits of protection too dispersed and the costs of lobbying not worth bearing. We use the four-firm concentration ratio as a proxy for this notion of an industry's ability to organize and pressure policymakers.

Country/Industry Biases

Evidence suggests that the identity of the named country in a antidumping or countervailing duty petition influences ITC decisions. We control for country-spe-

cific differences by including dummy variables for petitions against each of the following: Japan, newly industrialized countries, West European countries, and non-market economies. Petitions against Japan might be treated differently in ITC decision making because of the overwhelming negative attention that Japan received during the 1980s in trade-related matters. Given its situation, one might expect that petitions against Japan would be more likely to receive a positive ITC ruling. Similarly, the rapid export-oriented growth of the newly industrialized countries might hurt them in ITC hearings. On the other hand, the historically strong relationship and trade ties between Europe and the U.S. may lead to more favorable treatment for their industries. Finally, cases filed against non-market economies may tend to be more successful, both because of cold-war suspicions and also because of the heavy reliance on "constructed value" measures of home market performance when non-market economies are involved (see Tharakan [1991] for a discussion).

Finally, we also control for the fact that steel and steel-related industries were by far the largest users of Title VII laws during the 1980s. The notion here is that petitions filed by steel and steel-related industries are more successful due to this industry's frequency of filing (i.e., learning-by-doing) or the inordinate amount of public attention steel cases tend to receive.

IV. ESTIMATING ITC DECISION MAKING

Our data set is comprised of the 770 Title VII cases filed between 1980 and 1988. We drop cases rejected by the Commerce Department (since the ITC never makes a final decision when no unfair practice is found). We also drop withdrawn cases which receive no official ITC determination. In addition, since most of our measures of economic criteria are unavailable for the agricultural sector, we restrict our sample to manufacturing in-

---

7. See Grossman and Helpman [1994] for a model highlighting the importance of political contributions to the policymaking process.

dustries. We also drop countervailing duty cases against industries located in countries that have not signed the GATT subsidy code since an injury decision is not required for these countries. After dropping these cases, we have data for 317 ITC decisions. We estimate the ITC decision function for all Title VII cases, and separately for just antidumping cases.[8]

Our probit estimates are given in Table III and IV. In Table III we present four specifications of the estimated ITC decision function, allowing for different measures of political pressure and cumulation.[9] In Table IV we test whether discretionary and mandated cumulation had different effects on the ITC.

General Findings

Several general findings emerge from the estimations. First, we find that political pressure has an important influence on ITC decisions. Second, petitions are more likely to result in duties when the case is filed against non-market economies and less likely when filed against European countries. Third, we find that the U.S. steel industry has fared particularly well in ITC decisions. Finally, cumulation crucially influences the ITC. Below we briefly discuss the results. An extended discussion of the importance of the estimated effect of cumulation is contained in section V.

Political Pressure. Supporting the findings of Hansen [1990], industries with representatives on the Ways and Means Committee have a greater chance of receiving protection; Senate Finance oversight representation, however, appears to be unrelated to ITC decision making. It is not surprising that the House oversight influence

8. We also estimate the ITC decision function for just countervailing duty cases, but to keep the paper a reasonable length, we do not present the results here. These regressions are available upon request from the authors.

9. Year dummies are included but not reported clue to space limitations. They are available upon request.

is more significant because House members have a much more geographically narrow constituency and therefore more narrowly defined interests; a firm filing a trade petition will surely affect a larger fraction of a House member's constituents than a senator's.

PAC contributions also appear to be positively related to an industry's prospects for protection. In all four specifications and for both the antidumping-only data set and the entire Title VII data set, the impact of PAC contributions is positive, but it is significant only for antidumping cases.

Economic Criteria. The percentage change in capacity utilization and the percentage change in shipments are proxies for changes in the industry's economic health. While both variables have the expected sign (i.e., increases in either capacity utilization or shipments lowers the chance of protection) neither is significant. Although Hansen [1990] and Moore [1992] find some support for economic decline predicting ITC decisions, we feel that the insignificance of the economic criteria reflects the great degree of latitude that the ITC has in making its decisions—statutory guidelines, which define the factors that determine injury and what level of injury constitutes "material" injury are extremely vague. This also explains why well-defined political pressure variables play such an important role.

Import market share has a positive and significant effect on ITC decisions. This implies that the larger a country's import market share, the more likely the ITC will find injury. Given domestic industries' testimony preceding the cumulation amendment, this finding was expected.

Country- and Industry-Specific Effects. Importantly, we find the existence of country- and industry-specific biases. For instance the European dummy is consistently negative and significant, suggesting that the ITC is reluctant to find injury when imports are from the U.S.'s European allies. In contrast, cases against non-market economies fare particularly well; the coefficient on the non-market dummy is large, positive, and significant. We find that there is no significant country effect for Japan and newly industrialized countries. We do find, however, that the steel industry, the largest single user of Title VII law, does quite well at the ITC: the steel dummy is consistently positive and significant.

Estimating Pre- and Post-1984 Cumulation Effect

The data presented in Table II suggest that cumulation had a more protective effect once Congress mandated its use. The most straightforward way to test for this is to simply add a regressor that captures the post-1984 cumulation effect. In specification E (Table IV) we estimate

$$Outcome_i = \alpha + \beta_1 X_i + \gamma_1 C_i + \gamma_2(D_i C_i) + \varphi Y_i,$$

where X_i is a vector of all variables in the model except the cumulation effect, C_i, and year dummies, Y_i; D_i is a post-1984 dummy variable. Thus, γ_1 is the pre-1984 and $\gamma_1 + \gamma_2$ the post-1984 cumulation effect.

Specification E can be applied to any of the four specifications estimated in Table III; the results in Table IV should be compared with specification A. As in Table III, we omit year dummies from the table. In addition, to conserve space, we do not present t-statistics, but rather only indicate which variables are significant.[10]

The estimates suggest that once cumulation was mandated, it had a greater impact on ITC decision making. For both the Title VII and antidumping-only data sets, γ_2 is positive and significant, while

10. Complete estimation results are available upon request.

γ_1 is insignificant. However, in neither data set is the estimate of γ_2 statistically different from the cumulation effect estimated in specification A.

As discussed above, the ITC may have interpreted the passage of the Trade and Tariff Act of 1984 as a signal to become more protectionist, and this change in behavior may manifest itself in all of the exogenous variables. If this is indeed the case, we need to estimate a function that allows for more general structural changes in ITC decision making post-1984. In specification F we estimate

$$Outcome_i = \alpha + \beta_1 X_i + \gamma_1 C_i + \delta_1 D_i$$
$$+ \beta_2(D_i X_i) + \gamma_2(D_i C_i) + \varphi Y_i.$$

Once again, we report estimates that should be compared with those in model A. While a number of the exogenous variables have significant post-1984 effects, the most important finding for our purposes is that cumulation has a statistically greater effect after 1984. However, as was the case for specification E, the estimated post-1984 effects are not statistically different from those reported in specification A.

We perform a chi-squared test in order to investigate the overall significance of this more general model (specification F vs. A). We find that for the antidumping-only data set there is no evidence of a general change in ITC behavior (at the 95 percent confidence level). However, for the Title VII data set, there is evidence that the 1984 trade act may have caused the ITC to become more protectionist.

V. SIGNIFICANCE OF CUMULATION

Most relevant to this work is the fact that cumulation is positive and statistically significant across all specifications for both the Title VII and antidumping-only data sets. In Table V we present several measures of the importance of the

TABLE III
Probit Estimation*

	Title VII Cases Specification				Antidumping Cases Specification			
	A	B	C	D	A	B	C	D
Constant	-0.676 (-0.885)	-0.704 (-0.922)	-0.669 (-0.878)	-1.228 (-1.873)	-0.389 (-0.414)	-0.290 (-0.310)	-0.413 (-0.440)	-1.085 (-1.333)
# Representatives Ways & Means Districts	0.146 (2.292)	0.114 (1.744)	0.133 (1.985)		0.197 (2.844)	0.149 (2.102)	0.161 (2.225)	
# Representatives Senate Finance States	-0.056 (-1.190)	-0.064 (-1.384)	-0.057 (-1.245)		-0.052 (-1.029)	-0.062 (-1.218)	-0.056 (-1.106)	
Employment in Oversight Districts				-0.280 (-1.145)				-0.125 (-0.444)
Employment	-0.945 (-0.789)	-0.599 (-0.491)	-0.415 (-0.330)		-1.419 (-1.064)	-0.740 (-0.536)	-0.568 (-0.397)	
PAC Contributions	0.745 (1.262)	0.675 (1.145)	0.683 (1.172)	0.915 (1.558)	1.160 (1.791)	1.069 (1.654)	1.040 (1.623)	1.186 (1.835)
Concentration Ratio	-0.546 (-0.663)	-0.759 (-0.926)	-0.690 (-0.856)	-0.898 (-1.351)	-0.047 (-0.052)	-0.232 (-0.256)	-0.305 (-0.343)	-0.702 (-0.944)
Tariff	-2.537 (-0.797)	-2.921 (-0.924)	-2.373 (-0.749)	-2.582 (-0.889)	-1.610 (-0.451)	-2.474 (-0.695)	-1.948 (-0.544)	-2.465 (-0.743)
Foreign Penetration	0.047 (0.065)	-0.056 (-0.077)	0.082 (0.114)	-0.079 (-0.112)	0.094 (0.119)	-0.024 (-0.030)	0.175 (0.222)	0.064 (0.083)
% Change Trade Deficit	1.997 (0.403)	-0.835 (-0.173)	0.805 (0.163)	-3.703 (-1.031)	7.656 (1.341)	5.005 (0.905)	5.306 (0.947)	-1.243 (-0.289)
% Change Capacity Utilization	-0.554 (-0.950)	-0.609 (-1.023)	-0.628 (-1.067)	-0.891 (-1.518)	-0.637 (-0.961)	-0.785 (-1.148)	-0.735 (-1.083)	-0.935 (-1.387)
% Change Shipments	-0.017 (-0.020)	-0.106 (-0.126)	-0.024 (-0.029)	-0.581 (-0.709)	0.749 (0.702)	0.658 (0.620)	0.567 (0.536)	-0.107 (-0.104)
Named Country's Market Share	1.974 (3.936)	1.943 (3.882)	1.839 (3.701)	1.686 (3.425)	1.591 (2.815)	1.492 (2.669)	1.487 (2.655)	1.365 (2.457)
Less-Than-Fair-Value Duty	0.582 (1.754)	0.612 (1.802)	0.699 (2.030)	0.665 (1.978)	0.604 (1.721)	0.669 (1.854)	0.743 (2.025)	0.728 (2.040)
Non-Market Dummy	0.965 (2.319)	0.939 (2.191)	0.903 (2.141)	0.908 (2.067)	0.993 (2.284)	0.940 (2.077)	0.958 (2.138)	0.974 (2.118)

TABLE III continued
Probit Estimation*

	Title VII Cases Specification				Antidumping Cases Specification			
	A	B	C	D	A	B	C	D
Europe Dummy	-0.498 (-2.245)	-0.570 (-2.526)	-0.473 (-2.035)	-0.576 (-2.485)	-0.453 (-1.626)	-0.616 (-2.116)	-0.478 (-1.592)	-0.555 (-1.873)
Newly Indus. Country Dummy	0.068 (0.233)	0.139 (0.486)	0.123 (0.426)	0.244 (0.854)	0.081 (0.253)	0.151 (0.473)	0.164 (0.509)	0.271 (0.854)
Japan Dummy	-0.116 (-0.383)	-0.092 (-0.303)	-0.137 (-0.443)	-0.127 (-0.424)	-0.051 (-0.158)	-0.054 (-0.168)	-0.060 (-0.184)	-0.068 (-0.216)
Steel Industry Dummy	0.811 (3.169)	0.876 (3.404)	0.424 (1.450)	0.754 (2.492)	0.781 (2.773)	0.846 (2.977)	0.417 (1.249)	0.671 (1.927)
Cumulation Dummy	0.670 (2.969)				0.805 (3.103)			
Other Named Countries' Cumulated Market Share		2.121 (2.834)	1.292 (1.608)	1.945 (2.767)		3.126 (3.280)	2.263 (2.256)	2.807 (3.166)
Cumulation × Steel			0.994 (3.132)	0.817 (2.617)			0.866 (2.399)	0.731 (2.055)
Log Likelihood	-159.646	-159.807	-154.738	-156.874	-114.396	-113.032	-110.095	-113.024
Chi-Squared Test	114.232	113.909	124.047	125.553	88.645	91.374	97.247	96.274
# Observations	313	313	313	317	230	230	230	234
# Observations Positive	151	151	151	155	124	124	124	128
% Observations Positive	48.2%	48.2%	48.2%	48.9%	53.9%	53.9%	53.9%	54.7%
% Correctly Predicted	76.0%	74.8%	78.3%	76.7%	75.7%	75.2%	76.5%	75.2%

*t-statistics reported in parentheses

ECONOMIC INQUIRY

TABLE IV
Pre- and Post-1984 Effect

	Title VII Cases Specification		Antidumping Cases Specification	
	E	F	E	F
Constant	-0.527	-1.324	-0.541	-1.603
# Representatives Ways & Means Districts	0.122*	0.057	0.164**	0.145
# Representatives Ways & Means Districts × Post-1984 Dummy		0.22		0.12
# Representatives Senate Finance States	-0.027	0.092	-0.019	0.072
# Representatives Senate Finance States × Post-1984 Dummy		-0.271**		-0.223
Employment	-0.92	-1 08	-1.363	-2.597
Employment × Post-1984 Dummy		-0.435		1.667
PAC Contributions	0.842	0.782	1.168*	0.926
PAC Contributions × Post-1984 Dummy		-0.723		-0 972
Concentration Ratio	-0.316	-1.609	-0.001	-1.483
Concentration Ratio × Post-1984 Dummy		4.524**		4.243*
Tariff	-3.288	-0.779	-1.926	2.023
Tariff × Post 1984-Dummy		-5.659		-5.587
Foreign Penetration	0.04	2.054**	0.17	2.056*
Foreign Penetration × Post-1984 Dummy		-4.548**		-3.996**
% Change Trade Deficit	5.218	0.657	8.644	-0 061
% Change Trade Deficit × Post-1984 Dummy		1.095		2.981
% Change Capacity Utilization	-0.561	0.007	-0.618	0.076
% Change Capacity Utilization × Post-1984 Dummy		-1.606		-1.891
% Change Shipments	0.038	-0.828	0.429	0.662
% Change Shipments × Post-1984 Dummy		1.881		-0.662
Named Country's Market Share	1.931**	1.331*	1.562**	1 350*
Named Country's Market Share × Post-1984 Dummy		1.808		1 238
Less-Than-Fair-Value Duty	0.632*	0.165	0.635*	0.497
Less-Than-Fair-Value Duty × Post-1984 Dummy		0.77		0.247
Non-Market Dummy	0.894**	0.696	0.956**	0.701
Non-Market Dummy × Post-1984 Dummy		0.264		0 26
Europe Dummy	-0.560**	-0.373	-0.505*	-0 284
Europe Dummy × Post-1984 Dummy		-0.818		-0 751
Newly Indus. Country Dummy	0.117	-0.227	0.134	0.029
Newly Indus. Country Dummy × Post-1984 Dummy		0.396		0 064
Japan Dummy	-0.126	-0.118	-0.056	0.079
Japan Dummy × Post-1984 Dummy		-0.252		-0.372
Steel Industry Dummy	0.782**	0.045	0.732**	0.312
Steel Industry Dummy × Post-1984 Dummy		1.055*		0.493
Cumulation Dummy	-0.034	0.004	0.232	0.09
Cumulation Dummy × Post-1984 Dummy	1.152**	1.196**	0.949*	1.238*
Post-1984 Dummy		0 212		0 51
Log Likelihood	-156 671	-138.935	-112.975	-100.245
Chi-Squared Test	120.181	155.653	91.488	116.948
# Observations	313	313	230	230
# Observations Positive	151	151	124	124
% Observations Positive	48.2%	48.2%	53.9%	53.9%
% Correctly Predicted	77.0%	77.6%	77.0%	79.6%

*denotes significance at 10% level, ** significance at 5% level (two-tailed tests)

TABLE V
Effects of Cumulation

	Title VII Cases Specification						Antidumping Cases Specification					
	A	B	C	D	E	F	A	B	C	D	E	F
Change in probability of positive decision due to cumulation	26.2%	20.2%	20.1%	25.8%	42.0%	43.7%	30.6%	28.4%	29.4%	34.2%	38.8%	45.0%
Number of cases that are predicted affirmative with cumulation but would be predicted negative without cumulation	39	20	38	45	45	23	38	27	45	49	47	26
Number of cases cumulated	112	112	112	116	112	112	98	98	98	102	98	98
Percent of cumulated cases where outcome changed	34.8%	17.9%	33.9%	38.8%	40.2%	20.5%	38.8%	27.6%	45.9%	48.0%	48.0%	26.5%
Average duty for those cases where outcome changed	22.3%	22.2%	16.8%	18.0%	23.3%	23.3%	23.0%	25.9%	20.4%	23.2%	22.9%	24.0%

cumulation provision on ITC decisions. Using the parameter estimates presented in Tables III and IV we calculate the change in the probability of protection due to cumulation evaluated at the mean value of the other independent variables. The estimates imply that not only is cumulation significant, but also it has a substantial effect on outcomes. For instance, for all Title VII cases, cumulation increases the probability of protection by more than 20 percent, while for antidumping cases, cumulation increases the probability of protection by about 30 percent.

Given this dramatic effect on the probability of protection, it is not surprising that cumulation crucially determines whether or not protection is granted in a large number of cases. For instance, for the data set including all Title VII cases (specification C), 112 of the 313 observations were cumulated. Based on our parameter estimates, of these 112 cumulated cases, 38 (34 percent) would have been negatively decided without cumulation, but were affirmatively decided with cumulation. The percentage of cumulated cases where the outcome changes due to cumulation varies according to the specification (from 18 percent to almost 50 percent for the antidumping-only data set), but is always a sizable number.

Further, note that changing the outcome of cases is only the immediate impact of cumulation; ultimately, the affirmative ITC decision leads to the imposition of a duty and therefore an effect on trade. In the last row of Table V we report the average duty for cases where cumulation changes the predicted outcome. As evidenced, duties are quite large for these cases, averaging about 20 percent per case. Given that the average tariff level is about 4 percent, the additional protection due to cumulation is substantial.

Most interestingly, our results imply that cumulated imports have a super-additive effect on ITC decisions. To illustrate this point, in Figure 1 we plot the esti-mated probability of an affirmative anti-dumping decision as a function of the total market share of imports under investigation. All other independent variables are valued at the sample mean and the coefficients are from specification C. We plot three hypothetical scenarios. First, we imagine the petition is filed against a single country. Second, we suppose that the domestic industry files antidumping petitions against two countries, assuming that each country accounts for half the imports under investigation. Finally, we suppose that the domestic industry files multiple antidumping petitions against five countries, each accounting for 1/5 of the imports under investigation.

The figure makes the protective effect of cumulation clear. Even though equivalent amounts of imports are under investigation in each of the scenarios, the cases involving cumulation have a greater probability of succeeding. Furthermore, the effect of cumulation becomes more pronounced the greater is the share of imports under investigation accounted for by other named countries. That is, for all levels of market share the probability of an affirmative decision when imports from five countries are cumulated lies above that for two countries, which in turn lies above the probability when only a single country is being investigated.

Consider for instance, the probability of an affirmative decision when 40 percent of imports are under investigation. If the case involves a single country, the probability of an affirmative decision is estimated to be 0.60. If petitions are filed against two countries, each with 20 percent of the import market (yielding a cumulated market share of 40 percent) the estimated probability of an affirmative decision jumps to 0.72. If petitions are filed against five countries, each with 8 percent of the import market the estimated probability of an affirmative decision is 0.78.

This is a startling result. Under the 1984 statute the ITC should treat each of the

FIGURE 1

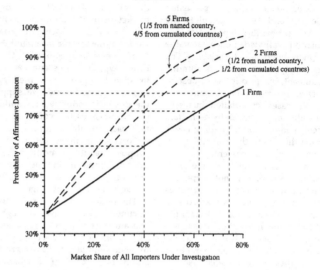

scenarios identically. Forty percent of the import market is under investigation in each scenario. If anything, one might expect the ITC to perceive an equivalent amount of cumulated imports as less injurious, since commissioners might not be inclined to punish small countries for the transgressions of others. To the contrary, our estimates imply that the ITC perceives cumulated imports as substantially more injurious.

In order for a case against a single country to be as likely to receive protection as when two countries (each with 20 percent of the import market) are under investigation, that single country would have to account for 62 percent of the import market; for a case against a single country to be as likely to receive protection as when five countries (each with 8 percent of the import market) are under investigation, that single country would have to account for 75 percent of the import market. In other words, cumulated

imports have a super-additive effect on ITC decisions. This surprising finding leads us to conclude that at least with respect to ITC decision making the sum of the parts is greater than the whole.

Table VI presents the effect of cumulation on predicted outcomes for several selected antidumping cases which had positive ITC decisions. For instance, consider again the "Brass sheet and strip" antidumping petition discussed above in Table I. The import market share for these countries ranged from West Germany's 21 percent to Sweden's 1 percent, and the cumulated import market share was 38 percent. With the cumulation provision in effect the ITC found that each of the seven named countries had caused injury to the U.S. industry and thus import duties of 7 percent to 42 percent were levied on brass sheet and strip imports. Without cumulation, however, some of the countries would not have been subject to duties. For instance, under the parameter estimates

TABLE VI
Predicted Outcomes without Cumulation*

Case	Country	Import Market Share	Cumulated Market Share	Market Share of Other Named Countries	Less-Than-Fair-Value Duty	A	B	Specification C	D	E	F
Potassium permanganate											
126	Spain	27.83%	49.72%	21.89%	5.49%	N	N	N	N	N	A
125	P.R. China	21.89%	49.72%	27.83%	39.63%	A	A	A	A	A	A
Color television receivers											
134	South Korea	31.29%	56.98%	25.70%	13.90%	N	A	A	A	A	A
135	Taiwan	25.70%	56.98%	31.29%	5.46%	N	N	N	A	A	A
Iron construction castings											
264	India	28.73%	68.88%	40.15%	0.90%	A	N	N	N	N	A
263	Canada	19.49%	68.88%	49.39%	10.20%	A	N	N	N	N	A
262	Brazil	12.66%	68.88%	56.22%	26.16%	A	N	A	N	N	A
265	P.R. China	8.00%	68.88%	60.88%	11.66%	A	A	A	A	A	A
Brass sheet and strip											
317	West Germany	21.27%	38.35%	17.08%	8.87%	A	A	N	N	N	N
311	Brazil	4.81%	38.35%	33.54%	40.62%	A	A	A	A	A	A
313	France	3.78%	38.35%	34.57%	42.24%	A	A	N	N	N	N
314	Italy	3.27%	38.35%	35.08%	12.08%	N	N	N	N	N	N
315	South Korea	2.20%	38.35%	36.15%	7.17%	A	A	A	A	A	A
312	Canada	1.83%	38.35%	36.51%	8.10%	A	A	N	N	N	A
316	Sweden	1.20%	38.35%	37.15%	9.49%	A	A	N	A	A	A
Granular polytetrafluoroethylene resin											
386	Japan	21.63%	29.97%	8.34%	91.74%	A	A	A	A	A	N
385	Italy	8.34%	29.97%	21.63%	46.46%	N	N	N	N	N	N**
Light-walled rectangular pipes & tubes											
409	Argentina	6.82%	8.41%	1.59%	27.71%	N	N**	N	N	N	N
410	Taiwan	1.59%	8.41%	6.82%	29.15%	N	N	N	N	N	N
Telephone systems and subassemblies											
426	Japan	23.72%	38.22%	14.51%	48.07%	A	A	A	N	A	A
428	Taiwan	9.43%	38.22%	28.79%	17.66%	N	N	A	N	N	A
427	South Korea	5.08%	38.22%	33.15%	8.63%	N	N	N	N	N	N

*Based on parameter estimates from antidumping-only dataset. All cases listed had affirmative ITC decisions
The predicted outcome (with cumulation) for all cases listed is affirmative, except where noted with **.
"A" denotes predicted outcome affirmative; "N" denotes predicted outcome negative.

from specifications A and B, we find that Italian imports would not have been found to have caused injury. Under specifications C and D, where we control for cumulation using the market share of the other named countries and allow for a cross-effect of cumulation with the steel industry dummy, we find that only Brazil and South Korea would have been subject to duties. In other words, without cumulation the vast majority (31 of 38 percent under investigation) of brass sheet and strip imports would not have been subject to duties.

While similar patterns emerge from the other cases, there are three points worth noting. First, cumulation appears to be less important for cases filed against non-market economies. This is because procedural and political biases against non-market economies are already so substantial that these cases would likely be affirmatively decided with or without cumulation. Second, the steel industry appears to have substantially benefited from cumulation, as evidenced by the large number of negative decisions predicted without cumulation, especially under specifications C and D. Cumulation appears to further enhance the already favorable treatment the steel industry receives by the ITC. Third for some petitions (e.g., telephone systems and light-walled rectangular pipes and tubes), our model implies that cumulation was the difference between an affirmative and negative decision for *all* of the named countries.

Finally, we use our estimates to calculate how many pre-1984 cases would have been affirmatively decided had cumulation been mandated during this period. To do this we restrict our data set to those pre-1984 cases that were *not* cumulated. We then consider what would have happened had the imports from all countries named in a multiple petition filing been cumulated by the ITC (i.e., what would have happened if cumulation had been mandated from 1980 onwards). While this

procedure is likely to overestimate the number of cumulated cases, since not all countries named in multiple petition filings always have their imports cumulated, it is as sensible as any alternative.

In Table VII we report the results of this pre-1984 scenario. We find that 16 percent to 60 percent of multiple petition cases that were negatively decided without cumulation would have been affirmatively decided with cumulation. While this result may be overestimated, the impact of cumulation on ITC decision making is clear; more affirmative decisions imposing protective duties on foreign imports would have occurred had mandatory use of cumulation been adopted prior to 1984.

VI CONCLUDING REMARKS

As we have shown above, after controlling for other factors, mandated cumulation has dramatically increased the likelihood that the ITC will grant U.S. industries protection. In fact, not only does mandatory cumulation increase the likelihood that the ITC will rule in favor of the domestic industry, but for a given cumulated import market share, it implies that the greater is the number of countries involved, the greater is the probability of receiving protection. This super-additive effect of cumulation would appear to stretch even beyond the intent of Congress in its impact.

There are a number of possible interpretations for our findings. First, as discussed above, the ITC may view Congress's decision to mandate cumulation as a signal to become more protectionist, especially for those petitions involving multiple countries. Second, cumulation may link cases together in a way that biases each country's chances of defending itself. For instance, a delay by any one of the cumulated countries in responding to the ITC's requests for information may hurt each of the countries' chances. In fact, it may be in the strategic interest of a country that expects to be subject to duties to increase

TABLE VII

Predicted Outcomes If Cumulation Had Been Mandatory Pre-1984

	Title VII Cases Specification						Antidumping Cases Specification					
	A	B	C	D	E	F	A	B	C	D	E	F
Number of cases with negative ITC decisions (and were not cumulated but were part of multiple petition filing)	93	93	93	93	93	93	49	49	49	49	49	49
Number of cases predicted negative (without cumulation)	83	82	86	84	81	85	41	40	44	43	40	41
Number of cases predicted negative if cumulation had been mandatory	68	64	34	35	28	28	20	28	21	21	16	15
Percentage of negative decisions with changed outcomes with cumulation	16.1%	19.4%	55.9%	52.7%	57.0%	61.3%	42.9%	24.5%	46.9%	44.9%	49.0%	53.1%

the likelihood that the other named countries are also sanctioned. In a noncooperative game, each country's profits will be higher if the other named countries are also subject to duties. If each country acts strategically, the final outcome might involve all of the countries being disadvantaged (as compared to when the countries are not cumulated).

There are several empirical concerns that should be mentioned. For example, occasionally cases are cumulated with cases that had been previously filed. A U.S. industry might file an antidumping petition against Taiwan and Brazil, and then several months later file another petition against Korea. In this circumstance, all three cases could be cumulated as long as the three criteria stipulated in the 1984 amendment are satisfied, even though the cases were not filed simultaneously. However, suppose that some information from the Taiwan and Brazil investigations has been revealed (e.g., say, a preliminary affirmative decision), then the likelihood of an affirmative decision against Korea might be affected. In the results presented, we would attribute the "increased probability" entirely to cumulation, where in fact the higher probability may be due in part to the sequential nature of the filings. In fact, even without the cumulation provision the cases might be linked due to the information revealed about the ITC's opinion on the health of the domestic industry. To check for this possibility, we drop cumulated cases that were cumulated with previously filed cases and estimate the model. Not surprisingly, since only seven cases were dropped, the parameter estimates are almost identical to those presented in Tables III and IV.

Another issue is the fact that a number of ITC commissioners have used "bifurcated analysis" when making their injury decisions. A commissioner choosing to use a bifurcated approach essentially makes a two-stage injury decision (see Kaplan [1991] for a discussion). First, the commissioner decides if injury exists. If so, then the commissioner decides whether or not imports are the cause. Under a bifurcated approach, cumulation would only affect the outcome if the test gets to the second stage. Thus, potentially our estimates of the cumulation effect might be biased if the following four criteria are met: (i) the case was cumulated, (ii) ITC commissioners used a bifurcated approach in making their injury decision (iii) the ITC's decision is negative, and (iv) the case was negative at the first stage of the bifurcated analysis.

However, we expect our parameter estimates to be robust whether or not a bifurcated approach was used since our exogenous variables control for both stages of the decision process. Nonetheless, we estimated our model dropping the potentially problematic cases (only twenty-one cases satisfied the above four criteria). The parameter estimates are essentially unchanged.

Finally, we should note that the 1984 Trade Act made a number of changes to Title VII statutes in addition to the cumulation provision. Allowing upstream subsidies to be countervailable and the expanded definition of "like" product were two of the more significant amendments. While it is conceivable that part of the protective effect that we attribute to the cumulation provision might be due these other amendments, we believe our estimation has identified the cumulation effect since the circumstances when these other amendments are relevant are unlikely to systematically coincide with cases that were cumulated.

In conclusion, we hope that our research draws increased attention to the protective effects of congressional amendments to the U.S. trade statutes. Other statutory and procedural amendments have likely also had a significant impact on the overall level of protection in the U.S. For instance, allowing the use of "best information available," making upstream subsidies countervailable, and expanding the definition of "like product" are all examples of revisions that were intended by Congress to make Title VII laws more protective, but whose ultimate impact is unknown.

We also hope that our research draws attention to the apparent movement towards procedural protectionism. While in recent years Congress has largely resisted the rising pressures from U.S. industries to grant them direct protection from foreign imports, it has in fact moved the U.S. towards a policy of greater protectionism. To appease U.S. industries, Congress amended existing U.S. trade laws in order to make them more accessible to industries subject to trade pressures. As the results of this paper indicate, these amendments may have unforeseen impacts on policy outcomes and international patterns of trade.

DATA APPENDIX

Basic Case Information: Case outcome, date of initiation, subject, and named country is available in the *Fed-Track Guide to Antidumping and Countervailing Duty Findings and Orders.* Imports subject to investigation are identified in the *Federal Register* by their TSUSA (line-item tariff) code. The less-than-fair-value duty is also found in the *Federal Register.* The four-digit SIC code corresponding to the TSUSA code can be found in *U.S. Foreign Trade Statistics, Schedule 6.*

Cumulation Data: The public ITC case reports contain information on which countries' imports were cumulated. Not all multiple country filings are cumulated. For example, due to quality differences some imports in multiple-country petitions were determined not to compete with one another, and thus were not cumulated. Petition filing data in the *Fed-Track* guides helped us construct the experiment involving mandatory cumulation for all pre-1984 multiple country petitions.

Capacity Utilization (practical rate) at the four-digit SIC level by year was obtained from the U.S. Bureau of the Census *Current Industrial Reports, Survey of Plant Capacity.*

Shipments and Employment at the four-digit SIC level by year was obtained from the U.S. Bu-

reau of the Census *Census of Manufactures, Subject Series.*

Concentration Ratio at the four-digit SIC level by year was obtained from the U.S. Bureau of the Census *Census of Manufactures, Industry Series.*

Civilian Unemployment Rate is given in the *Economic Report of the President.* The merchandise trade deficit (millions of dollars) is also given in the *Economic Report of the President*

Oversight Committee Data was measured by matching four-digit SIC industry location with congressional districts. Typically, each product (which is identified by a SIC code) is produced in a number of locations across the country. If a product is produced in a district whose congressional representative (House or Senate) is a member of the Trade Subcommittee of the House Ways and Means Committee or the International Trade Subcommittee of the Senate Finance Committee, then the industry is believed to have a greater ability to influence ITC policymaking through its political pressure. The *Almanac of American Politics* was used to determine subcommittee membership. Data for industry location (and employment) by district and year at the four-digit SIC level were obtained from the *Census of Manufactures, Geographic Area Series.*

PAC Contributions to oversight members were constructed using the Federal Election commission's publicly available *Campaign Expenditures in the United States Reports on Financial Activity (RFA)* data. The Federal Election Commission reports contributions by each PAC to each representative and each registered candidate. Each PAC is also coded with a (self-reported) "special interest group" classification. The major task is to construct a concordance between PACs and SIC industry definitions without biasing the estimation procedure. The Federal Election Commission's special interest group classification is inadequate, offering only a handful of different codes In order to create a concordance we used the Center for Responsive Politics PAC coding scheme (Makinson [1989]). The Center for Responsive Politics assigns each PAC one or more category codes which denote the industry and/or groups the committee represents. The first category is the PAC's primary industry affiliation, the second is the next most important, etc. The Center's categories are relatively detailed, offering almost 400 category codes and greatly help in identifying what industry is represented by which PACs. Unfortunately, the Center's categories were not developed with the aim of mapping into SIC industry codes, and so the classification process is still somewhat arbitrary. Where possible we assigned the Center's categories a four-digit SIC code, but it was often difficult to go beyond two-digit SIC codes. The results reported in this paper are based on PAC contribution at the two-digit SIC level. PAC data is coded in millions of dollars.

Country and Steel Dummies: Non-market economies are defined as East Germany, Czechoslovakia, Hungary, Estonia, Latvia, Lithuania, Poland, USSR, Yugoslavia, Romania, Bulgaria Vietnam, People's Republic of China, and North Korea. *West European economies* are defined as the United Kingdom, Ireland, the Netherlands, Belgium, Luxembourg, France, West Germany, Austria, Switzerland, Spain, Portugal, and Italy. The *newly industrialized economies* are defined as Singapore, South Korea, Hong Kong, and Taiwan (China). The *steel industry* was defined to include the following four-digit SIC codes: 3312, 3321, 3334, 3339, 3351, 3357, 3432, 3441, 3494, 3496, 3519, 3523, 3557, 3562.

REFERENCES

Baldwin, Robert E. *The Political Economy of U.S. Import Policy.* Cambridge: MIT Press, 1985.

Baldwin, Robert E., and Jeffrey W. Steagall. "An Analysis of ITC Decisions in Antidumping, Countervailing Duty and Safeguard Cases." *Weltwirtschaftliches Archiv*, 130(2), 1994, 290–308.

Bello, Judith Hippler, and Alan F. Holmer. "The Trade and Tariff Act of 1984: Principal Antidumping and Countervailing Duty Provisions." *The International Lawyer*, 192, 1985, 639–73.

Federal Election Commission. *Campaign Expenditures in the United States, various years: Reports on Financial Activity (RFA) Data,* (Computer file). Washington, D.C: Federal Election Commission (producer), 1977 through 1991. Ann Arbor, Mich. Inter-university Consortium for Political and Social Research (distributor), 1978 through 1992.

Finger, J. Michael, H. Keith Hall, and Douglas R. Nelson. "The Political Economy of Administered Protection." *American Economic Review,* June 1982, 452–66.

Finger, J. Michael, and Tracy Murray. "Policing Unfair Imports: The United States Example." *Journal of World Trade,* August 1990, 39–53

Grossman, Gene M., and Elhanan Helpman. "Protection for Sale." *American Economic Review,* September 1994, 833–50.

Hansen, Wendy L. "The International Trade Commission and the Politics of Protectionism." *American Political Science Review,* 84(1), 1990, 21–46.

Hansen, Wendy L., Renee J. Johnson, and Isaac Unah. "Specialized Courts, Bureaucratic Agencies and the Politics of U.S. Trade Policy." *American Journal of Political Science,* August 1995 (forthcoming).

Hansen, Wendy L., and Thomas J. Prusa. "The Road Most Taken: The Rise of Title VII Protection." *The World Economy,* March 1995, 295–313.

Hoekman, Bernard M., and Michael P. Leidy. "Dumping, Antidumping, and Emergency Protection." *Journal of World Trade Law,* October 1989, 27–44.

Horlick, Gary N., and Geoffrey D. Oliver. "Antidumping and Countervailing Duty Law Provisions of the Omnibus Trade and Competitiveness Act of 1988." *Journal of World Trade,* June 1989, 5–49.

Kaplan, Seth. "Injury and Causation in USITC Antidumping Determinations: Five Recent Approaches," in *Policy Implications of Antidumping Measures,* edited by P. K. M. Tharakan. Amsterdam: North-Holland, 1991, 143–73.

Lande, Stephen L., and Craig VanGrasstek. *The Trade and Tariff Act of 1984.* Lexington: Lexington Books, 1986.

Makinson, Larry. *Money and Politics: The Price of Admission.* Washington, D.C.: Center for Responsive Politics, 1989.

Mock, William B. T. "Cumulation of Import Statistics in Injury Investigations before the International Trade Commission." *Northwestern Journal of International Law & Business,* 7(3), 1986, 433–79.

Moore, Michael, "Rules or Politics? An Empirical Analysis of ITC Antidumping Decisions." *Economic Inquiry,* July 1992, 449–66.

Palmeter, David N. "Dumping Margins and Material Injury: The USITC Is Free to Choose." *Journal of World Trade Law,* August 1987, 173–75.

Prusa, Thomas J., "Why Are So Many Antidumping Petitions Withdrawn?" *Journal of International Economics,* August 1992, 1–20.

Shapiro, Martin M. *Who Guards the Guardian: Judicial Control of Administration.* Athens: University of Georgia Press, 1988.

Suder, Jonathan T. "Cumulation of Imports in Antidumping and Countervailing Duty Investigations." *George Washington Journal of International Law and Economics,* 17(2), 1983. 463–87.

Takacs, Wendy E. "Pressures for Protectionism: An Empirical Analysis." *Economic Inquiry,* October 1981, 687–93.

Tharakan, P. K. M. "East European State Trading Countries and Antidumping Undertakings," in *Policy Implications of Antidumping Measures.* edited by P. K. M. Tharakan. Amsterdam: North-Holland, 1991, 143–73.

Weingast, Barry. "The Congressional-bureaucratic System: A Principal Agent Perspective (with Applications to the SEC)." *Public Choice,* 44(1), 1984, 117–91.

Wilson, James Q. *Bureaucracy: What Government Agencies Do and Why They Do It.* New York: Basic Books, 1989.

Chapter 9

U.S. Anti-dumping: Much Ado about Zeroing*

CHAD P. BOWN AND THOMAS J. PRUSA[1]

1 INTRODUCTION

One of the Uruguay Round's more notable achievements was the establishment of the WTO Dispute Settlement Understanding (DSU). When the Uruguay Round negotiations were initiated in 1986 there was a growing consensus that the original GATT dispute settlement system was ineffective (Hudec 1993). Compliance was a key failing of the old system; GATT contracting countries either blocked or simply ignored the findings of panels.[2] This was particularly problematic and embarrassing for high-profile trade disputes involving both the United States and the EC over, for example, bananas, beef hormones and tuna-dolphin. The failure to resolve these prominent disputes undermined the credibility of the GATT dispute process.

Consequently, a dispute settlement process that improved on both the timeliness and enforceability of dispute decisions was one of the major goals of the Uruguay Round. In many respects, the WTO DSU does represent a significant advance over the toothless GATT system.[3] However, frustrations remain. In theory, the new system induces compliance by increasing the possibility that plaintiffs will obtain the right to levy compensatory/retaliatory tariffs against defendants who do not adjust their policies. In reality, compliance has, on occasion, continued to be a problem. Countries continue to argue about what

---

[1] The authors thank James Durling, Valerie Ellis and Edwin Vermulst for useful discussions. The chapter also benefited from useful comments by Will Martin, Petros Marvoidis, Niall Meagher, Mike Moore, William Nye, Hylke Vandenbussche and Deborah Winkler.

[2] The need to reach consensus also affected how panels constructed their rulings, as the three panelists knew that their report also had to be accepted by the losing party in order to be adopted. Accordingly, there was an incentive to rule not solely on the basis of the legal merits of a complaint, but to aim for a 'diplomatic' solution by crafting a compromise that would be acceptable to both sides.

[3] Hudec (1999) refers to the increasingly legalised WTO dispute settlement as one of 'jurist's jurisprudence' when compared with the GATT system's 'diplomat's jurisprudence' (Hudec 1970). Jackson (1997) and Hoekman and Kostecki (2009, Chapter 5) also provide useful discussions of the evolution of the GATT and WTO dispute systems. Bown (2009) emphasises the implications of WTO dispute settlement for developing countries.

---

*This article originally appeared in *Policy Research Working Paper Series*, 5352.

constitutes compliance, and half measures can delay even 'compensatory' tariffs for years.[4]

While the GATT dispute system was damaged by its failure in highly prominent cases, the shortcomings of the WTO DSU are most apparent in a series of seemingly minor disputes involving the esoteric practice of zeroing in anti-dumping investigations. Zeroing refers to the practice of replacing the actual amount of dumping that yield negative dumping margins with a value of zero prior to the final calculation of a weighted-average margin of dumping for the product under investigation with respect to the exporters under investigation. Zeroing drops transactions that have negative margins and, hence, increases the overall dumping margins and the resulting size of the applied anti-dumping duty. As we will show, zeroing makes it extremely difficult for a firm to avoid dumping. This makes zeroing a major irritant to exporters while being highly desired by import-competing industries.

Over the past decade, the WTO AB has heard more than a dozen disputes involving zeroing, and, *each* time, has found that the practice violates the WTO Anti-dumping Agreement (ADA).[5] The first zeroing case was initiated by India in 1998 against the EC (*EC - Bed Linen*).[6] All but one of the remaining cases has involved the United States as a respondent. The EC changed its anti-dumping procedures after losing at the WTO and no longer 'zeros'. The United States, by contrast, has not yet fully complied with the WTO decisions and many WTO AB cases involving the United States' zeroing practice remain unresolved.

The WTO's current inability to resolve the zeroing issue is reminiscent of the enforcement problems that plagued the GATT dispute system. While the DSU may be working more or less as designed, is the zeroing issue a first indication that the WTO DSU must be reformed? Put differently, is zeroing an

---

[4]Wilson (2007) notes that the respondent country has eventually brought itself into compliance in the vast majority of WTO disputes that have resulted in adverse panel and Appellate Body rulings. Bown and Pauwelyn (2010) provide a collection of research examining the WTO dispute settlement process for the roughly dozen cases over the 1995–2007 period that resulted in at least a period of non-compliance and, thus, WTO Article 22.6 arbitration rulings that authorised formal retaliation by the complainants. Examples of such disputes include *Brazil - Aircraft Subsidies (Canada)*, *Canada - Aircraft Subsidies (Brazil)*; *EC - Bananas (Ecuador)*; *EC - Bananas (US)*; *EC - Hormones (Canada)*; *EC - Hormones (US)*; *US - Anti-dumping Act of 1916 (EC)*; *US - Continuing Dumping and Subsidy Offset Act (Byrd Amendment) (Brazil, Canada, Chile, EC, India, Japan, Korea, Mexico)*; *US - Foreign Sales Corporations (EC)*; *US - Internet Gambling (Antigua and Barbuda)*; and *US - Upland Cotton (Brazil)*.

[5]At least four more cases involving zeroing are pending AB decisions.

[6]Janow and Staiger (2003) and Grossman and Sykes (2006) provide an analysis of a variety of legal–economic issues associated with the first zeroing dispute of *EC - Bed Linen*. See also Crowley and Howse (2010), who examine the zeroing issues in *US - Stainless Steel (Mexico)*.

U.S. Anti-dumping: Much Ado about Zeroing 357

issue that could be better resolved through multilateral negotiations? If so, who should be at the negotiating table and what is at stake? This chapter presents a positive analysis seeking to provide some perspective on the zeroing issue. How did we get here? What exactly is zeroing? Why was the EC able to stop zeroing, while the United States was not? Are developing-country exporters also exposed to zeroing? To date, zeroing disputes have been dominated by developed countries, not only on the respondent side, but also on the complainant side. Should we expect a blizzard of zeroing complaints filed by developing countries? Even if the disputes fail to arise, is there evidence that zeroing impacts exports from developing countries as much as those from developed countries? Finally, we will try to get a better sense of zeroing's importance. Is it a 'big' issue? Or perhaps is this whole mess over zeroing (with apologies to William Shakespeare) much ado about nothing?

Anticipating our conclusions, we find that a unique set of characteristics have conspired to make zeroing such a bothersome issue. The WTO legislative history and technical nature of the zeroing violation likely contribute to the United States' feeling that its current policy is in compliance. The United States' retrospective duty collection system complicates the task of complying with the WTO AB decisions. By contrast, the prospective nature of the EC's duty collection system made zeroing a much less economically important issue, which explains why it was relatively easy for the EC to comply.

Any U.S. intransigence cannot alone explain why zeroing consumes so much of the WTO dispute settlement caseload, which thus serves to heighten the political sensitivity to the issue. The United States has anti-dumping duties on thousands of companies, on hundreds of separate products, and on more than 50 different WTO members. Given that the United States 'zeros' in *every* anti-dumping margin review calculation, the scope of the potential violation is enormous. The WTO AB could become a full-time zeroing body.[7]

The rest of this chapter proceeds as follows. Section 2 provides a discussion of the economic relevance of the zeroing issue in the context of the U.S. anti-dumping caseload. In Section 3 we more formally introduce anti-dumping and zeroing, and we identify how key factors such as export price volatility are likely to accentuate the impact of zeroing on the calculation of dumping margins. Section 4 then reviews the WTO dispute settlement caseload over the zeroing issue. We describe in detail the United States' retrospective system for assessing anti-dumping margins and the impact that this has on zeroing in Section 5. Section 6 focuses on the existing evidence of impact of the zeroing

---

[7]It also should be mentioned that the AB may have inadvertently exacerbated the issue of a high volume of zeroing-related cases through its initial choice of addressing zeroing in a piecemeal fashion. Bown and Sykes (2008) describe the implications of the AB's narrow and iterative approach to ruling on zeroing, comparing it with a more expansive approach that might have clarified the full scope of permissibility and impermissibility of zeroing across all of the procedures of the anti-dumping process in which it might be used.

358   *Unfinished Business? The WTO's Doha Agenda*

methodology on dumping margins. Section 7 provides our own empirical evidence into the question of zeroing's impact, and we find that zeroing is as likely to impact the anti-dumping margins on developing-country exports (which has typically not been brought forward to WTO dispute settlement) as anti-dumping margins on developed economy exports (which has frequently been brought to the DSU). Finally, Section 8 concludes.

2   THE ECONOMIC RELEVANCE OF ZEROING

Whether zeroing is a 'big' or 'small' issue depends on one's perspective as well as recognition of the likely policy alternatives in a world without zeroing. We begin by discussing some factors that suggest that zeroing is a major trade issue.

2.1   Scope: Number of Cases

In Figure 14.1 we provide one measure of U.S. anti-dumping activity. Here we plot the number of products affected by U.S. anti-dumping actions since 1990.[8] The solid line depicts the stock of products under order, while the dashed line shows the number of new products being investigated in each year. As shown, the U.S. Department of Commerce (USDOC) currently has orders on more than 400 products. The dashed line reveals that about 75 products are subject to new investigations each year, though with fluctuations that are broadly consistent with macroeconomic fluctuations (Knetter and Prusa 2003). This means that, in addition to the large stock of products that have been 'zeroed', many new additional WTO zeroing violations probably occur each year.

Moreover, given that most products are exported by multiple firms and by multiple countries, these numbers are probably a lower bound on the number of potential zeroing complaints. This raises the real possibility that the United States (and the WTO AB) could potentially be confronted with hundreds of zeroing disputes.

2.2   Scope: Countries Affected

Despite a dispute settlement history that has mainly entailed industrialised countries challenging the United States' use of zeroing in anti-dumping cases, there is every reason to believe that zeroing is just as important for developing-country exporters. First, developing countries are increasingly affected by U.S. anti-dumping. In Figure 14.2 we report the stock of U.S. anti-dumping measures in effect for each year from 1990 through 2009. In this chart we include information for both the products and the exporting country.

---

[8]In this figure we follow the common practice of using the eight-digit tariff line to define what constitutes a product.

U.S. Anti-dumping: Much Ado about Zeroing   359

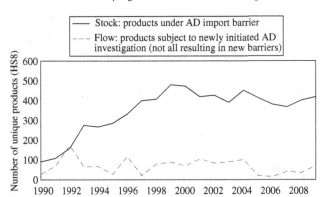

Figure 14.1: *Stock and flow of U.S. anti-dumping measures, 1990–2009.*
The stock is computed on a yearly basis as the number of eight-digit HS products subject to U.S. preliminary and/or final anti-dumping measures. The flow is computed on a yearly basis as the number of eight-digit HS products subject to U.S. anti-dumping investigations, some of which may not result in a duty. Since the data rely on the HS system, the stock does not reflect any imposed or removed anti-dumping measures that were imposed before 1988 under the annotated Tariff Schedule for the United States product classification system.
Source: compiled by the authors from Bown (2010a).

We divide the exporting countries into three groups: developed countries, China, and other (non-China) developing countries.[9] The information in Figure 14.2 indicates that over 60% of the stock of products covered by U.S. anti-dumping orders in place between 2006 and 2009 were on exports sourced from developing countries, more than doubling the share of total products affected at the onset of the WTO in 1995. The stock of measures affecting developing-country exports has been increasing over time, as exports from many emerging economies have continued to expand.[10] Looking forward, it is reasonable to think that this emerging pattern of anti-dumping measures

---

[9]We separate China due to the heavy incidence of anti-dumping cases brought against it (Bown 2010c).

[10]Note that it is notoriously difficult to compute estimates of the incidence of trade barriers such as anti-dumping. Thus, here we address this not by attempting to construct a measure in value terms but instead by examining the count of eight-digit HS and exporter combinations subject to U.S. anti-dumping measures. On a value-weighted basis, it is likely that a larger share of the incidence of the stock of U.S. anti-dumping activity falls on developed-economy exports, given the larger dollar values associated with their trade. It should also be noted that, while the United States frequently uses anti-dumping to restrict imports from middle-income economies such as Brazil, China, India, Indonesia, South Africa, Thailand and Turkey, the United States has typically not used anti-dumping to restrict imports sourced from low-income economies, with the exception of Vietnam.

Figure 14.2: *The stock of U.S. anti-dumping measures imposed and in place, 1990–2009.*

The stock is computed on a yearly basis as the number of eight-digit HS product-exporter combinations subject to U.S. preliminary and/or final anti-dumping measures. Since the data relies on the HS system, the stock does not reflect any imposed or removed anti-dumping measures that were imposed before 1988 under the annotated Tariff Schedule for The United States product classification system.

Source: compiled by the authors from Bown (2010a).

involving developing countries will also be seen in the pattern of zeroing complaints at the WTO AB. Although developing countries have currently only filed a few complaints challenging the practice, if the United States continues its non-compliance stance, there will, in all likelihood, be more and more zeroing cases against the United States, especially given that the AB's position towards zeroing is well established.

2.3 Impact and Incidence

To date, the best evidence we have suggests that, were the United States to stop zeroing, perhaps as much as half of all U.S. anti-dumping measures would be removed and the duties in the other cases would fall significantly. Our analysis also suggests that dumping margins calculated and, hence, duties imposed on developing countries are as likely to be affected by zeroing as

U.S. Anti-dumping: Much Ado about Zeroing   361

those imposed on developed countries. As we will explain, zeroing punishes suppliers with export price variation in particular. We collect import pricing data for a number of the biggest anti-dumping disputes over the past decade (many of which were the basis for WTO zeroing complaints) and review the price volatility for developed and developing countries. We find that developing countries have about the same price variation and, hence, their anti-dumping duties are likely to be similarly affected by zeroing.

While zeroing is likely to impact developing-country exporters and may lead to escalating tensions through WTO dispute settlement, there are other factors suggesting that zeroing may be less important than the above discussion indicates.

2.4   Anti-dumping and WTO AB

First, when it comes to dispute settlement, a broad and general point is simply that WTO disputes over anti-dumping are highly likely to continue to occur for reasons that have nothing to do with zeroing. Bown (2009, p. 80) estimates that, over the 2001–8 period, more than 30% of the entire WTO dispute initiation caseload involved challenges to just two policies: anti-dumping or countervailing duties, anti-dumping's sister 'unfair trade' policy.[11] Because much of this caseload of WTO anti-dumping disputes confronted other countries' (and not the United States') use of anti-dumping, it was not intended to address the specific issue of zeroing. Even if there were no disputes involving zeroing, a large fraction of the WTO AB's workload would still involve anti-dumping and countervailing duty issues.

There are a number of reasons why WTO disputes challenging anti-dumping frequently occur. Perhaps the most important explanation is the simple fact that the basic use of anti-dumping import restrictions has increased over time and across the WTO membership (Prusa 2001).[12] Dozens of economies now

---

[11] Only 15% of the dispute caseload during the WTO's first six years in existence (1995–2000) related to anti-dumping or countervailing duties. While a large share of the DSU caseload does involve challenges to many countries' use of anti-dumping, this is not to imply that most imposed anti-dumping measures get challenged through the DSU. In fact, it is quite the opposite. Bown (2009, p. 82) estimates that fewer than 7% of the total WTO membership's anti-dumping investigations that resulted in (more than 1600) imposed measures over the 1995-2008 period faced formal challenges through dispute settlement. Nevertheless, this figure is much higher for the United States; Bown and Crowley (2010) note that almost 21% (27 out of 130) of the U.S. anti-dumping measures imposed against WTO members over the 1997-2006 period were challenged through formal dispute settlement, including a number via the zeroing cases we describe below.

[12] Bown (2009) discusses a number of other reasons that contribute to anti-dumping being a frequent subject of WTO disputes, including the transparency of the policy and the fact that anti-dumping does not require political coordination of adversely affected firms and, hence, has fewer free-rider problems than those facing exporting firms subject to many other sorts of trade barriers.

have in place thousands of anti-dumping orders, and they are imposed and removed with great frequency. Nevertheless, it is unlikely that anti-dumping will go away any time soon, as most of the largest WTO members have adopted the policy and appear to appreciate its flexibility, for better or for worse. This is especially apparent in light of the global economic crisis of 2008–10 in which many WTO members increased their use of the policy (Bown 2010b), and yet this increased anti-dumping activity did not result in a massive and global protectionist backlash.

2.5 Trade Cost

Despite anti-dumping frequently being used in the United States, the total value of trade affected by anti-dumping (let alone zeroing) may be relatively small.[13] Furthermore, any single country subject to U.S. anti-dumping actions is likely to have a similar fraction of its exports affected. In many cases the elimination of zeroing would just reduce the margin, not eliminate the order, which means the impact of zeroing on the amount of trade affected is considerably smaller than the impact of anti-dumping. The small dollar value involved is one likely reason why the spectre of retaliation has apparently not induced the United States to alter its policy.

2.6 The Alternative Policy

Suppose that zeroing were eliminated and this policy change resulted in significantly less use of anti-dumping by the United States. Would this mean that U.S. imports would be subject to much less protection? Perhaps not. More likely is that some new type of protection would emerge. What would be the alternative to anti-dumping? Given that countries appear to desire access to flexibility with their trade policy and the historical evidence of episodes in which there is 'some' political-economy need for some form of discretionary import protection, anti-dumping may be less worrisome economically than many other scenarios that might emerge.

3 ANTI-DUMPING AND ZEROING: THE THEORY

If a company exports a product at a price lower than the price it normally charges in its own home market, it is said to be 'dumping' the product. If, in addition, the dumped imports are found to be causing, or threatening

---

[13]The issue is unresolved and two recent papers even provide different interpretations of the estimated impact of anti-dumping on trade flows. Vandenbussche and Zanardi (2010) argue that the costs of anti-dumping are larger than generally recognised because it depresses overall bilateral trade, whereas Egger and Nelson (forthcoming) provide evidence that the impact on overall trade is small.

U.S. Anti-dumping: Much Ado about Zeroing   363

to cause, material injury to the competing domestic industry, the WTO ADA allows governments to take action against dumping. The ADA contains rules that define how anti-dumping remedies should be implemented.[14] Of particular relevance for our discussion, the ADA states that the anti-dumping duty can be no greater than the calculated dumping margin. In the simplest terms, a dumping margin of, say, 5% means that on average the export price is 5% lower than the average home market price. The size of the dumping margin is therefore crucial, determining both whether there is a right to levy the duty and also the size of the duty.

In the process of computing the anti-dumping duty, a government must aggregate the results of comparisons between the normal value and export prices. Hundreds or even thousands of individual transactions are aggregated to produce a single anti-dumping duty. The ADA provides rules for how such calculations should be done. Zeroing refers to one particular step in the calculation. Zeroing is the practice of replacing the actual amount of dumping that yields negative dumping margins (ie export transactions for which the export price exceeds the calculated normal value) with a value of zero prior to the final calculation of a weighted-average margin of dumping for the product under investigation with respect to the exporters under investigation. Because the zeroing method drops transactions that have negative margins, it has the effect of increasing the overall dumping margins.[15]

In practice, zeroing is much easier to understand than the formal definition suggests. In Table 14.1 we present an example of a foreign firm's home and export sales in a given month.[16] We assume that the data in Table 14.1 represent net prices for separate transactions on a series of dates in the month of September.[17] To keep the example as simple as possible, we will assume that each transaction is for the same volume, ie one unit. Governments compute dumping margins on a weighted-average basis, but, for the purposes of our illustration, the introduction of different quantities on different dates just serves to complicate the computations, and needless complication is a primary reason why anti-dumping is so misunderstood.

As seen, prices vary from transaction to transaction in both markets. As is often the case in the real world, on some dates the export price is below the

---

[14]Blonigen and Prusa (2003) provide a survey of the economic research literature on anti-dumping.

[15]There are two zeroing methods: simple and model. For purposes of this chapter, we limit our discussion to simple zeroing. Readers interested in the fine details of both methods should consult Prusa and Vermulst (2009).

[16]The example is drawn from Prusa and Vermulst (2009).

[17]Net prices are the exporter's prices following a series of adjustments. For example, all expenses incurred to promote, sell, store and transport the products are deducted from both export price and domestic price. In addition, various other adjustments, such as level of trade and accounting for physical differences are made.

364   *Unfinished Business? The WTO's Doha Agenda*

Table 14.1: *An example of zeroing.*

Sales date	Export transaction	Home market transaction	Difference: no zeroing	Difference: zeroing
2 September	75	90	15	15
4 September	75	95	20	20
8 September	95	95	0	0
10 September	100	95	−5	0
12 September	105	95	−10	0
16 September	105	105	0	0
18 September	110	105	−5	0
20 September	115	110	−5	0
24 September	120	110	−10	0
Weighted-average price	100	100		
Dumping value			0	35
Dumping margin			0.0%	3.9%

home market price, on others the export price is above the home market price and, occasionally, the same price is charged in both the markets.

Under ADA rules, a government can calculate the difference in price on a transaction-by-transaction basis and then compute the weighted average of these price differences, *ie* the individual export transactions are compared with the individual domestic transactions made at or at about the same date as the export transactions concerned.[18]

In column 4 of Table 14.1 we compute the difference for each comparable transaction. Accordingly, for some comparisons the difference is positive (which means dumping) and for other comparisons it is negative. When we sum the weighted price differences we find that, for all comparable transactions, the cumulative difference is zero. Put differently, the dumping amount (35) for the two transactions with positive dumping is exactly equal to the amount (−35) for the five transactions with negative dumping. In this example, as long as the dumped and the non-dumped export transactions are allowed to offset each other, the conclusion, using the transaction-to-transaction method, will be that there is zero dumping.

As clean and simple as the above calculations are, the United States has long had a practice of not computing the margins as described. Instead, in the process of the transaction-to-transaction comparisons, the United States

---

[18]There are three common methods for calculating dumping margins: a weighted-average-to-weighted-average comparison, a transaction-to-transaction basis, and a weighted-average-to-transaction comparison. Zeroing has been used in all methods. For simplicity, we will just discuss zeroing in the context of the transaction-to-transaction approach. Prusa and Vermulst (2009) discuss all three methods.

U.S. Anti-dumping: Much Ado about Zeroing   365

employs the practice of zeroing. In our example, and, in fact, in most 'real world' cases, the use of zeroing leads to dramatically different margins. To see this, in the last column of Table 14.1 we have computed the difference for each comparable transaction using zeroing. Each of the five negative margins is set to zero. In our example, the amount of dumping is 35, which implies a dumping margin of 3.9% (35 divided by the total export value of 900 equals 0.039).[19]

Four important insights are gleaned from this example. First, zeroing can never lower the margin. Zeroing only drops negative margins. Second, zeroing treats some foreign prices as if they were something different than they actually are. On both 12 and 16 September the foreign firm charged $105, but a government using zeroing could treat the 12 September price as if it were just $95. Third, zeroing is driven by price variation over the sample period. If the foreign firm charged exactly the same price for all transactions, then zeroing would not matter.[20] Fourth, zeroing can be the difference between no dumping (or a *de minimis* margin) and a positive dumping margin, *ie* whether an anti-dumping duty is applied at all.

We elaborate on the last two insights in Figures 14.3 and 14.4. In Figure 14.3 we provide examples of hypothetical pricing data where zeroing does *not* change the anti-dumping duty. In the figure we provide two different pricing scenarios over a 12-month period. In both cases we assume that the foreign firm's home market price is constant at $100.[21] In Scenario A (solid line, circular markers) we consider a case when the foreign firm always charges an export price higher than $100. There is month-to-month variation but there is no dumping in any month. In Scenario B (dashed line, square markers) we depict the polar opposite situation. In this case the foreign firm always charges a lower export price than the comparable home market price. In this case the month-to-month pricing variation does not generate any potential offsetting margins.

Figure 14.4 depicts the more typical situation. We again assume that the foreign firm's home market price is constant at $100. We now assume that, in some months, the foreign firm's export price is above $100 and, in other months, it is below $100. The firm's actual export prices are depicted by the black dashed line and circular markers.[22] With zeroing, the government treats the foreign firm's prices as if they instead looked like the grey dotted line with

---

[19]We note that this approach as adopted by the United States does, however, include all comparable transactions in the denominator (even though it zeroes many transactions in the numerator).

[20]This statement can be generalised to account for 'model' zeroing (Prusa and Vermulst 2009).

[21]Alternatively, $100 could be the average home market price over the period.

[22]As with the example given in Table 14.1, without zeroing the actual export prices in Figure 14.4 would generate no dumping margin.

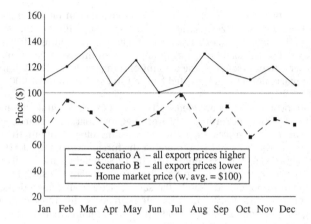

Figure 14.3: *Examples of export pricing when zeroing does not change dumping margin.*

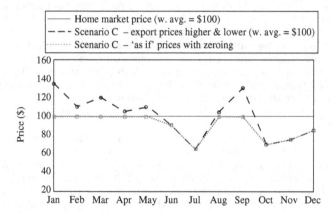

Figure 14.4: *Example of export pricing when zeroing alters dumping margin.*

square markers. In January, for example, a government practicing zeroing would act as if the foreign firm's price were $100 instead of $135.

As these examples show, zeroing makes it extremely difficult for a firm to avoid dumping. In January through May the foreign firm was making pricing decisions with no knowledge that those prices would be treated as something very different by the investigating foreign government. Unless a

U.S. Anti-dumping: Much Ado about Zeroing   367

firm's export prices are always high or low (relative to some home market benchmark), zeroing combined with price variation will generate dumping margins. Moreover, the reasons for the price variation (seasonality, exchange rates, variations in freight costs over time, *etc*) are irrelevant. In some cases, the product could be sold pursuant to a long-term contract, which might mean no price variation and, hence, zeroing might not matter. In other cases, the product could be sold on a spot basis, which could mean heightened price variation.

Price variation significantly affects the extent to which zeroing impacts the dumping margin. All else being equal, zeroing will have a larger impact for products with greater price variation. To see this, we will now compute dumping margins across distributions with different variation but holding the average price constant.[23] We assume the average *export* price is $100 in each scenario.

We begin by supposing that export prices are uniformly distributed between p^{low} and p^{high}.[24] In the first scenario we will assume that the weighted-average *home* market price is $100.[25] Hence, if there was no zeroing, the anti-dumping margin would be 0%. With zeroing, however, prices greater than $100 will be treated as if they were just $100. The extent of the zeroing impact depends on how much prices are adjusted: the greater the variation, the greater the adjustment. In Figure 14.5 we show the dumping margins as a function of different levels of price variation. The solid line depicts the anti-dumping duty with zeroing. As shown, price deviation of as little as 5% will generate margins in excess of the *de minimis* level.[26]

In the second scenario we consider a starker example of the impact of zeroing. Here we assume the weighted-average home market price is $90. In other words, in this scenario the average export price ($100) *exceeds* the home market price by 11%. Yet, as depicted by the dashed line, with zeroing a moderate amount of price deviation will again generate significant anti-dumping margins.

In the third scenario we consider a more extreme case when the weighted-average home market price is $75. In this scenario the average export price ($100) *exceeds* the home market price by 33%. However, zeroing combined with price deviation will nonetheless generate anti-dumping margins.

Two lessons emerge from these three scenarios. First we see that the greater the degree of over-selling (*ie* the bigger the difference between the average export price and the average home market price) the greater the required price

---

[23]Nye (2009) also points out that price volatility affects the zeroing distortion.

[24]For a uniform distribution the average price is $(p^{high} - p^{low})/2$ and the standard deviation is $(p^{high} - p^{low})/12^{1/2}$.

[25]For simplicity, assume one unit is sold at each transaction.

[26]For administrative reviews the United States imposes a *de minimis* margin of 2%.

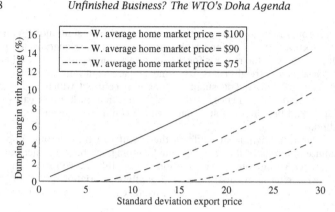

Figure 14.5: *Export price variation and zeroing (uniform distribution).*

variation before non-*de minimis* anti-dumping margins are created. Second, despite substantially higher export prices, zeroing can produce positive dumping.

The positive relationship between price variation and zeroing is quite general. In Figure 14.6 we depict dumping margins with zeroing for three different distributions of export prices: uniform, normal, and bimodal normal. As with the first scenario in Figure 14.5, we restrict the export prices so that the average is $100; this means there would be a zero dumping margin without zeroing. As shown, this is not the case with zeroing. For all three distributions the dumping margin increases with the pricing variation.

There are two key observations to be made from this discussion. First, export characteristics that are associated with *greater* price variation will tend to be more seriously affected by zeroing. These characteristics could be associated with the product (*eg* seasonality, volatile input prices), the exporting firm or industry (*eg* more or less competitive), or the exporting country (*eg* exchange rate regime).

Second, volatility will play a significant role in assessing whether zeroing is as relevant for developing countries as it has been for developed countries. As we will discuss in the following section, to date, most of the WTO cases involving zeroing have been initiated by developed countries. One possible explanation for this is that zeroing does not affect developing-country exports. Later in the chapter we review export price volatility, and our results suggest this is probably not the case. Consequently, the lack of zeroing cases involving developing countries is most likely explained by other reasons (*eg* unwillingness to increase trade tensions with the United States, inexperienced legal staff, *etc*).

U.S. Anti-dumping: Much Ado about Zeroing 369

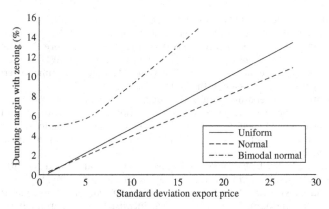

Figure 14.6: *Export price variation and zeroing (across distributions).*

4 WORLD TRADE ORGANIZATION DISPUTES INVOLVING ZEROING

There are four stages in the WTO dispute resolution system.[27] The first is the consultation phase, where the two complaining and respondent countries meet and attempt to negotiate a resolution. If they are unable to do so, they can request a 'panel' to hear the evidence (the second phase). Other WTO members with an interest in the dispute can join the process at this stage as an 'interested third party'. The panel hears the evidence and issues a legal ruling. If either of the primary countries is unhappy with any aspect of the panel's rulings, it can appeal the case to the WTO's AB (the third phase). After reviewing the case and hearing arguments from the parties, the AB will issue its final decision. At that point, if a country's policy has been found to be in violation of its WTO obligations, it is supposed to bring its policy into compliance. If the complaining party is unhappy with the compliance, it can request a compliance panel to rule on whether the respondent country has actually lived up to the AB's rulings (the fourth phase). If it has not, the AB can authorise the complainant to retaliate against the respondent, usually in the form of higher tariffs.

In Table 14.2 we list all WTO AB disputes that have involved zeroing. Between the first zeroing dispute of 1998 and early 2010, of the more than 260 disputes initiated during that time period, nearly 20 disputes have involved zeroing.[28] Furthermore, while 60% of all WTO disputes are resolved at the

---

[27] For a detailed description of the legal process, see Mavroidis (2007, pp. 398–445).

[28] Five of the cases are pending AB decisions. Zeroing was only a minor issue in several disputes. However, in most of the aforementioned disputes zeroing was the focal issue being adjudicated.

consultation phase, this has not been the case for any zeroing disputes. As a result, zeroing accounts for a greater share of panel and AB time than the above statistics suggest. Zeroing has been the subject of more than 13% of all WTO panel investigations (phase 2) and almost 20% of all WTO AB reports (phase 3). It is quite likely that the WTO AB has devoted more time to zeroing than any other single issue in the WTO.

The number of separate panel and AB decisions that have found the practice of zeroing to be inconsistent with the ADA is noteworthy. By our accounting, there have been at least 22 separate decisions finding the practice of zeroing to be inconsistent with the ADA (11 panel, 11 AB). Several comments about these decisions are warranted.

First, there has been some tension between the panels and the AB. The panels have sent mixed messages at least twice about zeroing. In two cases, (*US - Stainless Steel (Mexico)* and *US - Zeroing (Japan)*), the panel ruled that zeroing in original investigations was inconsistent but zeroing in review proceedings was consistent.[29] The panels' rationale hinged on their reading of Article 2.4.2 of the ADA, which states that

> the existence of margins of dumping during the investigation phase shall normally be established on the basis of a comparison of a weighted-average normal value with a weighted average of prices of all comparable export transactions or by a comparison of normal value and export prices on a transaction-to-transaction basis. A normal value established on a weighted-average basis may be compared with prices of individual export transactions if the authorities find a pattern of export prices which differ significantly among different purchasers, regions or time periods, and if an explanation is provided as to why such differences cannot be taken into account appropriately by the use of a weighted-average-to-weighted-average or transaction-to-transaction comparison.

The panels agreed with the United States' contention that the phrase 'during the investigation phase' limits the applicability to the original investigation, not to any type of review proceeding. However, in both cases the AB overturned the panel and found zeroing to be inconsistent in both original investigations and reviews.

The WTO AB has repeatedly determined that allowing zeroing in reviews but not in original investigations would lead to unequal treatment between prospective and retrospective duty systems. In the prospective system (used by most WTO members), the dumping margin is established on the basis of the original investigation. In the retrospective system used by the United States, the dumping margin calculated in the initial investigation only establishes the deposit rate. The actual dumping margin is established during an

---

[29] Adding more confusion, in *US - Continued Zeroing (EC)*, the panel stated their sympathy with the U.S. position but determined zeroing to be inconsistent only because of prior AB rulings.

Table 14.2: *World Trade Organization Jurisprudence on zeroing.*

Case	Dispute	Year initiated	Third parties	Panel	AB
US – Shrimp (Vietnam)	404	2010	—	—	—
US – Use of Zeroing (Korea)	402	2009	Japan	—	—
US – Stainless Steel (Mexico), Article 21.5	344	2009	—	—	—
US – Carrier Bags (Thailand)	383	2008	Argentina, Chinese Taipei, EC, Japan, Korea	Y	—
US – Orange Juice (Brazil)	382	2008	Argentina, Chinese Taipei, EC, Japan, Korea, Thailand	—	—
US – Zeroing (Japan), Article 21.5	322	2008	China, Chinese Taipei, EC, Hong Kong (China), Korea, Mexico, Norway, Thailand	Y	Y
US – Zeroing (EC), Article 21.5	294	2007	Chinese Taipei, India, Japan, Korea, Mexico, Norway, Thailand	Y	Y
US – Continued Zeroing (EC)	350	2006	Brazil, Chinese Taipei, China, Egypt, India, Japan, Korea, Mexico, Norway, Thailand	Y	Y
US – Shrimp (Thailand)	343	2006	Brazil, Chile, China, EC, India, Japan, Korea, Mexico, Vietnam	Y	N/A
US – Stainless Steel (Mexico)	344	2006	Chile, China, EC, Japan, Thailand	Y/N	Y
US – Shrimp Anti-dumping Measure (Ecuador)	335	2005	Brazil, Chile, China, EC, India, Japan, Korea, Mexico, Thailand	Y	N/A
US – Zeroing (Japan)	322	2004	Argentina, China, EC, Hong Kong (China), India, Korea, Mexico, New Zealand, Norway, Thailand	Y/N	Y
US – Softwood Lumber Anti-dumping Final (Canada), Article 21.5	264	2005	China, EC, India, Japan, New Zealand, Thailand	Y	Y
US – Zeroing (EC)	294	2003	Argentina, Brazil, China, Chinese Taipei, Hong Kong (China), India, Japan, Korea, Mexico, Norway	Y	Y
US – Softwood Lumber Anti-dumping Final (Canada)	264	2002	EC, India, Japan	Y	Y
US – Corrosion-Resistant Steel Sunset Review (Japan)	244	2002	Brazil, Chile, EC, India, Korea, Norway	N	Y
EC – Pipe Fittings (Brazil)	219	2000	Chile, Japan, Mexico, United States	Y	Y
EC – Bed Linen (India)	141	1998	Japan, Korea, United States	Y	Y

'—' indicates unavailable/pending. 'N/A' indicates cases where the panel's zeroing decision was not appealed to the AB.

Source: compiled by the authors from information on the WTO website.

administrative review. If the United States' position held, then a country with a retrospective system would be able to zero but a country with a prospective system (like the EC) would not.

Second, the nature of the WTO's jurisprudence has likely contributed to the number of disputes. The practice of the panels and the AB has typically been to craft very narrow determinations in an attempt to reduce accusations of 'judicial activism' and thus not limit infringement on member countries' sovereign rights. As a result, important issues are often left unaddressed for 'judicial economy', which opens the door for the respondent country to limit the applicability of a ruling. What the AB intended their decision to mean is often unclear until essentially the same issue is brought to the WTO DSU again (and again). With respect to zeroing, the judicial economy exercised by the AB in the initial cases meant that many issues (*ie* alternative methods of zeroing, appropriate use during different stages in a case) were not discussed. This allowed the United States to interpret the early rulings very narrowly and resulted in more cases being filed (Bown and Sykes 2008).

Any ambiguity stemming from the AB's piecemeal approach to decision-making should now be resolved in light of the recent decisions against zeroing. The first few cases challenging zeroing made claims just against the use of zeroing in original investigations as applied in specific cases. However, in more recent cases (*US – Continued Zeroing (EC)*; *US – Zeroing (Japan)*; and *US – Zeroing (EC)*), the complainants made very expansive claims against the practice. The WTO AB's decisions now imply that the practice of zeroing is inconsistent except under exceptional circumstances.

The number of countries complaining about the practice is also noteworthy. In Table 14.3 we list the number of countries who have either initiated a WTO dispute involving zeroing (*ie* the 'complainant') or have filed supporting briefs as interested third parties. In total, 19 countries have been involved in zeroing disputes, 10 as complainant parties.

5   THE UNITED STATES RETROSPECTIVE SYSTEM AND THE IMPACT OF ZEROING

Despite the ongoing cases against it, the United States argues that it has complied with the WTO AB rules and that its practice is now consistent with the ADA. The United States contends that it has brought its policy into compliance in response to the initial WTO AB decisions against zeroing. In January 2007 the USDOC decided to stop zeroing in original investigations. The USDOC has not agreed, however, to stop zeroing in reviews. This raises the question—why would the United States only take half-measures when resolving this trade issue? We believe the answer is inextricably tied to the retrospective duty assessment system using by the United States.

Compare the EC and U.S. response to the WTO AB's decisions regarding zeroing. As a general rule, no WTO member happily accedes to dispute

U.S. Anti-dumping: Much Ado about Zeroing   373

Table 14.3: *Economies involved in WTO jurisprudence on zeroing.*

	Number initiated	Number of third party
Argentina	—	4
Brazil	2	5
Canada	2	—
Chile	—	5
China	—	8
Chinese Taipei	—	6
EC	3	10
Ecuador	1	—
Egypt, Arab Rep. of	—	1
Hong Kong (China)	—	3
India	1	9
Japan	3	13
Korea	1	11
Mexico	2	8
New Zealand	—	2
Norway	—	6
Thailand	1	8
United States	—	2
Vietnam	1	1

Source: compiled by the authors from information on the WTO website.

settlement decisions that go against their existing policies. However, when the EC's zeroing practice was found to be inconsistent with the WTO ADA, it fairly quickly changed its procedures to eliminate zeroing. When the United States' zeroing methodology was found to be inconsistent, the United States has been unable (or unwilling) to fully change its procedures.

The duty assessment systems in the EC and U.S. partly explain why they responded differently to the WTO rulings. Under the prospective duty assessment system used by the EC (and all other WTO members), the exporter is assigned a duty calculated on past pricing data and the duty applies to future transactions. By contrast, under the U.S. retrospective system, the anti-dumping duty imposed at the end of the original investigation only constitutes an estimate of the future liability. The actual payment of anti-dumping duties will depend on the calculations made in the course of the annual administrative or duty-assessment reviews.

Under either system, zeroing will serve to increase margins. It is fair to say that import-competing industries in both the EC and the United States want zeroing because it serves to inflate the size of margins and, hence, leads to the imposition of larger import restrictions that shield them from foreign competition. The difference, however, is that the impact of zeroing is amplified when used in a retrospective system. Hence, the cost of eliminating zeroing in the United States is greater, thereby increasing U.S. reluctance to abolish the practice.

The retrospective system adds an element of uncertainty that is not present in the prospective system. Under a prospective system, an importer purchasing from an exporter under an anti-dumping order will know the exact size of its extra duty. Under a retrospective system, on the other hand, an importer purchasing from an exporter under an anti-dumping order only has an estimate of its extra duty. It is conceivable that the uncertainty could have as big an impact as the margin itself. Suppose, for instance, that the exporter is subject to a 5% duty and that duty exactly (or nearly) offsets her cost advantage relative to 'non-subject' suppliers, *ie* exporters which sell the same product in the U.S. market but that were not confronted with (subject to) the U.S. anti-dumping duty. An importer might be unwilling to purchase from the exporter under order because of the possibility of a higher liability once the administrative review is conducted. While uncertainty is inherent in the retrospective system, zeroing greatly compounds the phenomenon. As shown in Figure 14.4, the importer can have numerous purchases made during the period of review that are treated by the USDOC as if they were conducted at a different price than they actually were. This makes importers even more reluctant to purchase from subject exporters.

As a result, U.S. import-competing industries are much more opposed to eliminating zeroing than EC import-competing industries were. In turn, their strong opposition to reform makes it difficult for the USDOC to stop zeroing. Put differently, the current U.S. compliance—stopping zeroing in original investigations—is essentially costless. The *de minimis* dumping margin in original investigation is 0.5%. In other words, if the home market price is $100 and the export price is $99.49, then the case will be allowed to proceed. However, when the administrative review is conducted, the exact same transactions would result in a larger dumping margin because of zeroing. Thus, the real economic impact of zeroing—both in terms of the margin imposed and the uncertainty surrounding that margin—is driven by the *review* stage.

6   THE IMPACT OF ZEROING ON MARGINS AND DUTIES

We now turn beyond the theory to the empirical question of the impact of zeroing on anti-dumping margins.[30] Obtaining an accurate measure of the impact of zeroing on margins is difficult. The fundamental problem is that the USDOC uses firm-level pricing in both the home and export markets to calculate margins. What we would like to do is compute the counterfactual

---

[30]An important effect of zeroing is the additional uncertainty created for importers buying from subject suppliers. We know of no empirical evidence on this latter impact, so we will just focus on how zeroing affects the size of the margin.

U.S. Anti-dumping: Much Ado about Zeroing   375

'what if there were no zeroing?' and then compare the counterfactual margin with the actual margin with zeroing. The calculation of this counterfactual requires access to confidential firm-level pricing data, and that is something we do not have. We do, however, have results from previous studies that did have access to such data and were able to perform the counterfactual exercise.

We begin by reviewing the result from what we believe is the only published study of zeroing that utilises the same firm-level data as USDOC. We then examine evidence of the impact of zeroing as contained in submissions to the WTO AB where countries submit the results of the counterfactual calculations.

6.1   Firm-Level Evidence

The only published firm-level analysis of the impact of zeroing is contained in a series of papers by the Cato Institute (Lindsey and Ikenson 2002a,b; Ikenson 2004). Lindsey and Ikenson were able to get 18 firms from 5 different countries to share the exact pricing data they had submitted to the USDOC as part of their dumping investigations. The determinations covered 14 original investigations and 4 administrative reviews. For each of these determinations, Lindsey and Ikenson used the USDOC's own dumping calculation computer programs. They first recreated the dumping margins determined by the USDOC. They then altered those programs to gauge the effect of zeroing on margins. They state that

> using actual case data and the DOC's dumping calculation computer pro-
> grams, it was possible to calculate the actual effects of zeroing in these
> particular cases. In 17 of the 18 determinations, the dumping margin was
> inflated by zeroing. In 5 of the cases, the overall dumping margin would have
> been negative. On average, the dumping margins in the 17 cases would have
> been 86.41% lower if zeroing had not been employed.   Ikenson (2004, p. 2)

Due to confidentiality issues, Lindsey and Ikenson are unable to report the actual size of the original dumping margin. As a result we are unable to determine how great the 86% reduction is: it could imply a change in the actual dumping margin of 2, 20 or even 50 percentage points. While we do not know the identity of the individual firms, we do know what cases were involved (eg stainless steel bar from Germany) and we know the 'all others' duty reported for each case.[31] Using the 'all others' duty we estimate that the Lindsey and Ikenson estimate of an 86.41% reduction due to zeroing implies that the *average* impact of zeroing is at least 17.50 percentage points, ie a change in the margin of dumping from 20.2% to 2.7%.

Lindsey and Ikenson's results with respect to reviews are particularly noteworthy. Their results confirm that zeroing has a particularly powerful

---

[31]We note that the 'all others' rate often does not necessarily correspond to any individual firm's duty but is better thought of as the average margin for all firms involved in the case.

impact at the review phase. They had access to case data for just four review calculations and, in each instance, they found the margin to be *entirely* driven by zeroing. That is, without zeroing, there would have been no margin. Their results are consistent with the idea that firms subject to anti-dumping orders make an effort to comply with the dumping order but are ultimately bedevilled by the distortion created by zeroing: transactions that they thought would be treated as occurring at one price were assigned a lower price by USDOC, which, in effect, creates margins.

6.2 Evidence from WTO Dispute Documents

While the Lindsey and Ikenson study is compelling, it involves a small sample of firms. We have also reviewed the WTO disputes for evidence on the impact of zeroing. We found reports of the impact of zeroing in the public documents for only three cases: *US – Stainless Steel (Mexico)* (dispute 344); *US – Zeroing (Japan)* (dispute 322); and *US – Zeroing (EC)* (dispute 294). From these three disputes we have information on the impact of zeroing for 74 separate margin calculations.

The tabulation of the findings is given in Table 14.4. For each margin calculation, we report the name of the product under investigation, the name of the company subject to the investigation, and the anti-dumping duty as calculated by the USDOC (inclusive of zeroing). For original investigations this is the final anti-dumping duty for each firm, while for administrative reviews this is the duty margin actually imposed by USDOC. In the final column we report the results of the counterfactual exercise: what the margin would have been if zeroing were not performed. Given the individual firms' sensitivities about revealing confidential pricing information, in many cases we do not know the exact 'what if no zeroing?' margin. Instead, the public documents often simply report 'lower', 'negative', or *de minimis*. 'Lower' simply means the margin would have been lower but would have still been above the *de minimis* level; 'negative' means the margin would have been negative (*ie* no dumping); *de minimis* means the margin would be positive but sufficiently small to be considered zero. In either of these latter two cases, the case would have been terminated (if an original investigation) or no duties would have been paid (if an administrative review).

In Table 14.5 we summarise the information reported in Table 14.4. Without zeroing, the dumping margin would have been lowered in 30 instances, and the margin would have been eliminated (*ie* a zero margin) in 42 instances. Put differently, more than half of the cases submitted to the WTO would have no dumping but for the practice of zeroing.

One needs to be cautious in extrapolating the statistics from the WTO AB cases to all U.S. anti-dumping activity. There are two reasons why we are concerned that there is a possible selection issue that might result in the WTO AB evidence overstating the impact of zeroing. First, the cases submitted

U.S. Anti-dumping: Much Ado about Zeroing   377

to the WTO may have been selected precisely because they were particularly egregious examples of zeroing. While we have no evidence for this, it is nevertheless a concern given the complainants' desire to submit the most compelling cases to the WTO.

Second, the cases chosen for WTO appeal might have lower margins and, thus, be more likely to have a zero margin if the practice of zeroing ceased. There is some evidence that this is the case. Using information from Bown (2010a), we compared the dumping margins for cases that were the basis for WTO zeroing complaints with all other U.S. anti-dumping cases. The average margin for cases not brought to the WTO is 62.6%, while the average margin for cases that have been the basis for WTO zeroing complaints is 36.2%.[32] This does not mean that the practice of zeroing has not affected the margins in the other cases, but it does suggest that the margins for most cases are not entirely driven by zeroing. It also suggests that countries choose to file WTO appeal on cases where it is more likely that the elimination of zeroing could mean *de minimis* margins and the removal of anti-dumping duties altogether.

The more robust finding is that the impact of zeroing is to increase the dumping margin. In Table 14.6 we use the WTO disputes and calculate the impact on the margin due to zeroing. On average, dumping margins would have been 12.3 percentage points lower. While this is smaller than the Lindsey and Ikenson study estimates, we note that it is greater than the average margin (10.5%) for these cases. This is again compelling evidence that zeroing has a large and significant impact on margins.

If we focus solely on the WTO cases in Table 14.4 that involve administrative reviews, we have a sample of 45 dumping margins. Of this sample, the margin would have been eliminated in 35 of the 45 cases if zeroing were not employed. If one is willing to assume that this is a representative statistic for other cases, the evidence from the current WTO jurisprudence suggests that about 75% of review margins would be eliminated but for zeroing. This is consistent with the Cato study which also found the impact of zeroing at the review phase to be particularly significant.

We again urge caution in applying the WTO AB statistics to the overall sample of U.S. anti-dumping cases. As discussed above, the margins for cases brought to the WTO AB are generally lower than those for other cases. It may simply be the case that the low-margin cases give the complaining country the 'biggest bang for the buck' and, therefore, that they are more likely to result in WTO challenges.[33]

Moreover, given that non-challenged cases tend to have higher margins, it is uncertain what the impact of zeroing is on the trade volumes. That is, suppose that the United States stopped zeroing in all cases. The elimination of zeroing may result in lower margins but nevertheless have little impact on trade. This

---

[32]The difference is statistically significant at the 1% level.

[33]Bown (2005) argues that this selection issue applies more generally in WTO disputes.

218   *Economic Effects of Antidumping*

378   *Unfinished Business? The WTO's Doha Agenda*

Table 14.4: *World Trade Organization disputes: reported impact of zeroing (case by case).*

Case number	Case name	Company	Anti-dumping duty (with zeroing) (%)	Anti-dumping duty (without zeroing)[a]
DS294: No. 1	(OI) Certain hot-rolled carbon steel flat products from the Netherlands	Corus Staal BV	2.59	Negative
DS294: No. 2	(OI) Stainless steel bar from France	Ugine-Savoie Imphy	3.90	Negative
		Aubert & Duval S.A.	71.83	Lower
DS294: No. 3	(OI) Stainless steel bar from Germany	BGH	13.63	Lower
		Einsal	4.17	De minimis
		EWK	15.40	Lower
		KEP	33.20	Lower
DS294: No. 4	(OI) Stainless Steel Bar from Italy	Acciaierie Valbruna Srl /Acciaierie Bolzano D.p.A.	2.50	Negative
		Acciaiera Foroni SpA	7.07	Lower
		Rodacciai S.p.A.	3.83	Lower
		Cogne Acciai Speciali Srl	33	N/A
DS294: No. 5	(OI) Stainless steel bar from the United Kingdom	Corus Engineering Steels	4.48	Negative
		Crownridge Stainless Steel, Ltd/ Valka Ltd and Firth Rixson Special Steels, Ltd	125.77	N/A
DS294: No. 6	(AR) Industrial nitrocellulose from France	Bergerac NC	3.26	Lower
DS294: No. 7	(AR) Industrial nitrocellulose from the United Kingdom	Imperial Chemical Industries	3.06	Negative
DS294: No. 8	(AR) Stainless steel plate in coils from Belgium	ALZ NV	3.84	Negative
DS294: No. 9	(AR) Certain pasta from Italy	Pastificio Guido Ferrara S.r.L.	1.25	Lower
		Pastificio Antonio Pallante S.r.L.	1.78	Lower
		PAM S.r.L.	4.10	De minimis
DS294: No. 10	(AR) Certain pasta from Italy	Pastificio Garofalo S.p.A.	0.55	Lower

U.S. Anti-dumping: Much Ado about Zeroing 379

Table 14.4: *Continued.*

Case number	Case name	Company	Anti-dumping duty (with zeroing) (%)	Anti-dumping duty (without zeroing)[a]
DS294: No. 11	(AR) Stainless steel sheet strip in coils from Italy	Acciai Speciali Terni SpA	0.66	Negative
DS294: No. 12	(AR) Stainless steel sheet strip in coils from Italy	Acciai Speciali Terni SpA	5.84	Negative
DS294: No. 13	(AR) Granular polytetrafluoroenthylene resin from Italy	Ausimont SpA	2.15	Lower
DS294: No. 14	(AR) Granular polytetrafluoroenthylene resin from Italy	Ausimont SpA	12.08	Lower
DS294: No. 15	(AR) Stainless steel sheet and strip in coils from France	Ugine	3.00	Negative
DS294: No. 16	(AR) Stainless steel sheet and strip in coils from France	Ugine	1.44	Negative
DS294: No. 17	(AR) Stainless steel sheet and strip in coils from Germany	KTN	2.61	Negative
DS294: No. 18	(AR) Stainless steel sheet and strip in coils from Germany	TKN	4.77	Negative
DS294: No. 19	(AR) Ball bearings from France	SKF France SA and Sarma	8.51%	Negative
DS294: No. 20	(AR) Ball bearings from Italy	SKF Industrie SpA	3.70%	Negative
DS294: No. 21	(AR) Ball bearings from United Kingdom	FAG Italia SpA	1.42%	Negative
		NSK Bearings Europe Ltd	16.87%	Negative
		Barden Corporation U.K.	3.87%	Negative
DS294: No. 22	(OI) Stainless steel wire rod from Sweden	Fagersta Stainless AB	5.71%	Negative
DS294: No. 23	(OI) Stainless steel wire rod from Spain	Roldán SA	4.73%	Lower

Table 14.4: *Continued.*

Case number	Case name	Company	Anti-dumping duty (with zeroing) (%)	Anti-dumping duty (without zeroing)[a]
DS294: No. 24	(OI) Stainless steel wire rod from Italy	Cogne Acciai Speciali Srl	12.72%	Lower
DS294: No. 25	(OI) Stainless steel wire rod from Belgium	ALZ	3.84%	Lower
DS294: No. 26	(OI) Stainless steel sheet and strip in coils from France	Usinor	9.38%	Lower
DS294: No. 27	(OI) Stainless steel sheet and strip in coils from Italy	Acciai Spaciali Terni SpA	11.23%	Lower
DS294: No. 28	(OI) Stainless steel sheet and strip in coils from the United Kingdom	Avesta Sheffield	14.84%	Lower
DS294: No. 29	(OI) Certain cut-to-length carbon-quality steel plate from France	Usinor	10.41%	Lower
DS294: No. 30	(OI) Certain cut-to-length carbon-quality steel plate from Italy	Palini and Bertoli SpA	7.85%	Lower
DS294: No. 31	(OI) Certain pasta from Italy	Italpasta La Molisana Liguori Pagani	21.34% 14.78% 12.41% 18.30%	Lower Lower Lower Lower
DS322: No. 1	(OI) Certain cut-to-length carbon-quality steel plate products from Japan	Kawasaki Steel Corporation	10.58%	Lower (9.46%)
DS322: No. 2	(AR) Tapered roller bearings, four inches or less in outside diameter, and components thereof, from Japan	Koyo Seiko Co., Ltd	14.86%	Negative (−1.27%)

U.S. Anti-dumping: Much Ado about Zeroing   381

Table 14.4: *Continued.*

Case number	Case name	Company	Anti-dumping duty (with zeroing) (%)	Anti-dumping duty (without zeroing)[a]
DS322: No. 3	(AR) Tapered roller bearings and parts thereof, finished and unfinished, from Japan	NTN Corporation	17.58%	Negative (−6.01%)
DS322: No. 4	(AR) Tapered roller bearings and parts thereof, finished and unfinished, from Japan	Koyo Seiko Co., Ltd	17.94%	Lower (13.32%)
DS322: No. 5	(AR) Ball bearings and parts thereof from Japan	NTN Corporation	6.14%	Negative (−25.15%)
DS322: No. 6	(AR) Cylindrical roller bearings and parts thereof from Japan	NTN Corporation	3.49%	Negative (−25.24%)
DS322: No. 7	(AR) Spherical plain bearings and parts thereof from Japan	NTN Corporation	2.78%	Negative (−26.06%)
DS322: No. 8	(AR) Ball bearings and parts thereof from Japan	Koyo Seiko Co., Ltd	10.10%	Negative (−5.51%)
		NTN Corporation	9.16%	Negative (−15.21%)
		NSK Ltd	4.22%	Negative (−20.76%)
DS322: No. 9	(AR) Cylindrical roller bearings and parts thereof from Japan	Koyo Seiko Co., Ltd	5.28%	Negative (−11.70%)
DS322: No. 10	(AR) Spherical plain bearings and parts thereof from Japan	NTN Corporation	16.26%	Negative (−8.08%)
		NTN Corporation	3.60%	Negative (−10.31%)
DS322: No. 11	(AR) Ball bearings and parts thereof from Japan	NSK Ltd	6.07%	Negative (−18.78%)
		Asahi Seiko Co., Ltd	2.51%	Negative (−26.83%)
		NTN Corporation	9.34%	Negative (−12.17%)

Table 14.4: *Continued.*

Case number	Case name	Company	Anti-dumping duty (with zeroing) (%)	Anti-dumping duty (without zeroing)[a]
DS322: No. 12	(AR) Ball bearings and parts thereof from Japan	NTN Corporation NSK Ltd	4.51% 2.68%	Negative (−25.99%) Negative (−29.90%)
DS322: No. 13	(AR) Ball bearings and parts thereof from Japan	Koyo Seiko Co., Ltd NTN Corporation NSK Ltd	5.56% 2.74% 2.46%	Negative (−10.83%) Negative (−25.86%) Negative (−29.61%)
DS344: No. 1	(OI) Stainless steel from Mexico	ThyssenKrupp Mexinox S.A. de C.V.	30.85%	Lower
DS344: No. 2	(First AR) Stainless steel from Mexico	ThyssenKrupp Mexinox S.A. de C.V.	2.28%	Negative
DS344: No. 3	(Second AR) Stainless steel from Mexico	ThyssenKrupp Mexinox S.A. de C.V.	6.15%	Lower (1.83%)
DS344: No. 4	(Third AR) Stainless steel from Mexico	ThyssenKrupp Mexinox S.A. de C.V.	7.43%	Lower (4.96%)
DS344: No. 5	(Fourth AR) Stainless steel from Mexico	ThyssenKrupp Mexinox S.A. de C.V.	5.42%	Lower (1.54%)
DS344: No. 6	(Fifth AR) Stainless steel from Mexico	ThyssenKrupp Mexinox S.A. de C.V.	2.96%	Negative

[a]This column indicates what would have been the outcome if zeroing were not applied; 'lower' simply means the margin would have been lower; 'negative' means the margin would have been negative (*ie* no dumping) and as a result the case would have been terminated (for original investigations) or no duties would have been paid (for administrative reviews). '*De minimis*' means the margin is too small to be subject to an order. 'OI' indicates original investigation whereas 'AR' indicates administrative review.

Source: compiled by the authors from the public documents submitted as part of each AB dispute; case information available from the WTO website.

U.S. Anti-dumping: Much Ado about Zeroing   383

Table 14.5: *World Trade Organization disputes: reported impact of zeroing (summary).*

Dumping margin lower	30
Dumping margin eliminated	42
Dumping margin change 'N/A'	2
Total cases	74

Source: compiled from the information in Table 14.4.

Table 14.6: *World Trade Organization disputes: change in margin due to zeroing (percentage point change).*

	Median (%)	Mean (%)
Cases where dumping margin was lowered but not eliminated	3.9	3.3
Cases where dumping margin was eliminated	7.2	13.3
All cases	4.8	12.3

Source: compiled from the information in Table 14.4.

would be the case, for instance, if the computed margin without dumping was still quite high. Suppose a firm has a dumping margin with zeroing of 80% and that its margin without zeroing was 35%. It is not likely that a margin of 35% would result in a significantly different volume of imports than a margin of 80%: a duty can easily be prohibitive at 35%.

7   LIKELY IMPACT OF ZEROING ON DEVELOPING COUNTRIES

Until relatively recently, most of the WTO disputes over zeroing had been dominated by cases initiated by developed-economy complainants such as EC, Japan and Canada. While there have been a few cases involving developing-country complainants, zeroing was a side issue in many of these cases.[34]

Since 2008, however, a growing number of developing countries such as Vietnam, Korea, Thailand and Brazil have initiated zeroing complaints at the WTO. Can we expect other developing countries to join the fray? The answer seems to be yes. First, the United States applies its practice of zeroing against all subject import suppliers. Every developing country with products subject to U.S. anti-dumping orders has had zeroing applied. Second, as Figure 14.2 indicates, there are many developing-country exports subject to current U.S. anti-dumping orders. This means that there are many cases that could be the basis for a WTO complaint. Third (and perhaps the most compelling reason

---

[34]Disputes 206, 335, 343 and 345 all contained zeroing complaints but they were primarily about other procedures.

384   *Unfinished Business? The WTO's Doha Agenda*

why one should expect more zeroing cases), the WTO AB's views on zeroing are now well established. As discussed above, numerous decisions have been made against zeroing. Moreover, the most recent WTO decisions have clearly established the general inconsistency of zeroing and have responded to all criticisms by panels of the early zeroing decisions. Given these decisions, it is hard to see how the United States could win any zeroing dispute at the WTO. This reality is likely to embolden other countries to initiate their own actions against the United States.

The key unknown is the extent to which zeroing has a different impact on developed- versus developing-country margins. If zeroing has a smaller impact on developing countries, then arguably there is a smaller benefit to be gained from filing a costly WTO dispute. This might be the case, for instance, if developing-country prices are consistently low or consistently high (as shown in Figure 14.3). In these cases, even though zeroing is technically applied to the pricing data, it may not have any influence (or only a small impact) on the margin. It could also be the case that import prices for developing countries were subject to less volatility than those for developed countries. As shown in Figure 14.5, if this were the case, then, all else being equal, zeroing will have less of an impact on the anti-dumping duty for countries with less price variation. In these situations, developing countries will have a smaller stake in a WTO dispute and, hence, will be less compelled to initiate a dispute. Finally, and as discussed in the last section, it may also be the case that the counterfactual dumping margins applied in the absence of zeroing might still be so high that the applied U.S. anti-dumping duty is still prohibitive; that is, *de facto*, there is no positive trade-enhancing effect of eliminating zeroing from the dumping calculation.[35]

This discussion suggests that it is possible that both the benefits and costs of WTO disputes may differ for developing countries, and we might not see a lot of developing-country-initiated zeroing disputes as a result. Because the failure to initiate a dispute is not clear evidence that there has been no harm, whether or not the U.S. zeroing process is also likely to adversely impact developing-country exporters is therefore an important empirical question.

---

[35]Moreover, as Bown (2009) notes, in general, the cost relative to benefits for developing countries to challenge the United States at the WTO might be higher than for developed countries. Nevertheless, this does not appear to be much of an issue for potential developing-country complainants when the trade barrier at issue is the trading partner's use of anti-dumping, of which there are many disputes. Indeed, Bown (2009, Table 6.6) points out that, with access to the Advisory Centre on WTO Law—which provides DSU legal assistance to developing-country clients—there have been a number of disputes in which the imposed anti-dumping measure being challenged was restricting less than $3 million of trade per year.

U.S. Anti-dumping: Much Ado about Zeroing 385

For our purposes, we limit ourselves to the question of whether zeroing has a significant effect on any potential duty imposed on developing countries. To get a sense of the possible extent of zeroing's impact on developing countries, we gathered U.S. import data for some of the most prominent products subject to U.S. anti-dumping-duty scrutiny over the past decade.[36] Two factors influenced what products we included in our sample. First, we wanted to capture cases that were economically 'important' for developing countries and were in products most likely to be subject to anti-dumping examination. Second, we wanted to focus on products where we had strong independent evidence that there had been a WTO zeroing violation. With respect to the first criterion, we included cases where there was both significant anti-dumping activity and also substantial import supply by developing countries. With respect to the second criterion, we included products for which there already had been WTO disputes.

Once we selected the products to review, we then calculated the monthly price variation over the 12 months of the year prior to the filing of the case, a time generally used by the USDOC in its anti-dumping-duty calculations. Products were identified at the Harmonized Tariff Schedule (HTS) ten-digit level. To assist in comparability across the various products, we normalised the prices for each HTS product so that the mean price for each HTS product was 1 for the sample period. With that normalisation we then computed the pricing variation over the period.

We used the World Bank's country classification guide to divide countries according to their development status (World Bank 2010). We group countries designated by the World Bank as 'low income' and 'lower-middle income' as *low income* and those designated 'upper-middle income' and 'high income' as *high income*.[37]

We can use a regression analysis to test for the statistical significance of the difference in price variation. The ordinary least-squares results for a linear specification are given in Table 14.7. We also control for whether a supplying country was subject to the investigation in these regressions. For each product, suppliers fall into one of four categories: subject high income; subject low income; non-subject high income; and non-subject low income. All parameters are measured relative to the subject-high-income countries; *ie* the economies filing the zeroing disputes against the United States at the WTO. In specification A we include just the basic controls; in specification B we attempt to control for the possible correlation between price variation and price levels by also controlling for the general level of prices. In this specification 'low prices' (respectively, 'high prices') correspond to exporters with prices at least

---

[36] A list of cases included in the analysis is given in Appendix 14.1.

[37] Most countries in our sample that we call 'low income' fall under the World Bank's 'lower-middle income' category.

386   *Unfinished Business? The WTO's Doha Agenda*

Table 14.7: *Ordinary least-squares regression: month-to-month variation in prices, by supplying country.*

	A	B
Subject, low income	−0.164	0.026
	[0.122]	[0.802]
Non-subject, high income	0.379	0.331
	[0.000]***	[0.000]***
Non-subject, low income	0.197	0.341
	[0.070]*	[0.001]***
'Moderate' prices		0.297
		[0.000]***
'High' prices		1.174
		[0.000]***
Constant	1.070	0.608
	[0.000]***	[0.000]***
Observations	1,948	1,948
Adjusted R^2	0.021	0.105

p-values are shown in square brackets. '*', '**' and '***' denotes significance at the 10%, 5% and 1% levels, respectively.

30% below (respectively, above) the average for the product. The third category ('moderate prices') denotes export prices within 30% of the average price. In specification B moderate- and high-price suppliers are measured relative to low-price suppliers.

The table reveals several interesting insights. First, let us focus solely on the subject suppliers that were confronted with U.S. anti-dumping. The results indicate that there is no statistically significant difference in price variation for low-income and high-income countries. In specification A the estimate is negative and in specification B the estimate is positive. In both specifications the parameter estimates are statistically insignificant. This is important because it suggests that price volatility for developing countries is comparable with that of developed countries, at least with respect to the products in our sample. What does this mean for zeroing? Given that many products in our sample were the basis for WTO zeroing disputes, we know that zeroing has affected the margins for developed countries in the sample. All else being equal, the similarity in price volatility makes it likely that zeroing has affected the margins and duties that the United States imposes on *developing* countries. Thus, even though developing countries did not initiate the WTO disputes, they are quite likely to be affected by zeroing in the same way as the developed countries that did initiate the disputes. Put differently, the results suggest that the lack of WTO activity is not a sign that zeroing is less relevant for developing countries.

Second, both specifications show that price volatility for non-subject suppliers is higher than for subject suppliers. The parameter estimates are

U.S. Anti-dumping: Much Ado about Zeroing   387

statistically significant in both specifications. This suggests that the spectre of zeroing also looms over non-subject countries. While they were not investigated in these cases, their price variation is greater than for firms that were investigated, which makes it likely that zeroing would also have affected their dumping margins.[38]

Third, in specification B, we control for the suppliers' export price levels. This is an attempt to capture some of the insights from our earlier discussion about the impact of price levels on zeroing. While the estimates clearly show that higher volatility is associated with higher price levels, the main results with respect to subject and non-subject suppliers are consistent across both specifications.

Overall, the results from this analysis indicate that developed and developing countries have comparable price volatility. Thus, although developing countries have not yet initiated many WTO disputes about zeroing, the pricing evidence suggests that their margins have been similarly affected by zeroing.

8 CONCLUDING COMMENTS

Zeroing has emerged as a particularly irksome issue for all affected parties. For the United States, the numerous negative decisions fuel the belief in Congress that the WTO is biased and lessens U.S. support for the WTO. For U.S. trading partners, the United States' unresponsiveness to the zeroing decisions sends a signal that compliance is voluntary, and this effectively erodes the legitimacy of the WTO. At one level, the WTO's current inability to resolve the zeroing issue echoes of the enforcement problems that eroded support for the GATT dispute system in the 1980s.

The evidence suggests a real possibility that developing countries will also soon begin filing WTO complaints over the United States' use of zeroing. First, WTO AB has now a long series of decisions striking down virtually all use of zeroing.[39] This makes it far more likely that a developing country will prevail in a dispute against the United States. Second, the evidence indicates that the elimination of zeroing significantly reduces the anti-dumping margin. This means there is the potential for a large economic return to the filing dispute.

---

[38]One potential explanation for why the non-subject countries were not investigated is that they were not 'dumping'. However, without any information on home market prices, we cannot infer whether these suppliers are selling at less than fair value.

[39]The AB decisions suggest that zeroing in response to 'targeted dumping' is consistent with the WTO. What constitutes 'targeted dumping' is unclear. Recent actions by USDOC seem to indicate that the United States will try to use this exception in order to continue zeroing (eg zeroing was applied in the final determination of sales at less than fair value in a recent case involving polyethylene retail carrier bags from Taiwan (China), 75 Fed. Reg. 14569, March 26, 2010).

Third, the empirical evidence implies that developing countries' export prices are at least as volatile as developed countries. This makes it likely that zeroing has affected developing-country margins and, thus, the size of anti-dumping duties that their exporters face. Fourth, at this point in time, there is no clear sign that the United States is ready to stop zeroing. This means that the WTO violations will remain unless pursued by the affected developing countries.

All signs, therefore, point towards more WTO cases and more strain on the system. However, we do not believe that the zeroing problem will be the ruin of the WTO DSU. The WTO dispute mechanism is, to a large extent, working as designed. While complainant parties have every reason to be frustrated with the pace of compliance, the WTO dispute settlement process was designed to proceed at a somewhat ponderous pace. As of early 2010, several cases are in, or have just finished, the Article 21.5 compliance phase of the DSU. As specified by the WTO agreement, complainant parties will probably soon have the right to retaliate against U.S. trade to offset the damage due to zeroing.

Much to the frustration of the other WTO members, the retaliation value is likely to be quite small for most instances of violation. For most countries and most products, the value of trade subject to anti-dumping orders is quite small. Even if half the orders are removed, the dollar value of current WTO decisions against the United States is probably insufficient to spur action by Congress. While zeroing is consuming a large amount of AB time, the reality is that it might be too small a violation to induce a difficult policy change.

The resolution to the zeroing issue may well be that the retaliatory claims against the United States—likely including many by developing countries—will have to continue to amass until the impact is sufficient enough to spur the USDOC to change its policy. In effect, the large number of zeroing cases at the AB is one indicator that it is a small issue economically.

Nevertheless, for the WTO itself, the growing number of very similar, unimplemented decisions against a prominent and powerful member challenge the stature of the institution. If the WTO cannot resolve something as simple as zeroing, how can any of its members hope that the AB can help resolve truly complicated and politically charged issues like genetically modified organisms, intellectual property standards, agriculture reform, labour standards or border tax adjustments for climate change? From this perspective, it is in the WTO's best interests to see that the zeroing conflict is resolved sooner rather than later.

REFERENCES

Blonigen, B. A., and T. J. Prusa (2003). Antidumping. In *Handbook of International Trade* (ed. E. K. Choi and J. Harrigan). Oxford, U.K. Blackwell.
Bown, C. P. (2005). Trade remedies and World Trade Organization dispute settlement: why are so few challenged? *Journal of Legal Studies* **34**(2), 515–55.

U.S. Anti-dumping: Much Ado about Zeroing   389

Bown, C. P. (2009). Self-enforcing trade: developing countries and WTO dispute settlement. Brookings Institution Press, Washington, DC.

Bown, C. P. (2010a). Global Antidumping Database. World Bank URL: http://econ.worldbank.org/ttbd/gad/.

Bown, C. P. (2010b). Taking stock of anti-dumping, safeguards, and countervailing duties, 1990–2009. World Bank Policy Research Working Paper 5436 (September).

Bown, C. P. (2010c). China's WTO entry: anti-dumping, safeguards, and dispute settlement. In *China's Growing Role in World Trade* (ed. R. Feenstra and S. Wei). University of Chicago Press for NBER.

Bown, C. P., and M. A. Crowley (2010). Self-enforcing trade agreements: evidence from time-varying trade policy. World Bank Working Paper 5223 (March).

Bown, C. P., and J. Pauwelyn (2010). *The Law, Economics and Politics of Trade Retaliation in WTO Dispute Settlement.* Cambridge University Press.

Bown, C. P., and A. O. Sykes (2008). The zeroing issue: a critical analysis of Softwood V. *World Trade Review* 7(1), 121–42.

Crowley, M., and R. Howse (2010). *US – Stainless Steel (Mexico).* World Trade Review 9(1), 117–50.

Egger, P., and D. Nelson (forthcoming). How bad is anti-dumping? Evidence from panel data. *The Review of Economics and Statistics.*

Grossman, G. M., and A. O. Sykes (2006). European Communities. Anti-dumping duties on imports of cotton-type bed linen from India: recourse to Article 21.5 of the DSU by India. In *The WTO Case Law of 2003* (ed. P. Mavroidis and H. Horn). Cambridge University Press.

Hoekman, B. M., and M. M. Kostecki (2009). *The Political Economy of the World Trading System: The WTO and Beyond* (3rd edition). Oxford University Press.

Hudec, R. E. (1970). The GATT legal system: a diplomat's jurisprudence. *Journal of World Trade Law* 4, 615–65.

Hudec, R. E. (1993). *Enforcing International Trade Law: The Evolution of the Modern GATT Legal System.* Salem, NH: Butterworth Legal.

Hudec, R. E. (1999). The new WTO dispute settlement procedure: an overview of the first three years. *Minnesota Journal of Global Trade* 8(1), 1–53.

Ikenson, D. (2004). Zeroing in: anti-dumping's flawed methodology under fire. *Cato Free Trade Bulletin* 11 (April 27).

Jackson, J. H. (1997). *The World Trading System: Law and Policy of International Economic Relations* (2nd edition). Cambridge, MA: MIT Press.

Janow, M. E., and R. W. Staiger (2003). European Communities. Anti-dumping duties on imports of cotton-type bed linen from India. *The WTO Case Law of 2001* (ed. P. Mavroidis and H. Horn). Cambridge University Press.

Knetter, M. M., and T. J. Prusa (2003). Macroeconomic factors and anti-dumping filings: evidence from four countries. *Journal of International Economics* 61(1), 1–17.

Lindsey, B., and D. Ikenson (2002a). Anti-dumping 101: the devilish details of 'unfair trade' law. *Cato Trade Policy Analysis* 20 (November 26).

Lindsey, B., and D. Ikenson (2002b). Reforming the anti-dumping agreement: a road map for WTO negotiations. *Cato Trade Policy Analysis* 21 (December 11).

Mavroidis, P. C. (2007). *Trade in Goods.* Oxford University Press.

Nye, W. W. (2009). The implications of 'zeroing' on enforcement of US anti-dumping law. *Journal of Economic Policy Reform* 12(4), 263–71.

Prusa, T. J. (2001). On the spread and impact of anti-dumping. *Canadian Journal of Economics* 34(3), 591–611.

Prusa, T. J., and E. Vermulst (2009). A one-two punch on zeroing: *US—Zeroing (EC)* and *US—Zeroing (Japan).* World Trade Review 8(1), 187–241.

Vandenbussche, H., and M. Zanardi (2010). The chilling trade effects of anti-dumping proliferation. *European Economic Review* **54**(6), 760–77.

Wilson, B. (2007). Compliance by WTO members with adverse WTO dispute settlement rulings: the record to date. *Journal of International Economic Law* **10**(2), 397–404.

World Bank (2010). WTI country classification by region and income (July 2009–July 2010). URL: http://siteresources.worldbank.org/INTRANETTRADE/Resources/239054-1261083100072/Country_Classification_by_Region_Income_Dec17.pdf.

9 APPENDIX

Table A14.1: *U.S. anti-dumping cases used in price variation analysis.*

Product	Case ID (Bown 2010)
Ball bearings	USA-AD-391a, USA-AD-392a, USA-AD-393a, USA-AD-394a, USA-AD-399a
Brass sheet/strip	USA-AD-317
Certain frozen and canned warmwater shrimp and prawns	USA-AD-1063, USA-AD-1064, USA-AD-1065, USA-AD-1066, USA-AD-1067, USA-AD-1068
Chlorinated isocyanurates	USA-AD-1083
Citric acid and certain citrate salts	USA-AD-1151, USA-AD-1152
Cold-rolled carbon steel products	USA-AD-829, USA-AD-830, USA-AD-831, USA-AD-832, USA-AD-833, USA-AD-834, USA-AD-835, USA-AD-836, USA-AD-837, USA-AD-838, USA-AD-839, USA-AD-840
Cold-rolled steel products	USA-AD-964, USA-AD-965, USA-AD-966, USA-AD-967, USA-AD-968, USA-AD-969, USA-AD-970, USA-AD-971, USA-AD-972, USA-AD-973, USA-AD-974, USA-AD-975, USA-AD-976, USA-AD-977, USA-AD-978, USA-AD-979, USA-AD-980, USA-AD-981, USA-AD-982, USA-AD-983
Corrosion-resistant carbon steel sheet	USA-AD-617
Cut-to-length carbon steel plate	USA-AD-815, USA-AD-816, USA-AD-817, USA-AD-818, USA-AD-819, USA-AD-820, USA-AD-821, USA-AD-822
Cylindrical roller bearings	USA-AD-391c, USA-AD-392c, USA-AD-393c, USA-AD-394c, USA-AD-399c
Granular polytetrafluoroethylene resin	USA-AD-385
Hot rolled carbon steel flat products	USA-AD-806, USA-AD-807, USA-AD-808
Hot-rolled carbon steel products	USA-AD-898, USA-AD-899, USA-AD-900, USA-AD-901, USA-AD-902, USA-AD-903, USA-AD-904, USA-AD-905, USA-AD-906, USA-AD-907, USA-AD-908
Industrial nitrocellulose	USA-AD-443
Nitrocellulose	USA-AD-96

Table A14.1: *Continued.*

Product	Case ID (Bown 2010)
Oil country tubular goods	USA-AD-1000, USA-AD-1001, USA-AD-1002, USA-AD-1003, USA-AD-1004, USA-AD-1005
Oil country tubular goods	USA-AD-992, USA-AD-993, USA-AD-994, USA-AD-995, USA-AD-996, USA-AD-997, USA-AD-998, USA-AD-999
Pasta	USA-AD-734
Purified carboxymethylcellulose	USA-AD-1084, USA-AD-1085, USA-AD-1086, USA-AD-1087
Spherical plain ball bearings	USA-AD-394e
Stainless steel bar	USA-AD-913, USA-AD-914, USA-AD-915, USA-AD-918
Stainless steel plate in coils	USA-AD-788
Stainless steel sheet and strip	USA-AD-797, USA-AD-798, USA-AD-799, USA-AD-802
Steel concrete rebar	USA-AD-878
Tapered roller bearings	USA-AD-343

Chapter 10

The Economic and Strategic Motives for Antidumping Filings[*]

By

Thomas J. Prusa and Susan Skeath

Contents: I. Introduction. – II. Spread of Antidumping Use. – III. Motivations for Antidumping Use. – IV. Data Description. – V. Nonparametric Analysis of Filing Patterns. – VI. Concluding Comments.

I. Introduction

Despite the accomplishments of the Uruguay Round of the GATT,[1] there remains concern that nations are circumventing the agreements by means of various non-tariff barriers. One specific concern is that the "Antidumping Agreement,"[2] created to allow unilateral measures against dumped imports causing material injury to domestic firms, is being used more often as pure protection than as a trade remedy and that it is being used to excess by an increasingly large number of countries.

Antidumping (AD) use has increased dramatically over the last two decades (Miranda et al. 1998; Prusa 2001). For instance, more than three times the number of countries have been involved in AD disputes – both

Remark: The authors would like to thank Kyle Bagwell, Tom Pugel and Bernie Yeung for helpful conversations as well as seminar participants at the University of Otago, Australia National University, Hong Kong University of Science and Technology, and NYU for comments and suggestions on an earlier draft. We would also like to thank an anonymous referee for a number of very helpful comments. Work on this project was started while Skeath was a Commerce Divisional Visiting Fellow at the University of Otago. Financial support from the Class of '32 Social Sciences Fund at Wellesley College' is gratefully acknowledged. We would also like to thank WTO Rules Division and Jorge Miranda in particular for making the WTO AD Measures Database available.

[1] Since the end of the Uruguay Round in 1994, the General Agreement on Tariffs and Trade (GATT) has been administered by the World Trade Organization (WTO). This latest round of agreements reduced developed country tariffs on industrial products by 40 percent and increased the percentage of product lines with bound tariff levels from 78 to 99 percent in the developed countries and from 21 to 73 percent in the developing countries; further details on the agreements reached during the Uruguay Round can be found at www.wto.org/wto/about/agmnts2.htm.

[2] The Antidumping Agreement is formally known as the "Agreement on Implementation of Article VI of the General Agreement on Tariffs and Trade 1994."

[*]This article originally appeared in *Review of World Economics (Weltwirtschaftliches Archiv)*, **138**(3), pp. 389–413.

in terms of those filing cases and those being filed against – during the 1990s as compared with the 1980s. Perhaps the most interesting aspect of the growth and certainly the most crucial for the issues examined in this paper is the fact that the "traditional" users of antidumping (Australia, Canada, the E.U., New Zealand, and the U.S.) have been joined by an ever-growing group of "new" users, including South Africa, Brazil, and Mexico among others.

In theory, AD actions are intended for use only against importers suspected of unfair trade practices. In practice, there is considerable latitude in usage due to the manner in which most AD codes are written. As the number of users and cases filed annually grow, it is increasingly difficult to identify the motives of the users of AD and to argue that increased usage signals merely an increase in unfair trade.

This paper uses data on all antidumping cases filed and reported to the GATT/WTO between 1980 and 1998 to examine these motives of AD users. We identify two sets of motives to which AD usage can be tied, one "economic" and one "strategic," and analyze filing patterns over the two decades to determine which of the motives receive support in the data. In addition, we take a critical look at the differences in filing patterns and motives across the two groups of AD users.

The economic motives we consider are based on the traditional view of AD as a response to unfair trade and on the newer description of AD as "special protection" (Bagwell and Staiger 1990). Here we look for evidence of AD cases filed against "big" suppliers or against suppliers with large import surges. Our set of strategic motives follows work by Finger (1993) and Prusa (2001) in identifying "club" and "retaliation" motives for AD use. Countries who have used previously used AD protection (against any country) are considered club members. The retaliation motive is more narrowly defined and refers to a country filing AD actions specifically against those countries that had previously named it in the past.[3]

Our analysis consists of an overview first of the number of AD cases initiated during the 1980s and 1990s, including a breakdown by country of origin, and then of the number of cases consistent with the various economic and strategic motives we have identified. We also provide

---

[3] As we will discuss more in the following section, AD cases are usually filed by companies, not countries, and tests for motives for AD would do well to consider firm or industry-level data. The data available to us is limited to country-level observations, but we believe that retaliation may still play a role in AD filing decisions at that level. This would be true if previous cases created resentment toward another country, making decision-makers more likely to file against that country.

some formal non-parametric tests that allow us to quantify the statistical significance of the observed trends.

The results of the analysis are striking. The general picture we find is in full accordance with the concerns regarding increased usage of AD. That is, the growth in the number of cases has been tremendous and the use of AD is spreading rapidly across countries. Beyond those well-acknowledged figures, however, we find in the raw data evidence to support both economic and strategic motives for AD case filings for both traditional and new users, with the most support for use against big suppliers and AD club members. Formal tests for statistical significance of the various motives show greater variation across the two user types, with traditional users showing more significance in both the economic and strategic motive categories but with considerable support for the existence of strategic motives for AD use. While further research aimed at distinguishing the individual effects of each motive is warranted, we believe that our results here help to reject the notion that the rise in AD activity can be solely explained by an increase in unfair trade.

The remainder of the paper proceeds as follows. The next section provides a brief overview of the historical trends in AD use and its spread during the last two decades. Section III reviews the theoretical underpinnings for the various explanations for AD use. In Section IV, we describe our data, including a breakdown of cases consistent with each of the different motives, and in Section V we present the results of our non-parametric tests. Concluding comments are provided in Section VI.

II. Spread of Antidumping Use

The relatively recent upsurge in antidumping case filings and the attention it has received belies the longer history of antidumping policy and its use. Antidumping was, in fact, in use very early in the 20th century. The first modern antidumping law was passed in Canada in 1904 with Australia following close behind in 1906. By 1921, the U.S., France, Britain and most of the British Commonwealth had similar laws on their books (Finger 1993: 15–23).

Despite its long lineage, AD was not a widely used trade law until the late-1970s. For example, according to Finger and Fung (1994), fewer than a dozen cases were filed each year during the 1960s. The reason is two-fold. First, tariffs were higher so industries were less exposed to import competition and fewer industries perceived imports

392   Weltwirtschaftliches Archiv 2002, Vol. 138 (3)

as a threat. Second, during this period the rules for imposing AD duties were difficult to satisfy. The U.S., for instance, did not levy duties in a single AD case during the entire decade of the 1950s. The pattern during the 1960s was about the same with only about 10 percent of U.S. AD cases resulting in duties. The high standards were in effect among all contracting parties. In 1958, when the contracting parties canvassed themselves about the use of AD, the resulting tally showed only 37 AD decrees in force across all GATT member countries (Finger 1993).

However, AD's life in the backwater of trade policy ended with the 1979 Tokyo Round agreement. The agreement contained two key amendments that transformed this little used trade statute into the workhorse of international trade protection. First, the definition of "less than fair value" (LTFV) sales was broadened to capture not only price discrimination but also sales below cost.[4] Cost-based allegations now account for between one-half and two-thirds of U.S. AD cases (Clarida 1996) and for as much as ninety percent of EU cases against developing countries (Messerlin 1989). According to one noted legal expert cost-based AD petitions have become "the dominant feature of US antidumping law" (Horlick 1989: 136).[5]

Second, there was a change to the procedures involved in showing material injury to domestic firms. The Kennedy Round Code had required that the dumped imports be "demonstrably the principal cause of material injury" before duties could be imposed. In response to pressure from a number of the developed countries, the Tokyo Round Code revised this provision to render such a demonstration unnecessary.

There was an almost immediate increase in the number of AD disputes (Figure 1).[6] In 1980, 69 new AD cases were filed and more than 150 cases were filed the following year. In fact, in only one year since 1980 has the number of cases fallen below 100. In recent years, about 250 AD cases have been initiated each year. Over the entire 19-year period, over 3,500 AD cases were filed worldwide (an average

---

[4] The rule codified recent practice in several of the signatory states, including Australia, Canada, and the United States.

[5] Lindsey (1999) provides strong evidence for Horlick's view: over the four-year period 1995–1998, only 4 of 141 LTFV calculations were based on a true price-to-price comparison.

[6] All AD data reported in this paper are based on the mandatory "Reports of AD activity" required by the GATT/WTO.

of 185 cases per year), with the bulk of these being filed during the 1990s.

Figure 1: *Worldwide Use of Antidumping, 1980–1998*

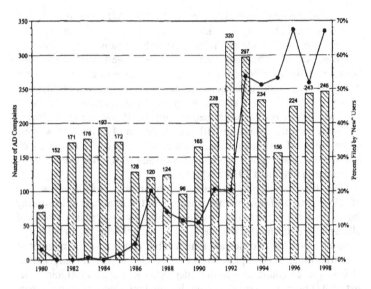

Despite the increase in its use, it did not initially appear that AD was a worldwide problem; it was an instrument wielded by only a handful of countries. Until the late 1980s, essentially all AD actions were initiated by the five "traditional" users: the U.S., Canada, the European Union, Australia, and New Zealand. Traditional users were responsible for a total of 99.4 percent of all of the AD cases filed between 1980 and 1985 as well as for more than 95 percent of the cases filed during the entire decade of the 1980s.

By the late 1980s, however, the AD club was no longer nearly as exclusive: the traditional users were being joined at an increasing rate by non-traditional or "new" users of AD. To highlight this point we also plot the percentage of AD cases filed by new users in Figure 1. New users first filed a significant fraction of all worldwide AD cases (20 percent) in 1987. Their prominent role in AD use has never abated; in every year since 1993 new users initiated over half of all AD cases

394   Weltwirtschaftliches Archiv 2002, Vol. 138 (3)

filed and were responsible for more than two-thirds of AD disputes in both 1996 and 1998. Overall, during the 1990s, new users accounted for more than 40 percent of the total number of cases filed, a considerable increase over the 4.5 percent of cases filed by new users during the 1980s.

It is informative to see which countries filed AD cases over the two decades covered by our study and to look at their changing roles in the international filing patterns. Table 1 provides details on the countries that filed AD cases between 1980 and 1989, as well as those that filed between 1990 and 1998, indicating the percentage of filings over each period that can be attributed to individual nations. For new users, the year of their first AD filing is also shown in the table. As mentioned above, over 95 percent of the cases filed during the 1980s can be attributed to the five traditional users. With the exception of Finland, new users began filing AD complaints only in the latter half of the decade, with South Korea starting in 1985 and Mexico and Brazil following shortly thereafter in 1987 and 1988, respectively.

The difference across the periods is remarkable. No single new user of AD accounted for more that 3 percent of the total cases filed during the 1980s and new users as a group accounted for fewer than 5 percent of all cases filed during that decade. During the 1990s the picture changed dramatically. That decade saw a noticeable increase in the number of countries filing AD complaints to a total of 33, compared to only 9 in the 1980s. The 24 countries that first filed AD cases after 1990 joined the list of AD users in a steady stream. Eleven countries (including Japan, Argentina, Turkey, and Israel) first used AD between 1991 and 1993; eight countries (including South Africa, Malaysia, and Trinidad and Tobago) first used AD between 1994 and 1996; a further five countries (including Egypt, Czechoslovakia, and Nicaragua) started using AD in 1997 and 1998.

Most of the new users filed a very small percentage of the total AD complaints lodged during the decade, with 21 countries filing fewer than 2 percent of the total cases each. Within those 21 countries were nations from all stages of economic development and from all parts of the world, ranging from Japan, Poland, Turkey and Egypt, to Nicaragua, Venezuela, Singapore and Thailand. The cumulative effect of this AD activity by new users was such that the five traditional users accounted for only slightly more than half (56 percent) of the cases filed in the 1990s. This fact emphasizes the manner in which the increased AD filings by non-traditional users eclipsed traditional user behavior over the last decade.

Table 1: *Antidumping Activity: 1980s vs. 1990s*

	Percent of total AD cases (worldwide) 1980–89	1990–98	Year country began using AD (GATT/WTO reports)	No. of AD actions against country prior to the adoption of own AD statute
U.S.	28.2	16.4	–	–
Australia	25.5	16.0	–	–
Canada	21.3	6.5	–	–
EU	19.8	14.6	–	–
New Zealand	0.7	2.4	–	–
Finland	1.4	0.1	–	–
Mexico	2.6	7.8	1987	10
South Korea	0.4	2.6	1985	39
Brazil	0.1	5.5	1988	55
Argentina		6.3	1991	16
South Africa		6.1	1994	20
India		4.2	1992	16
Turkey		1.6	1993	15
Colombia		1.2	1991	4
Poland		1.2	1991	43
Israel		1.1	1993	13
Indonesia		1.1	1996	31
Venezuela		1.0	1993	18
Peru		0.9	1994	1
Malaysia		0.7	1995	32
Philippines		0.7	1993	9
Chile		0.5	1993	5
Egypt		0.3	1997	7
Thailand		0.3	1993	35
Costa Rica		0.3	1996	1
Trin-Tobago		0.2	1996	3
Japan		0.2	1991	164
Czechoslovakia		0.1	1998	69
Nicaragua		0.1	1998	2
Panama		0.1	1998	0
Singapore		0.1	1994	34
Ecuador		0.1	1998	2
Guatemala		0.1	1996	0
TOTAL #	1401	2113		

One of the goals of this paper is to examine the motives behind the increasingly large number of AD complaints filed each year, especially by non-traditional users. Countries can always claim, of course, that

396   Weltwirtschaftliches Archiv 2002, Vol. 138 (3)

they are motivated only by a sincere desire to "level the playing field" and "fight unfair trade." The enthusiasm with which the new users have embraced AD, however, certainly makes us question whether other factors are involved.[7]

Along these lines we highlight one particularly interesting trend in the final column of Table 1. There we indicate, for each new user, the number of AD cases filed *against* that country between 1980 and the year of its first AD filing. For instance, when South Korea began to use AD law in 1985, it had been subject to almost 40 AD investigations since 1980. When Brazil started its AD program in 1988, it had been the subject of 55 investigations. With the exception only of Panama and Guatemala, every new user was subject to AD complaints before it initiated its own AD policy; many countries had been named in dozens of investigations. In fact, almost two-thirds of the 28 new users were subject to at least ten investigations before they began to initiate their own AD complaints.

This suggests that the new users were not unfamiliar with the implications of AD policy prior to their first filed complaints, that they had prior experience with the vagaries of the broad notions of injury and dumping, and that they would have been able to identify those countries that had successfully used AD against them in the past. If ulterior motives lie behind the increase in AD filings by new users in the 1990s, the data in the last column of Table 1 suggest why such countries might have felt that strategic retaliation was warranted. We will return to this issue in the following sections.

When considered as a whole package, the evidence on recent trends in AD use suggests that, to a large extent, the table has turned for the traditional users. The share of cases accounted for by the United States, the world's most prolific user of AD law, decreased by almost 50 percent during the 1990s as compared with the 1980s. In fact, the United States is now the second most *investigated* country, trailing only PR-China.[8] Countries such as Mexico, Argentina, South Africa, Brazil, and India have become some of the heaviest users of AD. And every year, new countries that have been investigated by others in the past make their own forays into the AD policy arena. Such striking trends certainly

---

[7] As we mentioned above, the flexibility of the cost standard is another explanation for why AD has proliferated. Given the discretion inherent in the cost standard, most normal business transactions today fall within its notion of "less than fair value."

[8] Leaving out cases brought by U.S. industries, the United States is the country most often alleged to have dumped.

raise the specter that countries are using AD law for reasons other than punishing unfair trade.

III. Motivations for Antidumping Use

Our look at the trends in antidumping use raises questions regarding the motivations that underlie the use of antidumping policy. Although AD actions, in their purest form, should occur only after an incident of dumping, AD statutes as generally written allow countries significant discretion in their application of the law, and implementation by authorities is often poor. Thus, the data reviewed in Section II lead us to ask whether the upsurge in AD case filings is truly indicative of an upsurge in unfair trading practices with the increased importance of global markets or whether there might be other incentives that drive each nation's decision to file, or begin to file, AD complaints. In reviewing the economic literature on antidumping, we find competing explanations for the use of AD, from the traditional analysis of AD as a response to unfair trade, through a more modern explanation of AD as special or safeguard protection, to the possibility that countries might use AD strategically.

The standard theoretical explanation for AD is based on the existence of dumped imports, goods that are sold either at a price below that set in the importer's domestic market or at a price below the importer's cost of production, implying that goods are not sold at "fair value."[9] In response to such unfair trade practices an importing country may then file AD actions. Such actions are consistent with the GATT/WTO code that provides for the imposition of AD duties in cases in which dumped imports are found to have caused material injury to domestic firms.

Given the level of detail at which the WTO records AD actions we are constrained to use country-level data in our current study. Therefore, we cannot directly identify instances of dumping or unfair trading practices. However, we can look for indirect evidence of such practices. For example, one could expect that exporting at unfairly low prices would result in large import volumes and/or large increases in imports. If AD cases were predominantly directed at trading partners with such trends, that fact could be construed as evidence of the use of AD to combat unfair trade.[10]

---

[9] For a formal theoretical treatment of dumping as international price discrimination, see Brander and Krugman (1983); for dumping as below-cost sales, see Ethier (1982).
[10] The injury requirement also makes it more likely that one would name countries with large imports or large changes in imports since such trends are usually taken as evidence of economic harm.

398					Weltwirtschaftliches Archiv 2002, Vol. 138 (3)

A newer explanation for the use of antidumping categorizes AD policy as an example of "special protection." Such protection has been argued to be an important component in achieving overall trade liberalization by allowing countries to suspend their tariff-reduction obligations for those industries that are more significantly injured by imports than trade negotiators anticipated. Bagwell and Staiger (1990) provide a formal game-theoretic model in which special protection arises as a short-term cooperative remedy for changes in the underlying trade flows.

The tariff reduction game between two countries has the structure of a prisoners' dilemma, with the "cooperative" tariff rate being at the low, trade-liberalizing level. In a repeated version of the game, countries could solve the dilemma by using contingent strategies that incorporate punishment schemes to handle instances of defection from the cooperative outcome, or by the creation of formal agreements that include third-party enforcement mechanisms, such as the GATT.[11] Bagwell and Staiger (1990) argue, however, that schemes such as these cannot account for the growing incidence of the use of special protection such as escape clause actions, VERs and AD. Their model incorporates observed random shocks to each country's output with positive shocks leading to higher volumes of trade. Crucially, they then show that the cooperative tariff rate is increasing in both import size and variance. In other words, Bagwell and Staiger formalize Corden's (1974) argument that special protection may be a tacitly agreed method to maintain cooperation in volatile trade periods.

When looking for Bagwell-Staiger incentives for the use of AD in our data, we check to see whether AD cases are being filed against a country's largest trading partners or against those trading partners with recent surges in import volume. Our indirect measures of such behavior include measures of trade volume and trade surges. Evidence of filings against countries would also be consistent with the use of AD to combat unfair trading practices.

A final possible explanation for the observed trends in AD filing behavior points to potential strategic motives on the part of the involved countries. Within the Bagwell-Staiger model, special protection-based changes in tariff levels are equilibrium responses to changes in the level or variance of imports. Yet, other work points out that there may be additional factors that should be considered. For example, Finger

---

[11] Papers by Dixit (1987), Jensen and Thursby (1984), and Riezman (1982) explore these issues.

(1993) argues that the countries that use AD form a type of "club," in that they tend to apply AD against one another rather than against non-club members. As evidence, Finger (1993: 7) notes that during the 1980s about two-thirds of AD cases were filed against countries who also used AD. Similarly, Prusa (2001) argues that many countries appear to file AD actions against countries that have previously investigated them, suggesting a type of retaliatory behavior.

Both of these arguments suggest that countries may be using AD in a strategic fashion to punish defectors from the cooperative (liberalized) equilibrium, or perhaps to deter such defection. Neither the club nor the retaliation motive for AD use is consistent with AD as protection against unfair trade, nor are they possible as equilibria within an unmodified Bagwell-Staiger model.[12] Another possibility is that worldwide AD use is not in equilibrium (in the Bagwell-Staiger notion of cooperative equilibrium). That is, the heavy use of AD law during the late 1970s and the early 1980s may have been too aggressive. Rather than maintaining the cooperative tariff level as implied by Bagwell and Staiger, such heavy use may have been perceived as a defection to the non-cooperative (one shot) prisoners' dilemma equilibrium. If this is the case, then recent AD actions might be "out of equilibrium" responses to the earlier defections.

We emphasize here that the club and retaliation incentives need not be directly motivated by the filing parties' own personal experience. AD cases are generally filed by companies within a given industry. Even if the companies filing the case have never been subject to AD actions themselves, they may nonetheless be aware of which countries have aggressively used AD in the past. Thus, the strategic incentives may impact filing patterns through perceived or actual biases at the decision-maker level or at the industry-level.

IV. Data Description

In order to investigate the motives for filing AD cases, we examine AD filing patterns in more detail. Before we begin our analysis we note that about one-fifth of the AD cases initiated between 1980 and 1998 were filed against non-market economies. This is noteworthy because the rules for determining the existence of dumping are quite different

---

[12] Extensions to the Bagwell-Staiger model might be made in order to generate club or retaliatory AD filings. Incorporating imperfect monitoring of demand shocks (following Green and Porter (1984)) or political economy incentives to misuse AD (following Grossman and Helpman (1994)) could give rise to observing AD cases filed as indirect (club) or direct (retaliatory) punishment for previous AD use.

when the affected country is a non-market economy (Boltuck and Litan 1991). As a result, the motivation for filing against a non-market economy is likely to be quite different than that for filing against a market economy. Therefore, from this point on we drop cases against non-market economies from our analysis. Furthermore, because of limited availability of bilateral import data, we must drop 1998 filings from our analysis.

We will be testing for two different explanations for AD filings, "economic" and "strategic." In terms of the economic incentives, we will be looking for evidence that AD cases are filed against the largest suppliers ("big supplier" hypothesis) and/or against suppliers who have the largest percentage change in imports ("import surge" hypothesis). Unfortunately, the Bagwell-Staiger model does not provide any guidance on how to define "big" so we test their theory as follows. For each year, we first rank each country's import suppliers from biggest to smallest. Suppliers who are above a specified cut-off percentile will be considered "big." This means that a country might be considered a big import supplier for the U.S. market in one year but not in other years. It also means that a country might be considered a big import supplier for one market but not another (e.g., big for the U.S. but not for Canada). We perform similar ranking (based on the percentage change in imports) to derive whether each supplier's "import surge" is big. For each hypothesis we present results for three cut-offs: 50th, 75th, and 90th percentile. As we will show, the results are not particularly sensitive to the choice of cut-off. We find this reassuring as it suggests that the main insights are not being driven by how we define "big."

As for the strategic explanations we will be looking for evidence for "club" and "retaliation" motives. Empirically, we will be looking for evidence that AD cases are filed against countries that also use AD (regardless of whom they have filed against). Such evidence would support the "club" hypothesis. For example, if in 1990 South Korea has previously used AD, then, under the club hypothesis, Mexico would be more likely to name South Korea than Uruguay (i.e., a country that had not used AD at all). For the "retaliation" hypothesis we will be looking for evidence that countries file AD cases against suppliers who have previously filed an AD case against them. For example, if Australia has filed cases against Mexico prior to 1990, then Mexico will be more likely to file cases against Australia in 1990 than against, say, Japan (i.e., a country that had not previously filed against Mexico).

For the strategic motives we also consider whether recent filing activity is more important for club and/or retaliation incentives. That is, it seems plausible that AD users might discount behavior in the relatively distant past and put more weight on recent actions. To be precise, consider Finland's use of AD. Finland filed about 20 AD cases during the 1980s but it has not filed any cases since 1991. It is possible that by the mid-1990s other countries no longer considered Finland a "club" member. Similarly, despite being the subject of a Finnish AD action in 1988, it seems reasonable to believe that Poland might no longer hold retaliation incentives against Finland after sufficient time had passed.

In order to address this concern, we consider two versions of the club and retaliation hypotheses, "long" memory and "limited" memory. Under the long memory scenario, club and retaliation incentives are never discounted. This means that Finland should be considered a club member throughout the 1990s and retaliation incentives should exist for all the countries Finland investigated during the 1980s. By contrast, under the limited memory scenario we hypothesize that the strategic incentives are only operative for the three years following the initiation of a particular case. In the case of Finland this means that it would be considered a club member only through 1994. Similarly, any retaliation incentives that Poland might have against Finland (due to the 1988 case) would be relevant only through 1991.

In Table 2 we report the percentage of cases consistent with the various hypotheses. This gives a feel for how the four hypotheses are reflected in the raw data. Several insights are quickly observed. First, we can see that regardless of the cut-off used, almost all AD cases are aimed at big suppliers. For instance, when we use the 75th percentile to define "big," over 90 percent of AD cases initiated by new users and over 97 percent initiated by traditional users are against big suppliers. When the 90th percentile is used, the share of cases for both new and traditional users falls to a still non-trivial 80 percent.

Second, there is far less support for the import surge hypothesis. Even when we use the 50th percentile cut-off – the most liberal interpretation of "big surge" – only about half of the AD cases over the sample are against suppliers whose imports have surged. When we use the more stringent cut-offs (75th and 90th percentiles) the fraction of cases against suppliers whose imports have surged falls dramatically. Fewer than 6 percent of all cases can qualify as having been filed against importers with surges when using the 75th percentile cut-off; fewer than 1 percent of all cases qualify at the 90th percentile.

Third, the club hypothesis receives strong support. More than 80 percent of AD cases filed by new users are against club members; almost

Table 2: *AD Actions Consistent with Alternative Hypotheses*
(Percentages)

Hypothesis	New users	Traditional users	Total
Economic incentives			
Big supplier			
Imports > 50th percentile	96.25	99.89	99.02
Imports > 75th percentile	90.12	97.57	95.78
Imports > 90th percentile	78.88	79.70	79.50
Import surge			
%Δ imports > 50th percentile	46.51	58.37	55.51
%Δ imports > 75th percentile	3.75	6.64	5.95
%Δ imports > 90th percentile	0.17	0.27	0.25
Strategic incentives			
Club effect			
Long memory	81.26	58.21	63.76
Limited memory	81.26	58.15	63.71
Retaliation			
Long memory	57.58	45.57	48.46
Limited memory	45.32	35.64	37.97

60 percent of AD cases by traditional users are against club members. The fact that there is almost no difference between the long and limited memory results reflects the fact that AD is an addictive habit; once countries begin using AD protection, they rarely cease using the statute for very long. In other words, the case of Finland is the exception to the rule.

Fourth, retaliation patterns are also reflected in the data. Overall, countries file about half of their cases against countries that previously had used AD against them, slightly more for new users, slightly less for traditional users. Even when we restrict retaliation incentives to only the previous three years (i.e., limited memory), we find that almost 40 percent of cases are consistent with the retaliation motive.

A few comments are in order. First, these statistics suggest that of the economic hypotheses, being "big" matters more than surges do. However, we need to be cautious before embracing this conclusion. First of all, it is more difficult for large suppliers to experience a large percentage change in imports (a surge) simply because they are starting with such a large base. The countries with "surges" tend to be those that are initially small suppliers, making it easier to experience a large "surge." This is a reminder that, while it often appears that AD actions are motivated by import surges, one must be careful to examine the entire universe of suppliers before drawing such a conclusion.

Second, AD cases are often aimed at quite narrow product categories, a particular type of steel, for example, rather than all steel products. Unfortunately the WTO does not require countries to report the exact categories, so we cannot identify trade at these disaggregated levels. As long as our trade measure is correlated with trade at the product category level, our analysis is accurate. If, however, trade at the disaggregated level consistently varies from our measure, we might be understating the importance of the surge hypothesis. Taken together, these two caveats lead us to be very cautious in interpreting results for the surge hypothesis.

Overall, we find the support for retaliation incentives quite striking. New and traditional users alike tend to file AD cases against those who have investigated them in the past. Because so many users apparently file partly due to these incentives, we can identify countries that are being named (or investigated) in AD disputes for apparent retaliatory motives. In Figure 2 we plot the shares of cases consistent with retaliation for each country (over the entire 1980–1998 period). On the x-axis we plot the share of *initiated* cases that are consistent with retaliation (i.e., the tendency for a country's use of AD to reflect retaliation incentives). On

Figure 2: *AD Filings Consistent with Retaliation, All Years*

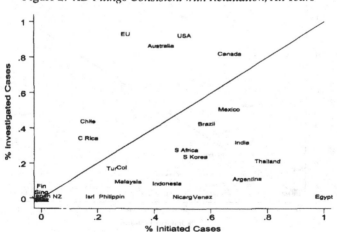

the y-axis we plot the share of cases in which the country is *investigated* that are consistent with retaliation (i.e., the tendency for a country to be named in a way consistent with retaliation incentives). The 45-degree line indicates countries that file and are subject to the same share of cases consistent with retaliation. Countries lying above (below) the line are subject to more (less) retaliation than their own filings suggest.

The figure is quite revealing. Even though about half of the AD actions initiated by traditional users (EU, Australia, U.S., Canada) are consistent with a retaliation incentive, a larger, near-90-percent fraction, of the cases in which they are investigated is initiated by countries that have a retaliation incentive. Only two new users, Chile and Costa Rica, demonstrate a similar pattern. The data for all the other new users reflect that their filings tend to be more retaliatory than the cases in which they are investigated. This pattern suggests that the traditional users are paying a high price for their refusal to strengthen AD rules. They are paying heavily for their past transgressions because they are now being regularly investigated in a retaliatory fashion.

In Figure 3 we also plot the shares of cases consistent with retaliation (initiated and investigated), but here we restrict ourselves to looking only at the 1994–1998 period. This allows us to control for the fact that the four major traditional AD users had a near monopoly on AD

Figure 3: *AD Filings Consistent with Retaliation, 1994–1998*

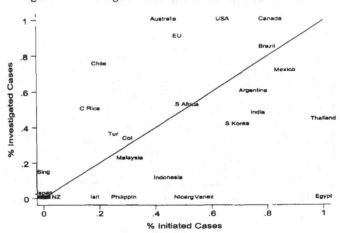

filings during the 1980s. In a sense, the analysis for the more recent years reflects a more level playing field because both new and traditional users were actively filing AD actions over the period. And as we can see, the story changes somewhat when we restrict ourselves to the more recent period. While the traditional users continue to be subject to a higher fraction of retaliatory cases, the new users have shifted up and now have a larger share of cases in which they are investigated consistent with retaliation. The lesson appears to be that as countries (both new and traditional users) embrace AD protection, they are subjecting themselves to long-run costs in the form of ongoing retaliation.

V. Nonparametric Analysis of Filing Patterns

The evidence from the raw data, presented in the previous section, provides support for both the economic and strategic incentives for AD filings. We now offer formal tests that allow us to quantify the statistical significance of the trends. In computing these tests we focus on the filings by country, and ask whether the cases filed by each country in each year are statistically consistent with each of our hypotheses.

In Table 3 we look at South Africa's filings in 1994 in order to illustrate the type of statistical tests that we use to determine whether each hypothesis is supported in the data. In 1994 South Africa filed 15 AD cases. Of these 15 filings, 11 (73 percent) were consistent with the retaliation hypothesis (i.e., 11 cases were against countries who had named South Africa in 1993 or earlier); 13 cases (87 percent) were consistent with the club hypothesis; 14 (93 percent) were against big suppliers (using the 50th percentile cut-off); only one case (6.7 percent) was against a big import surge supplier (again, using the 50th percentile cut-off).

The question is whether these filing patterns provide any support for the various hypotheses. Consider first the economic hypotheses. If economic motives were *not* present, then we would expect cases to be filed independently of the volume of imports from any particular country. Therefore, we would expect that the share of cases against big suppliers would be the same as the cut-off percentile used to define "big" (i.e., 50th, 75th, or 90th percentile).

In the case of South Africa in 1994, 93 percent of its cases were filed against big suppliers. Under the null hypothesis that economic motives were *not* present, we would expect only 50 percent of its cases to be filed against big suppliers when using the 50th percentile cut-off. Using the binomial test we can indeed conclude that such a large fraction of

406   Weltwirtschaftliches Archiv 2002, Vol. 138 (3)

Table 3: *South Africa AD Filings in 1994*

	Number	Percent
Total AD actions	15	
AD actions consistent with retaliation	11	73.33
AD actions consistent with club effect	13	86.67
AD actions against big suppliers (50th %tile)	14	93.33
AD actions against big %Δ imports (50th %tile)	1	6.67
Suppliers who had previously used AD		10.14
Suppliers who had previously named S. Africa		4.73
Binomial probability		
Retaliation (15, 11, 4.73%)	0.00000	
Club (15, 13, 10.14%)	0.00000	
Big suppliers (15, 14, 50%)	0.00049	
Big %Δ imports (15, 1, 50%)	0.99960	

cases against big suppliers is highly (99 percent) unlikely; the binomial probability Pr(15, 14, 50 percent) is essentially zero. Therefore, we can reject the null hypothesis and conclude that South Africa's 1994 filings provide statistical support for the big-supplier hypothesis.

Using the same logic as above, we can test the big-import-surge hypothesis after constructing a null hypothesis that there is *no* motive to use AD against big import surges. In this case, we would again expect the share of cases against big surge suppliers to be the same as the cut-off percentile used to define "big." In the case of South Africa in 1994 when using the 50th percentile cut-off, only one case was against a big surge supplier. Under the null hypothesis, however, we would expect 50 percent of the 1994 cases to be filed against big suppliers. Using the binomial test we find that we should expect (with 99 percent likelihood) that at least one case would be filed against a big surge supplier. Therefore, South Africa's 1994 filings do *not* provide any statistical support for the big-surge hypothesis.

Consider next the strategic hypotheses, beginning with the club hypothesis. Table 3 shows that only 10 percent of South Africa's suppliers had ever used AD (against any country) in the past, so only 10 percent of its suppliers qualify as club members. Under the null hypothesis that the club effect is *not* present, we would expect cases to be filed independently of whether a country is a club member. Given the information about South Africa's suppliers, we would expect that under the null hypothesis only 10 percent of South Africa cases should be against club members. We observe, however, that 13 of South Africa's 15 AD cases (87 percent) were against club members. To statistically confirm that this pattern is significant, we again use the binomial test. We conclude that such a large fraction of cases against club members is highly unlikely (essentially zero). Thus, South Africa's 1994 filings provide statistical support for the club hypothesis.

Finally, similar calculations can be performed to test for evidence of the retaliation motive. By 1994 only 4.7 percent of South Africa's suppliers had ever filed an AD case against it; yet, 73 percent of South Africa's cases were against countries that had named it in the past. Once again, formulating the null hypothesis that there is *no* retaliation motive we can use the binomial test to conclude that such a large fraction of cases consistent with retaliation is extremely unlikely. Thus, South Africa's 1994 filings also show support for the retaliation hypothesis.

We perform such binomial tests on the filing patterns for each country in each year.[13] For example, South Africa's AD activity gives us four years of filings (1994, 1995, 1996, and 1997) on which we can perform binomial tests. Over all countries and all years of their AD use, we have a total of 212 country-year pairs and we present results for 212 separate binomial tests of each of our four hypotheses. We use a significance level of 5 percent to determine whether a country-year observation supports a hypothesis. Depending on how many country-year observations have significant tests, we can determine the extent to which each hypothesis is supported by the data.

In Table 4 we report the binomial test results for the economic hypotheses. These results indicate that AD filings are far better explained by the big-supplier hypothesis than by the import-surge hypothesis. For instance, when we use the 50th percentile cut-off, about half of the annual observations (104 of 212) support the big-supplier hypothesis but only 13 percent of the annual observations (29 of 212) support the import-surge hypothesis. The same qualitative pattern exists regardless of what cut-off we use. Simply stated, the AD filings provide far more support for the big-supplier hypothesis than for the import-surge hypothesis.

There are also important differences between traditional and new user filing patterns. In particular, continuing to use the 50th percentile cut-off, we note that over 90 percent of the annual observations on traditional users' AD activity support the big-supplier hypothesis. In particular, 70 of the 77 country-year observations have binomial prob-

---

[13] Once a country begins using AD protection, we perform the tests in every year thereafter.

Table 4: *Binomial Tests for Economic Incentives for Using AD Law*

		Big supplier: imports					
		> 50th percentile		> 75th percentile		> 90th percentile	
		Significant at 5%		Significant at 5%		Significant at 5%	
Type of AD user	Total obs.	#	%	#	%	#	%
New user	135	34	25.19	30	22.22	22	16.30
Traditional AD user	77	70	90.91	70	90.91	52	67.53
Total	212	104	49.06	100	47.17	74	34.91

		Import surge: %Δ imports					
		> 50th percentile		> 75th percentile		> 90th percentile	
		Significant at 5%		Significant at 5%		Significant at 5%	
Type of AD user	Total obs.	#	%	#	%	#	%
New user	135	6	4.44	0	0.00	0	0.00
Traditional AD user	77	23	29.87	1	1.30	0	0.00
Total	212	29	13.68	1	0.47	0	0.00

ability less than 0.05. Interestingly, less than 30 percent (23 of 77) of the annual observations on traditional users' AD activity support the big-surge hypothesis.

By contrast, we find that new user AD activity provides far less statistical support for either economic hypothesis. For example, only about one-quarter of the observations on new users' AD activity support the big-supplier hypothesis. The big-surge hypothesis receives even less support. Less than five percent of the observations on new users AD activity support the big-surge hypothesis.

The qualitative results are the same for the 75th and 90th percentile cut-offs. Namely, traditional user AD activity strongly supports the big-supplier hypothesis and provides (at best) weak support for the import-surge hypothesis. On the other hand, new user AD activity provides no support at all for the import-surge hypothesis, and only weak support for the big-supplier hypothesis.

We report the binomial results for the strategic motives in Table 5. The first finding of note is that, overall, both the club and retaliation hypotheses receive strong support. Under either the long- or limited-memory scenarios, 56 percent (118 of 212) of the country-year observations are statistically significant with the club hypothesis at the 5 percent level. Between 40 and 50 percent of the observations support the retaliation hypothesis.

Table 5: *Binomial Tests for Strategic Motives for Using AD Law*

		Club effect hypothesis			
		Long memory		Limited memory	
Type of AD user	Total obs.	Significant at 5%		Significant at 5%	
		#	%	#	%
New user	135	51	37.78	51	37.78
Traditional AD user	77	67	87.01	67	87.01
Total	212	118	55.66	118	55.66
		Retaliation hypothesis			
		Long memory		Limited memory	
Type of AD user	Total obs.	Significant at 5%		Significant at 5%	
		#	%	#	%
New user	135	43	31.85	37	27.41
Traditional AD user	77	59	76.62	54	70.13
Total	212	102	48.11	91	42.92

Interestingly, there is a striking difference between the new and traditional users. A full 87 percent of the annual observations on traditional users' filings are consistent with the club effect, but only 38 percent of the annual observations on new users' filings are consistent with the club effect. Similarly, over 70 percent of traditional users' filings, but only about 30 percent of new users' filings, support the retaliation hypothesis.

Thus, even though in the raw data it appeared that new users' AD filings were more often consistent with the retaliation and club hypotheses, once we control for the expanding set of AD users we are able to conclude that statistically the club and retaliation motives are far more relevant for traditional users than for new users. Nevertheless, new user filing behavior is better explained by strategic motives than by economic motives.

There are several possible interpretations of these results. First, the finding that economic considerations are not the only explanation for AD filings is consistent with earlier studies. Other research has found that EU and U.S. AD decisions are influenced by political pressure, national security interests, and historical economic relationships (Hansen and Prusa 1996, 1997; Tharakan and Waelbroeck 1994a, 1994b).

Second, the finding that economic motivations do a poor job explaining the filing behavior of new users may partially reflect the weak rules and informal institutions governing AD proceedings in those countries. New users are particularly likely to determine injury using very simple methods, especially when compared with methods employed by traditional users (Santos 1998). Thus, it may be quite difficult for the new users to accurately evaluate economic injury. This would make it more likely that strategic considerations would play an unusually important role in new users' AD activity.

Third, measurement issues are a concern across all of the hypotheses. As mentioned above, GATT/WTO reporting limits the level of disaggregation at which we are able to measure imports. While we would like to utilize product-level import data, countries are not required to report which products are subject to AD case filings. As a result, our measures are more aggregated than we would like. Similarly, our variables capturing the strategic motives for AD use are also more broadly defined than the ideal. For instance, retaliation and club effects may play a particularly important role at the industry level, and less so at the country level. Once again, until the WTO collects AD filing data at the industry level this issue cannot be addressed.

Fourth, the results suggest that both economic and strategic considerations play a role in motivating national-level AD filings. The nonparametric tests performed in this paper do not let us separate these effects, however. While such a task is beyond the scope of the current paper, we use parametric techniques in related work (Prusa and Skeath 2002) and find results that are consistent with those discussed here. Namely, AD filing patterns cannot be explained completely by only economic considerations. Rather, a combination of both economic and strategic considerations is important in explaining trends in AD filings.

VI. Concluding Comments

Our review of the worldwide AD filing patterns between 1980 and 1998 indicates that strategic considerations are an important explanation for AD filings. After reviewing the filing patterns we find that three-quarters of all AD filings are consistent with the club effect and half are consistent with retaliation incentives. When we perform statistical tests on annual filings at the country level, we find that approximately 50 percent of observations provide statistically significant support for the strategic hypotheses. For traditional users we find evidence that both economic and strategic motives are important; however, for new users we find that strategic motives are more important than the economic motives.

Our results are consistent with evidence beginning to be reported elsewhere in the literature. Blonigen and Bown (2001) investigate the effects of the threat of foreign retaliation on U.S. antidumping case filing behavior. Their results indicate that retaliation exposure and, in particular, the threat of foreign reciprocal AD duties can reduce the likelihood of U.S. AD cases being filed against certain countries. Further work needs to be done in this area as our findings indicate that the growth of AD has not slowed down and that AD club members tend to file against one another. Our results suggest that the dampening effect implied by Blonigen and Bown's work may be statistically significant but not quantitatively important.

Taken together, the sources of evidence on the importance of retaliatory motives underscore the importance of including AD rules on the agenda in any future WTO negotiations. The fact that so many AD cases worldwide are apparently motivated by strategic considerations indicates that the rules currently in use are too broad and too easily subjugated to other forces. Improved AD rules and tighter guidelines for the implementation of AD legislation would greatly help in limiting the use of AD protection for reasons other than that intended by the WTO statute.

412   Weltwirtschaftliches Archiv 2002, Vol. 138 (3)

References

Bagwell, K., and R. Staiger (1990). A Theory of Managed Trade. *American Economic Review* 80 (4): 779–795.

Blonigen, B. A., and C. P. Bown (2001). Antidumping and Retaliation Threats. Mimeo. Brandeis University, October.

Boltuck, R., and R. E. Litan (eds.) (1991). *Down in the Dumps: Administration of the Unfair Trade Laws.* Washington, D.C.: Brookings Institute.

Brander, J. A., and P. Krugman (1983). A 'Reciprocal Dumping' Model of International Trade. *Journal of International Economics* 15 (3–4): 313–321.

Clarida, R. H. (1996). Dumping: In Theory, in Policy, and in Practice. In J. Bhagwati and R. Hudec (eds.), *Fair Trade and Harmonization: Prerequisites for Free Trade?* Cambridge: MIT Press.

Corden, W. M. (1974). *Trade Policy and Economic Welfare.* Oxford: Oxford University Press.

Dixit, A. K. (1987). Strategic Aspects of Trade Policy. In T. F. Bewley (ed.), *Advances in Economic Theory: Fifth World Congress.* New York: Cambridge University Press.

Ethier, W. J. (1982). Dumping. *Journal of Political Economy* 90 (3): 487–506.

Finger, J. M. (ed.) (1993). *Antidumping.* Ann Arbor, MI: University of Michigan Press.

Finger, J. M., and K. C. Fung (1994). Will GATT Enforcement Control Antidumping? *Journal of Economic Integration* 9 (2): 198–213.

Green, E. J., and R. H. Porter (1984). Noncooperative Collusion Under Imperfect Price Information. *Econometrica* 52 (1): 87–100.

Grossman, G., and E. Helpman (1994). Protection for Sale. *American Economic Review* 84 (4): 833–850.

Hansen, W. L., and T. J. Prusa (1996). Cumulation and ITC Decision Making: The Sum of the Parts is Greater than the Whole. *Economic Inquiry* 34 (4): 746–769.

Hansen, W. L., and T. J. Prusa (1997). The Economics and Politics of Trade Policy: An Empirical Analysis of ITC Decision Making. *Review of International Economics* 5 (2): 230–245.

Horlick, G. N. (1989). The United States Antidumping System. In J. H. Jackson and E. A. Vermulst (eds.), *Antidumping Law and Practice: A Comparative Study.* Ann Arbor, MI: University of Michigan Press.

Jensen, R., and M. Thursby (1984). Free Trade: Two Noncooperative Approaches. Ohio State University Working Paper.

Lindsey, B. (1999). The U.S. Antidumping Law Rhetoric versus Reality. Cato Institute Trade Policy Analysis Number 7. Washington, D.C.

Messerlin, P. (1989). The EC Antidumping Regulations: A First Economic Appraisal, 1980–85. *Weltwirtschaftliches Archiv* 125 (3): 563–587.

Miranda, J., R. A. Torres, and M. Ruiz (1998). The International Use of Antidumping: 1987–1997. *Journal of World Trade* 32 (5): 5–71.

Prusa, T. J. (2001). On the Spread and Impact of Antidumping. *Canadian Journal of Economics* 34 (3): 591–611.

Prusa, T. J., and S. Skeath (2002). Modern Commercial Policy: Managed Trade or Retaliation? Forthcoming in *Handbook of International Trade and Law*. Oxford: Basil Blackwell.

Riezman, R. (1982). Tariff Retaliation from a Strategic Viewpoint. *Southern Economic Journal* 48 (3): 583–593.

Santos, L. E. (ed.) (1998). *The Compendium of Foreign Trade Remedy Laws*. Washington, D.C.: The American Bar Association.

Tharakan, P. K. M., and J. Waelbroeck (1994a). Determinants of Anti-dumping and Countervailing Duty Decisions in the European Communities. In M. Dewatripont and V. Ginsburgh (eds.), *European Economic Integration: A Challenge in a Changing World*. Amsterdam: North-Holland.

Tharakan, P. K. M., and J. Waelbroeck (1994b). Antidumping and Countervailing Duty Decisions in the E.C. and in the US: An Experiment in Comparative Political Economy. *European Economic Review* 38 (1): 171–193.

* * *

Abstract: The Economic and Strategic Motives for Antidumping Filings. – This paper looks at worldwide antidumping activity during the last two decades. We examine the motives for AD filings by countries in an attempt to identify whether economic or strategic concerns are driving the recent upsurge in AD use. We begin by providing a comprehensive overview of the data on cases initiated in the 1980–1998 period. We then use nonparametric methods to identify motivations for the use of antidumping and find considerable support for strategic motivations. This suggests that the rise in AD activity cannot be solely explained by an increase in unfair trading practices. JEL no. F10, F13

Chapter 11

WTO Exceptions as Insurance[†]

Ronald D. Fischer and Thomas J. Prusa*

Abstract

The paper formalizes the notion that GATT exceptions such as antidumping and escape clause actions can act as insurance for import competing sectors affected by adverse price shocks. The authors use a general-equilibrium model with several import competing sectors and assume incomplete markets so that agents cannot contract insurance. It is shown that sector-specific contingent protection measures are superior to uniform contingent tariffs as an insurance mechanism. A tax-cum-subsidy policy (i.e., taxing all sectors in order to subsidize the shocked sector) also improves welfare and is superior to contingent protection.

1. Introduction

Thanks primarily to the tariff reductions negotiated under the auspices of the GATT and WTO, international trade is likely as unfettered by restrictions as at any other time in history. While the gains from free trade are widely recognized, it is also well known that openness makes economies more vulnerable to injury from adverse trade shocks. GATT founders were cognizant that injured import competing groups might use such shocks as an excuse to renege on GATT agreements; for that reason exceptions to tariff obligations were provided within the GATT. These exceptions allow governments to protect the injured sector while not abandoning the tariff liberalization achieved in other sectors.[1]

GATT exceptions allow governments to take actions in response to imports which are deemed to have harmed the domestic competing industry. If injury is caused by "fair" trade (e.g., an increase in imports due to tariff reductions), a government can invoke the escape clause to restrain imports; if injury is caused by "unfair" trade (e.g., dumping or government subsidization of imports), the policy response is antidumping or countervailing duties. Dam (1970) points out that these exceptions have been included in *every* GATT agreement. Moreover, he argues that the inclusion of these exceptions was crucial for the success of the early GATT rounds. His view is that exceptions greatly increased the number of sectors where tariffs were liberalized by diffusing domestic political opposition toward trade liberalization. In a sense, exceptions offered the promise of insurance for sectors injured by the liberalization.

Clearly then, for many years policymakers have taken for granted that trade policy can act as insurance. However, the notion that trade policy can act as insurance was not formalized until Eaton and Grossman (1985; EG hereafter).[2] In their model there is a single import competing sector and single export sector. The import competing sector is subject to price shocks. The goods are produced with two factors; one factor (labor) can be allocated after the price shock is realized while the other factor (capital)

---

* Fischer: Centro de Economía, Aplicada Departamento de Ingeniería Industrial, República 701, Santiago, Chile. Tel: 56-2-6784072; Fax: 56-2-6897895; E-mail: rfischer@dii.uchile.cl. Prusa: Department of Economics, Rutgers University, New Brunswick, NJ 08901-1248, USA. Tel: 732-932-7670; Fax: 732-932-7416; E-mail: prusa@econ.rutgers.edu. Fischer wishes to thank the Direccion de Investigacion de la Facultad de Ciencias Fisicas y Matematicas for the financial support of a research grant and FONDECYT #1010430. Fischer also thanks Rutgers University for its hospitality. We wish to thank an anonymous referee, Avinash Dixit, Jonathan Eaton, Gene Grossman, and especially Rich McLean for their comments and suggestions.

[†]This article originally appeared in *Review of International Economics*, **11**(5), pp. 745–757.

259

can only be allocated before the terms of trade are realized. EG demonstrate that a tariff can raise *ex ante* welfare if insurance markets are incomplete.

EG's insight has spurred a number of other papers, most notably those by Staiger and Tabellini (1987) and Dixit (1987, 1989a,b). These related papers also assume that markets are incomplete and that factors are not completely mobile *ex post*. Staiger and Tabellini use the basic EG framework to examine the time consistency of tariff protection. While EG and Staiger and Tabellini were willing to leave implicit the reasons for the incompleteness of insurance markets, Dixit argues that the source of the incompleteness can be important. For instance, he shows that when the market failure is explicitly tied to adverse selection or moral hazard, the laissez-faire equilibrium may be Pareto-optimal. Following EG's approach, we will leave the precise source of the market failure implicit, but note that unobservable actions and outcomes are not the only source of market incompleteness. Rather, the transaction costs of insuring agents against trade shocks are surely quite large and will likely preclude complete insurance. In addition, trade shocks may well give rise to bankruptcy concerns, implying that markets will likely be at least partially incomplete. Finally, there might be other distortions in the economy that preclude complete insurance.[3]

We believe, however, the EG model is not well suited to study GATT exceptions for at least two reasons. First, GATT MNF tariffs are typically negotiated years in advance and thus are very difficult to be levied in a contingent fashion. GATT exceptions, on the other hand, are precisely designed to be levied *after* the trade shock. Second, and the more troubling concern, exceptions like antidumping and the escape clause are sector-specific protection. With a single import-competing sector, EG's model cannot adequately characterize the conditions when sector-specific protection is desirable. In their model the tariff is levied on all import competing sectors; therefore their paper is better interpreted as formalizing the effect of a uniform *noncontingent* tariff.

In this paper we develop a model that allows us to better answer the question of whether GATT exceptions can act as insurance. With the EG model serving as the foundation for our analysis, we allow for multiple import competing sectors which are subject to sector-specific price shocks. This allows us to understand and contrast the distortions created across sectors. As in the EG paper, we assume capital is immobile *ex post* and markets are incomplete. We show that GATT exceptions raise welfare by providing insurance.

In addition, we compare the efficacy of sector-specific contingent measures with the traditional "across the board" *contingent* tariff protection *à la* EG. We show that sector-specific policies dominate uniform tariffs. In contrast with EG, we find that the optimal uniform policy may involve export taxes. The difference lies in the fact that in our somewhat more general model only one sector benefits from the imposition of a uniform tariff while the other sector is worse off. Since a sector-specific contingent tariff is targeted at the distressed sector, it reduces the negative effects on other sectors.

Thus, our model provides a theoretical foundation for the notion that GATT exceptions can provide insurance. Given the unprecedented use of GATT exceptions—in particular antidumping actions—during the past twenty years, many question whether insurance is the motivation for many of the actions (Bhagwati, 1988; Finger, 1993; Krueger, 1995).[4] Briefly stated, the concern is that antidumping procedures allow investigations to be conducted when there is little evidence of injury or unfair actions. Given the apparent capture of antidumping by protectionist interests, we also examine whether an alternative policy could also serve as insurance. In particular, we consider a policy wherein the adversely affected sector is offered a subsidy which is financed by (lump-sum) taxes on all sectors; we find that this "tax and subsidize" policy also increases welfare and is in fact welfare-superior to contingent protection. This suggests that even though it is possible to design alternative policies that have the beneficial risk-sharing properties of current GATT exceptions, these alternative policies are not used for political economy reasons (i.e., it is politically difficult to raise taxes).

2. The Model

We consider a three-sector model of a small open economy facing stochastic international prices.[5] The goods are X, Y^1, Y^2; all are consumed domestically. We also assume that in all states of the world all three goods are produced domestically. Following EG we assume that at the time capital must be allocated between productive sectors the terms of trade are unknown. In contrast, labor can move between sectors after the uncertainty is resolved and after the trade policy is implemented.

We assume that good X, the export good, is produced under constant returns to scale using only labor. We let X be the *numéraire* good; to simplify we assume that $X = G(L^X) = L^X$, so $w = 1$. The other two goods are imported and are produced using a CRS technology with capital and labor. The outputs of the import competing goods in state s are

$$Y^{1s} = F^1(K^1, L^{1s}), \quad Y^{2s} = F^2(K^2, L^{2s}),$$

where K^i and L^{is} denote the amount of capital and labor employed in the production of good i in state s. The production functions are quasi-concave and twice differentiable.

Each household has one unit of labor and k units of nondivisible capital. Each household must allocate its capital to one sector. We assume that total endowment of labor is one ($L = 1$) implying that $K = k$ is total capital. Full employment implies $L^{Xs} + L^{1s} + L^{2s} = 1$ and $K^1 + K^2 = K = k$. Let $\lambda^i \equiv K^i/K = K^i/k$ be the proportion of households that allocate their capital to sector i, so that $K^i = \lambda^i K$. Since we can associate the households to the sector in which they invest, it follows that there are λ^1 households in sector 1 and $\lambda^2 = 1 - \lambda^1$ households in sector 2.

Let P^{is} be the world price of good $i = 1, 2$ in state s. The domestic price can be written as $p^{is} = (1 + t^{is})P^{is}$, where t^{is} denotes the *ad valorem* tariff for good i in state s. Let C^{ijs} be the consumption of good i by households invested in sector j in state s. The value of imports are defined as

$$M^s = M^{1s} + M^{2s} = P^{1s}(\lambda^1 C^{11s} + \lambda^2 C^{12s} - F^1) + P^{2s}(\lambda^1 C^{21s} + \lambda^2 C^{22s} - F^2). \quad (1)$$

We will assume that an imported good never becomes an exported good, so $M^{is} \geq 0$. The per-unit return to a household from her capital investment in sector i is

$$r^{is} = p^{is} F_k^i(K^i, L^{is}),$$

where the subscript K indicates partial derivative. The income accruing to the typical household in industry i is

$$y^{is} = p^{is} F_k^i(K^i, L^{is})k + w + T^s, \quad (2)$$

where T^s denotes tariff revenue in state s. We assume the revenue is distributed equally among households in a lump-sum fashion.

There are three states of nature. State s occurs with probability π^s, $s \in S = \{A, B, C\}$. In state A (B), sector 1 (2) receives a negative price shock; in state C neither import competing sector receives a shock.[6] Throughout much of the paper we will suppress the superscript *s* unless doing so leads to confusion.

The key question we are concerned with is the welfare effects of tariff policy. Given the small-country assumption, free trade is the optimal policy unless there are terms-of-trade shocks. In light of the uncertainty, trade policy may now act as insurance and hence raise welfare. The desirability of such a policy depends in part on the nature of the tariff. In section 3, we examine the benchmark case when the government sets a uniform tariff. In this case $t^1 = t^2 = t$ and tariff revenue is simply $T = tM$. In section 4, we consider sector-specific contingent tariffs—such as antidumping and escape clauses. In this scenario the tariff is levied only on the injured sector, implying case tariff revenue is $T = t^i P^i M^i$.

Letting $V^{is} \equiv V(y^{is}, p^{1s}, p^{2s})$ denote the indirect utility function of a type i household in state s, we can define welfare as[7]

$$W \equiv \sum_{s \in S} \pi^s W^s = \sum_{s \in S} \pi^s (\lambda^1 V^{1s} + \lambda^2 V^{2s}). \tag{3}$$

Finally we assume that *ex ante* an investment in each sector produces the same expected utility, implying

$$\sum_{s \in S} \pi^s (V^{1s} - V^{2s}) = 0. \tag{4}$$

3. Uniform Tariff Policy

We begin by considering the effect of imposing a uniform tariff in case of a negative shock (and no tariff if there is no shock). Since we believe that anticipated policies are of greater interest, we assume that all agents internalize the existence of the uniform tariff.[8]

For notational convenience we will use dot notation to denote derivatives with respect to the tariff, e.g., $\dot{y} \equiv dy/dt$, $\dot{M} \equiv dM/dt$, etc. The following result will be useful in deriving the main welfare result. (Complete proofs are contained in the Appendix.)

LEMMA 1. *The effect of an anticipated uniform tariff on sector i income is*

$$\frac{dy^i}{dt} \equiv \dot{y}^i = \frac{P^i F^i}{\lambda^i} + M + t\dot{M}, \quad i = 1, 2;$$

that is, the effect of a uniform tariff on income can be expressed as the sum of the direct income effect and the tariff income effect.

LEMMA 2. *The effect of a small uniform tariff on welfare in state s is*

$$\left. \frac{dW^s}{dt} \right|_{t=0} \equiv \dot{W}^s \Big|_{t=0} = \lambda^1 \lambda^2 (V_y^{1s} - V_y^{2s})\{(\dot{y}^{1s} - \dot{y}^{2s})$$
$$+ P^{1s}(C^{12s} - C^{11s}) + P^{2s}(C^{22s} - C^{21s})\}; \tag{5}$$

that is, the welfare effect of the uniform tariff is composed of the differential impact on the indirect utility of the two types weighed by the income change and the implicit income cost of the price changes.

PROOF. *Consider the effect of a tariff on welfare in state s (for details see the Appendix):*

$$\dot{W}^s = \lambda^1 [V_y^{1s} \dot{y}_1^s + V_1^{1s} P^{1s} + V_2^{1s} P^{2s}] + \pi^s \lambda^2 [V_y^{2s} \dot{y}_2^s + V_1^{2s} P^{1s} + V_2^{2s} P^{2s}], \tag{6}$$

where we have denoted $dV/dp^i \equiv V_i$. Using Roy's identity, Lemma 1, and equation (1), we get

$$\dot{W}^s = \lambda^1 \lambda^2 V_y^1 \{(\dot{y}^1 - \dot{y}^2) + (t\dot{M}/\lambda^2) + P^1(C^{12} - C^{11}) + P^2(C^{22} - C^{21})\}$$
$$+ \lambda^1 \lambda^2 V_y^2 \{(\dot{y}^2 - \dot{y}^1) + (t\dot{M}/\lambda^1) + P^1(C^{11} - C^{12}) + P^2(C^{21} - C^{21})\}.$$

Evaluating at $t = 0$ and simplifying we get the desired expression. $\square$

Lemma 2 allows us to evaluate the welfare effect of a uniform tariff. Suppose there is a negative price shock to sector 1 (state A). We have that $y^{1A} < y^{2A}$; hence $(V_y^{1A} - V_y^{2A}) > 0$ because of diminishing marginal utility. We can also sign the consumption terms if the importables are not inferior (both terms are positive). Note, however, that the term $\dot{y}^{1A} - \dot{y}^{2A}$ is negative. Therefore we cannot sign the overall expression, $\dot{W}^s$. The same ambiguity exists in state B. Since the optimal policy in state C is free trade, we must conclude the following.

PROPOSITION 1. *A small uniform tariff has an ambiguous effect on welfare; that is*

$$\left. \frac{dW}{dt} \right|_{t=0} \gtreqless 0.$$

Proposition 1 contrasts with EG's (1985) finding that a small tariff raises welfare when there are negative import price shocks. The difference lies in the fact that our model allows for multiple import competing goods, and while a uniform tariff carries benefits to the injured sector (as in EG) it has a negative effect on the other import competing sector. This result helps explain why we do not observe countries using uniform tariff policies to safeguard domestic industries from sector-specific terms-of-trade shocks.

4. A Sector-Specific Tariff

We now consider the case when a sector-specific tariff is imposed whenever there is a shock to a particular sector. We will assume that the government reacts by imposing tariff t^i on good i when there is a shock to that sector. All other sectors remain unprotected. Formally, the domestic price of good i in state s is $p^{is} = P^{is}(1 + t^{is})$ and

$$t^{is} = \begin{cases} t^i > 0 & \text{if } i = 1 \text{ and } s = A \text{ or if } i = 2 \text{ and } s = B, \\ 0 & \text{otherwise.} \end{cases}$$

A sector-specific tariff has two effects: an *ex post* effect on the allocation of labor once the state and the applicable tariff are known, and an *ex ante* effect on the allocation of capital between sectors. For instance, suppose we are in state A. An increase in the state A tariff raises the attractiveness of sector 1, since the bad state turns out to be not so bad (since the tariff raises the expected return to sector 1 capital). This implies that more capital will be invested in sector 1 (and less in other sectors). Hence, a state contingent tariff will have an effect on the capital stocks in all states, in contrast to the case of a uniform tariff.

Without loss of generality we will study the welfare effect of a state A contingent tariff (i.e., a tariff $t^1 > 0$). All the results are directly applicable to a state B contingent tariff. Differentiating equation (3) with respect to a state A contingent tariff leads to

$$\frac{dW}{dt^1} = \sum_{s \in S} \pi^s \left\{ \left(\lambda^1 \frac{\partial V^{1s}}{\partial t^1} + V^{1s} \frac{d\lambda^1}{dt^1} \right) + \left(\lambda^2 \frac{\partial V^{2s}}{\partial t^1} + V^{2s} \frac{d\lambda^2}{dt^1} \right) \right\}. \quad (7)$$

The following lemma will be useful in solving for the effect of a state contingent tariff.

LEMMA 3.

$$\sum_{s \in S} \pi^s \left(V^{1s} \frac{d\lambda^1}{dt^1} + V^{2s} \frac{d\lambda^2}{dt^1} \right) = 0;$$

that is, all the effects on welfare of a state contingent tariff are due to the direct effect of the tariff on indirect utility; i.e., the effect due to changes in the capital allocation between sectors induced by the tariff is zero.

LEMMA 4. *The change in income due to a state A contingent tariff is*

$$\dot{y}^{1A} = \frac{P^{1A} F^1}{\lambda^1} + M^{1A} + t^1 \dot{M}^{1A}, \tag{8}$$

$$\dot{y}^{2A} = M^{1A} + t^1 \dot{M}^{1A}. \tag{9}$$

The effect of a state contingent tariff on sector income is composed of the direct income effect plus the tariff income effect for the case of the sector hit by the price shock. For the other sector, the only effect on income is the tariff income effect.

PROPOSITION 2. *A small state contingent sector-specific tariff increases welfare; that is*

$$\left. \frac{\partial W}{\partial t^{is}} \right|_{t^{is}=0} > 0.$$

We now show that contingent tariffs are preferable to uniform tariffs, as follows.

PROPOSITION 3. *Assume that $M^{2A} < p^{2A} C^{21A}$ and $M^{1B} < P^{1B} C^{12B}$. Then a small sector-specific contingent tariff dominates a small uniform tariff as a response to trade shocks.*

5. Sector-Specific Taxes and Subsidies

An alternative policy instrument are sector-specific taxes and subsidies. We consider an *ad valorem* production subsidy σ^{is} to sector i in state s. To fix ideas, producers receive price $p^{is} = (1 + \sigma^{is})P^{is}$ where

$$\sigma^{is} = \begin{cases} \sigma^i > 0 & \text{if } i = 1 \text{ and } s = A \text{ or if } i = 2 \text{ and } s = B, \\ 0 & \text{otherwise.} \end{cases}$$

In other words, producers in sector i receive the subsidy only when i receives a negative shock. We assume that consumers continue to face world prices and that the subsidy is paid by lump-sum taxation on all sectors, so that taxes in sector i are $\tau^{is} \equiv \lambda^i \sigma^{is} P^{is} F^{is}$.

Consider for instance when state A is realized and sector 1 receives the negative price shock. In the rest of the section we will omit the superscript denoting the state unless doing so leads to confusion. Let $\rho^i \equiv P^i F^i$; therefore the total value of the subsidy is $\sigma^1 \rho^1$. The income received by type i household is

$$y^i = w + p^i F_K^i k - \lambda^i \sigma^i \rho^i, \quad i = 1, 2. \tag{10}$$

We can show the following.

LEMMA 5. *The change in income due to a state A contingent subsidy-cum-tax is*

$$\dot{y}^1 = \frac{\rho^1}{\lambda^1} + \lambda^2(\sigma^1\dot{\rho}^1 + \rho^1) + \lambda^2\sigma^1\rho^1,$$

$$\dot{y}^2 = -\lambda^2(\sigma^1\dot{\rho}^1 + \rho^1) - \lambda^2\sigma^1\dot{r}^1.$$

PROPOSITION 4. *A small state contingent subsidy is welfare-improving; that is*

$$\left.\frac{\partial W}{\partial \sigma^{is}}\right|_{\sigma^{is}=0} > 0.$$

6. A Ranking of Sector-Specific Taxes-cum-Subsidies and Sector-Specific Tariffs

We now compare a sector-specific tariff with sector-specific taxes-cum-subsidies. As we have modeled the policies, the tax-cum-subsidy policy is financed with a nondistorting tax. Since the tariff is both a tax on consumption and a subsidy to producers, it will distort more by design. We show the following.

PROPOSITION 5. *Assume* $P^{1A}C^{11A} > M^{1A}$ *and* $P^{1A}C^{22B} > M^{2B}$. *A small sector-specific subsidy dominates a small sector-specific contingent tariff as a response to trade shocks.*

This is a nice result as it shows that there exist alternative instruments that also lead to improvements in welfare.[9] The result begs the question: "why do we observe so many countries using sector-specific tariffs rather than sector-specific subsidies?" We believe there are two reasons why sector-specific taxes and subsidies are not generally used as insurance against price shocks. First, from the point of view of the sectors requiring aid, subsidies are vulnerable to budgetary restrictions. In addition, there are political economy reasons which make the imposition of selective taxes unattractive. Second, over the past twenty years there is considerable support for the view that antidumping regulations have been captured by protectionist interests (Bhagwati, 1988; Krueger, 1995). Hence, from a protectionist viewpoint, the value of antidumping regulations lies not only in its insurance aspects, but also in the fact that it can be manipulated.

7. Conclusions and Extensions

Using a general-equilibrium model with incomplete insurance markets, we have shown that contingent protection on a sectoral basis will increase welfare when the economy is subject to sector-specific price shocks. Moreover, it is a more efficient instrument than uniform contingent tariffs. Our model thus provides a theoretical basis for the long-held notion that GATT exceptions can act as insurance. Trade negotiators have long argued that the inclusion of the most popular sector-specific tool—antidumping actions—is a precondition for the approval of any trade agreement. The main result of the paper affirms this intuition by showing that there is an insurance role for antidumping that had not been considered in the theoretical literature.

We also show that there exist alternative instruments that also lead to improvements in welfare, such as a set of lump-sum taxes on all sectors coupled to a subsidy to the sector that receives the shock. Moreover, these policies have a higher welfare impact. However, we believe political economy reasons explain the popularity of sector-specific tariffs.

One limitation of this paper is that it does not show why exceptions are needed in order to sign trade agreements. If protection is what is desired, why is that not included in the original agreements? Another caveat is that our results should be interpreted as second-best arguments for contingent protection. As a first best, policy should always be directed at removing the sources of distortion, if possible.

Appendix

Proof of Lemma 1

First note that

$$\dot{w} = P^i F_L^i + p^i F_{LK}^i \dot{K}^i + p^i F_{LL}^i \dot{L}^i = 0, \quad i = 1, 2. \tag{A1}$$

Differentiating equation (2) and solving yields

$$
\begin{aligned}
\dot{y}^i &= P^i F_K^i k + p^i F_{KK}^i k \dot{K}^i + p^i F_{KL}^i k \dot{L}^i + M + t\dot{M} \\
&= \left[P^i F_K^i k + P^i F_L^i \frac{L^i}{\lambda^i} \right] + \left[p^i F_{KK}^i k \dot{K}^i + p^i F_{LK}^i \dot{K}^i \frac{L^i}{\lambda^i} \right] \\
&\quad + \left[p^i F_{KL}^i k \dot{L}^i + p^i F_{LL}^i \dot{L}^i \frac{L^i}{\lambda^i} \right] + M + t\dot{M} \\
&= \frac{P^i}{\lambda^i} [F_K^i K^i + F_L^i L^i] + \frac{p^i \dot{K}^i}{\lambda^i} [F_{KK}^i K^i + F_{LK}^i L^i] \\
&\quad + \frac{p^i \dot{L}^i}{\lambda^i} [F_{KL}^i K^i + F_{LL}^i L^i] + M + t\dot{M} \\
&= \frac{P^i F^i}{\lambda^i} + M + t\dot{M}, \tag{A2}
\end{aligned}
$$

where we have used Euler's theorem three times. □

Proof of Lemma 2

Consider the effect of a tariff on welfare in state s:

$$\dot{W}^s = \lambda^1 [V_y^{1s} \dot{y}_1^s + V_1^{1s} P^{1s} + V_2^{1s} P^{2s}] + \pi^s \lambda^2 [V_y^{2s} \dot{y}_2^s + V_1^{2s} P^{1s} + V_2^{2s} P^{2s}], \tag{A3}$$

where we have denoted $dV/dp^i \equiv V_i$. Using Roy's identity, we get

$$\dot{W}^s = \lambda^1 V_y^{1s} [\dot{y}_1^s - P^{1s} C^{11s} - P^{2s} C^{21s}] + \lambda^2 V_y^{2s} [\dot{y}_2^s - P^{1s} C^{12s} - P^{2s} C^{22s}]. \tag{A4}$$

We now use Lemma 1 to get (we now suppress the superscript s to simplify the notation)

$$
\begin{aligned}
\dot{W}^s &= \lambda^1 V_y^1 \{ P^1 F^1 / \lambda^1 + t\dot{M} + M - P^1 C^{11} - P^2 C^{21} \} \\
&\quad + \lambda^2 V_y^2 \{ P^2 F^2 / \lambda^2 + t\dot{M} + M - P^1 C^{12} - P^2 C^{22} \}. \tag{A5}
\end{aligned}
$$

Using the import equation (1) we have

$$M - P^1 C^{11} - P^2 C^{21} = P^1 [\lambda^2 (C^{12} - C^{11}) - F^1] + P^2 [\lambda^1 (C^{22} - C^{21}) - F^2]$$

and a corresponding expression for $M - P^1C^{12} - P^2C^{22}$. Substituting these into (A5) yields

$$\dot{W}^s = \lambda^1 V_y^1 \{P^1(F^1/\lambda^1) + t\dot{M} + P^1[\lambda^2(C^{12} - C^{11}) - F^1] + P^2[\lambda^2(C^{22} - C^{21}) - F^2]\}$$
$$+ \lambda^2 V_y^2 \{P^2(F^2/\lambda^2) + t\dot{M} + P^1[\lambda^1(C^{11} - C^{12}) - F^1] + P^2[\lambda^1(C^{21} - C^{22}) - F^2]\}.$$

Using Lemma 1, note that

$$\dot{y}^1 - \dot{y}^2 = \frac{\lambda^2 P^1 F^1 - \lambda^1 P^2 F^2}{\lambda^1 \lambda^2}. \tag{A6}$$

Substituting this expression gives

$$\dot{W}^s = \lambda^1 \lambda^2 V_y^1 \{(\dot{y}^1 - \dot{y}^2) + (t\dot{M}/\lambda^2) + P^1(C^{12} - C^{11}) + P^2(C^{22} - C^{21})\}$$
$$+ \lambda^1 \lambda^2 V_y^2 \{(\dot{y}^2 - \dot{y}^1) + (t\dot{M}/\lambda^1) + P^1(C^{11} - C^{12}) + P^2(C^{21} - C^{22})\},$$

from which we obtain

$$\dot{W}^s = \lambda^1 \lambda^2 (V_y^{1s} - V_y^{2s})\{(\dot{y}^{1s} - \dot{y}^{2s}) + P^{1s}(C^{12s} - C^{11s}) + P^{2s}(C^{22s} - C^{21s})\}$$
$$+ t\dot{M}\lambda^1 \lambda^2 \left(\frac{V_y^{1s}}{\lambda^2} + \frac{V_y^{2s}}{\lambda^1} \right), \tag{A7}$$

where we again use superscript s to denote the state. Evaluating at $t = 0$, we obtain the desired expression. $\square$

Proof of Lemma 3

From $K^1 + K^2 = K$ it follows that

$$\frac{dK^1}{dt^1} = -\frac{dK^2}{dt^1}.$$

This implies

$$\frac{d\lambda^1}{dt^1} = \frac{d\lambda^1}{dK^1}\frac{dK^1}{dt^1} = -\frac{1}{k}\frac{dK^2}{dt^1}.$$

Substituting yields

$$\sum_{s \in S} \pi^s \sum_{i=1}^{2} V^{is} \frac{d\lambda^i}{dt^1} = \sum_{s \in S} \pi^s \left[(V^{2s} - V^{1s})(1/k)\frac{dK^2}{dt^1} \right]$$
$$= (1/k)\frac{dK^2}{dt^1} \sum_{s \in S} \pi^s (V^{2s} - V^{1s}) = 0,$$

where the last equality follows from (4). $\square$

Proof of Lemma 4

From the wage equation $1 = w = p^{iA}F_L^i$, $i = 1, 2$, we have that

$$\dot{w} = 0 = P^{1A}F_L^1 + p^{1A}F_{LL}^1 \dot{L}^1 + p^{1A}F_{LK}^1 \dot{K}^1 = p^{2A}F_{LL}^2 \dot{L}^2 + p^{2A}F_{LK}^2 \dot{K}^2. \tag{A8}$$

Differentiating (2), it follows that the change in income in state A is

754   *Ronald D. Fischer and Thomas J. Prusa*

$$\dot{y}^{1A} = \mathsf{P}^{1A}F_K^1 k + p^{1A}F_{KK}^1 \dot{K}^1 k + p^{1A}F_{KL}^1 \dot{L}^1 k + t^1 \dot{M}^{1A} + M^{1A}$$
$$= \mathsf{P}^{1A}F_K^1 k + p^{1A}F_{KK}^1 \dot{K}^1 k + p^{1A}F_{KL}^1 \dot{L}^1 k + t^1 \dot{M}^{1A} + M^{1A}$$
$$+ \left(p^{1A}F_{LL}^1 \dot{L}^1 \frac{L^1}{\lambda^1} - p^{1A}F_{LL}^1 \dot{L}^1 \frac{L^1}{\lambda^1} \right) + \left(p^{1A}F_{KL}^1 \dot{K}^1 \frac{L^1}{\lambda^1} - p^{1A}F_{KL}^1 \dot{K}^1 \frac{L^1}{\lambda^1} \right)$$
$$= \left(\mathsf{P}^{1A}F_K^1 k + \mathsf{P}^{1A}F_L^1 \frac{L^1}{\lambda^1} \right) + \left(p^{1A}F_{KL}^1 \dot{L}^1 k + p^{1A}F_{LL}^1 \dot{L}^1 \frac{L^1}{\lambda^1} \right)$$
$$+ \left(p^{1A}F_{KK}^1 \dot{K}^1 k + p^{1A}F_{KL}^1 \dot{K}^1 \frac{L^1}{\lambda^1} \right) + t^1 \dot{M}^{1A} + M^{1A}$$
$$= \frac{\mathsf{P}^{1A}F^1}{\lambda^1} + t^1 \dot{M}^{1A} + M^{1A},$$

where we have used Euler's theorem three times; and

$$\dot{y}^{2A} = p^{2A}F_{KK}^2 \dot{K}^2 k + p^{2A}F_{KL}^2 \dot{L}^2 k + t^1 \dot{M}^{1A} + M^{1A}$$
$$= p^{2A}F_{KK}^2 \dot{K}^2 k + p^{2A}F_{KL}^2 \dot{L}^2 k + t^1 \dot{M}^{1A} + M^{1A}$$
$$+ \left(p^{2A}F_{LL}^2 \dot{L}^2 \frac{L^2}{\lambda^2} - p^{2A}F_{LL}^2 \dot{L}^2 \frac{L^2}{\lambda^2} \right) + \left(p^{2A}F_{KL}^2 \dot{K}^2 \frac{L^2}{\lambda^2} - p^{2A}F_{KL}^2 \dot{K}^2 \frac{L^2}{\lambda^2} \right)$$
$$= \left(p^{2A}F_{KK}^2 \dot{K}^2 k + p^{2A}F_{KL}^2 \dot{K}^2 \frac{L^2}{\lambda^2} \right) + \left(p^{2A}F_{KL}^2 \dot{L}^2 k + p^{2A}F_{LL}^2 \dot{L}^2 \frac{L^2}{\lambda^2} \right)$$
$$- \left(p^{2A}F_{LL}^2 \dot{L}^2 \frac{L^2}{\lambda^2} + p^{2A}F_{KL}^2 \dot{K}^2 \frac{L^2}{\lambda^2} \right) + t^1 \dot{M}^{1A} + M^{1A}$$
$$= t^1 \dot{M}^{1A} + M^{1A},$$

using Euler's theorem two times.

Finally, recall that there is no income from a state A contingent tariff in states B or C. Thus, in states B and C, $y^{is} = w + r^{is}k$. Hence

$$\dot{y}^{is} = p^{is}F_{KL}^i k \dot{L}^i + p^{is}F_{KK}^i \dot{K}^i k = 0, \quad s = B, C$$

by Euler's theorem.   □

Proof of Proposition 2

As above, we will proceed by analyzing a state A contingent tariff. Recall that

$$\frac{\partial V^{iA}}{\partial t^1} = V_y^{iA} \dot{y}^i + V_1^{iA} \mathsf{P}^{1A}, \quad i = 1, 2,$$

and that

$$M^{1A} - \mathsf{P}^{1A}C^{11A} = \mathsf{P}^{1A}(\lambda^2 (C^{12A} - C^{11A}) - F^1),$$
$$M^{1A} - \mathsf{P}^{1A}C^{12A} = \mathsf{P}^{1A}(\lambda^1 (C^{11A} - C^{12A}) - F^1). \tag{A9}$$

Using Roy's identity, Lemmas 3 and 4, and equation (A9) we have

$$\frac{\partial W^A}{\partial t^1}\bigg|_{t^1=0} = \lambda^1 \frac{\partial V^{1A}}{\partial t^1} + \lambda^2 \frac{\partial V^{2A}}{\partial t^1}$$
$$= \mathsf{P}^{1A}F^1 \lambda^2 (V_y^{1A} - V_y^{2A}) + \mathsf{P}^{1A}\lambda^1 \lambda^2 (C^{12A} - C^{11A})(V_y^{1A} - V_y^{2A}) > 0. \tag{A10}$$

The last expression is positive. To see this, note that $y^{1A} < y^{2A}$; hence the first term on the right-hand side is positive because of diminishing marginal utility of income. The second term is positive because, whether or not $y^2 > y^1$, the terms $C^{12A} - C^{11A}$ and $V_y^{1A} - V_y^{2A}$ always have the same sign.

The only remaining step is to show that $dW^s/dt^1 = 0$ for $s = B, C$. But this is simple enough, since we have shown in Lemma 3 that $\dot{y}^{is} = 0$, $i = 1, 2$, for all states $s = B, C$. Since a state A contingent tariff has no direct effect on prices in the other states, it follows that

$$\frac{\partial V^{is}}{\partial t^1} = V_y^{is}\dot{y}^{is} + \sum_i V_y^{is}\frac{\partial p^{1s}}{dt^1} = 0, \quad i = 1, 2, \quad s = B, C. \qquad \square$$

Proof of Proposition 3

Let u or c subscript indicate a uniform or a contingent policy, respectively. Note that using (A6) in (5) we get

$$\dot{W}_u^A = (V_y^{1A} - V_y^{2A})\{\lambda^2 P^{1A}F^1 + \lambda_1\lambda_2 P^1(C^{12A} - C^{11A}) - \lambda_1 P^{2A}F^2 + \lambda_1\lambda_2 P^2(C^{22A} - C^{21A})\};$$

that is:

$$\dot{W}_u^A = (V_y^{1A} - V_y^{2A})\{\lambda^2 P^{1A}(F^1 + \lambda^1(C^{12A} - C^{11A})) + \lambda_1 P^{2A}(-F^2 + \lambda_2(C^{22A} - C^{21A}))\}.$$

Consider the difference $\Delta\dot{W}^A \equiv \dot{W}_c^A - \dot{W}_u^A$. We have

$$\Delta\dot{W}^A = (V_y^{1A} - V_y^{2A})\lambda_1 P^{2A}\{(F^2 - \lambda^2(C^{22A} - C^{21A})\}.$$

We know that the terms outside the brackets are positive. Thus

$$\begin{aligned}\text{sgn}(\Delta\dot{W}^A) &= \text{sgn}\, P^{2A}(F^2 - \lambda^2(C^{22A} - C^{21A})) \\ &= \text{sgn}(P^{2A}C^{21A} - M^{2A}) > 0\end{aligned}$$

because of our assumption that $M^{2A} < p^{2A}C^{21A}$. A similar proof applies in state B, with the corresponding condition. Finally, in the case $s = C$, both mechanisms do nothing, so that $E\Delta\dot{W} > 0$. $\qquad \square$

Proof of Lemma 5

Differentiating (10):

$$\dot{y}^1 = P^1 F_K^1 k + p^1 F_{KK}^1 \dot{K}^1 k + p^1 F_{KL}^1 \dot{L}^1 k + \lambda^2(\sigma^1\dot{\rho}^1 + \rho^1) + \dot{\lambda}^2\sigma^1\rho^1,$$
$$\dot{y}^2 = P^2 F_{KK}^2 \dot{K}^2 k + P^2 F_{KL}^2 \dot{L}^2 k - \lambda^2(\sigma^1\dot{\rho}^1 + \rho^1) - \dot{\lambda}^2\sigma^1\rho^1.$$

Adding and subtracting $p^i F_{KL}^i \dot{k}^i (L^i/\lambda^i)$ and $p^i F_{LL}^i \dot{L}^i (L^i/\lambda^i)$, using the fact that $\dot{w} = 0$, and using Euler's theorem gives the desired expression. $\qquad \square$

Proof of Proposition 4

Recall that consumers face world prices, so the subsidy does not change the prices they face. Hence $dV^i/d\sigma^1 = V_y^i\dot{y}^i$, and the total change in welfare in state A due to a small contingent production subsidy is

$$\begin{aligned}\frac{dW^A}{d\sigma^1}\bigg|_{\sigma^1=0} &= \lambda^1 V_y^1\left(\frac{\rho^1}{\lambda^1} + \lambda^2\rho^1\right) - V_y^2\lambda^2\rho^1 \\ &= ((1 + \lambda^1\lambda^2)V_y^1 - \lambda^2 V_y^2)P^1 F^1 > 0.\end{aligned} \qquad (A11)$$

Note also that $dW^B/d\sigma^1 = 0$, as in the previous section. The negative shock implies that $V_y^{1A} > V_y^{2A}$ and hence the effect of the subsidy is always positive. $\qquad \square$

756   *Ronald D. Fischer and Thomas J. Prusa*

Proof of Proposition 5

Recall from equation (A10) that

$$\left.\frac{\partial W^A}{\partial t^1}\right|_{t^1=0} = P^{1A}F^1\lambda^2(V_y^{1A}-V_y^{2A})+P^{1A}\lambda^1\lambda^2(C^{12A}-C^{11A})(V_y^{1A}-V_y^{2A}) > 0.$$

Similarly, from equation (A11), we have

$$\left.\frac{dW^A}{d\sigma^1}\right|_{\sigma^1=0} = \lambda^2(V_y^{1A}-V_y^{2A})P^{1A}F^1 + \lambda^1(1+\lambda^2)V_y^{1A}P^{1A}F^1;$$

so that

$$\left.\frac{dW^A}{d\sigma^1}\right|_{\sigma^1=0} > \left.\frac{\partial W^A}{\partial t^1}\right|_{t^1=0}$$

if

$$P^{1A}\lambda^1\lambda^2(C^{12A}-C^{11A})(V_y^{1A}-V_y^{2A}) < \lambda^1(1+\lambda^2)V_y^{1A}P^{1A}F^1.$$

Since $(C^{12A}-C^{11A})$ and $(V_y^{1A}-V_y^{2A})$ have the same sign and $(V_y^{1A} > V_y^{2A})$, we can write the condition as

$$\lambda^2 P^{1A}(C^{12A}-C^{11A})V_y^{1A} < (1+\lambda^2)V_y^{1A}P^{1A}F^1.$$

Since $V_y^{1A} > 0$ the condition becomes

$$\lambda^2 P^{1A}(C^{12A}-C^{11A}) < (1+\lambda^2)P^{1A}F^1.$$

Recall equation (A9):

$$M^{1A}-P^{1A}C^{11A} = P^{1A}(\lambda^2(C^{12A}-C^{11A})-F^1).$$

So the inequality holds if

$$M^{1A}-P^{1A}C^{11A} < 0,$$

because $P^{1A}F^1 > 0$. Analogously for a shock to state B.   □

References

Baldwin, Robert E., "The Political Economy of Protectionism," in Jagdish Bhagwati (ed.), *Import Competition and Response*, Chicago: University of Chicago Press (1982).

Bhagwati, Jagdish, *Protectionism*, Cambridge, MA: MIT Press (1988).

Corden, W. Max, *Trade Policy and Economic Welfare*, Oxford: Oxford University Press (1974).

Dam, Kenneth W., *The GATT: Law and International Economic Organization*, Chicago: University of Chicago Press (1970).

Dixit, Avinash K., "Trade and Insurance with Moral Hazard," *Journal of International Economics* 23 (1987):201–20.

———, "Trade and Insurance with Adverse Selection," *Review of Economic Studies* 56 (1989a):235–48.

———, "Trade and Insurance with Imperfectly Observed Outcomes," *Quarterly Journal of Economics* 104 (1989b):195–203.

Eaton, Jonathan and Gene M. Grossman, "Tariffs as Insurance: Optimal Commercial Policy when Domestic Markets are Incomplete," *Canadian Journal of Economics* 18 (1985):258–72.

Finger, J. Michael (ed.), *Antidumping: How It Works and Who Gets Hurt*, Ann Arbor: University of Michigan Press (1993).

Jackson, John, *World Trade and the Law of GATT*, New York: Bobbs-Merrill Co. (1969).

Krueger, Anne O., *The American Trade Policy: a Tragedy in the Making*, Washington, DC: AEI Press (1995).

Staiger, Robert W., "International Rules and Institutions for Trade Policy," in Gene M. Grossman and Kenneth S. Rogoff (eds.), *Handbook of International Economics*, Vol. 3, Amsterdam: North-Holland (1995).

Staiger, Robert W. and Guido Tabellini, "Discretionary Trade Policy and Excessive Protection," *American Economic Review* 77 (1987):823–37.

Staiger, Robert W. and Frank A. Wolak, "Measuring Industry Specific Protection: Antidumping in the United States," *Brookings Papers on Economic Activity, Microeconomics* (1994):51–103.

Notes

1. See Jackson (1969) for a description of the legal foundations for exceptions. Staiger (1995) discusses some economic issues relating to GATT rules and institutions.

2. The idea that trade policy might act as insurance was informally discussed for many years (Corden, 1974; Baldwin, 1982).

3. Consider the case where insurance against market shocks is expensive, owing to the existence of a monopoly in insurance. The first best would be to eliminate the monopoly, in which case it might not be necessary to have contingent protection. If this is impossible, contingent protection can be used as a second-best way to avoid the cost of not being able to insure against trade shocks.

4. Staiger and Wolak (1994) find that many US antidumping complaints are not primarily aimed at winning duties, but rather at hindering the foreign rival during the investigation (in their terminology, many industries are "process filers").

5. The results can be easily extended to the case of n import competing sectors.

6. By assumption, shocks never make an import good become an export good.

7. Good X also enters the utility function, but since it is the *numéraire* good it is convenient if we suppress it in the indirect utility function.

8. The effect of a uniform tariff when the tariff is unanticipated is similar. This is somewhat surprising since in general the tariff alters the return in each of the possible states of nature, which in turn means that the allocation of capital could depend on whether the tariff is anticipated. In the case of a uniform tariff, however, this effect does not exist. This rather surprising result is explained by the fact that the relative price of the import goods p^1/p^2, remains the same with or without the tariff. Given that *ex ante* investment in each sector provides the same expected utility, we find that anticipated and unanticipated protection has the same effect on income.

9. We note that the sufficiency conditions can be relaxed at the cost of more complexity.

Chapter 12

Using safeguard protection to raise domestic rivals' costs[†]

James P. Durling[a], Thomas J. Prusa[b,*]

[a]*Willkie Farr & Gallagher, New York, NY, USA*
[b]*Department of Economics, New Jersey Hall, Rutgers University and NBER,
New Brunswick, NJ 08901-1248, USA*

Received 5 April 2002; received in revised form 21 August 2002; accepted 16 September 2002

Abstract

The primary impact of import protection is to raise foreign firms' costs. We show that poorly designed protection also raises domestic rivals' costs. We find that simultaneously taxing both the upstream and downstream import markets results in a very small expansion in industry-wide downstream production. We use the US' recent steel safeguard action as a case study. Our analysis sheds new light on the controversial steel slab restrictions. We show that the primary effect of the steel tariffs is distributional. In particular, the steel tariffs will mainly benefit minimills and will provide relatively small benefits to traditional mills.
© 2002 Elsevier Science B.V. All rights reserved.

JEL classification: F10; F12; F13

Keywords: Raising rivals' costs; Protection; Steel

1. Introduction

The idea of "raising rivals' costs" is widely accepted by antitrust authorities as an important threat to competition (Salop and Scheffman, 1983, 1987; Brennan, 1988). The concept is easy to explain. A dominant firm executes some type of strategy to shift the supply curve of its rivals. This, in turn, shifts out the residual demand curve for the dominant firm's product and results in increased profits for the dominant firm. Crucially, shifting upward the the rivals' supply curve requires increasing the rivals' costs at the margin.

---

*Corresponding author. Tel.: +1-732-932-7670; fax: +1-732-932-7416.
E-mail address: prusa@econ.rutgers.edu (T.J. Prusa).

[†]This article originally appeared in *Japan and the World Economy*, **15**, pp. 47–68.

48   *J.P. Durling, T.J. Prusa/Japan and the World Economy 15 (2003) 47–68*

Although not discussed in Salop and Scheffman's original papers, import restrictions are arguably the most widely used (and abused) example of raising rivals' costs. For instance, Baumol and Ordover (1985) argue that the protection discourages firms from adopting technological improvements and instead encourages the firms to litigate against foreign firms who have innovated. In effect, trade protection, most notably antidumping, is a form of raising rivals' costs whereby foreign firms' efforts to lower their costs are "undone" by higher tariffs.[1]

In this paper, we argue that Baumol and Ordover's critique addresses only half of the problem. In particular, Baumol and Ordover's entire focus is on the impact of trade protection on *foreign* firms' costs. Policymakers sympathetic with antidumping protection discount such concerns as outside the intent of the law. Their view is that Congress has made a decision that low-cost imports are to be discouraged, regardless of their benefits.[2] Simply put, their view is that if foreign firms' costs are raised, so be it—it was Congress' intent that the ITC raise foreign rivals' costs.

We argue, however, that the cost-raising impact of administered protection is not solely limited to foreign firms. In fact, for vertically integrated industries, we believe that the cost-raising concerns of protection are more insidious, more widespread, and more anticompetitive than previously discussed. We argue that poorly designed, over-reaching protection will serve to raise not only foreign rivals' costs, but also *domestic* rivals' costs. Therefore, our findings are much more difficult for policymakers to ignore. Even the most ardent protectionists cannot argue that it was Congress' intent to harm one domestic firm so that another domestic firm will gain. But this is precisely what we find.

Our results are not merely a theoretical curiosity. Rather, the findings directly bear on the US's recent Section 201 investigation involving steel.[3] In truth, the steel safeguard case served as the motivation for this paper. In the 201 dispute almost all steel products were investigated in an attempt to determine whether imports were causing serious injury to the domestic steel industry. Steel is perhaps the archetypal example of a vertically related industry, where product A is the input for product B, which in turn is the input for product C, and so on.

The complicating factor is that different steel firms rely on different sources for their inputs. For instance, some firms like US Steel (USX) internally produce virtually all of their input needs. Other firms, like AK Steel and California Steel must purchase some (or all) of certain inputs on the open-market. In the 201 dispute, due to strong lobbying by the firms who are wholly internalized, the US government levied huge tariffs on the entire vertical chain of products. The huge tariffs were even levied on a vital input like steel slab. What makes this decision particularly troubling is that slab is not available domestically. At

---

[1] As articulated by Salop and Scheffman, the concept of raising rivals' costs can be interpreted a form of nonprice predation carried out by altering the rivals' supply curve, rather then the traditional (and prohibitively expensive) predatory tactic of reducing the market price by flooding the market. It is therefore more than a bit ironic that antidumping—a law originally intended to discourage predatory behavior—is the primary weapon used to raise foreign rivals' costs.

[2] For instance, ITC Commissioner Lynn Bragg wrote, "As a nation ... we have made the judgment that unfairly traded imports are to be discouraged, regardless of their 'benefits,' if they cause harm to competing domestic industries and workers" (USITC, 1995).

[3] Section 201 actions are also known as safeguard protection.

J.P. Durling, T.J. Prusa/Japan and the World Economy 15 (2003) 47–68   49

its core, our paper shows that firms who generally do not need (or use) imported slab—namely Nucor and US Steel—used the government to raise their rivals' costs.

As Salop and Scheffman note in their original article, a strategy of raising rivals' costs is most viable when the strategy increases rival costs more than those of the incumbent firms.[4] This condition is met in the present case, as the tariffs on slab increase the costs of rollers more than of the integrated firms and particularly the minimills. This asymmetry is what drives the strategy and makes it more likely to succeed than, for example, a typical predatory pricing strategy.

We will also show that cutting off the import market for upstream products does very little real good for the overall industry. We show that protecting the upstream product results in a very small increase in total industry production. The primary effect is distributional. Some firms (like Nucor) will expand their output while others (like many traditional integrated mills) will decrease their output. Ironically, given that the firms who benefit have very low unit labor requirements, we find that taxing the upstream product may actual lower domestic employment. All in all, given the technological characteristics of modern steel production, the decision to impose restrictions on upstream products is not only perplexing but also counterproductive to the objective of increasing steel industry employment.

The remainder of the paper proceeds as follows. In Section 2, we will describe the current state of the US Steel industry. In Section 3, we will give an overview of the Section 201 proceedings. In Section 4, we will report on the stated positions of the various domestic firms. In Section 5, we will US a stylized model of the competition with the steel industry. We then solve the model and show that the primary effect of the government's decision is to choose winners and losers. We make a few concluding comments in Section 6.

2. The steel industry: the emergence of new competitive pressures

To understand the current competitive dynamics of the steel industry, it is important to realize that not all steel firms are alike. Within the domestic flat-rolled steel industry, there are at least three distinct business models: the traditional integrated mills; the new low cost minimills; and the new lower cost rollers. The emergence of these two new lower cost segments has intensified the intra-industry competition in the domestic steel industry.

2.1. Traditional BF/BOF mills

The traditional business model for the domestic steel industry involved firms manufacturing steel by combining basic raw materials.[5] These "integrated mills" combine iron ore, coke, and other fuel sources in a large blast furnace (BF) to make pig iron and then refine that pig iron into raw steel in a basic oxygen furnace (BOF). Slabs and billets are then cast from the liquid steel (see Fig. 1). These two products are referred to as semi-finished

---

[4] According to Salop and Scheffman, "a sufficient condition for an (RRC) strategy to be profitable is for it to shift up the dominant firms' residual demand curve by more than it shifts up its average cost curve at the original output."

[5] For a useful historical overview, see Barnett and Crandall (1998).

50 *J.P. Durling, T.J. Prusa / Japan and the World Economy 15 (2003) 47–68*

Two Technologies for Making Steel

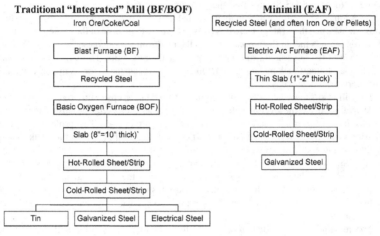

Fig. 1. Two technologies for making steel.

steel since these early stage products have not been sufficiently processed to have any real commercial use. The slabs and billets are then rolled or shaped into various finished steel end products. For example, a typical production flow would be to start by making steel slab, which is then processed into "hot-rolled steel" (steel rolled to less than 0.20 in. thick while still in a hot state), or further processed into "cold-rolled steel" (steel that is allowed to cool, and is then rolled even thinner and smoother) or even further processed with various coatings such as zinc or tin to create corrosion resistant steel and other specialized products.

In order for blast furnace technology to be economically efficient, the furnaces need to be large, by which analysts mean capable of producing at least 2–3 million tonnes per year. A BF/BOF mill of this scale requires substantial capital investments—according to study done by the US International Trade Commission (Yost, 1996) the cost of a new BF/BOF mill of efficient scale is on the order of US$ 3.5–5 billion.[6] A BF/BOF's high fixed costs create a particularly strong incentive to maximize output, so as to lower the average cost of the steel produced.

2.2. EAF minimills

The first major change to the traditional steel-making model is principally a techno-logical phenomenon—the emergence of electric arc furnace ("EAF") steel mills. Rather

---

[6] Donald Barnett, a leading industry analyst, estimates the cost of a new blast furnace is approximately US$ 2 billion (Ghemawat and Stander, 1992). The cost is so high relative to likely profits, no new greenfield BF/BOF has been built in the US in more than 20 years.

J.P. Durling, T.J. Prusa / Japan and the World Economy 15 (2003) 47–68   51

than making raw steel in a blast furnace, these so-called "minimills" use electricity to melt scrap steel and virgin iron units in an EAF (see Fig. 1). The recycled steel is then used to make various downstream products. By avoiding the time consuming and expensive process of making raw steel, the minimills can make downstream products faster and with substantially lower costs than integrated mills. Moreover, an EAF's minimum efficient scale is about 1/10 that an integrated's which means that successful minimills can set up EAF furnaces in geographically diverse locations, allowing them to be near customers and therefore minimize transportation costs.[7] An EAF's smaller scale also means that the capital costs are a fraction of a BOF.[8] After accounting for all of these factors, minimill costs are widely estimated to be 25–30 percent lower than even the most efficiently operated US integrated mills (Barnett, 2000).

Although US minimills have produced substantial quantities of steel using EAF technology since the 1960s, their output was traditionally confined to less technically complex steel products such as wire rod, bar, and rebar. And while the minimills' substantial cost advantages have resulted in the exit of traditional mills in the structural and long product segments, most traditional mills survived by specializing their operations in the one product segment that minimills were traditionally unable to produce: flat-rolled steel. Flat-rolled steel products, such as automobile panels, the exterior metal on home appliances, construction sheet metal, HVAC ducting, tin, etc., now accounts for more than 95 percent of traditional integrated mills' output. Flat-rolled steel also accounts for about 70 percent of all US steel consumption.

By 1989, however, EAF technology had evolved to the extent that minimills were finally able to produce flat-rolled products. In a technological breakthrough, Nucor pioneered the commercial application of thin slab casting. In contrast with integrated mills which produce thick slab (8–10 in. thick) minimills go from molten steel directly to 1–2 in. steel slab, skipping entirely the traditional thick slab stage. Moreover, not only do mini-mills using thin slab caster produce 1–2 in. slabs, the slabs are immediately hot-rolled in a continuous process. That is, they are not taken off-line and placed in inventory. This saves the cost of re-heating a cold slab.[9] As was easily predictable, the minimills' cost advantage has led to rapid market share growth in the flat-rolled segment. As of 2002, minimills are projected to account for 27 percent of domestic flat-rolled production (Barnett, 2000).

2.3. Rollers

The second major change in the US steel industry is not primarily technological (as is the case with minimills) but rather philosophical—namely, the use of imported slab to augment internal production or to overcome fundamental mill shortcomings. But in order to appreciate this new business model, a bit more background is needed.

---

[7] A typical EAF has an output of 1–1.5 million tonnes per year.

[8] Yost (1996) estimates the costs of a greenfield EAF minimill are US$ 460–500 million.

[9] This also means that Nucor does not produce slabs for inventory and does not purchase slabs. Thus, its production process precludes it from either buying or selling slabs. In addition, thin slabs cannot be transported because they are too long and thin.

Table 1
International cost comparison—thick slab (1999)

Country	Cost per tonne (US$)	Costs relative US (percent)
US	247	NA
Canada	205	−17
Japan	198.75	−20
EU	184	−26
Korea	166.25	−33
Brazil	141	−43

Source: Barnett (2000).

Over the past 20 years it has become increasingly clear that: (i) other countries can produce slab at far lower cost than the US;[10] and (ii) wholly self-contained (i.e. fully integrated) production limits a firm's ability to fully utilize its best assets.

Table 1 illuminates the first point. As one can see, world-class slab production has a cost advantage of more than US$ 100 per tonne (40 percent) even relative to efficient US production. Foreign producers' cost advantage stems from their proximity to high-quality, low-cost raw materials, their more modern facilities, and also their larger scale.

With respect to the second point, the rapid growth of minimills has accelerated what is often referred to as a "deverticalization" in the steel industry. That is, the minimills' success is not entirely technological, but rather is also heavily influenced by their belief in maximizing output per manhour. Accordingly, minimills sell a far greater fraction of their output on the open-market than the traditional integrated mills who prefer to handle most of the downstream processing themselves. In other words, primarily due to the success of Nucor, many now realize that there is neither a technological nor economic reason why a steel mill has to be a "one stop shop." Rather, profitability is driven by being the lowest cost producer in those product segments where you do participate. As a result, there are dozens of new steel firms who only produce cold-rolled steel, or only make pipe, or only produce galvanized steel. Rather than produce the upstream input required, these new firms simply purchase the input, usually from a US minimill or foreign suppliers.

This movement toward slab importing is simply the next step in this process. Given the substantial investment needed to construct and operate an integrated mill, the competitive advantages that other countries have at the slab stage, and the relatively more attractive operating margins on higher value-added downstream products, a number of firms have invested in downstream rolling capacity without any concomitant creation or expansion in their upstream blast furnace capacity. To the extent that these mills' new rolling facilities imply that they have a slab deficit, the firms can simply turn to the open-market and purchase slab.

There are two substantial costs savings associated with buying slab. First, the slab buyer (often referred to as a roller) has significantly lower fixed costs of investment. This is especially important during periods of slack demand when slab buyer can simply cut their purchases without worrying about the ongoing costs of maintaining and owning a BF/BOF.

---

[10] Put another way, the US has lost comparative and absolute advantage in slab production.

J.P. Durling, T.J. Prusa / Japan and the World Economy 15 (2003) 47–68   53

Indeed, in the early 1990s when AK Steel made the choice of where to invest money in their steel operations, they chose to invest in state-of-the-art rolling mills rather than their furnaces.

Second, as demonstrated in Table 1 the cost of buying slab is lower than the cost of making slab. Blast furnaces in Brazil and other countries—large, modern, efficient mills near sources of high quality iron ore and substantial transportation infrastructure—produce high quality slabs at a lower cost than any American blast furnace. Importing slab thus gives the rollers significant cost savings.

Mills have adopted this new approach to steel making in two ways. Firms such AK Steel, Oregon Steel and Ispat Inland buy imported slab to *supplement* their own steel slab production. Other firms such as California Steel and Duferco-Farrell rescued the rolling operations of shuttered mills, but did not purchase the highly inefficient melting operations. Without *any* ability to produce raw steel, these two firms became pure rollers.

This new business model has exerted competitive pressure on both the high- and and low-ends of the steel market. Let's first think about the implications for the high-end. Given that minimills use scrap steel, and the difficulty of controlling the purity and consistency of the scrap, some types of steel—particularly higher quality grades of cold-rolled and coated steels—still need to be produced by the BF/BOF method. At this point minimills simply cannot profitably make these high-end types of steel.[11] As a result, minimill market share gains have been primarily confined to commodity-grade products. Not surprisingly, BF/BOF mills who compete in that part of the market are struggling to stay in business.

However, BF/BOF mills who compete in the high-quality part of the market have done much better. The slab roller business model threatens this safe haven.[12] Depending on the quality of slab imported and the quality of the rolling lines, slab rollers can compete quite successfully at the high-end of the steel market. AK Steel is the preeminent example of a slab buyer competing at the highest end of the market. AK Steel invested more than US$ 1 billion to build a large capacity, state-of-the-art rolling mill and is now the most profitable US steel producer (on a per tonne basis). But, these new rolling lines mean that AK Steel must augment its own internally produced slab with open-market purchases.

What are the implications of the rollers on the low-end of the market. Simply put, if roller mills purchase commodity grade slab, they can compete quite successfully at the low-end or commodity-grade part of the market. But this is precisely the market segment where the Nucor and the rest of the minimills dominate. As a result, roller mills like California Steel and Duferco-Farrell pose a serious competitive challenge to the minimills' dominance.

2.4. The risk of vertical foreclosure

The rollers have proven that it is no longer necessary for a successful steel firm to make all of its own raw steel; the feedstock can be purchased. The only caveat, of course, is that there needs to be firms willing to supply the slab. This seemingly obvious stipulation is the

---

[11] Although there are public reports that the best minimills are very close to making and selling higher quality grades.

[12] We note that the many firms merely augment their own internal slab production and are not really rollers. In order to keep the terminology simple, we will use the term roller to refer to both types of firms.

huge risk associated with this new business model. Why? Domestic integrated mills never offer commercial quantities of slab on a regular basis—they would rather roll the slab into higher value-added products before selling the steel.[13] Besides, domestic integrated firms have no incentive to enable their rivals to compete for downstream higher margin sales. In addition, all of the new roller firms' operations require thick slab which means that minimills are not potential suppliers. In other words, if left to their own devices, domestic mills can and do choke off the supply of slab and thus can largely eliminate the competition from these new firms.

This business situation means that rollers depend almost entirely on imported slab.[14] Large-scale internationally competitive mills in other countries—most notably Brazil and Mexico—are willing and able to supply large quantities of slab on a regular basis.[15] Over the past few years, slab imports have increased to meet the growing demand by rollers.

In summary, these new segments—both the minimills and the rollers—have fueled competitive pressures in the market. The integrated mills for years experienced only limited rivalry, mostly from other integrated mills. This industry spent decades expecting annual price increases. Yet in the past two decades, minimills have captured larger and larger shares of more and more product segments. Now in the past decade, the rollers have begun to capture a larger portion of even the higher valued-added segments. The competitive rivalry within the domestic industry has intensified. Even more troubling for traditional integrated mills, both the minimills and the rollers have significant cost advantages, and thus have more flexibility to adjust prices. The problem posed by the rollers could be solved, of course, if the traditional mills and minimills could find a way to eliminate the supply of imported slab.

3. The Section 201 proceeding: targeting competitive rivals

Under international trade rules, countries may impose so-called "safeguard" measures. Under WTO rules, countries normally should not raise tariffs[16] or impose quantitative restrictions. Under Article XIX of the GATT and the Agreement on Safeguards, however, countries can impose such restrictions in exceptional situations if a domestic industry is suffering serious injury substantially caused by rapidly increasing imports. The importing country is allowed to take a temporary break from its trade obligations to allow its domestic industry time to restructure.

---

[13] Domestic mills do make "courtesy" shipments to each other, say, when a blast furnace needs to shut down for relining. But such shipments are sporadic at best, often of undesirable chemistries, and almost always for relatively small volumes.

[14] It should be noted that the unavailability of domestic slab means that *all* BOF mills purchase at least some imported slab. There is simply no other source.

[15] In contrast to the situation in the US, many other countries can produce more slab than they can roll. Thus, selling slab to other markets is a viable option for mills in other countries. The supplies of slabs will remain available in the long-run and are not contingent upon a downturn in the demand for finished steels in foreign countries.

[16] Technically, countries may not raise tariffs beyond the legally "bound rate;" in practice, most countries set actual duty rates at the bound rate.

J.P. Durling, T.J. Prusa/Japan and the World Economy 15 (2003) 47–68   55

Under US law, the Senate, the President, or a domestic industry can request safeguard measures under Section 201. The Trade Act of 1974 allows the imposition of safeguard measures if certain statutory factors are met. The first stage of a Section 201 proceeding involves an investigation by the International Trade Commission ("ITC"), an independent regulatory agency, of whether the domestic industry is suffering serious injury caused by increasing imports. The second stage is for the ITC to consider the alternative remedy options, and to make a recommendation to the President. The third and final stage consists of the President's decision, who can accept, reject, or modify the ITC recommendations. In many cases, the President exercises the statutory right to consider the broader national interest and not impose restrictions.

The domestic steel industry has a long history of obtaining trade protection, going back to the 1970s. This history includes prior safeguard proceedings. In 1984, the steel industry filed a Section 201 case. Although President Reagan technically rejected the recommended import relief, he then proceeded to negotiate a series of voluntary export restraint agreements with all the US trading partners. These quantitative restrictions protected the steel industry from 1984 to 1992.[17]

In the summer of 2001, the US began its second major safeguards investigation of steel imports. The domestic industry had been pushing for such an investigation for some time as a way to limit imports. The campaign for a Section 201 case began in 1998. In the early stages, the industry chose not to file a formal request and instead pushed for President Clinton to self-initiate a case. The Clinton Administration, however, felt that the domestic industry had sufficient protection from the hundreds of antidumping cases and that additional protection was neither necessary nor appropriate. To the very end, even in the election year, President Clinton rebuffed calls for a self-initiated case.

With the election of President Bush, the dynamics would soon change. In theory, the Bush Administration should have been even more committed to resisting calls for protection. But when Senator Jeffords of Vermont changed parties and gave control of the Senate to the Democrats, the political dynamic changed dramatically. The Senate Finance Committee was posed to initiate the Section 201 case that the Republicans on the committee had blocked for so long. Under these circumstances, President Bush decided to initiate the case himself. Like all politicians, President Bush wanted to be able to take credit for an action that was now inevitable.

This proceeding was unique in several respects. First, the position of the minimills had changed over the years. In trade disputes in the 1980s, minimills had consistently opposed trade protection. In the 1984 safeguards case, for example, the leading minimill Nucor testified in opposition to any special protection for the steel industry.[18] By the late 1990s, however, management changes and new competitive realities (and rivalries) changed the minimill position. Now minimills joined the domestic industry crusade to seek protection.

Second, the competitive dynamics surrounding trade in slab had changed. The emergence of rollers had created larger and growing demand for slab imports. Unlike the 1984 safeguards case, in which slab imports were only 3–4 percent of total imports under

---

[17] For this history of protection, see Barringer and Pierce (2000) and Moore (1996).

[18] Ken Iverson, then CEO of Nucor, published at article in *The Wall Street Journal* on 21 August 1986 with the subtitle "Protection ensures stagnation."

56 *J.P. Durling, T.J. Prusa/Japan and the World Economy 15 (2003) 47–68*

investigation, in the 2001 safeguards case, slab imports accounted for more than 9 percent of the total imports under investigation.[19] Moreover, the rate of growth in slab imports was one of the highest of all the steel products being investigated. In fact, while most products were showing declining imports, slab imports were still increasing.

Third, the slab import issue split the domestic industry. Although the industry largely agreed on the demand for protection on finished goods, the industry was sharply split over semi-finished goods. The most extreme position—take by the United Steelworkers—called for an investigation of all semi-finished products, including both "pig iron" (an early stage material) and slab. The minimills wanted to exclude pig iron—a product that could be used in some EAF technologies—but include everything else. The economic rationale for the minimills' position is that high quality pig iron allows them to produce cleaner steel and higher value downstream products which ultimately makes them even more competitive with integrated mills. The rollers, in contrast, fought hard to exclude slabs from the Section 201 case. The minimills's position prevailed on both counts—pig iron was excluded; slab was included.

In the end, the ITC found serious injury caused by imports. The ITC grouped together into one "like product" most flat carbon steel—including slab, plate, hot-, cold-rolled, and corrosion resistant steel into a single category. The plurality remedy recommendation from the ITC was for 20 percent tariffs on all finished flat-rolled steel, and a tariff rate quota on slab that allowed the first 7 million tonnes to enter duty free with a 20 percent tariff applying to imports in excess of the quota. The President ultimately imposed a 30 percent tariffs on all finished flat-rolled steel, and a tariff rate quota on slab that allowed the first 5.4 million tonnes to enter duty free with a 30 percent tariff applying to imports in excess of the quota.[20]

4. Using government regulation to vertically foreclose domestic rivals

Despite early assurances from minimill producers that historical levels of slab imports would be allowed, once the case proceeded to the ITC, the minimills pressed hard to have large tariffs imposed on slab.

For instance, shortly before the initiation of the 201 investigation (June 2001) *New Steel* magazine published the following exchange between the CEO of Nucor and the CEO of California Steel (emphasis added):

New Steel: What is the impact of President Bush's decision to initiate a Section 201 investigation? What are the implications for the US industry and for steelmakers around the world?

Gonçalves (CEO, California Steel): The 201 is not supposed to create losers, especially here among US steel companies. 'If restrictions are applied to slabs, of course, California Steel would be a loser'.

New Steel: People are wondering if semi-finished steel might be included. You [Gonçalves] must have quite an interest in this issue. Slabs are your bread and butter.

---

[19] See USITC (1984) and (USITC, 2001).

[20] The slab TRQ was not designed to merely stop a surge of slab imports. Rather the TRQ was set at an amount less than the average 1998–2000 level.

J.P. Durling, T.J. Prusa / Japan and the World Economy 15 (2003) 47–68   57

Gonçalves: Absolutely. It's my raw material . . . Even if the slabs are included, we have . . . to teach the ITC what slabs mean, the importance of slabs for companies such as California Steel.

DiMicco (CEO, Nucor): Slabs will be allowed in at certain levels that will grandfather companies like CSI, AK, and other people who have been using slabs regularly for running their businesses . . . The industry is fairly unanimous on that.

Mr. DiMicco's statement warrants two comments. First, his statement that "the industry is fairly unanimous" on restricting slab is demonstrably false. The slab issue was arguably the most hotly contested aspect of the 201 case. We sumrise that he means the Steel Manufacturers Association, a trade association of EAF steel makers and perhaps a few integrated producers who import little slab.

Second, the statement demonstrates that Mr. DiMicco is well versed in the politics of protectionism. Early on in the case Mr. DiMicco did not want to publicly reveal his anticompetitive intent. However, once the case proceeded to the remedy phase, there was no longer any talk of allowing slab imports at "certain levels" and instead Mr. DiMicco and his allies pushed for uniform, across-the-board 40 percent tariffs on all products.

For instance, in *Metal Center News* (December 2001), Thomas J. Usher, CEO of USX Corporation stated

We urge the President to act quickly to adopt 40 percent tariffs on all flat-rolled imports, including slabs.

In February 2002, Mr. Thomas J. Usher pursued this argument further; testifying before the US Senate Finance Committee he stated:

Relief on slab is critical . . . The only fair remedy is to put everyone on an even footing—including slab re-rollers, hot band re-rollers, integrated mills, etc.—and insure that any imported feedstock is subject to a consistent remedy.

At the same hearing Mr. DiMicco testified and stated:

It is crucial that the same tariff be applied to all product categories, from semi-finished slab to rebar.

Thus, at the end of the process, the minimills were revealing their true intentions—namely, the foreclosure of their most threatening competitors.

5. A modelling framework

5.1. General description

Minimills neither produce nor consume traditional "thick" slab. Nevertheless, the minimills, most notably Nucor, lobbied long and hard to have prohibitive tariffs levied on all slab imports.[21]

---

[21] Integrated mills like US Steel that source their feedstock internally also lobbied hard to restrict slab imports. These mills sell very little, if any, slab in the open-market.

58   *J.P. Durling, T.J. Prusa / Japan and the World Economy 15 (2003) 47–68*

Vertically Related Production

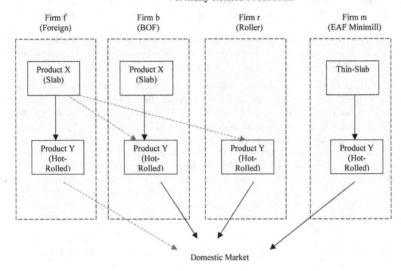

Fig. 2. Vertically related production.

Was their position only an attempt to project industry solidarity to the President? Or, were the minimills' motivated in the 201 case by a desire to raise their rivals' costs? If their lobbying efforts were successful, for all intents and purposes they would have induced the government to foreclose input supply from their domestic rivals.

In order to formally discuss this issue, we will now setup and analyze an oligopoly model with vertically related production.[22] The model setup is illustrated in Fig. 2. There are four firms in the market: (i) a domestic integrated BF/BOF mill (firm *b*); (ii) a domestic EAF minimill (firm *m*); (iii) a domestic roller mill (firm *r*); and (iv) a foreign integrated BF/BOF mill (firm *f*). The outer dotted lines indicate vertical integration.

For simplicity, we will confine our analysis to only the first two stages of flat-rolled steel production: slab and hot-rolled steel. In our model, we will simply refer the products as upstream (X) and downstream (Y) products. The model can be easily, if somewhat tediously, extended to additional downstream product lines. Also, throughout our exposition, we focus exclusively on the domestic market.[23]

In our model, the vertically integrated foreign firm, denoted as firm *f*, controls the exports of both products. That is, firm *f* can export both X and Y to the domestic market. In keeping with actual practice in the domestic steel industry, we will assume that the foreign firm is the *only* source for buying the upstream product on the open-market. Once firm *f*

---

[22] The structure of the model is similar to that in Spencer and Jones (1992) and Rodrik and Yoon (1995).

[23] More precisely, we are assuming that the domestic and foreign market are segmented. Given our assumptions on the foreign firm's costs, this has little impact on the analysis.

J.P. Durling, T.J. Prusa / Japan and the World Economy 15 (2003) 47–68   59

sets a price for the upstream product, the integrated BF/BOF mill (firm b) and the roller (firm r) can then choose a volume to import.[24] We will assume firm m uses an alternative technology and thus will not purchase the upstream product from firm f.

We will assume that 1 tonne of the upstream product is required to produce 1 tonne of the downstream product.[25] We will also assume that a fixed number of laborers are required to produce 1 tonne of the upstream product. We will use the parameter α_i to denote the unit labor requirement at firm i.[26] We denote the unit labor requirement of downstream production as β_i.[27] We now turn to the issue of capturing costs of upstream production. As we discussed above, the US integrated mills operate at substantially higher costs than either minimills or their foreign rivals. In addition, we want to capture the incentive for firm b to purchase at least some of its upstream product from the open-market. To capture both issues, we will assume that firm b is characterized by increasing marginal costs. In contrast, the three other firms have constant marginal costs. With increasing marginal costs, firm b may both import and and internally produce the upstream product.[28]

The subgame perfect equilibrium between the firms involves two stages of decision. At stage 1, the foreign firm (f) announces a price for the upstream product. At stage 2, the output of each of the four firms is determined by Cournot competition. At this second state, firm b will choose the cost minimizing combination of imports and internal production and firm r will choose how many tonnes of X to import. In setting the upstream product price at stage 1, firm f takes into account the effect of the price on the second stage Cournot quantity competition.

Finally, we will allow the home government to levy a tariff on the upstream product, t^X, and also on the downstream product, t^Y.

Before discussing the solution to the model, it seems appropriate at this point to make a couple of comments on our our modelling approach. First, our goal is to show how different steel firms had different economic stakes in the design of the Section 201 restraints. We believe that an oligopoly approach is a useful tool for highlighting the differing incentives. Toward this end, our model assumes that only a single firm sells the upstream product on the open-market. While it is true that a few domestic firms occasionally participate in the slab market, in reality there are dozens of firms from many countries who sell slab on the open-market. The ITC's recommendations subjected all foreign slab producers to the same

---

[24] Since the the price and the export quantity of the upstream product are related, it does not really matter whether we model the foreign firm setting the price or quantity of upstream product. The presentation is a bit more straightforward if we assume the foreign firm sets the price of the upstream product.

[25] This is consistent with actual steel industry technology, where about 1.05 tonnes of slab is required to produce 1 tonne of hot-rolled steel.

[26] According to Barnett (2000), minimills require about 1 man-hour to produce 1 tonne of steel and integrated mills require about 4 man-hours.

[27] Following industry wisdom we assume that the minimills have the lowest unit labor requirement for downstream production, followed by rollers (predominantly non-union operations), and then integrated (mostly union mills).

[28] We note that in circumstances where demand for steel is weak, integrated mills can expand production with decreasing marginal costs. However, US BF/BOFs are small which means that at normal demand levels integrated mills operate at or near practical capacity, particularly with respect to many grades of steel. At this point the firms have increasing costs—substantial capacity investments—unless they augment their needs with slab imports. For simplicity, we model this alternative as increasing marginal costs. In related work we examine alternative cost technologies.

tariff treatment. Loosely speaking, lumping all the foreign suppliers into a single firm captures the notion that all of the foreign suppliers would be subject to the same tariff. In practice, however, the various foreign slab suppliers cannot coordinate their actions. Hence, our model gives substantially more market power to firm f than any slab seller has.

A similar stipulation applies to the downstream market, namely we assume that there are only four firms. Just as in the upstream market, this likely means that we are endowing each firm with more market power than any one firm has in practice. Of the two markets, however, our sense is that the model's "deviation" from actual market behavior is more serious for the slab market. We are endowing firm f with monopoly power in the slab market. As a result, we believe that our model more severely overstates the extent of firm f's strategic behavior.[29]

Second, we have deliberately abstracted away from any capacity constraint issues. In practice, capacity constraints—especially at the upstream product level—can have an important impact on market behavior. For simplicity we model integrated firms as importing slab when the marginal cost of internal production exceeds the open-market price of slab. In practice, fixed capacity also explains the open-market purchases of slab. Ignoring the capacity constraint means that our model understates the true cost of tariffs on the upstream product. Our modelling approach allows domestic firms to expand their output. A high tariff simply induces firm b to expand its internal production but at a higher marginal cost. In reality, it is impossible to expand beyond a BF/BOF's maximum capacity regardless of cost. The fixed capacity will mean that a high tariff has a bigger impact than our model captures.

Despite these caveats, we believe our model captures important economic forces in the steel market. What we take from these limitations is that although the model may overstate/understate the impact of the tariff policy, the sign or direction of the impact (i.e. which firm's output expands) is accurate. Said differently, we feel strongly that the economic intuition and lessons from the analysis are accurate, but the quantitative estimates are more illustrative than precise predictions.

5.2. Formal description

5.2.1. The downstream (hot-rolled) market

As is customary in two-stage models, we setup and solve the model backwards, first characterizing the downstream market and then the upstream market.

Thus, we begin by looking at the downstream market. We will assume that the downstream products are perfectly substitutes, so we can write the price as the inverse demand curve $P^Y = P^Y(Q_b^Y + Q_m^Y + Q_r^Y + Q_f^Y)$. Letting w (w_f) denote the exogenous cost of home (foreign) country labor, we can write the firm b's profit from producing Y as

$$
\Pi_b = \begin{cases} R_b(Q_b^Y, Q_m^Y, Q_r^Y, Q_f^Y) - P^X(Q_b^Y - Q_{bi}^X) - C_b(Q_{bi}^X) - \beta_b w Q_b^Y - \alpha_b w Q_{bi}^X, & \text{if augment,} \\ R_b(Q_b^Y, Q_m^Y, Q_r^Y, Q_f^Y; t^Y) - C_b(Q_b^Y) - (\beta_b + \alpha_b) w Q_b^Y, & \text{otherwise,} \end{cases}
$$

$$(1)$$

---

[29] While not an absolute monopoly, Brazil has about 50 percent of the non-NAFTA slab market. The degree of concentration in slab far exceeds other flat steel markets. To keep the exposition simple, we model the upstream market as a monopoly.

J.P. Durling, T.J. Prusa/Japan and the World Economy 15 (2003) 47–68 61

where $R_b(\cdot)$ denotes the revenue from selling Q_b^Y. $C_b(Q_{bi}^X)$ is the total cost of internally producing Q_{bi}^X tonnes of X. The firm will choose to augment when $P^X = C_b'(\cdot)\alpha_b w$.[30]

Firm m's profit from producing Y is

$$\Pi_m = R_m(Q_b^Y, Q_m^Y, Q_r^Y, Q_f^Y) - (\beta_m w + \alpha_m w + c_m)Q_m^Y, \tag{2}$$

where c_m denotes the constant marginal cost of producing 1 tonne of the alternative upstream product (i.e. thin-slab).

Firm r's profit from producing Y is

$$\Pi_r = R_r(Q_b^Y, Q_m^Y, Q_r^Y, Q_f^Y) - (\beta_r w + P^X)Q_r^Y, \tag{3}$$

and firm f's profit from producing Y is

$$\Pi_f = R_f(Q_b^Y, Q_m^Y, Q_r^Y, Q_f^Y; t^Y) - (\beta_f w_f + \alpha_f w_f + c_f)Q_f^Y. \tag{4}$$

The first-order conditions can be written as

$$\frac{\partial R_b}{\partial Q_b^Y} = \begin{cases} P^X + \beta_b w, & \text{if augment,} \\ C_b'(\cdot) + \beta_b w + \alpha_b w, & \text{otherwise.} \end{cases} \tag{5}$$

$$\frac{\partial R_m}{\partial Q_m^Y} = \beta_m w + \alpha_m w + c_m \tag{6}$$

$$\frac{\partial R_r}{\partial Q_r^Y} = P^X + \beta_r w \tag{7}$$

$$\frac{\partial R_f}{\partial Q_f^Y} = \beta_f w_f + \alpha_f w_f + c_f. \tag{8}$$

The second stage Cournot equilibrium can be characterized by the equilibrium output levels $\{\tilde{Q}_b^Y(P^X, t^Y), \tilde{Q}_m^Y(P^X, t^Y), \tilde{Q}_r^Y(P^X, t^Y), \tilde{Q}_f^Y(P^X, t^Y)\}$, which simultaneously solve the four first-order conditions, (5)–(8). We will assume that the parameters are such that there is a unique Cournot equilibrium wherein the integrated firm imports some X and that the relevant second order conditions are satisfied. Substituting the Cournot equilibrium quantities into (1)–(4), we denote the second stage equilibrium profits as[31]

$$\{\tilde{\Pi}_b^Y(P^X, t^Y), \tilde{\Pi}_m^Y(P^X, t^Y), \tilde{\Pi}_r^Y(P^X, t^Y), \tilde{\Pi}_f^Y(P^X, t^Y)\}.$$

5.2.2. Workers' objective

It will be useful to also discuss the impact of the various policies on workers. Our sense is the workers' objective function (or at least as articulated by the union leaders) can be roughly stated as "maximize jobs." It is unclear, however, how broadly the employment objective is defined. Most of the minimills and even some of the rollers have little/no union

---

[30] We note that there are substantial sunk cost of BF/BOF operations. Without these sunk costs in practice some integrated mills would find it optimal to purchase all their slab on the open-market. The sunk costs, however, mandate that the BF/BOFs stay in operation. We abstract from these issues.

[31] For notational convenience, we suppress the exogenously given wage levels w, w_f, and technology parameters, $c_j, \alpha_j, \beta_j, j = b, m, r, f$.

representation. It seems reasonable to believe that union leaders only care about union jobs. Moreover, given that the disproportionate share of steel-making jobs are at the upstream stage, it is arguable that the union only cares about upstream employment.

Hence, we will consider several potential objective functions for the workers:

$$\text{firm}B\text{—all jobs}: \quad \beta_b Q_b^Y + \alpha_b Q_{bi}^X$$

$$\text{firm}B\text{—upstream jobs}: \quad \alpha_b Q_{bi}^X$$

$$\text{all firms—all jobs}: \quad \beta_b Q_b^Y + \alpha_b Q_{bi}^X + (\beta_m + \alpha_m)Q_m^Y + \beta_r Q_r^Y$$

$$\text{all firms—upstream jobs}: \quad \alpha_b Q_{bi}^X + \alpha_m Q_m^Y$$

5.2.3. The upstream (slab) market

We now turn to the stage 1 decision of the establishing the open-market price of X. Given the strategic interaction between the markets, firm f will choose the price of X incorporating its impact on both the upstream and downstream markets.

Firm f's total profits can be written

$$\Pi_f^{\text{tot}}(P^X) = (P^X - t^X - c_f - \alpha_f w_f)(Q_b^Y - Q_{bi}^X + Q_f^Y) + \tilde{\Pi}_f(P^X, t^Y). \tag{9}$$

Maximizing total profits with respect to P^X gives rise to the first-order condition $d\Pi_f^{\text{tot}}/dP^X = 0$. The solution to which we will denote as as $\tilde{P}^X(t^X, t^Y)$.

5.3. Simulating the impact of trade restrictions

In order to quantify the strategic incentives for firms to lobby for tariffs on the upstream and downstream products we will numerically solve the model described above. Parametric details are provided in the Appendix A.[32] Most of the computational details are relatively unimportant, but one key simplification should be noted. In our simulations we assume that demand is linear, $P^Y = \theta - \lambda(Q_b^Y + Q_m^Y + Q_r^Y + Q_r^Y)$.

Table 2 summarizes our findings. We consider two scenarios which differ in the extent to which firm b augments its internal production with imports. In the first scenario we study a situation where firm b imports a large quantity of its total requirements of X (more than half in free trade). In the second scenario firm b imports a small quantity of its total requirements of X (about 10 percent).

5.3.1. High import volume/high tariff scenario

In the high import scenario, we analyze a policy where very high specific tariffs are imposed (equivalent to about a 30 percent ad valorem tariff) on one or both of the products. In each of the columns we report the impact relative to the free trade benchmark. Hence, positive (negative) numbers mean the variable of interest expands (contracts) relative to its free trade level.

5.3.1.1. Tariff on upstream imports (slab).
Lets begin by looking at column 1. Here we consider a tariff on product X (slab) alone. In this case, firm f absorbs about a half of the

---

[32] Maple code is available upon request.

J.P. Durling, T.J. Prusa / Japan and the World Economy 15 (2003) 47–68   63

Table 2
Summary: impact of tariffs relative to free trade

	Slab tariff only (percent)	Hot-rolled tariff only (percent)	Tariff on slab and hot-rolled (percent)
BOF High import volume scenario, high tariff scenario (30 percent ad valorem equivalent)			
Price slab	17.5	−4.5	13.0
Price hot-rolled	6.0	5.1	11.2
Firm b—slab imports	−97.4	96.7	−0.7
Firm r—slab imports	−86.0	85.5	−0.5
Total slab imports	−91.4	90.8	−0.6
Firm b—slab internal	12.7	−3.4	9.5
Firm b—hot-rolled production	−96.7	96.1	−0.6
Firm m—hot-rolled production	7.3	6.2	13.6
Firm r—hot-rolled production	−86.0	85.5	−0.5
Firm f—hot-rolled exports	6.9	−32.1	−25.3
Total hot-rolled sales	−3.2	−2.7	−5.9
Firm b—profit	−95.7	275.5	−0.4
Firm m—profit	15.2	12.9	28.9
Firm r—profit	−98.0	244.1	−1.1
Firm f—profit	−3.0	−32.2	−40.3
Workers—firm B, all jobs	−95.3	94.8	−0.5
Workers—firm B, upstream jobs only	12.7	−3.4	9.5
Workers—all firms, all jobs	−9.8	20.9	11.1
Workers—all firms, upstream jobs only	7.3	6.2	13.5
BOF low import volume scenario, low tariff scenario (10 percent ad valorem equivalent)			
Price slab	5.8	−1.3	4.5
Price hot-rolled	1.9	1.6	3.5
Firm b—slab imports	−49.8	42.8	−7.0
Firm r—slab imports	−20.5	19.1	−1.4
Total slab imports	−29.7	26.6	−3.1
Firm b—slab internal	5.2	−1.2	4.0
Firm b—hot-rolled production	−22.4	20.9	−1.5
Firm m—hot-rolled production	2.3	1.9	4.3
Firm r—hot-rolled production	−20.5	19.1	−1.4
Firm f—hot-rolled exports	2.2	−9.7	−7.5
Total hot-rolled sales	−1.0	−0.8	−1.8
Firm b—profit	−8.0	16.2	4.5
Firm m—profit	4.7	3.9	8.7
Firm r—profit	−36.8	41.9	−2.7
Firm f—profit	−1.6	−11.6	−13.7
Workers—firm B, all jobs	−8.6	9.9	1.2
Workers—firm B, upstream jobs only	5.2	−1.2	4.0
Workers—all firms, all jobs	−2.1	5.2	3.1
Workers—all firms, upstream jobs only	3.0	1.2	4.2

tariff and passes the rest through to the buyers. This tariff dramatically reduces trade in product X. Specifically, firm b reduces its purchases by 97 percent. Firm r reduces its purchases by 86 percent. Overall, the imports of the upstream product fall by 91 percent.

Not surprisingly, the large tariff on the upstream product has an impact on downstream production. In particular, total (foreign + domestic) downstream production falls by about 3 percent. This modest fall masks a huge change in fortunes among domestic mills. Both firm b and r's output falls dramatically. Firm m's output, on the other hand, expands by 7 percent. In other words, the main impact of a tariff on the upstream product is its effect on the *distribution* of production, not total output. Given the vertical nature of production, taxing the upstream product is nothing short of having the government pick winners and losers. Taxing the upstream product puts firms b and r at a competitive disadvantage and firm m in a favorable position.

The output changes correspond to observed profit changes—namely, firm b and r's profit falls while firm m's profit increases.

Interestingly, protecting the upstream product is not a panacea for workers. We find protecting X may well hurt workers.[33] Whether a high tariff on X makes workers worse off depends on the relative unit labor requirements and on what jobs the union focuses. Protecting X does increase upstream jobs, but total industry employment falls. This seemingly paradoxical result is driven by the fact that minimills have such low unit labor requirements. Protecting X raises firm b and r costs and thus indirectly encourages firm m to expand its output. And, since firm m has a relatively low unit labor requirement relative to the rest of the industry, then even though firm b increases its internal production and firm m grows, total jobs will lost in the industry. Put another way, taxing X encourages an expansion of the firm who has the smallest unit labor requirement. And, as firm m expands, firm b and r strategically respond by reducing their output (and employment). Overall, there are two reasons why taxing upstream imports lowers domestic employment: (i) raising input costs results in a reduction in total domestic production; and (ii) the firm with low unit labor requirement (firm m) expands its production at the expense of the firm with a high unit labor requirement (firm b).

5.3.1.2. Tariff on downstream imports (hot-rolled).

Lets look next at column 2. Here we consider a tariff on product Y (hot-rolled) alone. In this case firm f absorbs about four-fifths of the tariff. Relative to the above scenario, competition from the other three firms significantly restricts the extent to which firm f can pass through the tariff. Importantly, protection in the downstream market has an impact on upstream input prices; in this case, lowering the price of X by about 4 percent. The tariff on Y reduces firm f's exports by about 32 percent.

As one would expect, reducing firm f's presence in the market results in expanded production by the three domestic firms. This in turn leads to greater trade in product X. Specifically, in order for both firm b and r to efficiently expand output they need to import more X. As a result, firm m is only able to expand its production by about 6 percent.

---

[33] We also modelled the objective as jobs at both the upstream and downstream product level, i.e. depending on total output. Our results are the unaffected—namely, workers can be made worse off by reducing upstream imports.

J.P. Durling, T.J. Prusa / Japan and the World Economy 15 (2003) 47–68 65

However, in comparison with firm b and r, firm m loses market share. Overall, all three domestic firms production and profits increase as a result of the tariff on Y. Thus, these results suggest that firm m would prefer not to have only downstream protection because relatively speaking, its rivals do better.

Finally, protecting Y benefits workers (i.e. raises domestic employment). Not only does overall industry output expand, but the output of each firm grows. While there is a small distributional impact, it favors the firms with higher unit labor requirement, which further bolstering workers.

5.3.1.3. Tariff on both upstream and downstream imports. We now turn to column 3. Here we consider a large tariff on both product X (slab) and product Y (hot-rolled). This is the scenario that most closely matches the policy recommendation of Nucor, the minimill coalition, and the United Steelworkers. In this case, firm f absorbs most of the upstream and downstream tariff. The large tariffs reduce trade both products, but has an especially big impact on product Y, lowering import volume trade by more than 25 percent. The impact on upstream sales is muted because the price increase on the downstream product.

Relative to a tariff on the downstream product alone (column 2), the addition of restrictions on the upstream product harms firm b and r. Specifically, when the tariff is levied on the downstream product alone, both firm b and r's output expands significantly; when the tariff is levied on both the upstream and downstream products, both firm b and r's output *falls* by about 1 percent. In terms of profitability, firm b and r both prefer a policy involving a tariff on Y only.[34]

The fact that restrictions on the upstream product hurt domestic firms is not entirely unexpected. After all, the policy essentially raises the costs of production for firms b and r. What might be surprising, however, is that workers are also worse off when the tariff is levied on the upstream product. When comparing all three policies, the most preferred policy for the workers is simply the policy where a tariff is levied on the downstream product alone. Perhaps to the surprise of the workers, taxing upstream trade hurts their cause. Why? Because it tilts the playing field in favor of firms who have low unit labor requirements.

Well, if firm b and r are worse off, and the workers are worse off, who benefits from taxing both upstream and downstream products? The firm with the alternative technology—firm m. Taxing upstream imports results in firm m looking relatively more efficient than it is under free trade. The tax on product X has no impact on firm m's costs, but raises the costs of its rivals. Intuitively, this means that the best response function of the other three firms (f, b and r) all shift in, and induce an expansion in firm m's output. As a result, firm m's output and profit increase relative to a policy where only the downstream product is taxed.

In summary, the model suggests that only one domestic constituent is unambiguously better off when the government taxes both upstream and downstream trade—firm m. All other interested parties are worse off, either relative to free trade (firm r) or relative to a policy where only downstream trade is taxed (firm b and workers).

---

[34] This result reflects the fact that both b and r import a high volume of slab. If firm b imports no slab, it would prefer protection on both X and Y.

5.3.2. Low import volume/low tariffs scenario

In the preceding analysis the benchmark free trade equilibrium involved a substantial quantity of X imports. As an alternative we now simulate a situation where in free trade imports augment only about 10 percent of firm b's production. We believe this scenario is interesting since in recent years the US imports about 10 percent of its slab requirements. However, given the relatively low volume of the upstream product imported, a 30 percent tariff is prohibitive. In fact, any tariff much larger than 10 percent ad valorem results in firm b ceasing to purchase any imports. Because we believe that technological restrictions and capacity limitations imply that BF/BOF firms must import slab, we restrict ourselves to studying the impact of tariffs of only about 10 percent ad valorem.

As it turns out, the qualitative results are remarkably similar to those presented above. Generally speaking, all of the key results continue hold. Namely, taxing the upstream product benefits firm m at the expense of firms b and r. In fact, adding upstream tariffs to a policy with tariffs on the downstream product essentially leaves firms b and r output unchanged relative to the "no tariff" scenario. Their profits are higher due to the downstream price distortion, but these means consumers are being taxed with no real production benefit to a large set of the domestic industry. On the other hand, adding upstream tariffs to a policy with tariffs on the downstream product doubles the impact on firm m. Both the high and low tariff simulations make it clear that taxing the upstream product serves primarily to raise the costs of domestic firms in order to benefit another part of the domestic industry.

As we saw in the above scenario, taxing upstream production has an ambiguous impact impact on steelworkers. Specifically, taxing upstream imports only benefits steelworkers if their objective is simply to maximize upstream jobs.

More precisely, not all sectors of the domestic industry use the same upstream inputs which implies that, in taxing imports of finished steels and imports of slab, the government is taxing all downstream trade but only *some* kinds of upstream trade. So perhaps more accurately, the problem in the steel 201 case is in large part due to the selective protection of upstream trade. Relative to free trade, taxing X lowers overall steel employment but does result in gain at the upstream stage. Relative to only taxing Y imports, taxing X reduces overall employment.

6. Conclusions

In this paper, we have examined that a decision made even before the steel 201 case was initiated—to include slab as part of the investigation—has led to a remedy that likely poses serious competition/antitrust policy concerns. Our results suggest that the Justice Department should carefully scrutinize the conduct of such investigations.[35] Whereas Congress may have intended to disadvantage to foreign rivals, it is far less clear that Congress intended the trade authorities to pick winners and losers among domestic firms.

The results in this paper suggests that the industry definition used in the investigation was overly broad and inevitably forced the President to make a choice over what set of

---

[35] Note that the problems are from an economic perspective. We realize that from a legal perspective, efforts to petition the government (i.e. seek protection) are largely protected under the Noerr–Pennington doctrine.

J.P. Durling, T.J. Prusa/Japan and the World Economy 15 (2003) 47–68   67

firms he wanted to favor. If he excluded slab from the remedy, he would allow capacity constrained BF/BOF mills and rollers to continue to operate profitably. If he included slab in the remedy, he would put those mills at jeopardy and encourage the expansion of the minimill sector.

In contrast with the rhetoric, our analysis indicates that there was really no "fair" remedy. In deciding whether or not to include slab the President was in effect making a decision whether or not to hurt one set of firms. As it turned out, the President chose to favor the minimills at the expense of the mills that rely on imported slab.

Our analysis also indicates that the restricting slab is not a panacea for workers. Raising the costs of slab puts all integrated mills at a competitive disadvantage, not just the rollers. Even mills like US Steel who import relatively small quantities of slab will be faced with higher marginal costs of production. As a result, the minimills will expand their production. While bolstering domestic production sounds good to the steelworkers, the firms experiencing the greatest gains are mills who use the fewest workers. And, as the minimills expand, the BF/BOF mills will lose sales. On net, we show that levying tariffs on slab may well reduce the number of steelworkers jobs.

The findings of this paper should not be viewed as only applying to the recent US steel safeguard case or safeguard cases more generally. Rather, the message is equally applicable to antidumping protection. When cases are selectively filed on upstream and downstream products the government ends up picking winners and losers instead of promoting overall industry health.

Acknowledgements

We would like to thank Joe Dorn, Ben Goodrich, Jorge Miranda, Kazuo Mino, Marty Perry, Bob Stoner and the participants of the NYU Technical Symposium on IO and Trade for their helpful comments. We would also like to thank Matt McCullough for sharing his knowledge of the US steel industry. The views presented are solely those of the authors and do not necessarily represent those of Willkie Farr and Gallagher or its clients.

Appendix A

We make the following assumptions:

- (Inverse) demand for downstream product

$$P^Y = \theta - \lambda(Q_b^Y + Q_m^Y + Q_r^Y + Q_r^Y),$$

where $\theta = 5000$, $\lambda = 1/100$.
- Firm b cost function $C_b(Q_{bi}^X) = \rho(Q_{bi}^X)^\eta$, where we will set
  ○ Cost function-high volume scenario $\rho = 0.5, \eta = 2.5$
  ○ Cost function-low volume scenario $\rho = 0.005, \eta = 2.25$.
- Constant marginal costs $c_f = 140, c_m = 225$.
- Wages $w = 40$, $w_f = 10$.

- Unit labor requirement—upstream product $\alpha_m = 1, \alpha_b = 4, \alpha_f = 5$.
- Unit labor requirement—downstream product $\beta_m = 1, \beta_r = 1.5, \beta_b = 2, \beta_f = 2$.

References

Barnett, D.F., 2000. Seizing the competitive advantage. World Steel Dynamics.

Barnett, D.F., Crandall, R.W., 1998. Steel: decline and renewal. In: Deutsch, L.I. (Ed.), Industry Studies. M.G. Sharpe, Armonk, NY.

Barringer, W.H., Pierce, K.J., 2000. Paying the Price for Big Steel: $100 Billion in Trade Restraints and Corporate Welfare. American Institute for International Steel, Washington, DC (available online at http:www.aiis.org).

Baumol, W.J., Ordover, J.A., 1985. Use of antitrust to subvert competition. Journal of Law and Economics 28, 247–265.

Brennan, T.J., 1988. Understanding 'raising rivals' costs. Antitrust Bulletin 33, 95–113.

Ghemawat, P., Stander, H.J., 1992. Nucor at a Crossroads. Harvard Business School Case Study No. 9-793-039 (revised 1998).

US International Trade Commission, 1984. Carbon and Certain Alloy Steel Products-Investigation No. TA-201-51. USITC Publication, 1553.

US International Trade Commission, 1995. Economic Effects of Antidumping and Countervailing Duty Orders and Suspension Agreements. USITC Publication, 2900.

US International Trade Commission, 2001. Steel-Investigation No. TA-201-73. USITC Publication, 3479.

Moore, M.O., 1996. Steel protection in the 1980s: the waning influence of big steel? In: Krueger, A.O. (Ed.), The Political Economy of American Trade Policy. University of Chicago Press, Chicago, pp. 73–125.

Rodrik, D., Yoon, C.H., 1995. Strategic trade policy with potential for import substitution. Journal of Economic Development 20, 37–56.

Salop, S.C., Scheffman, D.T., 1983. Raising rivals' costs. American Economic Review 73, 267–271.

Salop, S.C., Scheffman, D.T., 1987. Cost-raising strategies. Journal of Industrial Economics 36, 19–34.

Spencer, B.J., Jones, R.W., 1992. Trade and protection in vertically related markets. Journal of International Economics 32, 31–55.

Yost, C., 1996. Thin-Slab Casting/Flat-Rolling: New Technology to Benefit US Steel Industry. USITC Industry, Trade, and Technology Review.

Printed in the United States
by Baker & Taylor Publisher Services